CONSTITUTION-MAKING AND TRANSNATIONAL LEGAL ORDER

Since the rise of the nation-state in the nineteenth century, constitutions have been seen as an embodiment of national values and identity. However, individuals, ideas, and institutions from abroad have always influenced constitutions, and so the process is better described as transnational. As cross-border interaction is increasing in intensity, a dominant transnational legal order for constitutions has emerged, with its own norms, guidelines, and shared ideas. Yet both the process and substance of constitution-making are being contested in divergent and insurgent constitutional orders. Bringing together leading scholars from the United States, Europe, Latin America, and Asia, this volume addresses the actors, networks, norms, and processes involved in constitution making, as well as the related challenges, from a transnational and comparative perspective. Drawing from the research on transnational legal orders, this work explores and examines constitution-making in every region of the world.

Gregory Shaffer is Chancellor's Professor of Law, University of California, Irvine School of Law.

Tom Ginsburg is Leo Spitz Professor of International Law at the University of Chicago Law School and a Research Professor at the American Bar Foundation.

Terence C. Halliday is a Research Professor at the American Bar Foundation.

COMPARATIVE CONSTITUTIONAL LAW AND POLICY

Series Editors

Tom Ginsburg *University of Chicago*
Zachary Elkins *University of Texas at Austin*
Ran Hirschl *University of Toronto*

Comparative constitutional law is an intellectually vibrant field that encompasses an increasingly broad array of approaches and methodologies. This series collects analytically innovative and empirically grounded work from scholars of comparative constitutionalism across academic disciplines. Books in the series include theoretically informed studies of single constitutional jurisdictions, comparative studies of constitutional law and institutions, and edited collections of original essays that respond to challenging theoretical and empirical questions in the field.

Books in the Series

Hybrid Constitutionalism Eric C. Ip

The Politico-Legal Dynamics of Judicial Review Thenuis Roux

The Invisible Constitution in Comparative Perspective Edited by Rosalind Dixon and Adrienne Stone

Constitutional Courts in Asia: A Comparative Perspective Edited by Albert H. Y. Chen and Andrew Harding

Judicial Review in Norway Anine Kierulf

Constituent Assemblies Edited by Jon Elster, Roberto Gargarella, Vatsal Naresh, and Bjorn Erik Rasch

The DNA of Constitutional Justice in Latin America: Politics, Governance, and Judicial Design Daniel M. Brinks and Abby Blass

The Adventures of the Constituent Power: Beyond Revolutions? Andrew Arato

Constitutions, Religion and Politics in Asia: Indonesia, Malaysia and Sri Lanka Dian A. H. Shah

Canada in the World: Comparative Perspectives on the Canadian Constitution Edited by Richard Albert and David R. Cameron

Courts and Democracies in Asia Po Jen Yap

Proportionality: New Frontiers, New Challenges Edited by Vicki C. Jackson and Mark Tushnet

Constituents before Assembly: Participation, Deliberation, and Representation in the Crafting of New Constitutions Todd A. Eisenstadt, A. Carl LeVan, and Tofigh Maboudi

Assessing Constitutional Performance Edited by Tom Ginsburg and Aziz Huq

Buddhism, Politics and the Limits of Law: The Pyrrhic Constitutionalism of Sri Lanka Benjamin Schonthal

Engaging with Social Rights: Procedure, Participation and Democracy in South Africa's Second Wave Brian Ray

Constitutional Courts as Mediators: Armed Conflict, Civil–Military Relations, and the Rule of Law in Latin America Julio Ríos-Figueroa

Perils of Judicial Self-Government in Transitional Societies David Kosař

Making We the People: Democratic Constitutional Founding in Postwar Japan and South Korea Chaihark Hahm and Sung Ho Kim

Radical Deprivation on Trial: The Impact of Judicial Activism on Socioeconomic Rights in the Global South César Rodríguez-Garavito and Diana Rodríguez-Franco

Unstable Constitutionalism: Law and Politics in South Asia Edited by Mark Tushnet and Madhav Khosla

Magna Carta and Its Modern Legacy Edited by Robert Hazell and James Melton

Constitutions and Religious Freedom Frank B. Cross

International Courts and the Performance of International Agreements: A General Theory with Evidence from the European Union Clifford J. Carrubba and Matthew J. Gabel

Reputation and Judicial Tactics: A Theory of National and International Courts Shai Dothan

Social Difference and Constitutionalism in Pan-Asia Edited by Susan H. Williams

Constitutionalism in Asia in the Early Twenty-First Century Edited by Albert H. Y. Chen

Constitutions in Authoritarian Regimes Edited by Tom Ginsburg and Alberto Simpser

Presidential Legislation in India: The Law and Practice of Ordinances Shubhankar Dam

Social and Political Foundations of Constitutions Edited by Denis J. Galligan and Mila Versteeg

Consequential Courts: Judicial Roles in Global Perspective Edited by Diana Kapiszewski, Gordon Silverstein, and Robert A. Kagan

Comparative Constitutional Design Edited by Tom Ginsburg

Constitution-Making and Transnational Legal Order

Edited by

GREGORY SHAFFER

University of California, Irvine

TOM GINSBURG

University of Chicago

TERENCE C. HALLIDAY

American Bar Foundation

CAMBRIDGE
UNIVERSITY PRESS

CAMBRIDGE
UNIVERSITY PRESS

University Printing House, Cambridge CB2 8BS, United Kingdom

One Liberty Plaza, 20th Floor, New York, NY 10006, USA

477 Williamstown Road, Port Melbourne, VIC 3207, Australia

314-321, 3rd Floor, Plot 3, Splendor Forum, Jasola District Centre, New Delhi - 110025, India

79 Anson Road, #06-04/06, Singapore 079906

Cambridge University Press is part of the University of Cambridge.

It furthers the University's mission by disseminating knowledge in the pursuit of education, learning and research at the highest international levels of excellence.

www.cambridge.org
Information on this title: www.cambridge.org/9781108460989
DOI: 10.1017/9781108561792

First published 2019
First paperback edition 2020

A catalogue record for this publication is available from the British Library

ISBN 978-1-108-47310-1 Hardback
ISBN 978-1-108-46098-9 Paperback

To Brooks and Sage
GS

To the memory of the Martman
TG

To Felix
TH

Contents

Figures

Tables

Contributors

COLIN J. BECK is Associate Professor of Sociology and the Chair of Sociology at Pomona College.

JAVIER COUSO is Professor of Law at the Universidad Diego Portales in Chile.

PAUL CRAIG is Professor of English Law at Oxford University.

GILI S. DRORI is Associate Professor of Sociology and Anthropology at the Hebrew University of Jerusalem, Israel.

TOM GINSBURG is Leo Spitz Professor of International Law at the University of Chicago Law School and a Research Professor at the American Bar Foundation.

TERENCE C. HALLIDAY is Research Professor at the American Bar Foundation.

RALPH I. HOSOKI is Assistant Professor, College of International Professional Development, Kansai Gaidai University, Japan.

H. KUMARASINGHAM is Lecturer in Politics at the University of Edinburgh.

DAVID E. LANDAU is Mason Ladd Professor and Associate Dean for International Programs at Florida State University College of Law.

DAVID S. LAW is Charles Nagel Chair in Constitutional Law and Political Science at Washington University in St. Louis and Sir Y.K. Pao Chair in Public Law at the University of Hong Kong.

JOHN W. MEYER is Professor of Sociology at Stanford University.

ABRAK SAATI is Senior Researcher at the Department of Political Science at Umea University.

KIM LANE SCHEPPELE is Laurence S. Rockefeller Professor of Sociology and International Affairs in the Woodrow Wilson School and the University Center for Human Values at Princeton University.

GREGORY SHAFFER is Chancellor's Professor at the University of California, Irvine School of Law.

1

Constitution-Making as Transnational Legal Ordering

Tom Ginsburg, Terence C. Halliday, and Gregory Shaffer

In January of 2011, after several decades of civil war, the largely Christian population of South Sudan voted overwhelmingly in a referendum to declare independence from predominately Muslim Sudan. As the country celebrated its independence six months later, it marked the occasion with the adoption of a written constitution. This document served to signal the country's independence on the international stage, to provide a framework for governance and, it was hoped, to underpin an era of peace. It contained a good number of rights, a presidential system of government, and detailed provisions covering everything from local governance to accountability institutions.

Things have not worked out very well for South Sudan on the ground, but it was hardly alone in pinning its hopes to a written constitution. Since at least the turn of the twentieth century, it has become an established norm for new countries emerging on the world stage to adopt such a text. Constitution-making is the quintessential national project, a moment when "We the People" come together to adopt fundamental rules that will govern our collective life and express our distinctive values. In the American telling, constitutional "government proceeds directly from the people," and "is emphatically, and truly, a government of the people."[1]

This common way of conceiving of constitution-making, however, is simply wrong. It ignores the long history of transnational flow of ideas about constitutions and how they should be made. Indeed, the very idea of a formal written constitution is foreign in many parts of the world, including in South Sudan. When one examines the actual processes by which constitutional documents are made, one sees an array of transnational influences, actors, and ideas that provide the very grammar for the project.

[1] *McCulloch* v. *Maryland*, 17 U.S. (4 Wheat) 316, 403–5 (1819).

South Sudan provides a perfect example in this regard. The referendum described above was the product of international negotiations to end the civil war, brokered by the neighboring countries in the Intergovernmental Authority on Development, a regional organization. This produced a Comprehensive Peace Agreement among the warring parties and an Interim Constitution for Sudan as a whole. As documented by Cope (2013), the process of drafting the Provisional Constitution for the new country involved myriad outside actors and advisers, including the United Nations, a Washington-based group called the Public International Law and Policy Group (PILPG), the US Institute of Peace, and many others. When the Provisional Constitution came into effect the day after independence, the occasion was widely celebrated in the country, and numerous advisers came in to help with implementation of the new constitutional framework. In short, the very idea of making a constitution was transnational: the drafting was a transnational process; and the implementation was also to some extent transnational.

While perhaps exceptional in the *degree* of transnational involvement, South Sudan is hardly alone in the engagement of transnational actors, ideas, and institutions in national constitution-making. Indeed, one of our claims is that this is the state of affairs in any contemporary constitution-making exercise, to a greater or lesser extent. This volume seeks to explore these forces, both at the moment of constitution-making and the subsequent practice of constitutionalism in context. Our theoretical framework draws on recent work by Shaffer (2013), working with Halliday (2015; in press) on Transnational Legal Orders (TLO). The TLO framework provides a framework for analyzing "legal norms that are exported and imported across borders and that involve transnational networks and international and regional institutions that help to construct and convey the legal norm within a field of law" (Shaffer 2013: 5).

Drawing on the idea of recursivity, as put forward by Halliday and Carruthers (2007; 2009), the TLO framework recognizes that norms and institutions at different levels interact across time, and mutually inform each other. In the spirit of recursivity, our book seeks not only to investigate what the TLO theoretical framework offers for the study of constitution-making and practice, but also how the study of constitution-making and practice reciprocally informs TLO theorizing.

The remainder of this introduction proceeds as follows. First, we trace the brief history of transnational constitution-making, to counteract the powerful myth of exclusively national content and process. Next, we lay out TLO theory. We then assess how the two interact, arguing that both have something to contribute to the other. We then briefly summarize the chapters, and conclude with an assessment of what they mean for TLO theory.

THE NATIONALIST MYTH AND TRANSNATIONAL REALITY OF CONSTITUTION-MAKING

Since the rise of the nation-state in the nineteenth century, law has been seen as an embodiment of national values and identity. As Oliver Wendell Holmes (1881) famously put it "[t]he law embodies the story of a nation's development." Or as the inscription of the classic 1815 Courthouse (Domhus) in Copenhagen states, "With Law We Shall Build the Land."

Of course, no law plays this role more than that of the constitution, the fundamental law. Constitutions are often viewed as engaging the "constituent power" of "We the People" (Landau 2013; Roznai 2017: 123–5). This suggests a distinct fit between a constitution and a particular national community. As Montesquieu might have put it, a constitution must be appropriate for the soil into which it is embedded to be successful. But it also suggests a certain recursivity or feedback between the norms of the constitution and the identity of the people. As reported by Ginsburg in his contribution here, this was a point emphasized by Jean-Jacques Rousseau, namely that a constitution had not only to reflect the norms of the population but could also play a role in building national identity. This two-way interaction suggests something more complicated than simply national norms being reflected in a unidirectional manner in a constitutional text.

One can press on this image in two ways: not only does a constitution interact with its domestic context, but it also interacts with the broader environment of ideas and institutions outside a nation's borders. In practice, we know empirically that there is a long transnational practice that has become more institutionalized over time in the creation of constitutions (Ginsburg, Chapter two; Couso, Chapter nine). Lanni and Vermuele (2012) report that the ancient Greeks would sometimes designate foreigners to draft their constitutional texts. This was not simply a matter of convenience, but promised a certain neutrality in terms of the provisions that were being drafted. Foreigners may be less likely to know the particular culture in which a constitution must operate, but they are also more likely to provide a disinterested view, and to be able to step outside the local milieu of interests and passions. In terms of Elster's (1995) classic framework, foreigners might get us closer to a constitution based on reason, rather than mere passions and interests.

Constitution-making in the modern era begins, of course, with the American experiments from 1776–89. The numerous state constitutions and the two federal ones drafted during this period surely influenced each other, but also drew from ideological currents from across the Atlantic (LaCroix 2010). Madison himself read widely about the experiences of other republics so as to inform his thoughts on how the new country could survive. Even the authors of the canonical phrase "we the people" were informed by experiences of prior countries. They also influenced and inspired republicans abroad for the next two centuries (Billias 2009). Similarly, the French Declaration of the Rights of Man, with its ringing tones of universality, influenced constitutional thinking throughout Europe as well as Latin America and the Caribbean. Since those early experiences, a rich practice in the diffusion of ideas and institutions has continued and accelerated over time.

Not only do ideas flow across borders but the triggers of constitution-making do as well. As documented by Elkins, Ginsburg, and Melton (2009) and Elster (1995), constitution-making tends to come in waves, often triggered by major geopolitical events. The collapse of the Spanish empire following Napoleon's invasion of Spain, the "springtime of nations" in 1848, World War I, World War II, ensuing decolonization, and the Cold War were each followed by a wave of constitution-making. The timing of constitution-making, then, is to some extent dictated by global and regional forces. In the modern era, this takes the form of post-conflict constitution-making (Hart 2001; Wallis 2013). Increasingly constitution-making is seen as an essential part of post-conflict reconstruction and renewal, and integrated temporally into peace negotiations, as the South Sudan example illustrates. An interesting literature has developed on particular cases, in which the fingerprints of the international community can be found.

Beyond the level of ideas and timing, specific constitutional institutions flow across borders in what scholars call the process of diffusion (Simmons & Elkins 2004). Scholars have noted that the content of these contemporaneous documents tends to be fairly similar, and a similar effect can be found for regions. Globally, Elkins, Ginsburg, and Simmons (2013) have identified a certain set of "core" norms, found in the vast majority of constitutions, to be contrasted with more peripheral ones that may be seen as optional. For most countries, the image of constitution-making as the work of a small group of national authors debating first principles could not be farther from reality.

Consider the spread of rights, a canonical symbol of universalism that also retains local character. Law and Versteeg (2011) have shown that rights provisions have spread around the globe. Elkins and his co-authors (2013) show that some rights, such as freedom of expression, have become nearly universal, while others have not. Some have argued that there is a kind of global script at work, whereby nation-states use constitutions to participate in global discourses. Scholars in the world society tradition of sociology, for example, emphasize the global interdependence of policy and institutional choices, so that constitutional texts respond to external forces as much as internal ones (Boli-Bennett & Meyer 1978; Go 2003). In this vein, Beck et al. in this volume show that constitutional rights provisions are not selected at random but are drawn from global templates such as the Universal Declaration of Human Rights. Elkins, Ginsburg, and Simmons (2013) show how the rights provisions of national constitutions are coordinated through the content of international treaties, such as the International Covenant on Civil and Political Rights, and the International Covenant on Economic, Social and Cultural Rights. Thus, the very menu from which designers choose is internationally constituted, influenced by global norms, and embodied in human rights treaties. The proliferation of international law and institutions enhance and support these transnational diffusion and modeling processes (Shaffer & Coye in press).

Even the parts of constitutions most conventionally thought of as reflecting national content – the preambles – are themselves transnationally constructed. Ginsburg, Rockmore, and Foti (2014) show that the language in preambles tends to flow across time and space. One can discern global trends in constitutional thinking by examining preambles: socialism rises in the twentieth century but falls in the twenty-first, to be replaced by references to the market, or to God who had earlier fallen in popularity after the nineteenth century. Similarly, Law in this volume identifies ideological clusters found in the latent patterns of language used in the texts.

The *process* of making constitutions is also affected by transnational norms and forces. International organizations with constitution-building programs have emerged, including International IDEA. These not only shape the content of constitution-making but the very process of making them. External organizations compile handbooks about how to design processes (Interpeace 2011) and case studies of how they operate (Miller & Aucoin 2010). Especially important in this regard is the norm that participation is required in constitution-making. The United Nations, in particular, has been pushing participatory constitution-making, and some ground it as a right in international law (Hart 2001). As Saati (2015) discusses, this norm rests on thin empirical grounding – participatory constitutions are not always more enduring or more effective (see also Moehler 2010). But the fact that even process is subject to transnational involvement shows the depth to which the field has been transformed.

Finally, constitutional implementation is increasingly a transnational enterprise. External actors – states, human rights organizations, international organizations, religious groups, and others – monitor the performance of constitutions. The Organization of American States, for example, was quick to judge the 2009 deposing of Honduras' sitting President Manuel Zelaya as a coup. One novel actor in this regard, described by Craig in this volume, is the Venice Commission, an organ of the Council of Europe, which has built a good deal of moral authority as a monitor of constitutions in the 47 nations in its ambit, and has now spread its activities beyond Europe to provide constitutional advice.

The involvement of international actors has become increasingly intense in recent decades, with more diverse sets of actors and norms entering the field. In every phase of the constitutional process – the triggering of constitution-making; design of the constitution-making procedures; drafting the text; adoption of the constitution; and implementation – constitution-making involves interaction between transnational actors and local parties. It involves both importers and exporters of norms, resistance, adaptation, normative settlement and unsettlement.

The constitutional process involves not just the design of a national legal system, but debates over particular norms that engage transnational actors in particular sub-fields, such as property rights, individual and social rights, gender rights, minority rights, the place of religion, and so forth. Contests and debates arise over the alignment of particular constitutional norms and practices with the underlying issues conceived as problems that law must address. While intense clashes arise in many of these areas, others exhibit normative settlement. A consensus exists, for example, on the need to have some rights provisions in a constitution, as well as on the need to at least give lip service to democratic processes. But the entire dynamic raises important empirical questions. To return to the South Sudan example, has the constitution not worked out very well because of its shallow local roots?

THEORIZING TRANSNATIONAL ASPECTS OF CONSTITUTION-MAKING

As the above description makes apparent, there is a burgeoning literature on constitution-making but to date little attention to characterizing the processes as a transnational legal practice. This book aims to build and apply transnational socio-legal theory regarding these practices to enhance collective research and understanding, including for normative interventions.

We are not, of course, the first to tackle this problem. Existing theoretical approaches include world society theory, which has documented how constitutions embody what they characterize as global forms; neo-colonial theory

(Hardt & Negri 2000; Fitzpatrick 2006; Gordon 1999); and theories of transnational expertise that document and critique expert governance (Kennedy 2016). These theories tend to be top down in their appraisal. To the extent they are applied to constitution-making, they also tend to stop at the moment of the creation of constitutional texts, rather than integrate constitution-making into a broader process of constitutional construction and ordering.

TLO theory, in contrast, aims to address the overall process through which norms settle and unsettle, and how these norms align with issues to be addressed.[2] These processes are dynamic and often recursive, and allow for the tracing of dynamics over time. The processes often involve constitution-making episodes, which (a) stretch from initiation of a constitutional writing/revision episode through ultimate settling or unsettling, and thereby (b) take into account recursive cycles in which "constitution-writing" is one, but only one, of many key constitution-making moments and activities. TLO theory thus pushes students of constitution-making to identify moments of settlement, and to define the relationship among discrete episodes of constitutional activity.

This volume applies the theoretical framework of TLOs to the study of constitutional norms to assess what the TLO framework can help reveal for the analysis of, and engagement with, constitution-making and practice, and how the study of constitution-making can inform TLO theory. The TLO framework brings together three concepts: (i) it focuses on the issue of *order*, a central concept in the sociology of law regarding the creation and settling of generalized normative behavioral expectations; (ii) it studies the role of *law* in such ordering processes, involving the use of legal form and legal institutions; and (iii) it examines the *transnational* nature of the normative ordering. Bringing these three concepts together, it defines a transnational legal order as "a collection of formalized legal norms and associated organizations and actors that authoritatively order the understanding and practice of law across national jurisdictions" (Halliday & Shaffer, 2015). That legal order could be the constitutional order itself, or it could be legal norms included within constitutions, such as human rights, women's rights, minority rights, property rights, religion, and so forth. In the latter case, a single constitution can comprise norms that are part of multiple TLOs.

The book reveals how these norms and patterns are rhetorically constructed. For example, there are core norms in a liberal, democratic constitutional prototype addressed by Scheppele and Landau. Similarly, there are central

[2] On the issues of normative settlement and issue alignment, see Halliday and Shaffer, *Transnational Legal Orders*, Chapter 1.

features pushed by a socialist TLO, such as existed in the Soviet era, and in Bolivarian constitutions involving different transnational networks (as discussed in the chapter by Law). Taking the chapters together, the book investigates the extent to which we see moves either toward the transnational emergence of a single constitutional TLO; or to rival liberal and socialist constitutional TLOs; or to multiple, competing TLOs addressing distinct sub-issues; or to insurgent TLOs, such as the authoritarian one addressed by Scheppele and Landau that takes a liberal form, but compromises liberal norms.

A transnational legal order is not static, and the concept does not posit an international or transnational form that is simply transposed in a top-down manner. Rather, a TLO results from processes of transnational legal ordering that involve the interaction of international, national, and local law and practice on each other (Shaffer 2013). From a TLO perspective, one assesses the role of importers and exporters of constitutional norms and how they interact over time, leading to the rise and fall of different constitutional orders. Constitution-making dynamics, in other words, can be viewed as multi-directional. They involve dynamics inside states (Kumarasingham and Couso chapters), across states, between states, and with international organizations, and transnational networks.

TLO theorizing assesses attempts, successes, and failures of creating TLOs in different issue areas to address "problems." Such problems are social constructions that reflect different interests, values, perspectives, and social understandings. Participants in transnational legal ordering aim to address and order "problems" through law, often in contests among actors. Problems addressed in constitution-making range from reduction of tribal or religious conflict, the mitigation of social conflict, the reduction of poverty, the subjugation of women, and the arbitrary exercise of power by the coercive powers available to a state. There is no inherent teleology in TLO theory; many efforts at TLO construction fail locally, nationally, and transnationally because they are successfully contested and blocked.

TLO theory calls on scholars to address practice as well as form. In the context of constitution-making, research will be directed to the development of constitutional conventions through practice, as well as constitutional texts. Written constitutions only tell us so much, and so TLO theory calls us to address constitutional practice that gives rise to conventions that are normalized, but that later can become contested. In this way, the TLO framework addresses, from a sociological perspective, how settlement and unsettlement give rise to a new normal.

This focus on iteration maps onto one of the interesting features identified by comparative constitutional scholars. In his account of "post-sovereign constitution making," Andrew Arato (2016) explains how constitutions are now produced in a more iterative manner, with multiple steps that allow for learning and adjustment. Not only has the process opened up spatially, through transnational influences, but it has also opened up temporally.

One of the virtues of this more dynamic approach is that it integrates the international and local levels. One of the phenomena that comparative scholars have identified is that constitutions tend not to last very long in most environments, but also that sequential constitutions in a country's history tend to borrow from each other as well as from international norms. The TLO orientation by treating international and national dynamics in the same framework, promises a richer understanding of how processes unfold over time.

To traditional black-letter scholars, the constitution as written stands by itself and is presumed to be effective; to some critical scholars, it results from some set of (dark) forces imposed on innocent and pure local contexts; and to some historical scholars, it sets in motion dynamics of refinement and development over time. The promise of the recursive approach to TLO construction is that it builds all these attributes into a dynamic framework that brings the insights of each temporal fragment of the process together.

The recognition of more dynamism raises important questions for legal theory. We are accustomed to thinking about constitutions as embodying a nationally situated constituent power that provides the basis for the making of law. Constitutions provide the *grundnorm*, the rules for the making of other rules (Kelsen 1960). H. L. A. Hart (1961), for example, places the constitution at the center of his concept of a legal system in that the constitution provides the secondary norms that give validation to primary norms that regulate behavior and facilitate coordination. In this way, the constitution constitutes a legal system. But if these constitutional norms are themselves constituted in a recursive and transnational manner, then their normative grounding as foundational (from the perspective of legal theory) becomes less clear.

In addition, the view of national constitutions as frameworks for legal systems of distinct sovereign states makes possible the field of comparative law (Michaels in press). In the last decades, the sub-field of comparative constitutional law has flourished (Hirschl 2014). Yet, once constitutions are viewed as part of dynamic processes of transnational legal ordering, the comparators become less stable. The very practice of comparative constitutionalism can participate in the dynamic shaping of the constitutions being compared. These practices can catalyze and contribute to constitutional change as part of ongoing transnational processes.

IDENTIFYING TLO BOUNDARIES

A central but challenging step in TLO analysis is to identify the boundaries of any given TLO. From the studies in this book, one can see different TLOs in competition with each other regarding constitution-making and practice, as well as efforts to establish a dominant liberal TLO.

With regard to constitutional texts, the chapter by Law finds evidence of different prototypes with different constitutional cores. Broadly speaking, one can see rival liberal-democratic and socialist constitutional orders. In addition, they show evidence of different heritages in constitutional orders involving colonial legacies and legal families. These give rise to parliamentary and presidential systems, and different roles for judicial review. Alternatively or complementarily, one sees evidence of constitutions as vehicles and opportunities to advance different substantive norms that themselves involve differentiated TLOs, such as TLOs for different human rights (Beck et al.), for gender, for property rights, for intellectual property protection, and for stakeholder participation (Saati).

In other words, the TLO framework opens the possibility of imagining constitution-making and implementation as social sites for contests among competing actors, each championing distinctive ideals which converge on some norms but deviate sufficiently on others that they appear as rivals. Ginsburg (Chapter two), Scheppele (Chapter seven), and Landau (Chapter eight), in particular, show that constitution-making can bring into tension multiple contenders for TLO primacy. Ginsburg suggests that the constitution-making process can be conceived of as an arena in which norm entrepreneurs in multiple TLOs – such as over different types of rights – contest substantive norms. In this sense, a constitution, conventionally conceived as the embodiment of national values and a framework for a national legal order, is in fact a transnational legal arena for contests over particular legal norms. The constitution-making process is, in other words, an arena for political and social struggle over the rules of the game. At any constitution-making moment local, national, and transnational actors are all drawn into this contest.

If the national and global enterprises of constitution-making are to be seen through a lens of contesting actors who champion norms for rival TLOs, then the core norms that are contested will include: (i) substantive norms (e.g., different human rights); (ii) procedural norms about the operation of governance (e.g., representation and modes of decision-making, such as elections); (iii) institutional norms (such as the structural allocation of power among institutions); and (iv) process norms about the very ways in which constitutions are written and adopted. In terms of substantive and institutional norms, Elkins et al. (2013) show that certain norms in the constitution are "core" and certain ones are "peripheral" and that these change over time. For example, eighteenth-century constitutions said little about political parties, and focused on what are known as "first generation" rights; twentieth-century constitutions introduced new concepts, like "self-determination," and had much lengthier lists of rights. They also introduced new machinery, including "fourth branch institutions" to monitor and supplement the classical three-branch structure of government. Even if there is no "end of history" in terms of the norms of liberal democracy, it is noteworthy that even dictatorships in our era try to legitimate themselves with elections. Nonetheless, because of the stakes, Couso finds that settling on institutional norms that affect the structural allocation of power is particularly difficult.

LEVELS OF CONSTITUTION-MAKING

TLO theory asserts that lawmaking in an interdependent world requires empirical inquiry simultaneously into the interaction of international/transnational, national, and local levels of lawmaking and practice. The manifest significance of the transnational in national constitution-making highlights the connections between legal orders and the sociology and politics of international organizations. Here the politics of TLOs intersect with an emerging sociology of international organizations that draws on social ecology theories of social spaces beyond the state for norm-making actors in general (Abbott, Green, & Keohane 2016) and global lawmaking in particular (Block-Lieb & Halliday 2017).

As regards national constitution-making, this requires tracing regularities in transnational influences on the development of national constitutional texts, such as through international human rights treaties (Beck et al., Chapter four; Elkins, Ginsburg, & Simmons 2013), and substantive and procedural soft law norms regarding gender and participation (Saati, Chapter ten). Similarly, it is necessary to discern patterns in the engagement and influence of external advisors and consultants from international organizations, foreign governments, and non-governmental organizations, as Ginsburg (Chapter two), Couso (Chapter nine), and Craig (Chapter six) observe. Yet, to study the interaction of these processes with national and local practice is a greater challenge.

A significant empirical challenge, from the perspective of TLO theory, is how to assess the settling of a TLO. In contrast to the conception of a normative order that exists only in written transnational norms, by definition a TLO can be said to be institutionalized only where there is concordance among transnational, national, and local legal norms in terms of practice (Block-Lieb & Halliday 2015). A preponderance of attention in constitution-making has been focused on the settlement of norms by a state. Partly as a matter of convenience this settlement can be observed in a written constitutional text that is stable over a number of years. It is quite another matter to establish empirically whether the norms in the national text are adopted locally, by the populace at large, or by the translators and conveyors of norms into everyday life within the nation-state.

Three possible modalities offer empirical insights into the degree to which national norms reach beyond settlements agreed by national leaders and flow outside the national capital. First, evidence of subnational and local settling of norms can be observed insofar as legal elites and practitioners, such as judges, police, prosecutors, and civil servants develop and internalize constitutional understandings, and local lawyers utilize constitutional constraints, rights, and conventions on behalf of their clients. Second, evidence can be found in the ways civil society and social movements lobby for constitutional norms, and then seize upon them in practice through legal complaints, media campaigns, and other means. Third, the penetration of norms deep into a society can be seen in the development of broader popular consciousness and references to the constitution that reflect a form of popular constitutional discourse (such as through surveys and discourse analysis).

DIACHRONIC PROCESSES: THE TRANSNATIONAL STRENGTHENING OF A TLO AND THE ADVENT OF A RIVAL TLO

Constitutional orders rise and fall (Halliday & Shaffer 2015: Chapter fourteen). One can see this with the Soviet socialist order that rose after World War II, was consolidated during the Cold War, and collapsed after the fall of the Berlin Wall. Scheppele (Chapter seven) and Landau (Chapter eight) provocatively suggest that the liberal, democratic constitutional order is under challenge in many countries. This raises the question that TLO theory insistently poses for all legal orders: what are the facilitating circumstances and precipitating conditions under which constitutional orders not only rise but also fall?

Constitution-making is iterative, leading to new opportunities for settlement and unsettlement of constitutional norms (Lerner 2013; Arato 2016). Recursive processes involving the interaction of international, transnational, national, and local lawmaking and practice often catalyze successive episodes of norm-making. As constitutions operate within a broader transnational institutionalized environment, when national leaders attempt to change, evade, and undermine settled constitutional norms, international and transnational actors respond. When they do so, they attempt to counter the undermining of the core norms that they view as part of the constitutional TLO. This at times can involve the strengthening of an institutionalized transnational constitutional TLO, or calls for it, as reflected in the chapters by Scheppele, Landau, and Craig. International institutions – such as the European Union, the Venice Commission of the Council of Europe, and the Organization of American States – develop varying powers to bolster constitutional constraints.

Efforts by national actors, however, can also be viewed in transnational context as attempts to create a rival TLO (involving shared norms and practices) that retain the liberal, democratic TLO in form, but find ways to fend off its constraints in practice. Scheppele and Landau respectively document these efforts in Eastern Europe and Latin America. These national actors often attempt to legitimate their practices within the conventional frame, while stealthily changing or evading it. Yet, even for them, some moves are off-limits or subject to greater normative constraints. Presidents Zelaya of Honduras and Morales of Bolivia confronted such constraints when attempting to free themselves from term limits. Actors develop rival transnational models to bolster their positions in transnational context.

MECHANISMS

Consistent with sociological theory on globalization and law, transnational legal ordering occurs through diverse mechanisms, such as coercion, reciprocity, modeling, negotiation, persuasion, learning, and socialization. Such is the case with the settlement and alignment of constitutional norms to address particular issues. Beck et al. examine the role of socialization processes; Kumarasingham of modeling; Ginsburg and Craig of expertise and persuasion through a sort of "invisible college" of experts who provide outside consultations. Others shows the role of coercive mechanisms, where aid or access to credit may be withdrawn, as following the ouster of Honduran President Zelaya (Landau), or force used, as in East Timor and a number of cases in West Africa. Constitution-making, though, doesn't typically involve reciprocity or peer review, mechanisms that have been identified in other international relations contexts.

From a TLO perspective, these mechanisms operate not simply in a top-down direction. They include the conveyance and uploading of norms from below into international treaties, soft law texts, and the practices of international organizations. They also include processes of horizontal diffusion through socialization, persuasion, modeling, and learning, as well as coercive threats.

INTERACTION OF LAW AND OTHER FORMS OF ORDERING

Legal ordering does not take place in a vacuum. Constitution-making involves high stakes (Couso, Chapter nine, and Kumarasingham, Chapter three). This raises the question of how transnational constitutional legal orders confront other forms of ordering, such as political orders (e.g., authoritarian regimes; Cold War politics), economic orders (e.g., neoliberal markets), and religious orders. What is the boundary work between the political, economic, religious, and the legal? How can one engage in such boundary work given the often porous borders between law, politics, the economy, and religion? Understanding the settlement and unsettlement of a constitutional TLO, or of TLOs for particular legal issues incorporated within a constitution, calls into question how the boundary of the legal order is affected by these other forms of ordering.

The high stakes in this area raise the question of whether constitutional TLOs are different in kind or degree from other TLOs, such as those identified in Halliday and Shaffer (2015). Since constitutional orders aim to constitute a legal system, a particularly pressing challenge following war and internal civil conflict, they at times confront fundamental issues of social peace affecting the very existence and organization of a state. In this way, they differ from technical areas of law that are subject to transnational legal ordering, such as customs regulation, secured transactions law, or securities regulation. When they implicate societies where religion plays a defining role, they can catalyze considerable social contestation or remain paper norms at the level of local practice because religion implicates most social practices, whether involving property rights, individual and social rights, the treatment of minorities, and so on. In this sense, the interaction of constitutional legal norms with political and religious orders is simply more salient than in other areas of law.

SUMMARY OF THE CHAPTERS

Our book includes a range of chapters that tackle these themes. First, Tom Ginsburg explores the history of external constitutional advice. He demonstrates that constitution-making has always had a transnational quality, with experts crossing borders to contribute to nominally sovereign processes. Using a series of individuals to illustrate some of the dynamics at work, he goes on to wrestle with the TLO concept, arguing that constitution-making episodes are often sites for contestation by (other) TLOs. Battles for influence among interest groups, forms of expertise, and normative ideas are routine in this process, rendering constitution-making an arena more than an institution.

Continuing the focus on agents of transnational norm transmission, Harshan Kumarasingham's chapter, using archival material, highlights Ivor Jennings' role in Pakistan's 1954 constitutional crisis. Jennings was an English lawyer and constitutional law scholar, who was consulted by many nations attempting to write a constitution styled on the Westminster model. The roadblock that many Asian countries ran into when they were trying to implement the Westminster system was disputes over the ceremonial head of state, which several systems modified to give the head of state more power. Jennings was asked to consult with the Constituent Assembly of Pakistan in July 1954, when it was attempting to build a system with a strong legislature along the lines of the Westminster model. In retaliation, the Governor-General Ghulam Muhammad, with the advice of Jennings, dissolved the Constituent Assembly for reasons of national security because the "constitutional machine has broken down." When the President of the Constituent Assembly took the Governor-General to trial, Jennings helped Muhammad to justify the seizure of power. While Jennings' argument lost in the Sindh High Court, he won in Federal Court, establishing a precedent and a doctrine of necessity that has bedeviled Pakistani constitutionalism to this day. Jennings and the Pakistani Chief Justice were able to harness the vast precedents of the Westminster model and manipulate traditional Westminster conventions to suit their purpose. Britain's parallel export of its common law tradition provided a means to distort the Westminster constitutional TLO model to legitimize authoritarian executive power. The chapter highlights that nominally neutral international expertise can be used in local contexts to shape institutional practices in very different ways from those of the "model" jurisdiction.

The chapter by Colin Beck, John Meyer, Ralph Hosoki, and Gili Drori draws on the "world society" school, which has provided sustained evidence that constitutions, once thought of as distinctly national documents, are produced in a transnational process. The chapter demonstrates the massive growth of human rights language and law in national constitutions. Drawing on data from the Comparative Constitutions Project, the authors produce an original measure of the human rights content in constitutions and use it to demonstrate the transnational origin of human rights inclusion in constitutions.

David Law uses a distinctive, cutting edge technique to analyze the content of national constitutions. The chapter demonstrates the utility of automated text analysis in uncovering latent patterns of similarity among constitutional texts, and argues that they are ideologically driven. Each of the major themes they uncover is associated with a transnational network of constitutional production, suggesting some robustness to the results and the existence of multiple, competing constitutional TLOs.

One of the modalities of transnational constitution-making in the contemporary era is the Venice Commission on Law and Democracy, a body of experts operating under the auspices of the Council of Europe, on which Paul Craig serves as an alternate member. In his chapter on the contribution of the Venice Commission to constitution-making, Craig explains the history, role, and working methodology of the Commission. He goes on to apply TLO theory to provide a framework for studying the Venice Commission's "transnational role in the dispersion of legal norms concerning democracy, human rights and the rule of law." Besides playing a central role as a TLO, the Commission provides a case study of the interaction of transnational bodies with other international actors and with national authorities, where norms must eventually settle to be effectuated. While there are some shortcomings that are apparent in any normative evaluation of the Commission's efficacy, the chapter concludes that it is ultimately a force for good in terms of preserving democracy, human rights, and the rule of law.

Kim Lane Scheppele's chapter on "Autocracy under Cover of the Transnational Legal Order" demonstrates that all that is transnational is not normatively attractive. The recent backsliding of constitutional democracies in Central and Eastern Europe has garnered a good deal of attention, and Scheppele points out that there may be a good deal of transnational learning among these countries. By working within the formal frameworks of the liberal, democratic constitutional TLO, leaders in these countries have been able to systematically undermine the spirit of constitutional democracy, seeking to entrench their coalitions. A counter-TLO can be viewed at work – one that retains the form of the democratic constitutional TLO but subverts it in practice – as these governments learn and borrow from each other's practices.

In his chapter on "Democratic Erosion and Constitution-Making Movements: The Role of Transnational Legal Norms," David Landau explores the risks constitution-making movements pose to democracy. The first part of his chapter argues that the constitution-making process is often fraught with a lack of legal restraint because of domestic legal and institutional circumstances: constitution-making often occurs during times of crisis and political turmoil, in which institutions have broken down or are fragile. Would-be authoritarian leaders can use this power vacuum to take over the constitutional process to strengthen their power. TLOs can be a part of the problem because the dominant legal theory of constitution-making is that it is grounded in the *pouvoir constituent*, an act of the people outside of the normal legal structure. Constituent assemblies are difficult to regulate, leading to the risk of democratic breakdown. Landau goes on to propose several possible tools to ameliorate risk, including democracy clauses, international norms, best practices, and advisory bodies that would further transnational legal ordering along a liberal, democratic model. While he sees no panacea, his hope is that solutions can consolidate over time and inform a transnational TLO that provides effective constraint on authoritarianism.

In her chapter on "Participatory Constitution-Making as a Transnational Legal Norm" Abrak Saati recounts the emergence of the new norm of participatory constitution-making. She both analyzes the concept from a TLO theoretical perspective and assesses how it has been implemented in practice. Building from a range of empirical cases, Saati analyzes the conditions under which participation produces the democratizing effects that it is posited to, instead of being subject to manipulation. She argues that a key condition is localization, in which norms and processes are institutionalized and internalized by the local population. In TLO terms, this would allow for the settlement of the transnationally articulated norms.

Finally, Javier Couso examines the role of transnational norms in the recent unsuccessful attempt to replace the Constitution of Chile, initiated by the government of Michele Bachelet. He identifies a process-oriented TLO, centered around International IDEA and other international actors, that focuses on rights, but has little to say about the forms of government. He speculates that this is because of political pushback when it comes to structuring the exercise of public power, which go to the core of state authority. While Chile is a relatively sophisticated legal culture, the dynamics he identifies may have broader implications for the stability of any transnational constitution-making TLO. There is likely to be continued unsettling on core issues about the form of government, even as norms on rights are more stable. One factor that might lead to this outcome is the presence of a well-established TLO on international human rights, which is linked to constitution-making processes (Elkins, Ginsburg, & Simmons 2013). Perhaps it is the linkages among TLOs, and their complex interactions, that predict the impact of constitution-making.

CONSTITUTION-MAKING AS A SITE FOR TLO THEORY-MAKING

TLO theory emerged as an analytic framework to study and understand legal responses to social, economic, and political problems, as they are constructed, framed, and applied in ways that span and transcend nation-states. Going beyond the initial empirical sites of research (which focused on discrete areas in human rights, private business, and regulatory law) (Halliday & Shaffer 2015), the studies in this volume open up a new issue-area to test and refine the theoretical power of TLO theory. How do they do so?

Attention to constitution-making contributes to TLO theory in two ways. First, the empirical site of constitution-making itself may have properties that are distinctive or *sui generis* and thus press TLO theory beyond its previous bounds. Second, attention to constitution-making promises to push forward frontiers of TLO theory that have already been partially explored in earlier scholarship (Halliday & Shaffer 2015). Here, we point to both sets of contributions.

The studies on constitution-making in this volume highlight social, political, and legal aspects of constitutions that, arguably, differ qualitatively from instances of legal change previously analyzed empirically through a TLO lens. While some national and transnational attention to a state's constitution focuses narrowly on an issue within a broader constitutional frame, as Craig has shown for issues that come to the Venice Commission, there are other instances (for example when constitutions are written anew) in which the "issue" is of a magnitude and complexity that seems to be qualitatively different from any TLO analyzed in previous work. The underlying problems reach to a broad range, and possibly almost every politically and socially contentious issue within a state's national boundaries. In so doing, any endeavor to produce a *legal* order that relies on a written constitutional text to be interpreted subsequently by designated *legal* institutions confronts every other kind of order and every kind of institutional logic within those orders. In these respects, constitution-making may be generic, foundational, and transformational in its aspirations unlike any other TLO. Indeed, a constitutional TLO has characteristics of a meta-TLO of as great a scope as the rule-of-law TLOs previously treated by Rajah (2015).

This distinctiveness manifests in direct encounters of a constitutional TLO with other forms of order in a society. Constitutions conventionally create rules for political life, but the extent to which logics of political life enter constitution-making can be controversial, both in their presence and absence (see Landau, Chapter eight; Saati, Chapter ten; Kumarasingham, Chapter three). A failure to reconcile legal and political processes for creating social order can contribute to legitimation deficits in a constitution or to a constitution's early demise. Constitutions increasingly, it appears, also confront religious orders and religious institutions and religious logics of action. Constitution-making and constitutional reforms therefore become fraught with negotiations between institutional leaders whose logics of action, modes of thought, and fundamental epistemological premises may be incommensurate. Economic orders, too, have their own logics (e.g., competition), their own ordering principles (e.g., efficiency, profit), their own institutions (e.g., property rights, firms, banks), and these too can lie within the jurisdiction of modern constitutions.

Not only does constitution-making bring into the same deliberative arena all other institutions in a society, but the means by which order is shaped in each social institution is presided over by elites with different forms of authority who use different modes of reasoning. The work of constitution-making at its core relies heavily on a legal complex of lawyers, judges, law professors, and lawyer-civil servants, among others. They confront other elites who are also authoritative, but whose mentalities, logics, and modes of leadership differ radically – priests and shamans, tribal leaders and generals, political party leaders, and banking tycoons. To design a national constitutional architecture invariably confronts one mode of producing order, i.e., through law, with contesting modes of order production that strain or compete with the producers of *legal* order. These incipient and sometimes overt contests affect the institutionalization of TLOs, since elites in competing orders effectively shape the prospects that nationally-inscribed norms in a written constitution will penetrate locally into the mentalities – the legal consciousness – of a broader population.

This juxtaposition of orders comes into stark relief in one feature of constitutional orders as TLOs – the confrontation between orders that rely on coercion and those that rely on rules. As Elkins, Ginsburg, and scholars of constitution-making over the *longue-durée* demonstrate, a substantial proportion of constitutions emerge from the breaking away or dissolution of empires, giving rise to political institutions that rest foundationally on military conquest and force. In fact, the initial moment of national constitution-making for a substantial proportion of states over the past two centuries emerges from armed conflict as the colonized rise against colonizers, as in decolonization from the 1950s to 1970s, or from wars that led to the collapse of empires, such as the Austro-Hungarian and Ottoman empires after World War I. International organizations and other transnational actors also rush to constitution-making as one component of the institutional packet of responses in the aftermath of bitter civil wars.

Arguably this particular kind of transition – from an order/disorder based on force and arising out of armed conflict to an order based on consent, consensus, and collective deference to civil resolution of deep societal differences – confronts constitutional lawmakers with a qualitatively greater challenge than TLO lawmakers who deploy law to order discrete issues involving markets, the environment, or other regulatory areas.

Moreover, constitution-making relies inherently on meta-narratives, past interpretations of a state's or people's history and its locus within regional and global discourses. TLO construction of constitutional orders therefore brings them into incipient engagement with powerful discourses grounded in centuries or millennia-long religious beliefs (e.g., Islam, Buddhism, Hinduism), in political ideologies (e.g., seventeenth- and eighteenth-century western liberalism or nineteenth- and twentieth-century Marxism), in economic discourses (e.g., liberalism and neoliberalism, state capitalism, and socialism in their various manifestations), and in historical tradition-making by emergent states (e.g., China's fictive 5,000 years of history or Pakistan's claim to the cultural distinctiveness of Indus Valley peoples). Thus a *legal* order that is articulated in contemporary constitution-making confronts to an unparalleled degree both transnational and historical narratives that are deeply embedded in discursive frames that infuse the mentalities and norms of the peoples to whom new legal norms are directed. In these ways, struggles over framing (see Halliday & Shaffer 2015: 481–4) are magnified, certainly at the onset of constitution-making and inevitably in the process of institutionalization of new constitutions in an attempt to embed extant transnational norms.

Here again the distinctiveness of constitution-making TLOs comes to the fore. The number and scope of issues covered by a constitutional TLO are extensive. The norms may seek to penetrate every social space, even if only to define limits of the state's penetration of those spaces. It most often reaches to every social institution. It impinges on every cultural identity, past and present. The "reason" inscribed in transnational scripts meets not only "reason" in national settings, but passions, emotions, and interests whose impulses, if not heeded, may subvert constitutional change that conforms to transnational norms. Couso (Chapter nine) asserts that the political stakes in constitution-writing are so high that one should expect *more*, not less conflict, in domestic constitutional politics. This, in turn, may lead to settlements that are inherently unstable because they do not resolve deep political rivalries within a society.

The empirical site of constitution-making also extends TLO theory built from research on business, regulatory, and human rights law (Halliday & Shaffer 2015, Chapter fourteen). Chapters in this volume underline the importance of attending to actors, their qualities, and relationships. A shift from portmanteau terms such as "diffusion" to the identification of particular classes of actors and the processes that knit them together, whether cooperatively or competitively, reinforces the significance of agency in TLO dynamics and thus one's ability to tease out fundamental forces in constitution-making. While it is valuable to map patterns of diffusion and their outcomes (Law; Beck et al.), it is also critical to disentangle contexts, conditions, and contingencies so as to develop conditional theory. Craig, Ginsburg, Kumarasingham, and Scheppele point to the extraordinary diversity of actors in TLO dynamics – UN bodies, intergovernmental organizations, national aid organizations, non-state transnational bodies, and, not least, democrats and autocrats, and notable norm entrepreneurs.

The empirical cases demonstrate that a robust theory of TLOs, in constitution-making and beyond, requires specification of domestic conditions that influence degrees of constitutional concordance and settlement. One set of contingencies relates to the circumstances that lead to the onset of a constitution-making episode. It makes a difference in domestic politics if constitution-writing was precipitated by the fall of an empire or by civil war and by which passions were inflamed in a civil conflict. It may be consequential if the drafting of a constitution is a novel conjunction of law and politics in a given society. Contingencies include the process of constitution-making itself, whether participation is shallow or deep, whether emotions, passions, and reason are given their due. It matters whether the agreements reached in constitutional processes authentically address grievances to the satisfaction of key groups and the general population within the state.

The contingencies of concordance with transnational norms are influenced by which actors mobilize effectively in national and local constitution-making practices. The chapters, especially those on participation in constitution-making, point to the methodological challenge of identifying actors within states who are initially excluded or defeated in diagnostic struggles and other aspects of the constitution-making process, but subsequently impede the institutionalization of the resulting norms. They thereby impel further recursive rounds of lawmaking and law implementation if a new constitution and its norms are to be institutionalized. Couso (Chapter nine) makes a strong case for paying close attention to national power configurations. In circumstances that would have otherwise seemed propitious, Chile's constitutional reforms foundered because there was entrenched and ultimately unassailable resistance to the reconstruction of central political institutions and the redistribution of power within the state. The "vices" of "normal politics," the "miseries of everyday politics (with its harshness, abuse of positions of power, and influence peddling)" were magnified to subvert an extraordinarily inclusive deliberative process.

The result was only a partial concordance of Chile's constitutional norms with transnational liberal constitutional ideals.

Previous studies show that discursive forms matter for TLO dynamics (Halliday & Shaffer 2015: 481ff). This book elaborates why the formal properties and rhetorical construction of transnational and national constitutional norms influence the rise and fall, the consolidation or contestation of TLOs. On the one hand, the very terminology of state constitutions reveals the degree of embeddedness of each state's self-understanding in relation to ideological movements beyond the state (Law, Chapter five). Yet the evocative comparative finding that constitutional dialects appear in clusters broadly derivative of the ideologies of British colonialism or socialist discourse respectively raises the question of the degree to which particular constitutional topics and terms reflect authentic ideological commitments or are empty signifiers.[3] Do they embed a given constitution in an already legitimate transnational discourse or is their purpose entirely served by gestures to satisfy otherwise skeptical audiences? On the other hand, formal properties matter not only because they have consequences for the probability of constitutional settlement, but also because the form of norms may enable insurgents to subvert the spirit of the law by selectively emphasizing certain transnational norms over others (Scheppele, Chapter seven).

The chapters in this book touch upon many moments of constitution-making. By imagining these many moments as connected parts of iterative recursive processes, as they unfold from the beginning to end of a constitution-making episode, the book reinforces the methodological and theoretical value of approaching legal ordering in terms of the many shifts from the local to national to transnational and back again. As a result, the book impels scholars to conceptualize the rise and fall of TLOs over the *longue durée*, while concomitantly examining constitution-making episodes within states as they go through the back and forth of local and national lawmaking and implementation that produces more or less institutionalization. Too little research on TLOs follows episodes from beginning to end. If connected, sequenced, and interrelated, the many moments identified in this book show the promise of such a dynamic and temporally-inflected approach. The rich attributes of constitution-making as a site of TLO research and theory propel scholarship toward processual theories of the transnational in the social sciences.

[3] A question raised by Mark Tushnet in his oral commentary on papers in this volume, LSA International meeting, Mexico City, June 2017.

REFERENCES

Abbott, Kenneth W., Jessica F. Green, and Robert O. Keohane. 2016. "Organizational Ecology and Organizational Strategies in World Politics." *International Organizations* 70(2): 247–77.

Arato, Andrew. 2016. *Post-Sovereign Constitution Making*. New York: Oxford University Press.

Beck, Colin, Gili Drori, and John Meyer. 2012. "World Influences on Human Rights Language in Constitutions: A Cross-National Study." *International Sociology* 27: 483–501.

Billias, George Athan. 2009. *American Constitutionalism Heard Round the World, 1776–1989: A Global Perspective*. New York: New York University Press.

Block-Lieb, Susan and Terence C. Halliday. 2017. *Global Lawmakers: International Organizations in the Crafting of World Markets*. New York: Cambridge University Press.

Block-Lieb, Susan and Terence C. Halliday. 2015. "Settling and Concordance: Two Cases in Global Commercial Law Settling in Transnational Legal Orders: Corporate Bankruptcy Law and International Trade by Sea." Pp. 80–110 in *Transnational Legal Orders* edited by Terence C. Halliday and Gregory Shaffer. New York: Cambridge University Press.

Boli, John. 1987. "Human Rights or State Expansion? Cross-National Definitions of Constitutional Rights, 1870–1970." Pp. 131–2 in *Institutional Structure: Constituting State, Society, and the Individual* edited by Francisco Ramirez et al. Beverly Hills: Sage Publications.

Boli-Bennett, John and John W. Meyer. 1978. "The Ideology of Childhood and the State: Rules Distinguishing Children in National Constitutions, 1870–1970." *American Sociological Review* 43: 797–8.

Cope, Kevin L. 2013. "The Intermestic Constitution: Lessons from the World's Newest Nation." *Virginia Journal of International Law* 53: 667.

Elkins, Zachary, Tom Ginsburg, and James Melton. 2009. *The Endurance of National Constitutions*. Cambridge: Cambridge University Press.

Elkins, Zachary, Tom Ginsburg, and Beth Simmons. 2013. "Getting to Rights: Treaty Ratification, Constitutional Convergence and International Law." *Harvard International Law Journal* 54: 61–95.

Elster, Jon. 1995. "Forces and Mechanisms in the Constitution Making Process." *Duke Law Journal* 45: 364–96.

Fitzpatrick, Peter. 2006. "The 'New Constitutionalism': The Global, the Postcolonial and the Constitution of Nations." *Law, Democracy and Development* 10: 1–20.

Ginsburg, Tom, Zachary Elkins, and Justin Blount. 2009. "Does the Process of Constitution-Making Matter?" *Annual Review of Law & Social Science* 5: 201–24.

Ginsburg, Tom, Daniel Rockmore, and Nick Foti. 2014. "'We the Peoples': The Global Origins of Constitutional Preamble." *George Washington International Law Review* 46: 305–40.

Go, Julian. 2003. "A Globalizing Constitutionalism? Views from the Postcolony, 1945–2000." *International Society* 18: 90.

Gordon, Ruth. 1999. "Growing Constitutions." *University of Pennsylvania Journal of Constitutional Law* 1: 528–82.

Halliday, Terence C. and Bruce G. Carruthers. 2009. *Bankrupt: Global Lawmaking and Systematic Financial Crisis*. Palo Alto: Stanford University Press.

Halliday, Terence C. and Bruce G. Carruthers. 2007. "The Recursivity of Law: Global Normmaking and National Lawmaking in the Globalization of Bankruptcy Regimes." *American Journal of Sociology* 112: 1135–202.

Halliday, Terence C. and Gregory Shaffer, eds. 2015. *Transnational Legal Orders*. New York: Cambridge University Press.

Hardt, Michael and Antonio Negri. 2000. *Empire*. Cambridge: Harvard University Press.

Hart, H. L. A. 1961. *The Concept of Law*. Oxford: Clarendon Press.

Hart, Vivienne. 2001. "Constitution-Making and the Transformation of Conflict." *Peace and Change* 26: 153–76.

Hirschl, Ran. 2014. *Comparative Matters*. New York: Oxford University Press.

Holmes, Oliver Wendell. 1881. *The Common Law*. London: MacMillan.

Interpeace. 2011. *Handbook on Constitution-making and Reform: Options for the Process*. Stockholm: Interpeace.

Kelsen, Hans. 1960. *Pure Theory of Law*, 2nd edition. Berkeley: University of California Press.

Kennedy, David. 2016. *A World of Struggle*. Princeton: Princeton University Press.

LaCroix, Alison. 2010. *The Ideological Origins of American Federalism*. Cambridge: Harvard University Press.

Landau, David. 2013. "Constitution-Making Gone Wrong." *Alabama Law Review* 64: 923.

Lanni, Adriaan and Adrian Vermeule. 2012. "Constitutional Design in the Ancient World." *Stanford Law Review* 64: 907–51.

Law, David S. and Mila Versteeg. 2011. "The Evolution and Ideology of Global Constitutionalism." *California Law Review* 99: 1163.

Lerner, Hanna. 2013. *Making Constitutions in Deeply Divided Societies*. New York: Cambridge University Press.

Michaels, Ralf. In Press. "Transnational Law and Comparative Law," in *Oxford Handbook of Transnational Law*, edited by Peer Zumbansen. Oxford: Oxford University Press.

Miller, Laurel and Louis Aucoin. 2010. *Framing the State in Times of Transition*. Washington: United States Institute of Peace Press.

Moehler, Devra. 2010. *Distrusting Democrats: Outcomes of Participatory Constitution-Making*. Ann Arbor: University of Michigan Press.

Negretto, Gabriel. 2013. *Making Constitutions*. New York: Cambridge University Press.

Rajah, Jothie. 2015. "'Rule of Law' as Transnational Legal Order." Pp. 340–73 in *Transnational Legal Orders*, edited by Terence C. Halliday and Gregory Shaffer. New York: Cambridge University Press.

Roznai, Yaniv. 2017. *Unconstitutional Constitutional Amendments: The Limits of Amendment Powers*. New York: Oxford University Press.

Saati, Abrak. 2015. *The Participation Myth: Outcomes of Participatory Constitution Building Processes on Democracy*. Umea, Sweden: Statsvetenskapliga institutionens skriftserie.

Shaffer, Gregory, ed. 2013. *Transnational Legal Ordering and State Change*. New York: Cambridge University Press.

Shaffer, Gregory and Carlos Coye. In Press. "From International Law to Jessup's Transnational Law; From Transnational Law to Transnational Legal Orders," in *Oxford Handbook of Transnational Law*, edited by Peer Zumbansen. Oxford: Oxford University Press.

Shaffer, Gregory and Terence C. Halliday. In Press. "With, Within, and Beyond the State: The Promise and Limits of Transnational Legal Ordering," in *Oxford Handbook of Transnational Law*, edited by Peer Zumbansen. Oxford: Oxford University Press.

Simmons, Beth and Zachary Elkins. 2004. "The Globalization of Liberalization: Policy Diffusion in the International Political Economy." *American Political Science Review* 98(1): 171–89.

Wallis, Joanne. 2013. *Constitution-Making During State Building*. New York: Cambridge University Press.

2

Constitutional Advice and Transnational Legal Order

Tom Ginsburg

From Bangkok to Barcelona, from Juba to Johannesburg, and from Sana'a to Santiago, the process of making national constitutions has garnered a good deal of attention from the academic and policy communities in recent years (Eisenstadt et al. 2017; Negretto 2013; Cope 2013a; Ginsburg, Elkins, & Blount 2009). The ubiquity of constitution-making processes – and the belief that constitutions can help advance myriad goals, from economic revitalization to post-conflict reconstruction – has generated demand for new forms of expertise as well as efforts to supply it. In this chapter, we consider the field of constitution-making as a transnational legal order (TLO) (Halliday & Shaffer 2015). We argue that the TLO framework is fruitful in that it illuminates aspects of the process, but also that this prominent field of legal activity brings into relief aspects of the framework that may need further elaboration. In that sense, the exercise is a recursive one, in which I juxtapose TLO theory and the constitution-making field to say something about each.

Constitution-making is a description for an activity that occurs in a vastly diverse set of contexts, attacking an array of very different problems. Some constitutions are made in situations after violent conflict; others are designed to prevent conflict from ever emerging; yet others involve minor revisions to political bargains in otherwise stable orders. One could easily and fairly refine these subcategories to discuss different kind of problem-driven approaches. It is also the case that constitution-making exercises are highly contested. Notwithstanding the persistent dualist imagery in which "higher" interests align (Ackerman 1992; Negretto 2013), constitutional politics are intense, high stakes, and occasionally violent.

This chapter begins with a brief history of constitution-making to describe the setting, then turns to the specific topic of transnational constitutional-advice giving. It then turns to a mapping of the contemporary terrain, with an informal accounting of the assets and capacities various repeat actors bring to the endeavor. Constitution-building has become a nascent form of expertise, with its own programs and experts. When one visits myriad constitution-making sites, one runs into a relatively limited set of repeat actors. Clearly, the field, and the world, have become more institutionalized since the end of the Cold War.

Does this make constitution-making a TLO? Halliday and Shaffer (2015) define a TLO as a set of "formalized legal norms and associated organizations and actors that authoritatively order the understanding and practice of law across national jurisdictions." While there is no central institution that authoritatively structures the practice of constitution-making, there is a loose network of institutions and actors that work in the field in multiple contexts, and the United Nations (UN) often seeks (sometimes unsuccessfully) to assert its dominance (Elmi 2012). Some institutions attempt to promote substantive norms, while others focus on the process of constitution-making; however, all of this is relatively under-institutionalized at the moment, and there is not, nor will there be, a transnational legal instrument or binding legal text on constitution-making.[1]

Indeed, it might be best to think about constitution-making as a field in which *other* TLOs come to engage in contests over outcomes. A contemporary constitution-making situation in a developing country might involve: various internal groups seeking a stake in power; several different units within the UN pushing for various sets of norms that might even be inconsistent with each other; the human rights community; a "transitional justice" legal order; a group pushing for federalism; a gender audit group; international financial institutions; bilateral donors arguing over religion clauses and oil rights; and various others. These different legal groups will have different agendas and not be aligned with each other. The result is a bounded set of contests that takes place in a temporally and geographically defined field. The chapter concludes with speculation on the implications of this analysis for the TLO framework.

THE SETTING

National constitutions have become one of the key components of a modern nation-state. Despite our imagery of a constitution as the quintessential expression of the values of a particular political community, constitutions are – and always have been – embedded in a transnational context. Written

[1] The United Nations Secretary General's note described below is the closest thing. But this is in essence an internal administrative order, articulated as a vague set of principles, to the vast bureaucracy of the UN, not purporting to bind outsiders.

constitutions in the modern sense are a particular form that emerged in the eighteenth century, borrowing upon earlier ideas and institutions (Elkins, Ginsburg, & Melton 2009). The form, which crystallized with the adoption of revolutionary constitutions in the United States, Poland, and France at the end of the eighteenth century, spread transnationally, partly because of the influence of revolutionary and liberal thought in Latin America (Gargarella 2010). New nation-states began to adopt constitutions as one of their first acts in existence. The documents play both symbolic and functional roles, defining a government and regulating the relationship between a government and its citizens. They also serve, in theory, to bind together the people. And importantly, they also serve as a signal to the international community that the government is a legitimate one.

Constitutional drafting is often undertaken in less than ideal conditions. Constitutions are often produced in situations of political uncertainty and under great time pressures, and the task is exacerbated by the fact that few constitutional drafters have any experience in the field. Repeat players are rare, even in countries in which constitutions do not last very long. This means that drafters often look for shortcuts.

This leads to two dynamics. First of all, constitutions tend to adopt a common set of core institutions. Look at the tables of contents of national constitutions and one will see a good deal of similarity. Virtually all constitutions have a separate section on a bill of rights, as well as sections on government, the judiciary, the legislature, local government, and, increasingly, accountability institutions. There are core institutions, found in almost every constitution, and also peripheral institutions which are found in relatively few. For example, 98 percent of constitutions stipulate how the head of state is to be selected, while something like 2 percent provide for a right to bear arms.[2] The former is a core provision, the latter a peripheral one. One might think of these core elements as the settled component of the transnational legal order of constitution-making.

The second dynamic is in part related to the first. Because constitutions are in part directed outside the nation-state, drafters often pay attention to the perceived demands of the international community. This leads drafters to adopt norms embodied in *other* constitutions written around the same time. Indeed, along with my co-authors in the Comparative Constitutions Project, I have shown that the best predictors of constitutional form are the era and region in which the constitution was drafted, as well as the contents of previous constitutions in the country's history (Ginsburg & Melton 2015). But the

[2] Data on file with author.

transnational nature of the process also means that countries frequently turn to outsiders to provide substantive advice.

A BRIEF HISTORY OF TRANSNATIONAL CONSTITUTIONAL ADVICE

This section provides a thumbnail history of transnational advice-giving through the experiences of several prominent practitioners. The idea here is not by any means to be comprehensive, but to be suggestive of some of the enduring themes and debates. As can be seen, the practice of constitutional advice engages a kind of dialectic between universal forms, of which written constitutions are themselves an embodiment, and local context. The major point of this section is that before 1990, most of the efforts involved one-off engagements with particular individuals and institutions, rather than a discrete social field. But since then the field is becoming more densely populated and institutionalized.

Antecedents

Constitutional advice has a long and distinguished history in the modern period. No less a figure than Jean-Jacques Rousseau was called on to advise constitution-making processes in Corsica and Poland in the late-eighteenth century. Each of these proto-countries was struggling for independence, and thought that a constitution would help to cement its claim to nationhood (Qvortrup 2003). Who could be better than the leading political theorist of the day to help in the process? By inclination, Rousseau was prone to abstraction, and he did not focus much on concrete institutions. Indeed, he was unable to finish his "Plan for a Constitution for Corsica" before the French Government took over the island (Damrosch 2005). Rousseau (1772) had a bit more influence in Poland, where his essay on *Considerations on the Government of Poland* apparently had some impact on the nobles who negotiated the short-lived Constitution of 1791. His advice was modest, noting that "institutions for Poland can only be the work of Poles," such that a "foreigner can hardly do more than offer some general observations for the enlightenment, but not for the guidance, of the law-reformer." Rousseau emphasized the importance of cultural activities like sports in building a common identity as a nation (Rousseau 1772). It was hardly his fault that Poland was eliminated as an independent state within a few years: no constitutional arrangement could change the country's unfortunate location between the expanding empires of Prussia and Russia.

Goodnow and China

As more and more countries became independent in the nineteenth century, demand for advice grew, and Western experts were well situated to provide it.[3] One early story of constitutional advice illustrates the potential pitfalls. Frank Goodnow, Columbia professor and the first president of the American Political Science Association, was asked by the Carnegie Endowment for International Peace in October 1912 to advise the Chinese Government on constitutional reform (Kroncke 2016: 135–40). On paper, Goodnow seemed to embody just the kind of interdisciplinary approach that should have been ideal. His area of expertise was administrative law, the area of law that deals with government organization and communication with citizens, and he took an explicitly political approach. He had studied in France and Germany as well as the United States. A believer in the power of technocratic expertise, he was known as a powerful figure in progressive thought.

As a comparative scholar, Goodnow knew better than to simply promote American-style institutions for China. Indeed, his scholarly work had posited that the United States had much to learn from constitutional and administrative models in other countries, especially Britain. Systems of government, he concluded, "are matters which must very largely be governed by the history and political needs of the particular country, and any attempt to impose on a country any hard and fast rule derived either from *a priori* reasoning or from any inductive generalization, based upon the experience of other countries, is rather more apt to meet with failure than success" (Pugach 1973: 501; Krocke 2016: 132–57).

As a believer in technocracy, Goodnow did not pay much attention to local politics, and by his own account was not deeply informed about China. He quickly became a proponent of executive power in the Chinese context, believing that the complexity of the country required strong central authority, and was amenable to a parliamentary system (Pugach 1973: 503). This view fit the interests of the warlord Yuan Shikai, who had taken over as president in 1914 after a struggle with Sun Yat-Sen's new Kuomintang Party. Yuan adopted a new constitution that was heavily influenced by Goodnow's draft. It included several western-style concepts like equality and privacy, but also featured strongly centralized power.

Still, Goodnow was frustrated. In one letter he noted, somewhat patronizingly, "as I look at it these Chinese have hardly the faintest idea of what a

3 For example, Harvard Law Professor Simon Greenleaf drafted the Constitution of Liberia in 1847. See Billias (2009) at 483. (Interestingly, it is one of the few constitutions outside the United States which included a right to bear arms!)

constitution is. They do not, I think, even know what law is" (Kroncke 2012: 560). He grew increasingly frustrated by the unwillingness of Chinese to engage his advice:

> My feeling was and is that the Chinese, the experience of all the advisers here would seem to show, have really no serious intention of following the advice of their advisers, unless that advice agrees with their own conclusions. Indeed, they regard their advisers as almost entirely ornamental in character and seldom let us know what is really going on. All we do is to write essays which are translated into Chinese and then what happens to them Heaven only knows. (Kroncke 2012: 563)

But this was not to be the case with his final essay. In 1915, after having returned to the US to become president of Johns Hopkins University, Goodnow drafted a short memo for Yuan entitled "Monarchy or Republic?", answering the rhetorical question in favor of the former (Kroncke 2012: 570–1). Monarchy, after all, was consistent with Chinese tradition and resolved problems of executive succession. Noting that the Chinese context was more similar to that of the troubled republics of Latin America than to the United States or England, Goodnow noted that "It is not susceptible of doubt, that a monarchy is better suited than a republic to China" (Kroncke 2012: 571).

Goodnow's views meshed perfectly with those of Yuan, who had been toying with establishing himself as a new emperor. His faction used Goodnow's endorsement to push forward a new draft of a monarchical constitution. Yuan's proposal could not have been further from the views of prominent Chinese intellectuals like Liang Qichao and Kang Youwei, who had been writing about the optimal form of Chinese government for decades. As a prominent Chinese intellectual said in the pages of the New York Times, "Dr. Goodnow was used simply as a tool. He is a great scholar, a professor, a citizen of a great republic, but he was duped by the monarchist faction, because he did not have a real insight into the situation" (Kroncke 2012: 574). Goodnow's friend Paul Reinsch wrote that "Advisors had been so generally treated as academic ornaments ... that Doctor Goodnow did not suspect that in this case his memorandum would be made the starting point and basis of positive action" (Pugach 1973: 500). Yuan Shi'kai ultimately decided to try to ascend the throne as a new emperor. However, he died before he could actually be enthroned, and China's long period of chaos, civil war, and failed governments continued for several more decades. Goodnow's constitutional project failed, and his return home was marked by criticism over his endorsement of monarchy. Goodnow's story illustrates the pitfalls and politics of advice-giving. While he sought to tailor his advice to local conditions, he was unaware of the uses to which it would be put. Expertise, we are reminded, is always political, but the experts may sometimes not be able to deploy it effectively or intentionally (Kennedy 2015). Clients for expertise have their own interests and tools that they bring to the game.

Biting the Hand that Feeds? Ivor Jennings and the End of Empire

Sir Ivor Jennings was a British academic and already a star constitutional lawyer when he was asked to take an appointment as Principal of Ceylon College (Jennings 2005; Kumarasingham 2015). He then moved to Sri Lanka and presided over the creation of the University of Peradeniya. On arriving in Sri Lanka, he confronted an educational system in high colonial mode. Students were given standard textbooks from England, in which geography lessons stopped at the Suez Canal. They were asked to memorize lists of plants and animals they would never see. Jennings recalled an English lesson in British Malaya in which the students were being asked to memorize the lines "O fair daffodils we weep to see you haste away so soon" (Jennings 2005: 100). When the students asked what daffodils were, they were told not to worry about it, as it would not be on the exam (Jennings 2005: 100–1). Jennings was shocked by such imperialist modes of education, and from the beginning, he sought to develop education that would be locally useful in Sri Lanka.

Constitutions, of course, are a bit like educational systems – they need to include common elements with the rest of the world, but also to be tailored to local conditions. With this view in mind, Jennings became a key constitutional advisor for the Sri Lankans, serving from 1942–8. His closest interlocutor was D. S. Senanayake, who eventually became the first prime minister of Ceylon in 1947. With his intimate knowledge of British political culture, Jennings would prep Senanayake and other leaders as to how to make their case to the colonial office. He analogized the process to a game of bridge, in which the British would obey the rules (Jennings 2005: 175–6). With Jennings advising them, the analogy suggested, Sri Lankans could play the right cards, but Jennings's role was not appreciated by the British Foreign Office, which sought to control the negotiations (Parkinson 2007).

The basic constitutional problem Jennings confronted was that the Ceylonese wished for independence immediately, while the colonial authorities thought they were still unfit for self-governance. Jennings came down on the side of the locals, and targeted the British idea of Dominion status, applicable to countries like Australia, Canada, and New Zealand, allowing for independent statehood within the British Empire, while retaining the British Crown as head of state (Jennings 2005: 174). Senanayake's political powers of persuasion helped convince the Colonial Office to support this view. Jennings was later involved in constitution-making in Pakistan, Malaysia, Singapore, Malta, the Maldives, Ghana, Guyana, Eritrea, and Nepal (Parkinson 2007: 29). He continued, on occasion, to bite the hand that fed him, siding with the king in Nepal against the foreign office. A relentless workaholic, he noted that "what troubles me is that there is so much to be done and so little time to do it" (Jennings 2005: 83).

The New Americans

The period after World War II was one of American dominance in international affairs, and this was reflected in constitutional design as in other fields. It was most apparent in cases of military occupations. Carl Friedrich, a Harvard political scientist, worked on the postwar German Constitution; the more famous case of the postwar Constitution of Japan reflected the direct influence of the American drafters working for the Supreme Commander of the Allied Powers (SCAP) (Moore & Robinson 2004; Elkins, Ginsburg, & Melton 2008; Law 2010). Unsurprisingly, some of the draft language made little sense in the local idiom. The description of rights as the "fruit of mankind's age-old struggle to be free" – included at the insistence of MacArthur's aide General Whitney – is almost unintelligible in Japanese, and clearly a tip-off for the foreign origin of the document (Elkins, Ginsburg, & Melton 2008). To be sure, the Japanese Government pretended to have written the text. For several months over the summer of 1946, the Japanese Diet debated the draft, making a few amendments, but preserving the basic core. The charade that Japanese had drafted the text is itself telling. Even if foreigners did write constitutions, it would undermine the legitimacy and probability of adoption of the resulting document to talk about it. Since local ownership is required to make constitutions work, foreign bragging tends to be counterproductive.

The immediate postwar period saw the writing of dozens of new constitutions as former colonial empires broke up. The United States played a role in some of these, but in other cases, the political dominance of the United States led some to *avoid* the American model (Scheppele 2003). The drafters of the Constitution of India, in particular, were intent on avoiding American approaches (Austin 1966: 27–39). Their decision to opt for a parliamentary rather than presidential form of government and their commitment to using the constitution for social transformation reflect this inclination. The drafters of India's constitution included a plethora of British-trained lawyers: indeed, one account suggests that two of three of the important players were lawyers (Austin 1966: 337–44). Yet even in this case, foreigners had some indirect influence. B. N. Rau, the constitutional advisor to the Indian Constituent Assembly, discussed the draft with several American professors as well as members of the United States Supreme Court. (He also visited England, Ireland, and Canada in his research, and looked at dozens of other countries' constitutions in formulating his recommendations.) Justice Felix Frankfurter successfully encouraged Rau to eliminate the general phrase "due process of law" from the Indian Constitution, informed by his dislike of judicial activism involving so-called "substantive" due process. The Indians instead borrowed the phrase "except according to procedure established by law," from the just-adopted 1946 Japanese Constitution (Austin 1966: 104). But that, of course, was itself an American product.

Later-Justice Thurgood Marshall played a role advising Kenya on its independence constitution in 1960, borrowing extensively from the Universal Declaration of Human Rights, and the constitutions of two newly independent countries, Nigeria and Malaya (Parkinson 2007: 221–5). Other American advisors played similar roles in various parts of Africa and Asia, but the much more prevalent model was a negotiated constitutional exit managed by the British or French colonial authorities. Constitutions in many countries were simply colonial gifts, a quid pro quo in exchange for granting independence, and they sometimes reflected colonial interests.

In the early years of the Eastern European constitution-making exercises after 1990, some American lawyers became highly sought after. One was A. E. Dick Howard, a professor at the University of Virginia Law School who had played a major role in drafting his state constitution in 1971. Howard traveled to many of the countries in Eastern Europe on behalf of USAID, and worked on the constitutions of ten countries (Perry 1991: 767–8). "The great ideals of American freedom," he wrote, "travel well" (Howard 1991: 8) and so, it seems, did he. Another peripatetic figure during this period was Albert Blaustein, a law librarian from Rutgers Law School. His first involvement in this kind of work came in the 1960s when he was asked to help build a law library for a new law school being created in Liberia (Perry 1991: 778). He later compiled a large collection of constitutional texts that was an important scholarly resource for many years (Flanz & Blaustein 2007). He parlayed this experience into a second career as a constitutional advisor including in his resume advisory roles in Bangladesh, Brazil, Mozambique, Namibia, Cambodia, Liberia, Niger, Peru, Fiji, Uganda, and Zimbabwe. He also contributed to processes in Romania, Poland, Slovenia, Eritrea, Ethiopia, and Lithuania. Blaustein later produced a "checklist" for constitutional designers, and some assert that he used "cut-and-paste" techniques from the compendium of other texts in dispensing his advice. When a reporter called him "The Johnny Appleseed of

Constitutions," Blaustein immodestly replied, "I prefer the Jewish James Madison" (Avery 1990).

Localism and Universalism

In some cases, advisors bring their own political biases and concerns to bear on supposedly national texts. Take the Constitution of Malaysia (originally known as Malaya). As the country was preparing for independence from Britain in 1956, British and Malaysian politicians agreed to form a drafting commission for a new constitution (Fernando 2016: 141–2). Headed by Sir William Reid, a distinguished British jurist, it included Ivor Jennings along with a former governor-general of Australia and judges from India and Pakistan. (No Malaysian was included in the Reid Commission, but it was understood that the local rulers and politicians would have to sign off on its product.)

Malaysia is a complicated place, with a majority of Muslim Malays but also substantial minorities of people of Chinese and Indian descent who moved there during the colonial period. Relations among these groups have varied over time, and the British established a system of privileges for the "indigenous" Malays, who were seen as economically backward relative to the other groups. Much like a contemporary affirmative action program, these privileges included land reservations, and quotas for public sector jobs, business licenses and university scholarships. The challenge for the Reid Commission was to reconcile these privileges with principles of equality, and it proposed that the privileges be temporarily extended for fifteen years. In this case, the drafters were trying to preserve a set of local institutions that were themselves of colonial origin. The consequences were significant, as Malaysia largely retains the affirmative action scheme more than five decades later, arguably a major factor in keeping it in the "Middle-Income Trap" (Ginsburg 2014: 26).

In recognition of the multi-ethnic nature of Malaysian society, the first draft of the constitution did not mention an official religion, and the various princes of the component states supported this position. However, the Pakistani delegate, a judge named Abdul Hamid, who had served as a drafter on his own country's constituent assembly, strongly insisted that Islam had to be the official religion (Fernando 2006: 256). Hamid's motives may have had more to do with the justification for the creation of Pakistan a decade earlier than his views as to what was appropriate for Malaya, which was less than 60 percent Muslim at the time. Whatever the motive, Hamid's insistence had significant consequences for Malaysia down the road. Today, all ethnic Malays are defined as Muslim, and until recently could not convert out of the religion.

This position was confirmed in an important legal case 2007 when a young Malay woman, Lina Joy, sought to have the state recognize her conversion to Christianity.[4] The courts refused to allow this. Malaysia remains an ethnically and religiously polarized place. Might it have been different if the status of religion had been left to the locals?[5]

The People Are the Client: Yash Ghai

The world's leading constitutional drafter today is Professor Yash Ghai, a Kenyan of East Indian origin who taught at the University of Hong Kong for many years. This cosmopolitan background and a deep knowledge, from both personal and academic experience, of situations of ethnic diversity have rendered him the leading person in the field. Frequently working with his wife, the distinguished law professor Jill Cottrell, Ghai has been involved in constitutions in Kenya, Papua New Guinea, Nepal, Libya, Somalia, Fiji, and many others.[6] He has taken an admirable and rare interest in the constitutions of small developing countries. Such countries may be more open to outside assistance in formulating their constitutions, and Ghai has frequently been asked to chair drafting commissions in quite public circumstances. This sometimes gets him into trouble.

In 2012, Ghai traveled to Fiji, where strongman Voreqe Bainimarama sought to legitimate his rule with a transition to a new constitution. (He had overthrown the previous constitution in a coup and had been appointed prime minister in 2009 after a constitutional suspension.) Ghai's good friend and former student Aiyaz Sayed-Khaiyum was a senior Indo-Fijian politician, and suggested that Ghai become involved in the Constitutional Commission that was to draft a new document. What better way for the Fijians to legitimate the transition to democracy than having the world's leading constitution-maker at the head of the process? At the same time, the presidential decrees promised a restoration of true democracy, and mandated that the constitution protect

4 *Lina Joy* v. *Majlis Agam Islam Wilayah Persekutan and Ors*. [2004] 2 MLJ 219, available at www.malaysianbar.org.my/selected_judgements/lina_joy_v_majlis_agama_islam_wilayah_persekutuan_2_ors_2005_ca.html.

5 If Abdul Hamid's views on religion seem to privilege one of Malaysia's groups over others, he also brought with him a prescient awareness of the dangers of emergency rule. He argued for strictly limited emergency powers, though this suggestion was rejected. Emergency powers were abused for many years thereafter in Malaysia (and in Pakistan as well).

6 In a 2005 paper he lists Seychelles, Papua New Guinea, Solomon Islands, Vanuatu, Fiji, East Timor, Afghanistan and reviews in Tanzania, Kiribati, Cook Islands, Maldives, Zambia, and Kenya. Ghai (2005).

human rights and be built through popular participation. It seemed a good gamble.

The formal mandate of the Constitutional Commission was to produce a draft which would be submitted to a constituent assembly, and to engage in wide consultations. The government insisted that the drafting process would give "every Fijian a voice." There were a few red lines given to the commission by the government: these included the need to grant immunity for the coup-makers in previous governments, a one-person one-vote electoral scheme, and human rights protections (Ghai 2005: 2). The immunity requirement, along with prime ministerial control of the review process, and gag orders on the constituent assembly that was to approve the draft, generated some international controversy, as it seemed to provide for veto points for the current power holders.

This assignment obviously posed some risks for Ghai, but, perhaps out of a deep optimism, he went ahead and agreed to participate in the drafting process. Foreign donors, including Australia, New Zealand, and Britain provided funding, which helped ensure that at least some degree of independence could be maintained. Joining Ghai on the commission was Christina Murray, who had worked on the South African Constitution and the Constitution of Kenya 2010, as well as three Fijians picked by the government. Ghai's spouse Jill Cottrell was a researcher. The group proceeded to engage with a broad range of civil society actors, and to organize training sessions in the basic approaches to institutional design. It received over 7,000 submissions from the public with ideas for the constitution, a remarkable number in a semi-literate country.

Things began to go south when Ghai sought to push in a democratic direction and to appeal directly to the people over the government. This meant that he stepped out of the role of being a mere advisor, to become a political actor in his own right. In part this reflects Ghai's view of the constitution-making mission. Whereas a practicing lawyer might see the client as the government or funding agency that hired him or her, Ghai's view has always been that constitutions are written for the people, and should be written on their behalf to the extent possible. In other words, the people, not the government, are the client.

The government's view differed. It saw Ghai's Commission as merely advisory to the government. It threatened Ghai with expulsion, and although the Commission then took a lower profile, things never got back on track. By December 2012, the Commission had produced a document with plenty of democratic protections (Draft Constitution Explanatory Report, 2012). This was surely a heroic achievement accomplished in a very short period of time, but all the work went to naught. The Commission's draft deviated from the instructions put to it on immunity. It only offered immunity for coup participants who took an oath renouncing their support of illegal regimes and, crucially, offered no immunity at all for those who had committed human rights violations. Furthermore, the proposals on land and transitional provisions generated controversy. As a result, the draft never saw the light of day. The Constitutional Commission ordered some copies of the draft printed, but as it waited for the books to come back from the printers, the government burned the printers' proofs. There was significant controversy over the precise sequence of events, but some asserted that one of Ghai's fellow commissioners had not known about the printing. Political and media attacks followed. Bainimarama spuriously accused the Commission, especially Professor Ghai, of consorting with individuals interested in making Fiji a Christian state. Ghai was also accused of working with the political opposition. On March 21, 2013, Bainimarama's government published its own draft constitution, which had largely been written largely by Ghai's former student, the attorney general.

This was hardly Ghai's only experience with failure, yet many of his projects have had an afterlife even beyond the death of the formal draft. He was extensively involved in producing a draft for his native Kenya in 2004–5, a project that ultimately was rejected by politicians who had much to lose (Ghai 2005: 828). The process involved a huge constituent assembly of 600 people, and extensive efforts to educate the public. Reflecting on the situation in 2005, he asked, "[m]ight it have been wiser to have opted for less radical change and carried the politicians with use, even if it meant ignoring the people?" (Ghai 2005). However, in the aftermath of electoral violence and a significant international effort to get the country back on track, many of his ideas made it into the 2010 constitution, which was a watershed in Kenyan history.

Ghai is noteworthy for recognizing an evolution in the role for constitutional advisors. Whereas someone like Jennings saw himself as primarily a technician trying to tailor a text to a particular set of local circumstances, Ghai sees the role of the modern constitutional advisor as much more complex. The advisor, in his view, must sometimes be an educator, sometimes be a negotiator, and sometimes play the role of facilitating broader participation beyond a narrow set of elites (Ghai 2005: 805). As an educator, the advisor must help to explain what has and has not worked to the political forces negotiating the constitution. As a negotiator, the advisor must sometimes engage in conflict resolution to help discover shared interests. And as a facilitator, the advisor must remember that the people are the ultimate source of sovereignty, whose participation can help to ensure that the constitution is successful.

The Lefties

Constitutional advice is a subsidy of information and ideas, and so it is perhaps unsurprising that the providers will have motives of their own. An important source of ideas for recent constitution-makers in Latin America has been a Spanish think tank, the Centro de Estudios Políticos y Sociales (CEPS), based in Valencia and dedicated to critique of capitalism and encouraging processes of social transformation. These include Professor Roberto Viciano Pastor, a prolific scholar who had a role in advising constitution-makers in Ecuador 1998, Venezuela 1999, Ecuador 2008, and Bolivia 2008, and his colleague Rubén Martínez Dalmau, who worked on the latter three constitutions. Their involvement led to controversy in both Spain and Latin America. One Spanish newspaper described Viciano as the "gray matter" for controversial president Hugo Chavez of Venezuela (Partlow 2009). While the advisors tended to focus more on abstract ideas, on occasion they had significant impact. For example, they successfully argued for a unicameral legislature in Venezuela, though Chávez initially wanted a bicameral legislature (Partlow 2009).

The advisors portrayed their role as more technical than substantive. But concerns over Viciano's role in advising the president of Ecuador's constitutional assembly led him to deny that the Spaniards played a role. Kinnto Lucas, who later had his fifteen minutes of fame as the deputy foreign minister to grant asylum to Wikileaks founder and accused rapist Julian Assange, noted, "I always disagreed with their presence, because I believed that they truly didn't know the country" (Partlow 2009).

Indeed, Viciano criticized the final Bolivian Constitution as involving too many concessions to the rightist political opposition. "This is what those who call themselves revolutionary sometimes don't understand: In the revolution, you can't always reach consensus," Viciano was quoted as saying, "[y]ou either have revolution or you don't. But you can't force consensus" (Partlow 2009). The point is that even governments that decry the role of transnational empire are customers for transnational constitutional advice, in this case from ideological allies in the country of the conquistadores, who were purer than the pope. So much for a neat division of the world into south and north.

Agents and Structure

The above vignettes identify individual advisors and their influence, but one must also consider the role of structure in the selection and empowerment of advisors. No doubt the selection of individuals is not random but responds to the conditions of the situation. Frank Goodnow spoke patronizingly of his Chinese interlocutors, but it is also clear that they were using him to legitimate their own goals in the eyes of outside constituencies. Foreigners can both provide and signal genuine disinterest, a real virtue in constitutional design (Lanni & Vermuele 2012: 932–4). In that sense, constitutional advice-giving should be understood not just as transnational transplant of ideas from outside, but also as a version of "palace wars" involving internal and external struggles among different groups (Dezalay & Garth 2010). The TLO framework highlights such struggles, which might involve transnational coalitions of those involved in transitional justice, economic liberalization, and human rights.

Notwithstanding these structural determinants, it also seems to be the case that individuals do have consequential impact. Had a Pakistani Sikh rather than a Muslim been brought in to advise on Malaysia's Constitution, the product might have been profoundly different. But there are real and genuine constraints on what is possible in any given situation. Our focus on the agent should not distract from the structures that drive outcomes, and here there may be room for further elaboration within the TLO framework.

TOWARD TRANSNATIONAL INSTITUTIONALIZATION

The pace and intensity of transnational involvement in constitution-making has intensified since 1990. That year saw the end of the Cold War and the beginning of a set of major overhauls of constitutions in many countries. It coincided with the "rule of law revival" in which foreign development agencies were increasingly concerned with the role of law in fostering economic development and political stability (Carothers 2006; deLisle 1999). Two key features of the new era are first, that it is institutions rather than individuals that are the primary vehicles for advice, and second, that the field is increasingly crowded and competitive.

In the early years after 1990, American organizations like The Asia Foundation and the newly established National Endowment for Democracy engaged in constitutional support in multiple countries. Bilateral donors too sought to get involved. Both the American military and USAID have had a bias toward constitutions, while other donors have focused on institutions like the civil code or judicial reform. In situations like post-conflict Cambodia or East Timor, where the UN has an official role in transitional administration, it plays an active role to be described in a bit more depth below. In major instances of invasion and occupation, as in Afghanistan and Iraq, the UN and United States are major players in some tension with each other, while myriad other actors are also involved (Sripati 2009).

To give one example of how these forces interact, the Comprehensive Peace Agreement between the warring Sudan and South Sudanese factions in 2005 featured an extensive bill of rights reportedly drafted by an American legal advisor to the Intergovernmental Authority on Development (IGAD) Secretariat for Peace in Sudan, sponsored by the US State Department (Cope 2013b: 692). IGAD is a regional organization, primarily funded by outside countries, which among other tasks served to facilitate the peace negotiations between the north and south regions of Sudan (Cope 2013b). The Comprehensive Peace Agreement in turn led to an interim constitution, and then a transitional constitution that still governs the young nation of South Sudan today (Cope 2013b: 302–3). Several organizations, including an American law firm, the National Democratic Institute, and the German Max Planck Institute for Comparative Public Law and International Law, claimed to have influenced the rights provisions in the Interim Constitution. Later, the Transitional Constitution of South Sudan 2011 was drafted with the assistance of the Public Interest Law and Policy Group (PILPG) based in Washington, DC, as well as other international organizations like the Max Planck Institute for Comparative and Foreign law, the US Institute of Peace, and the International Development Law Organization. The involvement of all these players meant that the South Sudanese drafters had to spend a good deal of time coordinating with the donors, while trying to soak up the myriad and sometimes conflicting advice they received. It is not surprising that they found the drafting process challenging at times.

Similarly, the recent wave of constitution-making in the aftermath of the Arab Spring generated demand for outside assistance. Constitutional exercises in Libya, Tunisia, and Yemen featured an array of foreign actors. International IDEA, Democracy Reporting International (a German NGO) the UN and the American party organizations – the National Democratic Institute and the International Republican Institute – were all involved in various countries. In Tunisia, various German foundations, like the Konrad Adenaeur and Hans Siedel Foundation, were also involved, as were French institutions and the Max Planck Institute for Public Comparative Law and Public International Law in Heidelberg.

Only in Egypt were foreign organizations shut out. As the Muslim Brotherhood-dominated constituent assembly sought to produce a draft in 2012, it made quite clear that it was not interested in foreign advice. No doubt their culture of distrust toward Western states that had supported the Mubarak regime for three decades was part of the motive. The broader conspiracy theories that inform Egyptian political life did not help. But ultimately, they may have been afraid of the message that international actors might have delivered: to be more inclusive.[7] Had foreign advisors been involved, they would likely have argued what has become a standard line: constitutions should be produced in an open process with participation from as broad a swath of the population as possible. Constitutions that are produced in open processes are likely to be more legitimate, it is often asserted. What is surprising is that this message is often delivered by the ultimate international actor, the UN, which has become an important player in the world of constitutional advice, and to which we now turn.

SPEAKING FROM ABOVE FOR THOSE BELOW: THE UNITED NATIONS AND CONSTITUTIONS

The end of the Cold War has seen the re-invigoration of the UN as a central actor in state building. Frequently called on to help countries transition out of civil war and conflict, the UN has set up missions in countries as diverse as Kosovo, East Timor, Somalia, Yemen, Iraq, Afghanistan, and Cambodia. In the course of these interventions, the UN has accumulated considerable experience in constitutional design, though its internal efforts (and their external legitimacy) vary from context to context. Cambodia's 1993 Constitution, for example, was formally produced by an elected constituent assembly, but was organized by the United National Transitional Authority for Cambodia (UNTAC), which was charged for conducting elections and organizing a process of state transformation (Marks 2009). Similarly, in 1990 Namibia was midwifed by the UN, and its constituent assembly used the 1992 Constitutional Principles contained in a report from the secretary-general and endorsed by UN Security Council Resolution 435 (Wiechers 2009: 81). Many of these situations involve countries emerging from violent conflict, leading to an emerging field of "peace-building."

Beyond knowledge, foreign institutions in general, and the UN in particular, can play a role in encouraging agreement among local factions that are often at the verge of violent conflict. The UN is a large, often-dysfunctional bureaucracy, but it does bring special resources to bear in terms of international legitimacy that, say, a bilateral donor may not have. Many members of its staff have extensive negotiating experience.

[7] Perhaps this attitude explains the extraordinarily short life of their product, which was suspended in mid-2013, just seven months after coming into effect. After all, with few international actors invested in the process, the military may have thought little of suspending the Egyptian Constitution in June 2013.

This is not to say that it is a truly neutral actor, whatever that might mean. The UN claims to respect national ownership of sovereign processes, and on the ground it emphasizes the role of public participation (Sripati 2009). But the UN is also bound by its charter to promote adherence to international human rights and the rule of law. There is an obvious tension here – global standards will sometimes conflict with local cultural norms.

In 2006, in recognition of this increasing demand for involvement in constitution-building, a high-level committee in the UN endorsed a program to review its constitution-making assistance and prepare further guidance. This culminated in 2009 in the release of a Guidance Note from the Secretary General on United Nations Assistance to Constitution-Making Processes. This in turn reiterates that constitution-making is "a sovereign national process, which, to be legitimate and successful, must be nationally owned and led."[8] Yet it also requires its agents to promote particular values:

> The UN should consistently promote compliance of constitutions with international human rights and other norms and standards. Thus, it should speak out when a draft constitution does not comply with these standards, especially as they relate to the administration of justice, transitional justice, electoral systems and a range of other constitutional issues ... The UN should address the rights that have been established under international law for groups that may be subjected to marginalization and discrimination in the country, including women, children, minorities, indigenous peoples, refugees, and stateless and displaced persons. For example, the principle of equality between men and women should be embedded in constitutions, and states should be encouraged to consider special provisions on children recognizing their status as subjects of human rights.[9]

All this seems unobjectionable from an international perspective, but in some societies may be deeply resisted by conservative social and religious forces. There is an irony that an international organization which is itself involved in imposing certain ideas is also the body that urges local participation in the process, and safeguards participation as a key process value (Saati, Chapter ten).

Notwithstanding its internal tensions, the secretary general's note is a kind of soft law guidance, with actual regulatory effect for internal UN actors. These are myriad, and the internecine UN politics in any given situation

8 *See* U.N. Secretary-General, *Guidance Note of the Secretary General: United Nations Assistance to Constitution-Making Processes* (April 2009), www.un.org/ruleoflaw/files/Guidance_Note_United_Nations_Assistance_to_Constitution-making_Processes_FINAL.pdf, at 2.

9 *Ibid.* at 4.

can be intense. Beyond whatever country mission has been established, the UN Entity for Gender Equality and the Empowerment of Women will seek to ensure compliance with global gender norms, the Mediation Support Unit will seek to provide technical advice, and the United Nations Development Program (UNDP) will often be involved as the lead agency in-country. This has led to the creation of a Constitutional Focal Point within the UN. Institutionalization is proceeding; but there are many drafting situations in which the UN is not a preferred partner, having antagonized locals with its heavy-handed normative biases, its bureaucratism, and its alliance with particular actors.

NORMATIVE ASSESSMENT: A QUALIFIED DEFENSE OF ADVICE

The ideal role of the constitutional advisor might seem to be to provide information to local decision-makers. The locals represent "We the People" who will make the final choices about what institutions are appropriate for the local context. But all constitutional drafters bring their own perspectives and backgrounds, and these may sometimes affect the advice they are giving.

One need not dig far to find those who style themselves constitutional advisors. In a recent interview, a law school applicant claimed to have played a major role in drafting the proposed constitution of Tunisia on the basis of a student project at Cambridge University.[10] Harvard law professor Noah Feldman is regularly asserted to have drafted the Constitution of Iraq,[11] notwithstanding the fact that he was nowhere near the country during the period when all the crucial provisions were negotiated.[12]

To judge from these and many others, foreigners play a major role in constitutional design. What are we to make of these claims? Clearly they are yet another indicator of our Twitter-laden era of self-promotion. They also reflect the natural interest of the public and the media in constitutions, which have an appeal as the highest legal acts of the state. In the case of academics and foreign donors, showing policy impact can be important professionally,

[10] Indian Helped Draft Tunisia's Constitution, Times of India, Feb 9, 2014 available at http://timesofindia.indiatimes.com/nri/other-news/Indian-helped-draft-Tunisias-constitution/articleshow/30079524.cms (discussing Riddhi Dasgupta).

[11] *See After You (Review of* Cool War *by Noah Feldman)*, THE ECONOMIST (July 15, 2013), www.economist.com/news/books-and-arts/21579430-will-bipolar-world-be-peaceful-after-you.

[12] Feldman served as a senior advisor to the Coalition Provisional Authority from April to July 2003 (Diamond 2007) but does not seem to have been involved in the actual process of drafting either the Transitional Administrative Law of 2004 or the Constitution of 2005. Bremer (2006), and none of the major accounts mention him. *See* Deeks & Burton (2007); Hamoudi (2013); and Al-Ali (2014).

and there is no higher-impact enterprise than constitution-making. But fundamentally these claims reflect a complete misunderstanding of the way constitutions are – and always have been – written. Constitutions are collective products, not written by single individuals. And while outsiders have always played an important role, the ultimate acts of adoption must by definition be done by insiders with the requisite political authority. We the People always trumps Me the People.

The need to balance between local and international norms has been a constant theme in constitution-making. The reason for seeking outside expertise is simple. Writing a constitution is a tough task, even at a purely technical level. Trying to figure out the myriad trade-offs involved among different institutions, and the likely effects of particular provisions, is a complex matter, requiring a sense of both local context but also what is sometimes called "social science knowledge." Even if interests of the main stakeholders can be aligned, they need to be able to estimate the likely effects of their institutional choices. To do the job requires knowing a lot about the local context, about different institutional designs, and about what is politically possible to achieve. Surely it is a project that takes a proverbial village.

In such a context, outsiders have a role to play. Local constitution-makers could, in theory, adopt the view that their situation is unique and that there is little to be learned from other countries. Some drafters do create innovative institutions from local tradition. But the very categories used in government tend to be similar across countries: most countries will adopt a legislature and an executive headed by a president or prime minister; most will promise their citizens "rights"; and most will consider how the national government interacts with those from lower levels. We might put local names on these institutions: the Mongolian legislature, for example, is called a "hural" after the traditional Mongolian assemblies. The first modern government of the country used the term in the 1920s and so it stuck. In societies with Persian influence the legislature is called a majlis. But regardless of the name, it is still a legislature.

Once it is recognized that institutions have been used in other countries, it would be quite irrational to ignore prior experience, even if it is foreign. Furthermore, unlike normal "products," there is little incentive for innovation. Unlike producers who seek to maximize profits in a competitive marketplace, drafters of constitutions do not acquire a property right in any new ideas they come up with. Nor can they easily sell their ideas to other countries. Once embedded in a new constitution, ideas and institutions are publicly available for all to see.

One way to think of the role of foreign advisors is that they offer a *subsidy* of knowledge. The international community can quickly bring a lot of relevant information to bear, not to dictate choices but to help lay out options for local drafters. Subsidizing the gathering of information can save a local drafter a lot of time and effort. Consider the alternative option for drafters. They could sit down with the myriad texts that have been produced by other countries. They could study comparative law and politics. But surely it makes far more sense to bring in an outsider or two who has some comparative knowledge.

If one danger is imposing an overly rigid archetype without tailoring to the local conditions, there may be another danger in being too sensitive to the interests of those currently in power. After all, the drafters of a constitution have enormous opportunities for enhancing their own authority and power. The advisor is usually hired by someone. Who is the client? Is it the nation as a whole, or the particular individual who hires the advisor? There has been very little attention to the ethics of advice-giving, and occasionally, as in the case with Peter Galbraith in Iraq, unethical behavior occurs.[13] One might expect that if constitutional advice is to emerge as a full-blown field of expertise, akin to other TLOs, it might be accompanied by pressures to adopt professional ethics.

COMPETITION FOR CONSTITUTIONS

In a contemporary drafting situation, many different actors – states, academics, international organizations, advocacy groups – are in some sense competing with each other to influence the final shape of the constitutional document, just as local political forces compete for advantage in negotiating the outcome. Each outside actor brings particular strengths and weaknesses. Whereas the UN brings a particular form of international legitimacy, and the weight to negotiate with powerful actors like the United States, bilateral donors may bring greater speed and flexibility. Norway, for example, has established an expertise in international conflict resolution that has allowed it to play outsized roles in constitutional-conundra like Israel/Palestine and Sri Lanka. However, bilateral donors are also constrained by their own national interests, which naturally weigh heavily on the choice of content and the local partners who are favored.

In Europe, the European Union has played a role in constraining constitution-making, especially in recent years when Article 2 of the treaty has come into play in the rightward turn in Central and Eastern Europe

[13] In a slightly different context, *see* Menkel-Meadow (2009).

(Scheppele 2013). The Venice Commission on Democracy through Law, part of the Council of Europe, has played an active role in formulating advice to constitutional reform efforts in Europe and beyond (de Visser 2015: 963–4; Craig, Chapter six). It has expanded its role since allowing the extension of membership by countries from outside the region, and now has nearly sixty member states. The Venice Commission has no binding power, but has the advantage of an association with Europe, giving it implicitly the pull of the European Union, and perhaps an implicit threat of collateral consequences from European governments. The downside is that its composition is overwhelmingly composed of senior academics and constitutional court judges; there is no social science expertise, and few have any experience drafting constitutions. Furthermore the membership is overwhelmingly male.[14]

Smaller international organizations like International IDEA also have developed specialized programs in constitution-making.[15] The IDEA program focuses on knowledge products, including a series of primers on constitutional issues, as well as tailored constitutional advice to particular drafting situations. Interpeace, a non-governmental organization based in Stockholm, has a program focusing on constitutional processes. Region-specific organizations are also involved. In addition, there are organizations that focus on substantive issues. Besides the crowded human rights space, there is the Forum on Federations, based in Canada, which promotes federal governance.

The point is that constitution-making is no longer as simple as gathering representatives into a New England town hall to deliberate fundamental principles. It involves a much more complex, transnational process. One way to think about this process is that it is not only a competition among different actors, but a competition among *different forms of expertise* (Abbott 1998). Law competes with political science, economics, and other disciplines; technocrats compete with interest groups to articulate their positions. Myriad international organizations, both governmental and intergovernmental, want to play a role in supporting constitution-making. A national constitution is in some sense the ultimate achievement – it allows the donor organization to claim credit, and show a track record of success. So there is a good deal of supply-side pressure for constitutional advice, and subsidies for the constitution-making process.

[14] 29 out of 128 members listed on the website appear to be female (Visser 2015).

[15] Disclosure: I serve as a Senior Advisor to the Constitution-Building Program of International IDEA. *Constitution-Building*, International IDEA (Dec. 14, 2016, 10:03 PM), www.idea.int/our-work/what-we-do/constitution-building.

Constitution-making in this sense is part of a much broader movement that has occurred over the last three decades, sometimes called the "rule-of-law" movement or the "law and development" movement (Carothers 2006). Building on earlier efforts, Western agencies, lawyers, and universities sought to transfer legal knowledge to the developing world. As time has gone on, this movement has seen a gradual empowerment of the "recipients" of legal knowledge. "Local ownership" is the holy grail for donors, as they rightly understand that nothing can work if simply imposed from outside. As more and more "suppliers" entered the field, the "buyers" of information have more to choose from and are in a stronger position to negotiate the terms of assistance. The availability of electronic tools and the growth of human capital in some developing countries mean that elites and drafters are also able to be more sophisticated consumers.

All this competition to influence constitutional language should make it abundantly clear that individuals do not draft these documents at all, and the individual advisor is embedded in larger structural and institutional frameworks. Of course, an individual drafter could conceivably do a better job than a committee of political representatives who often foist incoherent compromises in to constitutional documents. The Ancient Greeks used to regularly appoint single individuals to draft laws, including constitutions (Lanni & Vermuele 2012: 918). Coming from outside of the political structure, and usually being drawn from the middle class, these were the ancestors of modern technocrats. But in the modern era, it is hard to imagine a single individual having the wisdom and expertise to do so. There are, to put it bluntly, no more Solons. Me, the People is always less legitimate than We, the People. Constitutions must garner the consent of the people who are to live under them, and this increasingly is seen to require a healthy dose of public participation.

As an aside, I cannot resist pointing out that the claims of foreign individuals to have drafted particular documents are particularly ironic in the case of Iraq. The Constitution of Iraq reflected a set of compromises achieved without the participation of one of the major political forces of the country. Pushing a constitution before there was a political agreement led directly to the horrific violence and civil war of 2005–9 (Al-Ali 2014). Furthermore, the constitution is objectively an incomplete document. It postpones major issues – the federal system, the distribution of oil, the nature of the upper house of parliament – to future laws which in many cases have never been passed. It is, at a technical level, a bad piece of work. Why anyone would want to take credit for it is unclear. To use a medical analogy, anyone who claims to have produced that document ought to be sued for institutional malpractice. Far better to admit that the process is a collective one, in which the credit – and blame – is shared.

Constitutions are always drafted in collective processes – and have to be. The process involves various kinds of expertise – legal, political, technical. It requires knowledge of international factors, including the different institutional options that have been tried in foreign countries, and their performance. It also requires local knowledge about what is politically and culturally possible. And it ultimately requires bringing all these things together, to make informed choices about the likely outcomes of institutions in a particular local context. It then requires a process of soliciting local input into the design process, and a process of negotiating with powerful stakeholders.

IS CONSTITUTION-MAKING A TRANSNATIONAL LEGAL ORDER?

We have described an increasingly institutionalized social field, in which constitution-building is become its own field of expertise. Let us now turn to the question posted at the outset: Does it qualify as a transnational legal order? To answer this we should isolate each element of the definition of the TLO. We have, I think, demonstrated that the field is an inherently transnational one, and that it is becoming increasingly institutionalized as transnational. But is constitution-making a *legal* process? It clearly involves law, but the process is not itself governed by transnational law. This exposes that the Halliday-Shaffer framework is a bit fuzzy on the legal. Their definition characterizes something as legal if it involves a transnational legal organization or network, directly engages multiple national legal institutions, and assumes a recognizable legal form (Halliday & Shaffer 2015: 11–12). This is a somewhat circular definition in that it includes legal concepts in the elements that constitute something as legal. Clearly the constitution-making network does act on law in multiple countries, but does it "assume legal form?"

There is very little law that governs the constitution-making process itself. To be sure, some norm entrepreneurs and the UN itself have sought to assert that there is a *right* to public participation in the constitution-making process (Hart 2003; Saati, Chapter ten). Yet no one would really question the idea that a constitution, made without participation but universally recognized by its own subjects as in force, was in fact a constitution. Normatively, the international community would surely prefer such a constitution that was perfectly congruent with international substantive norms to one that was highly defective but adopted in a participatory fashion. Even at a purely national level, we do not always observe legal continuity in the sense that new constitutions are produced under the rules set out in prior documents (Arato 2012: 178). In short, applying the framework to constitution-making seems to call into question some aspects of the definition, but the authors of the framework might respond, fairly enough, that the legal nature of constitutions means that the TLO definition is satisfied on this point.

Third, is it a transnational legal *order*? Constitution-making as a field is highly fragmented, with different organizations and individuals competing to provide advice and to influence the process. There is intense competition in the process, and many of the actors are themselves TLOs.[16] For this reason, we prefer to treat constitution-making as a field which serves as an arena for *other* TLOs to engage. The forces at play in the arena are by no means limited to TLOs, for the major political players are by their nature intensely local. But the constitution-making world is one in which all these actors compete, with some gaining advantage and others losing out.

Yet at the same time, we do see an increasingly dense network of specialists emerging in the field. These actors seek to create a kind of epistemic field, and to provide order to the messy world of constitution-making. We might thus say without exaggeration that constitution-making is a field in which order is emerging. But there are also, by nature of the policy problem being confronted, elements of disorder at play. Constitution-making exercises regularly fail; there is no guarantee of success, and there is no agreed upon set of norms, discrete from other TLOs that one could identify as being exclusive to constitution-making. We hope that trying to use the TLO framework to understand constitution-making has also illuminated aspects of the very concept of the TLO itself.

REFERENCES

Abbott, Andrew. 1998. *The System of Professions: An Essay on the Division of Expert Labor*. Chicago: The University of Chicago Press.

Ackerman, Bruce. 1992. *We the People*. Cambridge: Harvard University Press.

Arato, Andrew. 2012. "Conventions, Constituent Assemblies, and Round Tables: Models, Principles and Elements of Democratic Constitution-Making." *Global Constitutionalism* 1(1): 173–200.

Austin, Granville. 1966. *The Indian Constitution: Cornerstone of a Nation*. New York: Oxford University Press.

Avery, Ron. "A Man of Strong Constitution Law Prof Helps Ex-Reds Rewrite Framework of Government." *Philadelphia Daily News*. Sept. 17, 1990. Retrieved (http://articles.philly.com/1990-09-17/news/25877043_1_new-constitution-oleg-g-rumyantsev-law-professor).

[16] For example, Transnational Legal Orders for human trafficking or human rights accountability are identified in the Halliday and Shaffer book. Halliday & Shaffer (2015).

Billias, George. 2009. *American Constitutionalism Heard Round the World 1787–1989: A Global Perspective*. New York: New York University Press.
Bremer, Paul. 2006. *My Year in Iraq: The Struggle to Build a Future of Hope*. New York: Simon and Schuster.
Bugarič, Bojan. 2014. "Protecting Democracy and the Rule of Law in the European Union: The Hungarian Challenge." LEQS Paper No. 79/2014. *London School of Economics Europe in Question series*.
Carothers, Thomas, ed. 2006. *Promoting the Rule of Law: In Search of Knowledge*. Washington, DC: Carnegie Endowment for International Peace.
Constitution-Building. *International IDEA*. Dec. 14, 2016, 10:03 PM. Retrieved (www.idea.int/our-work/what-we-do/constitution-building).
Cope, Kevin. 2013a. South Sudan's Dualistic Constitution. Pp. 295–320 in *The Social and Political Foundations of Constitutions*, edited by Denis J. Galligan and Mila Versteeg. New York: Cambridge University Press.
Cope, Kevin. 2013b. "The Intermestic Constitution: Lessons from the World's Newest Nation." *Virginia Journal of International Law* 53: 667–724.
Damrosch, Leo. 2005. *Jean Jacques Rousseau: Restless Genius*. New York: Houghton Mifflin Company.
de Visser, Maartje. 2015. "A Critical Assessment of the Role of the Venice Commission in Processes of Domestic Constitutional Reform." *American Journal of Comparative Law* 63(4): 1–35.
Deeks, Ashley and Mathew Burton. 2007. "Iraq's Constitution: A Drafting History." *Cornell International Law Journal* 40(1): 1–87.
DeLisle, Jacques. 1999. "Lex Americana: United States Legal Assistance, American Legal Models, and Legal Change in the Post-Communist World and Beyond." *University of Pennsylvania Journal of International Law* 20: 179–308.
Dezalay, Yves and Bryant Garth. 2010. *The Internationalization of Palace Wars*. Chicago: University of Chicago Press.
Diamond, Larry. 2005. *Squandered Victory: The American Occupation and the Bungled Effort to Bring Democracy to Iraq*. New York: Henry Holt and Company.
Eisenstadt, Todd A., Carl LeVan, and Tofigh Maboudi. 2017. *Constituents before Assembly: Participation, Deliberation, and Representation in The Worldwide Crafting of New Constitutions*. New York: Cambridge University Press.
Elkins, Zachary, Tom Ginsburg, and James Melton. 2008. "Baghdad, Tokyo, Kabul: Constitution-making in Occupied States." *William and Mary Law Review* 49: 1139–78.
Elkins, Zachary, Tom Ginsburg, and James Melton. 2009. *The Endurance of National Constitutions*. New York: Cambridge University Press.

Elmi, Afyare. 2012. "Revisiting the UN-Controlled Constitution-Making Process for Somalia." *E-International Relations*. Retrieved Jan. 11, 2017 (www.e-ir.info/2012/09/02/revisiting-the-un-controlled-constitution-making-process-for-somalia/).

Fernando, Joseph. 2006. "The Position of Islam in the Constitution of Malaysia." *Journal of Southeast Asian Studies* 37: 249–66.

Fernando, Joseph. 2016. "Constitutionalism and the Politics of Constitution-making in Malaya." In *Constitution-Making in Asia – Decolonisation and State-Building in the Aftermath of the British Empire*, edited by Harshan Kumarasingham. New York: Taylor and Francis.

Flanz, Gisbert and Albert Blaustein. 2007. *Constitutions of the Countries of the World*. New York: Oceana.

Feldman, Noah. 2013. "After You: Will a Bipolar World Be Peaceful?" *The Economist*. Retrieved July 15, 2013 (www.economist.com/news/books-and-arts/21579430-will-bipolar-world-be-peaceful-after-you).

Gargarella, Roberto. 2010. "The Constitution of Inequality: Constitutionalism in the Americas 1776–1860." *International Journal of Constitutional Law* 3(1): 1–23.

Ghai, Yash. 2005. "A Journey around Constitutions: Reflections on Contemporary Constitutions." *South African Law Journal* 122: 804–31.

Ginsburg, Tom, Zachary Elkins, and Justin Blount. 2009. "Does the Process of Constitution-Making Matter?" *Annual Review of Law and Social Science* 5(5): 201–23.

Ginsburg, Tom. 2014. "The Politics of Law and Development in Middle-Income Countries." Pp. 21–35 in *Law and Development in Middle Income Countries*, edited by Randall Peerenboom and Tom Ginsburg. New York: Cambridge University Press.

Ginsburg, Tom and James Melton. 2015. *Writing Rights* (unpublished manuscript) (on file with author).

Guhal, Subhabrata. "Indian Helped Draft Tunisia's Constitution." *Times of India*. Retrieved Feb. 9, 2014 (http://timesofindia.indiatimes.com/nri/other-news/Indian-helped-draft-Tunisias-constitution/articleshow/30079524.cms).

Halliday, Terence and Gregory Shaffer. 2015. *Transnational Legal Orders*. New York: Cambridge University Press.

Hamoudi, Haider. 2013. *Negotiating in Civil Conflict: Constitutional Construction and Imperfect Bargaining in Iraq*. Chicago: University of Chicago Press.

Hart, Vivian. 2003. "Democratic Constitution Making, Special Report 107." *U.S. Institute of International Peace*. Retrieved (www.usip.org/sites/default/files/sr107.pdf).

Howard, Dick. 1991. *Democracy's Dawn: A Directory of American Initiatives on Constitutionalism, Democracy, and the Rule of Law in*

Central and Easter Europe. Virginia: University of Virginia Press. Retrieved (www.lse.ac.uk/europeanInstitute/LEQS%20Discussion%20Paper%20Series/LEQSPaper79.pdf).

Kennedy, David. 2015. *A World of Struggle: How Power, Law and Expertise Shape Global Political Economy*. New Jersey: Princeton University Press.

Kroncke, Jedidiah. 2016. *The Futility of Law and Development: China and the Dangers of Exporting American Law*. New York: Oxford University Press.

Kroncke, Jedidiah. 2012. "An Early Tragedy of Comparative Constitutionalism: Frank Goodnow and the Chinese Republic." *Pacific Rim Law and Policy Journal* 21: 533–90.

Kumarsingham, Harshan, ed. 2015. *Constitution-Maker: Selected Writings of Sir Ivor Jennings*. New York: University of Cambridge.

Landau, David. 2013. "Constitution-Making Gone Wrong." *Alabama Law Review* 64: 923–80.

Lanni, Adriaan and Adrian Vermeule. 2012. "Constitutional Design in the Ancient World." *Stanford Law Review* 64(4): 907–49.

Law, David. 2010. "The Myth of the Imposed Constitution." Pp. 239–68 in *Social and Political Foundations of Constitutions*, edited by Denis Galigan and Mila Versteeg. New York: Cambridge University Press.

Marks, Stephen. 2009. "The Process of Creating a Constitution for Cambodia." Pp. 207–44 in *Framing the State in Times of Transition: Case Studies in Constitution Making*, edited by Laurel Miller. Washington, DC: United States Institute of Peace Press.

Menkel-Meadow, Carrie. 2009. "Are there Systemic Ethics Issues in Dispute Settlement System Design? And What We Should [Not] Do about It: Lessons from International and Domestic Fronts." *Harvard Law Review* 14: 195–232.

Moore, Ray and Donald Robinson. 2004. *Partners for Democracy*. New York: Oxford University Press.

Negretto, Gabrielle. 2013. *Making Constitutions: Presidents, Parties, and Institutional Choice in Latin America*. New York: Cambridge University Press.

Parkinson, Charles. 2007. *Bills of Rights and Decolonization*. New York: Oxford University Press.

Partlow, Joshua. "Latin America's Document-Driven Revolutions." *Washington Post*, Feb. 17, 2009. Retrieved (www.washingtonpost.com/wp-dyn/content/article/2009/02/16/AR2009021601468_2.html).

Perry, Barbara. 1991. "Constitutional Johnny Apple Seeds." *Albany Law Review* 55: 767–92.

Pugach, Noel. 1973. "Embarrassed Monarchist: Frank J. Goodnow and Constitutional Development in China, 1913–1915." *Pacific Historical Review* 42: 499–517.

Qvortrup, Mads. 2003. *The Political Philosophy of Jean-Jacques Rousseau: The Impossibility of Reason*. Manchester: Manchester University Press.

Rousseau, Jean-Jacques. 1772. *Considerations on the Government of Poland and on Its Proposed Reformation*. Retrieved (www.constitution.org/jjr/poland.htm).

Scheppele, Kim Lane. 2003. "Aspirational and Aversive Constitutionalism: The Case for Studying Cross-Constitutional Influence through Negative Models." *International Journal of Constitutional Law* 1: 296–324.

Scheppele, Kim Lane. 2013. "What Can the European Commission Do When Member States Violate Basic Principles of the European Union? The Case for Systemic Infringement Actions." *European Commission*. Retrieved (http://ec.europa.eu/justice/events/assises-justice-2013/files/contributions/45.princetonuniversityscheppelesystemicinfringementactionbrusselsversion_en.pdf).

Jennings, Sir William Ivor. 2005. *The Road to Peradeniya*, edited by Henry Alfred Ian Goonetileke. Michigan: University of Michigan.

Sripati, Vijayashri. 2009. "UN Constitutional Assistance: An Emergent Policy Institution." Working Paper 5, York Centre for Public Policy & Law. Retrieved (http://digitalcommons.osgoode.yorku.ca/cgi/viewcontent.cgi?article=1004&context=ycppl).

U.N. Secretary-General. 2009. *Guidance Note of the Secretary General: United Nations Assistance to Constitution-Making Processes*. Retrieved (www.un.org/ruleoflaw/files/Guidance_Note_United_Nations_Assistance_to_Constitution-making_Processes_FINAL.pdf).

Wiechers, Marinus. "Namibia's Long Walk to Freedom: The Role of Constitution Making in the Creation of an Independent Namibia." Pp. 81–111 in *Framing the State in Times of Transition: Case Studies in Constitution Making*, edited by Laurel Miller. Washington, DC: United States Institute of Peace Press.

3

A Transnational Actor on a Dramatic Stage – Sir Ivor Jennings and the Manipulation of Westminster Style Democracy in Pakistan

H. Kumarasingham*

Across first Asia and then Africa new states rose from colonial rule in the post-war era that sought to build *New Westminster* constitutions. The Westminster model was the transnational trend after 1945 in constitution-making for much of the world emerging from colonial rule, and was promoted by the Colonial Office, Indigenous leaders and constitutional advisers such as the ubiquitous Sir Ivor Jennings. However, this flexible and ambiguous regime type caused many political and constitutional crises that questioned the wisdom of applying Westminster to these states. Jennings worked across Africa and Asia including Ceylon, Nepal, Malaya, Singapore, the Maldives, Sudan, Ethiopia, South Africa, and the Federation of Rhodesia and Nyasaland. It is Pakistan, however, that sticks out as Jennings' most controversial role where he effectively, legally, and politically, contentiously defended a "constitutional coup" by the Governor-General against the Constituent Assembly in 1954. The case also serves to demonstrate how the manipulation and divisive interpretations of Westminster conventions and institutions in the first decade of Pakistan led to the breakdown of democracy and laid conspicuous precedents for dictatorship and military rule, which have explanatory value in understanding the country's prevalent fragility in embedding accountability and democracy.

* I would like to acknowledge the comments and guidance from this tremendous transnational constitution-making group convened by Greg Shaffer, Tom Ginsburg, and Terry Halliday in Irvine, California in September 2016. I'm particularly grateful to Paul Craig for his thoughtful and entertaining comments at UCI on an earlier version of this chapter. Maryam Khan and Arun K. Thiruvengadam were very helpful to me on matters of Pakistan and law. Their advice strengthened this chapter.

INTRODUCTION

"[W]e shall have to go far back in history and to trace the origin and subsequent development of the British Empire itself."[1] So stated the opinion of the Chief Justice of Pakistan, Muhammad Munir, when searching for the legal justification of the controversial dissolution of the Constituent Assembly on October 24, 1954 by the Governor-General to forestall the adoption of a new constitution that would have curbed his powers. In a context where the country was attempting to craft a republic based on Islamic principles in South Asia the case and crisis it passed judgment on relied on templates from the settler states where few, if any Muslims resided. Decisions and actions of English monarchs stretching back to the seventeenth century were employed. It was Halsbury's not Hammurabi's laws that guided the proceedings.[2] It remains the most dramatic court case in Pakistani history following one of the most controversial constitutional crises in the common law world. Sir Ivor Jennings believed the case "dealt with fundamental principles of constitutional law of interest throughout the Commonwealth" (Jennings 1957: vii). Jennings would know. Not only as the world's foremost expert on the constitutions of the Commonwealth at the time, but in his direct role in Pakistan as adviser, advocate, and author of critical legal, political, and academic writings on a crisis that many Pakistani scholars angrily denounce the crisis as the real beginning of that country's decent into dictatorship and its ruling elites' enduring attraction to martial rule.

Jennings, as the Governor-General's adviser, colluded to ex post facto justify a constitutional coup d'état that crushed democratic saplings, ridiculed the rule of law and exposed the dangers of adopting the Westminster model and the conventions and prerogatives that came with it (Kumarasingham 2013b: 579–96). As a constitution-maker of transnational influence and scope the role of Jennings in Pakistan provides an insight into how selective precedents and interpretations from across the British Empire and Commonwealth were used to justify what appeared unjustifiable. In turn the "Pakistan Formula," as Jennings confidentially called his contentious fix there, was drawn upon for other states around the world that he advised – primarily, as was the case in Pakistan, to frustrate, if not suspend, the will of parliament to the advantage of unelected elites.[3] The actions of Jennings in Pakistan, using Halliday and Shaffer's Transnational Legal Order (TLO) definition, are that of an actor

[1] Federal Court of Pakistan, Constitutional Civil Appeal No 1 of 1955.

[2] Multiple editions of *Halsbury* were used in these cases before the Pakistani courts.

[3] For example Nepal.

who, with the willful cooperation of bureaucratic and judicial officers, authoritatively forged the understanding and practice of transnational common law for employment in Pakistan. The consequences of this enhanced a socio-legal environment that dented the rule of law and re-orientated it toward more illiberal "behavioral" ends while impacting on legal orders in the country ever since (Halliday & Shaffer 2015: 8–11). In the case study the critical and intimate interaction between law and politics can be seen. The boundary between legal and political orders in Pakistan were permeable and without robust norms which enabled a corresponding weakening of democracy and strengthening of executive power. The practices here observed of the Pakistani political elite with the help of figures like Jennings crafted behavioral expectations and political orders that justified authoritarian exercises of power under the cover of legal order. As such in TLO terms old norms surrounding democracy became unsettled and instead new political norms and legal behavioral orders emerged that aligned with dynamics and the expectations of those who held and wielded power. The transnational expertise and advice Jennings provided considerably enabled the Pakistani elite to disable democracy and engineer Pakistan's first "constitutional coup" in October 1954 with post facto legal justification, thereby establishing a detrimental legal norm for future rulers to evoke when subverting constitutional government.

JENNINGS IN ASIA

Sir Ivor Jennings was one of the twentieth century's most influential constitutional scholars and became, additionally, from the 1940s until his death in 1965, one of its most established "constitution-makers."[4] Before the term was employed Jennings was undoubtedly transnational in his scholarship and had near omnipresence across the British world. The vast British domains in Asia proved his most important and significant arena for constitution-making (see Kumarasingham 2016: 1–35). Starting from his arrival in Colombo in March 1941, to head what would become the University of Ceylon, he soon became an unofficial adviser to D. S. Senanayake, the pre-eminent political leader in the island destined to be its first prime minster. Jennings, with Senanayake and the local panjandrum O. E. Goonetilleke, formed the "nucleus of a Reforms Ministry" where the new vice-chancellor acted as the constitutional adviser "on tap" giving expertise that unquestionably improved Ceylon's (and especially Senanayake's) case (Kumarasingham 2015b: 10). This

4 For an introduction on his life and this aspect of his career, see Kumarasingham 2015a; Bradley 2016.

famous trio relied on each other and with near exclusivity conducted and formulated the Ceylon side of the negotiations with the British. Jennings, just 38 when he arrived, played a major role in the articulation of Ceylon's independence demands and relished it. Jennings' role went well beyond the academic and ventured into the political. It was a role he craved, but also one that elicited jealousy and deep suspicion as to how much this Englishman was influencing high politics, especially when not only the citizenry, but even the leading local politicians were kept out of deciding Ceylon's future. Jennings had, in fact, no formal role. As he admitted "Officially I did not exist" (Kumarasingham 2015b: 16). Official or not, locals noted his presence and sway. Prominent Ceylonese journalist Mervyn de Silva sardonically penned a portrait of Jennings in the press, which some Pakistanis could well have recognized.

> As Vice-Chancellor Jennings went from success to success in this country, from Commission to Commission, and finally to the exalted position of one of the architects of Ceylon's independence, and thence to a knighthood, the patronising air with which he looked upon the campus was extended to cover the whole nation. And when, with Ceylon as a base, his influence broadened out to cover neighbouring countries Pakistan, Malaya, the Maldives which consulted him on constitutional matters, he found it possible to patronise a whole continent. It is a fact that at least two of these countries have been riddled with constitutional crises and catastrophes since Sir Ivor left their shores. But to match Sir Ivor's own manifest modesty if for no other reason, we refuse to credit our ex-Vice-Chancellor with responsibility for these historic events! (*Ceylon Daily News*, June 13, 1957, quoted in Kumarasingham 2015b: xxvi–xxvii)

The "immature democracies" of Asia, as Jennings termed them, nonetheless sought his counsel and he became from Punjab to Penang an Asian transnational constitution-maker and adviser (Jennings 1956: 32). Jennings was well regarded and employed for three main reasons. First, he had the reputation as the pre-eminent expert on Commonwealth constitutions with several of his major (and best) publications completed before the Second World War. Second, he had substantial experience of Asia as Ceylon's vice-chancellor from 1941–55 and university business across the region. He was also known to some of the leaders and leading lawyers of the region in an era that was flush with Oxbridge men. Finally, he was very hardworking and had form in getting things done quickly, however thorny the situation. His ability and versatility to draw upon the constitutional wealth of British and Imperial precedents was legendary. This naturally pleased the elites that dominated the upper echelons of Asian states and who employed him to give a solution with the imprimatur of a British academic who nonetheless was not in the pocket of Her Majesty's Government.

The constitutional form the Westminster model afforded enabled multifarious versions and styles to sprout globally. Westminster consciously avoided rigid constitutional and institutional forms and instead nurtured convention and context to provide the constitutional order. While not *the* determining political factor in the crises that will be detailed below in Pakistan, Westminster style government was nonetheless a regime type, with its deliberate ambiguity and tacit assumptions, that greatly assisted the actions and objectives of the Pakistani elite in retarding democracy and for Ivor Jennings to creatively give legal cover for them. Transnational legal expertise was critically deployed for narrow national political ends. Jennings was able to draw on Common Law and Commonwealth political history to service the needs of the Pakistani establishment despite the unlikely and unsuitable transferability of much of his advice for the major political crises that confronted the young state.

THE CONSTITUTIONAL AND POLITICAL CONTEXT IN PAKISTAN

The Indian Independence Act 1947 that crafted the Pakistani state facilitated a Constituent Assembly to sit and create a constitution for the Dominion. As Alan Gledhill put it, while "India succeeded to the capital, the instrumentalities, and the accommodation of the central government, Pakistan had to improvise" (Gledhill 1957: 65). The division of the state with 1000 miles of hostile territory between West and East Pakistan aggravated an already difficult task of managing multiple strong ethnic and linguistic identities (see Khan 2014). Unique outcomes occurred in this tense context. An example of this was when M. A. Jinnah, who was the unquestionable founder of Pakistan, became, without precedent, both Governor-General and President of the Assembly. Pakistani politicians and the population accepted and largely revered Jinnah as the Quaid-i-Azam, the Great Leader, and did not question this concentration of power and influence. In contrast to every other part of the Commonwealth at that time, and with no other twentieth century example, the Crown in Pakistan and its representative were endowed with critical political power supplemented by the ambiguous conventions surrounding the office, giving ample ground to interpret awesome authority unheard of in any other Westminster style state. Pakistan was no dictatorship in 1947, however, and it was believed that its exceptional creation allowed for exceptional actions from its creator to cement the foundations and interests of the state. This context allowed extraordinary political power in the hands of the Governor-General. Jinnah chaired and directed Cabinet, instructed provincial governors, and gave orders to the Civil and Military services. He also moved swiftly against provincial and political opposition and augmented Punjabi dominance over the state. All of this was not meant to carry on after the Jinnah's death in September 1948 – just over a year after independence (see Jalal 1985). Nonetheless, precedents and personalities existed for the dramas of 1954.

The above also illustrates a key characteristic of the Westminster model – with its ambiguity and flexibility – its transnational ability to be manipulated and forged for very different purposes in very different places. Pakistan was an *Eastminster* – a state that consciously had institutional and political resemblances to Britain's system, but with critical cultural and constitutional "deviations" (Kumarasingham 2016: 1–35). For states like Pakistan, in the formative state-building period, Eastminster confronted the state with conditions that made Westminster-style government of the variety exhibited in London or Ottawa arduous. Thus Pakistan's state had to deal with five major deviations from Westminster that tested its newly won freedom:

1. A population and leadership unused to sovereign power or cohesive parliamentary participation due to colonialism.
2. A "Ceremonial" Head of State that routinely interfered in all areas of politics without "advice."
3. A leadership and legislature that often operated without popular mandate.
4. Majoritarian tendencies accentuated with critical linguistic, ethnic, and regional actors unable to be either represented or accommodated.
5. Colonial powers continued and extended after independence in favor of the Executive, which often wilfully abused traditional Westminster conventions. (Kumarasingham 2016: 11–26)

These above factors actively fueled the situation and crises Pakistan faced in the mid-1950s.

Constitution-making was a very lackluster affair compared with India (Kumarasingham 2013a: 25–45). The Assembly hardly concerned itself with its constitution-making task. In the first fourteen of its sixteen sessions it only managed to clock up fifty-seven days between 1947 and 1953.[5] Instead much of the real political activity occurred beyond the legislature at the desks of the Bureaucracy, canteens of the Officer's mess, and the Governor-General's

[5] Based on table from Callard 1958: 80.

residence. Political parties were largely incidental. The Muslim League, once the great minority party of undivided India, began in the new state of Pakistan to crack under the pressures and fissions of the country's ethnic and linguistic diversity as well as operating with the factionalism and impatience political leaders had for party democracy. As Andrew Harding has argued the two-party system was meant to be part of the Westminster export model, but rarely could be found anywhere, especially in Asia (Harding 2004: 160). In to the breach were old institutions of the Raj now largely manned by local elites. Viceregalism was in vogue, evoking the "oriental despotism" of India's Viceroys, and colonial era practices not only continued, but were often accentuated. Even Viceroys during the Colonial era were restrained by the India Office and Parliament in London. Evidence of accentuation and the non-party executive constellation that ruled the country can be seen with the former Indian Civil Servant Ghulam Mohammed, Governor-General since 1951, openly sacking the Muslim League party Prime Minister, Khwaja Nazimuddin, due to policy and personal differences in April 1953 without advice and without reference to the legislature where the Prime Minister claimed a majority. Nazimuddin, himself a former Governor-General, was replaced by a non-politician, Mohammed Ali Bogra, who was then serving as Ambassador to Washington, and was expected to carry out the wishes of the bureaucratic-military axis, which he largely did. The Governor-General instructed the Law Minister to issue a statement to quell constitutional mutterings attaching "undue emphasis on certain conventions as they are known to the British constitutional practice" (McGrath 1996: 98). Most, however, were very pleased with the action since the government had grown unpopular and had lost control of East Pakistan. The American Ambassador reported to Washington that the Governor-General's action against Nazimuddin was "one of the most popular coups in history" (McGrath 1996: 97). A coup nonetheless, and one that breached not the law, but convention.

Sir Ivor Jennings noted of the dismissal that "on all British precedents, this action was completely unjustifiable" (Kumarasingham 2015a: 136). Nonetheless the Cambridge-educated public law scholar had been selected in July 1954 to advise the Constituent Assembly. His name had been discussed since the idea of Pakistan became a reality.[6] Despite not having explicit expertise of Pakistan he was selected. Indeed he confessed to the Secretary of the Ministry of Law and fellow Englishman, Sir Edward Snelson, after

6 His name, for example, was mentioned for the role as early as July 4, 1947. H. L. Ismay to Liaquat Ali Khan July 4, 1947, F. 2/175 in Zaidi 1996: 85.

receiving a request to help advise the Governor-General, that "I am not sufficiently familiar with the law of Pakistan to advise what legal form proceedings should take" (Jennings to Snelson, November 10, 1954, ICS 125/BXV/4, JP). Jennings prided himself, however, on his adaptability: "Clearly one cannot sit in the Constituent Assembly Building in Murree or Karachi and draft a Constitution for the Gold Coast. There are, however, common elements which make it possible to at least define the problem" (Jennings 1956: 11). The new prime minister expressed to the population in a broadcast on 1 April 1954 that Pakistan was "being advised by Sir Ivor Jennings, one the greatest constitutional authorities in the world" (see Pirzada 1995: 42).[7] This could have been a rather "normal" role for Jennings providing advice on constitutional matters, as he had done already across the world. However, in Pakistan it was not his role as constitutional adviser to the Assembly which draws the focus of this chapter, but instead his highly secretive and crafty role in advising the Governor-General and bureaucracy on the dissolution of the Constituent Assembly and the subsequent political and legal justifications of a power most scholars and lawyers believed the Crown no longer possessed and did not exist in Pakistan. This role, therefore, compelled Jennings to find defenses, precedents, and prevarications that only someone of his immense transnational and comparative knowledge of constitutional practices across the world could bring to the rescue of what even he thought unlawful. As Jennings admitted:

> There is ... no power in GOI [Government of India] Act to dissolve the Federal Legislature. It was in GOI Act s. 19, but was removed in 1947. Nor is there power to dissolve CA in I.I. [India Independence] Act. In other words, this is a revolutionary act ... This illustrates the general principle that *an act of illegality compels other acts of illegality*. ("Revolution in Pakistan," ICS 125/B/15/6, October 25, 1954, JP)

However, this did not perturb Jennings who afterwards would even congratulate his legal finesse: "There is no provision in the Government of India Act for the dissolution of the Constituent Assembly. The action taken was therefore both unconstitutional and illegal. This raised certain problems, which seem to have been solved at least temporarily with considerable success" (Kumarasingham 2015a: 132). As Paula Newberg argues, these years where

[7] Sir Kenneth Roberts-Wray, Legal Adviser to the Colonial Office and later author of *Commonwealth and Colonial Law* (London, 1966) for one did not have a high opinion of Jennings and considered his draft constitution for Ceylon "quite useless" – an opinion he repeated in 1956 when Jennings was about to go to Malaya as part of the Reid Commission. See Kumarasingham 2015a: 9; Kumarasingham 2015b; Simpson 2001: 859.

Jennings operated showed a period that "took refuge in the presumed impartiality of inherited constitutional instruments without recognizing their deficiencies and structural partialities' with disastrous consequences for future constitution-making" (Newberg 2002: 65). Jennings was no creature of the Pakistani elite; he knew what he was doing and the local elite knew whom they were employing. This was not a neo-colonial plot to destabilize a non-western state, though there were political gains for Pakistan's Anglo-Saxon allies, but instead an example of internal political machinations given extra fuel from external actors like Jennings. Arguably the crises and its immediate outcome legitimized both Jennings and the Pakistani establishment that directed him. The Queen on the advice of her Pakistani Ministers even felt the emboldened to make Jennings a Knight Commander of the Most Excellent Order of the British Empire at the end of his mission in the country and he would go on to collect further academic and national honors with his advice sought from Nigeria to New Zealand (see Kumarasingham 2015a: 3). While Pakistan's rulers no doubt congratulated themselves that their coup against parliamentary democracy was not only defended by Jennings, but lauded in the international press. In London the oldest journal of international affairs, *The Round Table*, congratulated the Governor-General from "stopping the rot" by dissolving the "irresponsible" Constituent Assembly and concluded that the "common man and the country have suffered long; and if we now have people at the helm of affairs who we know are clear in their visions and have honesty of purpose we are inclined to wish them god-speed and forget everything else" (The Round Table 1954: 44–50).

Looking at the crisis and the context surrounding the dissolution it is evident how much the Westminster system was being used and interpreted in different ways to suit the Pakistani elites' purposes. The Westminster model became, as Woodrow Wilson predicted, the "world's fashion," especially after 1945 (Norris 2001: 877; Kumarasingham 2016: 2–3). However, as A. F. Madden reminds us, countless British Colonial Reports, Statesmen and Officials counselled strongly against the suitability of Westminster as transnational regime type. Most in Whitehall until the twentieth century shared the view of the redoubtable senior nineteenth-century Colonial Office mandarin, James Stephen, that to create "miniature" British constitutions across the world, especially for places with substantial non-European populations, was "the grossest of absurdities" (Madden 1979: 19). The 1930 Simon Report into Indian constitutional reform perceived the experiment in introducing Westminster to the East was dangerous. "The introduction into an oriental country, with a long history of autocracy, of methods of self-government evolved during centuries of experiments by a Western nation for its own conditions and people was a momentous and even hazardous enterprise" (Indian Statutory Commission 1930: 4).

Nonetheless, for much of the twentieth century the Westminster model traveled far and wide, not as an imposed form of constitution-making, but instead as one that both British and indigenous politicians desired in order to achieve ambitions of geopolitical connection, a belief that this system was the best and most understood, and local intentions to wrest away the awesome power of the colonial state into their waiting hands. As De Smith argued, another characteristic which critically made this all possible and enabled the system's export to far corners of the globe of improbable suitability was that "uniformity is neither sought nor achieved." Conventions were critical therefore, but this still meant that for those across the world that chose Westminster style government the "dichotomy of law and convention was preserved, and most of the really important conventions were left to the interpolator" (De Smith 1961: 4).

Ivor Jennings was, and remains, one of the most critical sources on British and Commonwealth conventions, and in some cases was not just advising or read on the subject, but became its "interpolator" himself, critically so in the case of Pakistan. Famously he opined that in the Westminster system conventions were "the flesh which clothes the dry bones of the law" (Jennings 1959b: 81). Transnational constitution-making in such a style of government was far from a rigid and mechanical transferal. Instead conventions for one constitution were anathema for others – despite having comparable institutions and origins. The conventions that surrounded the Crown were a bone of contention in Pakistan throughout the 1947–56 period when it was a Dominion with a Governor-General representing the monarch in Buckingham Palace. The Westminster model often experienced "dyarchical malfunctions" in Asia (Harding 2004: 104). The critical position of Head of State in Asia was rarely ceremonial and apolitical as Westminster convention dictates, instead the Eastminsters of Asia took on a major "deviation" from the settler cases. Asian Heads of State routinely interfered in politics, wielded significant executive power, frustrated policy, and had a very different definition of the Westminster maxim of "responsible advice" (Kumarasingham 2016: 16–19).

This central element of Westminster government faced problematic transnational translation, and it forms the crux of the crisis and where Ivor Jennings, constitution-maker par excellence, played a formidable role in bringing down the constitutional order of Pakistan. As W. J. M. Mackenzie observed on the task of constitution-making "A lawyer's constitution is dead until it strikes roots in the political soil" (Mackenzie 1975: 60). Elkins, Ginsburg, and Melton argue in their wide-ranging survey on the content of authoritarian constitutions that not only are there "few systematic differences across the formal constitutions of democracies and dictatorships," but instead the "most important determinants of constitutional form are the era and the region in which the constitution was written and the set of institutions chosen for the first constitution in the country's history" (Elkins, Ginsburg, & Melton 2013: 162). A difficulty of transnationalism in a legal framework is, as Jothie Rajah argues, that it risks "homogenising" and can perpetuate "notions of nation as the unproblematic vehicle of sovereign equality." This is especially problematic when there are nations and states subsequent to the "Westphalian moment," namely the post-colonial variety (Rajah 2015: 346–7). Pakistan was about to cultivate its democratic constitution for one more resembling dictatorship thanks to the ambiguity of the Westminster model and the ingenuity of Ivor Jennings.

Since the tabling of Basic Principles in 1949 by then Prime Minister Liaquat Ali Khan, Pakistan had the aim of becoming a republic with Islamic character (see Choudhury 1970: 35–58). As mentioned above the Assembly, as a constitution-making body, was very desultory. The activity increased in its last two sessions when framing, finally, a new constitution with the total days spent as a constitution-making body before its dissolution in October 1954 more than the previous fourteen sessions put together – though still just fifty-nine days.[8] Though there were key American constitutional ideas concerning executive accountability, Jennings observed a preference, still, for English constitutional practices, observing that many Pakistani legislators resembled the Barons at Merton in 1236 pronouncing "nolumus leges Angliae mutare" – "we do not want to change the laws of England" (Jennings 1956: 12). Critically, though, the new constitution explicitly aimed to curb the powers of the Head of State and make legally conspicuous the need for the Head of State to follow advice. The dismissal of Nazimuddin the previous year was clearly on the minds of those in the Assembly. The influential paper *Dawn* approvingly carried the headline "Parliament Made Supreme Body" (McGrath 1996: 124). In essence much of what the Assembly approved on September 21, 1954 was the codifying of conventions, which would close off opportunities for the Governor-General to act except on advice of his ministers and the assertion of the supremacy of parliament. The draft constitution was submitted to Jennings who made "extensive but minor changes" and was sent to the Government Printers on October 15 with the aim that the country would have a new constitution based on a more stable form of parliamentary democracy (McGrath 1996: 124). As Geoffrey Marshall argued of Pakistan "the lawful

[8] Based on table from Callard 1958: 80.

seat of sovereignty was in dispute for more than seven years after the Independence Act of 1947" (Marshall 1957: 133). The Assembly was attempting to clear the constitutional confusion.

Meanwhile Ghulam Muhammad was not impressed and unlikely to accept a recalibration of his powers that would compel him to act as a traditional Westminster head of state. Ghulam Mohammed, as Karl Newman contends, "was not only active, ambitious and somewhat given to intrigue but he was also the product of the Indian Civil Service with all its traditions of vigorous executive action, especially in times of crisis or failures of political leadership" and therefore in the crisis that he saw in Pakistan felt legitimately emboldened and "left the path of constitutional government" (Newman 1959: 24–5). Pakistan's military and bureaucracy, including the Governor-General, were keen to cement financial and defense support from the Americans, who had been wary of the country's political instability. While in Washington in September 1953 and afterwards Ghulam Mohammed with Ayub Khan and the backing of Iskander Mirza, both future military rulers, assured American officials in that critical Cold War climate that Pakistan would be its ally not become a "fanatical theocracy," which apparently the Constituent Assembly promoted when recommending the Islamic influence over the constitution. Instead they would withstand political pressures of "religious zealots" and offered the prospect of a "constitutional dictatorship" which envisioned the Governor-General at the helm with the support of the military and all provinces under Governor's Rule except East Bengal, which the military would directly control – in addition the Constituent Assembly would be dissolved (Jalal 1990: 185–7). This indeed was largely what happened on October 24, 1954. The passing in the Assembly of the draft constitution alerted him to action. The Governor-General "scorned the idea of any parliamentary government in Pakistan. Though he pretended to favour the American executive system his real model was the vice-regal pattern of the British period" (Choudhury 1970: 32). With the support of the military and civil service and after browbeating the prime minister in the early hours, who was dramatically summoned from Washington, Ghulam Muhammad acted defiantly and issued a proclamation on October 24, 1954 that extinguished hopes for Pakistani parliamentary democracy. The defeated acquiescence of Muhammad Ali Bogra as prime minister enabled his puppet-master, Ghulam Mohammed, to produce someone to take political responsibility for actions the prime minister had no part of and appease the radical reformation of the Cabinet he supposedly headed.[9]

> The Governor-General having considered the political crisis with which the country is faced, has with deep regret come to the conclusion that the constitutional machinery has broken down. He therefore has decided to declare a state of emergency throughout Pakistan. The Constituent Assembly as at present constituted has lost confidence of the people and can no longer function. The ultimate authority vests in the people who will decide all issues including constitutional issues through their representatives who are to be elected; fresh elections will be held as early as possible. (*Governor-General's Proclamation*, October 25, 1954)

The Prime Minister, who had only days earlier praised the Assembly for completing its principal constitution-making task, now felt compelled to announce to the world –

> Constitution-making by the present Constituent Assembly has resulted in developments which threaten to imperil our national unity. It has provoked personal, sectional and provincial rivalries and suspicions. These have to be curbed, and Pakistan's interests must be put above everything else. This is what the Governor-General's action envisages. (*The Times*, October 25, 1954)

It was reported that Muhammad Ali Bogra's acceptance of Ghulam Muhammad's invitation to re-form the Government meant he was in agreement with the dramatic actions taken by the Governor-General in his absence abroad (*The Times*, October 25, 1954). The *Times* correspondent speculated a day later that

9 Jennings recorded in his diary "When PM Ali arrived in London on 22/10, he was met by Ispaham (H.C.) and Iskander Mirza. They had arranged for him to leave immediately by RAF Hastings for Cyprus, where a second Hastings was waiting. For some reason unknown he refused the services of the RAF and, after a delay of four hours, chartered a BOAC plane. He arrived in Karachi on the night of the 23/11. Two government Hare cars were waiting, + with them the C. in C. Ali was invited to get into one of the cars, which he did, sitting between the two generals. When Mrs. Ali tried to follow, she was politely requested to get into the other car. Ali was whisked off to GH and Mrs. Ali to the PM's house. Ali was asked to wait downstairs while the generals talked to GG. He was then sent for + told what GG wanted. He refused to agree. He was again asked to wait while a further discussion took place. This went on until 2.30 a.m., when he finally agreed. The impression I got, though I did not exactly say so, was that Ali was given a choice between agreement and arrest. Next morning the Secretaries were sent for + the Proclamations issued. The new Ministers were sworn in that night (24/10). From then on, GG and PM have worked together." November 10, 1954, ICS 125/BXV/6, JP.

> Pakistan would not be true to herself if not every lawyer busily rereading constitutional law to define the legality of the action taken by the Governor-General last Sunday. It is not unlikely that the legal argument will continue for months, but a recently arrived observer, bemused by seemingly contradictory acts, sections and clauses, can quickly come to one conclusion: whatever the Opposition lawyers may have to say – and it seems it will be unending – Karachi at least has accepted Mr Ghulam Muhammad's intervention calmly and perhaps with relief. (*The Times*, October 26, 1954)

Time magazine called Ghulam Muhammad the "Reluctant Dictator" (April 11, 1955). The President of the Constituent Assembly, Moulvi Tamizuddin Khan, disagreed with the "reluctance" and challenged the dissolution in the Courts. Into this context Ivor Jennings was summoned back.[10] The constitution-maker was to be the constitution-breaker.

ENTER JENNINGS AND TRANSNATIONAL COMMON LAW INTO THE PAKISTANI CRISES

Though the crisis is well known to Pakistani historians and legal scholars (less so outside) the role of Jennings has never been substantially addressed or exposed through his papers. The preeminent and most well-known historical and political account of Pakistan's road to military rule, Ayesha Jalal's *State of Martial Rule*, for example has no mention of Jennings' role. Similarly the best legal study of Pakistan's courts, Paula R. Newberg's *Judging the State – Courts and Constitutional Politics in Pakistan*, while astutely getting to the heart of the legal-political quagmire of the dissolution, finds no place for Jennings' substantial influence on the crisis.[11] Jennings did publish his own account of the events in Pakistan, *Constitutional Problems in Pakistan*, but this emphasized the constitutional soundness of dissolution and minimized his own effect giving little attention to critical or alternative views of the dissolution (Jennings 1957). Perhaps for this reason the book is uncharacteristically sober and without the usual flourish and mordant words that can be found in most of his work with the majority of it reproducing memoranda and judgments. Allen McGrath's *Destruction of Pakistan's Democracy* has been one of the few works that have given an important place to Jennings in the 1954 crisis as a "scholar-turned-advocate" who provided "constitutional ideas which were used to legitimize autocracy in Pakistan" (McGrath 1996: xii). This chapter utilizes

[10] Jennings since July 1954 had been advising the Constituent Assembly to devise a new constitution, but had returned to Ceylon.

[11] Both of those significant works do, however, cite his work concerning Pakistan.

material from the Jennings archive that have never been used before and in so doing gives crucial insight into one of the most destructive forms of post-war constitutional advice, which flowed from Jennings' scholarly experience and transnational authority.

After the dissolution the Governor-General reformed *his* Cabinet and invited the Commander-in-Chief of the Army, General Ayub Khan, to join as Defense Minister. The open inclusion of a serving officer set a grievous precedent and opened the door to what Tayyab Mahmud terms praetorianism, that would usher in military rule over the country becoming its dominant governance style (Mahmud 1993: 1234). *Dawn* captured that time a few years later when military rule was soon unveiled:

> There have indeed been times – such as that October night in 1954 – when with a General to the right of him and a General to the left of him, a half-mad Governor-General imposed upon a captured Prime Minister the dissolution of the Constituent Assembly and the virtual setting up of a semi-dictatorial Executive. (*Dawn*, August 11, 1957 cited in Sayeed 1980: 35)

Just days after the dissolution Sir Edward Snelson, Secretary to the Ministry of Law, sent a telegram on November 1, 1954 to Jennings stating, for cover, that he was to be on "holiday" in Ceylon, but, nonetheless, wanted to see Jennings, where he was vice-chancellor, urgently on the third of the month. Jennings sent a car for Snelson to bring him straight to Peradeniya and from there they saw Ceylon's Governor-General, Sir Oliver Goonetilleke, (no stranger to vice-regal and political intrigue) on the fifth for almost two hours evidently to discuss the political and constitutional machinations in Pakistan. Snelson and Jennings then flew the same day to Karachi (Note, November 10, 1954, ICS 125, BXV/6, JP). Jennings had already heard rumors that the Governor-General would dissolve the Assembly while still in Pakistan. Jennings confided to his diary on the day of the dissolution.

> Once you start on illegality you can never stop. This is not 1688: in England everybody tried to keep as close to the law as possible and there was no party conflict. Even so the non-juror movement was quite substantial. Before I left Karachi I pointed out … how fine was the line between law and anarchy. There is, of course, an alternative to anarchy, dictatorship. At the moment that seems to be where Pakistan is heading … Further consideration brings out another point. CA was to have met on the 27th, and I think PM Ali was to have returned that day. The Draft Constn. was to have been reported on the same day. It seems, therefore, that GG recalled Ali in order to get the coup d'etat effected before the CA members returned from their Provinces. They

> will not even be provided with their travelling expenses. The question is whether Nazimuddin and Nishtar will acquiesce or whether they will organise an opposition. If they do, they will probably be arrested under GOI rules, or the rules succeeding them. Note that Nehru is in China. In his absence, nobody is likely to order the Indian Army into East Bengal. What a chance he has missed! West Pakistan could then become a small unitary State. ("Revolution in Pakistan," [Note] October 25, 1954, ICS 125/B/XV/6, JP)

Jennings added that he was worried he would not get paid for the consultative work he did for the Assembly, though Snelson assured him he would! Following the intensive discussions in Ceylon Jennings was happy to help but wanted formal instructions. After even more discussions about fees, housing, allowances, and currency preferences Jennings was asked informally and then formally to answer the following questions at the request of the Governor-General and Law Ministry:

1. Did the Governor-General act constitutionally in (a) dissolving the Constituent Assembly and (b) inviting the Prime Minister to "re-form" the Cabinet?
2. Was the reconstituting of the Ministry by the Governor-General and Prime Minister unconstitutional?
3. On what grounds could a challenge be brought into the Courts as to the legality or constitutionality of (a) the dissolution (b) the re-forming of the Ministry and what would be the issues?
4. How should any challenge be met?
5. If Courts accept the "challenge" from Tazimuddin what should be done to meet the resulting situation? (Snelson to Jennings, 6 November 1954, ICS 125/BXV/4, JP)

The challenge came swiftly. Just days after Jennings arrived back in Pakistan a petition was delivered to the Sindh High Court. As Ginsburg, Elkins, and Blount argue the use of international actors in constitutional design can have critical effect. One major potential effect is where external participation "may lead drafters to adopt suboptimal or inappropriate provisions designed for the needs of others" (Ginsburg, Elkins, & Blount 2009: 214). Extrapolating this for Pakistan, Jennings had been brought in to solve the Ghulam Mohammed's dilemma of how to constitutionally and politically justify his actions in a context of ambiguous constitutional status. Jennings may have succeeded in creatively fulfilling his "brief" to the Governor-General, but it is no large step to see this more importantly as having "suboptimal" effects for Pakistani democracy. For one Pakistani academic the action utilized relied on powers available in all Westminster democracies, it was only evoked to "nourish" democracy.

> All this should cause no surprise or alarm to students of constitutional history. The plant of parliamentary government is delicate and sensitive. It needs care and nourishment ... The Governor-General had to step in and act as the guardian of the Constitution. The reserve powers that he used are available to executives in nearly all democratic constitutions. (Sayeed 1955: 338–9)

The situation was full of farce and risk as recounted over forty years later by S. S. Pirzada, one of the Assembly President's counsel – who unlike Jennings took the case gratis. Tamizuddin

> left his house through the back door disguised as a burqa-clad woman and in a rickshaw reached the Court through the side gate. The main gates of the Court were watched by Intelligence personnel. I drove to the Court in a diplomat's car which had dark glasses and was able to enter without being noticed. My junior Homi Nicholwala scaled side wall and received minor injuries. (Pirzada 1995: 54–5)

The petition to the Sindh High Court was made on the night of November 7, 1954 and the affidavit was signed by Manzar-i-Alam as the identifying advocate. When Manzar-i-Alam duly turned up in his own car at the main gates of the Court to present the petition, he was taken into protective custody and only when the Sindh Chief Justice, Sir George Constantine, ordered the police to release him or face contempt was Manzar-i-Alam allowed to join the others. An alleged unsuccessful attempt was also made on the life of Pirzada on November 11, 1954 by the Government Security Officers (Pirzada 1995: 54–5).

As the Government's adviser Jennings, in the opening session, was questioned by the Court due to his constitutional experience. However, the Assembly's legal team then wanted to understandably cross-examine him, which then convinced Jennings to refrain from speaking in court and instead allow his arguments to pervade through instructions (McGrath 1996: 168). D. N. Pritt QC with his remarkable political and legal career was called urgently to represent Tamizuddin. Waiving most of his fee and keeping with the dark comedy of the situation Pritt pretended to be a surgeon in all cables to Pakistan "who might be required for a difficult operation in Karachi" and like the opposing side he met in clandestine circumstances in Ceylon to discuss the case, and flew to Pakistan thence taking an omnibus to avoid attention (Pritt 1966: 48). Pritt argued "that a somewhat remarkable feature of the proclamation was that it did not give any legal authority to support it: it was just an announcement of intentions. It made no attempt to rely on prerogatives or statutory provisions" and did not even mention the word "dissolution." He also countered the Government's reliance on the Royal prerogative by asking "whether it was right to destroy the Constituent Assembly on the basis of a prerogative right which existed 250 years ago" by a Governor-General who is not part of the constitution-making body in a way that the Queen is part of the UK legislature ("Summary of the Arguments" to the Sindh High Court in Pirzada 1995: 106–9). Despite such unpropitious circumstances the Sindh High Court found in favor of Tamizuddin that the Governor-General did not have the authority to dissolve the Assembly since this was not part of the India Independence Act. The Chief Justice found

> There is no case throughout the Commonwealth outside England where dissolution of a Legislature takes place except by express provision in the Constitution, whether granted by statute or order in council. The prerogative of dissolution in my opinion extends only to the parliament of the United Kingdom: elsewhere dissolution is dependent upon statute or order in council ... It follows, therefore, that the Constituent Assembly's purported dissolution is a nullity in law, and that both it and the office of its President are still existent ... I would therefore issue a writ of mandamus restraining the respondents from preventing the petitioner from performing the functions of his office of President of the Constituent Assembly. (All Pakistan Legal Decisions, PLD 1955, Sind 96, in Pirzada 1955: 126–7)

The drama then moved to the Federal Court because there was no chance the Governor-General could admit wrong in this high-stakes performance. Even a compromise formula which would have saved face for both sides and maintained the dissolution was ruled out by Ghulam Mohammed for fear it would unravel the legitimacy of his past actions (McGrath 1996: 175). Politics was at the fore, which demoted law to a position of expedience. As a study of British legal thought contends Jennings was "primarily concerned with the architecture of power" over doctrine and procedure (McLean 2012: 234). A. W. Brian Simpson notes Jennings was "a firm believer in the right of states to protect themselves against subversion" (Simpson 2001: 860 n178). In Pakistan an English Don was behind the subversion of the constitution from above. Jennings recorded that

> There is thus initial dictatorship. It seems very unlikely that either the Governor-General or the Prime Minister would wish to perpetuate this

> position: but, now that there has been departure from strict legal principles, there is no great practical difficulty about going further. So long as the Army and the police support the Governor-General, anything whatever may happen. (Kumarasingham 2015a: 133)

With such thinking in mind Jennings efficiently prepared not only a new creative defense, but also plans to suspend the constitution and enable emergency rule should the Federal court uphold the lower court's ruling. Proficient as ever Jennings gave four options for the Cabinet to legitimize the actions of the Governor-General as well as four immediate steps to make this easier including the suspension of habeas corpus (Note for Cabinet, B/XV/3/1, JP). In a very matter of fact way he drafted an order to transfer all legislative powers to the Governor-General "excluding the jurisdiction of the Courts. I have explained that this cannot be legally justified, but that it is easy enough for the Govt. to refuse to give effect to judicial decisions" (Diary 31 March 1955, B/XV/8, JP). In this dangerous legal situation was an even more dangerous political one. Few wanted to challenge the Governor-General as democrats wilted.

> HM [Honourable Minister] Law gave me a copy of a telephone message from A.G. at lunch, + after lunch HM Interior joined us in conference. They wanted a Proclamation assuring a dictatorship, which I drafted after lunch + had ready for a Cabinet at PM's house. The Cabinet decided nothing but moved to GG's house at 6 p.m., where also nothing was decided. HM Law and Interior were alone in their anxiety for dictatorship, though HM Communications spoke up for them at the GGs. PM was obviously disturbed at the suggestion, but had no views of his own. The others also lacked decision of any kind. (13 April 1955, B/XV/8, JP)

TRANSNATIONAL SOURCES FOR LOCAL COURSES

Jennings, of course, was the major source of Westminster constitutional practice and his published works seemed to contradict his arguments in Pakistan. As an illustration of this Jennings noted in his widely read manual of Cabinet Government that the monarch cannot "secure a dissolution without 'advice'" without bringing conspicuous damage to the Crown (Jennings 1959a: 412–13).[12] Interestingly in the third and final edition of the volume

12 Though he records that Queen Victoria made "vague suggestions" about it in regard to the political dynamite that was Gladstone's Irish Home Rule. She was dissuaded from doing so by all her advisers since with even Gladstone's arch rival Lord Salisbury believing it would "injure the authority" of the sovereign.

published in 1959 Jennings inserts a bare footnote that in Pakistan the Queen's Representative did in fact dissolve the legislature without advice, but only because Pakistan "did not import British constitutional practice" (Jennings 1959a: 412 n1).[13] Indeed Jennings, while in Pakistan, had been meeting the Chief Justice, Muhammad Munir, "off the record" as had the Governor-General. The Chief Justice recommended "that GG must take over Government under 'natural law' powers" (March 28, 1955, B/XV/8, JP). After getting a Royal Pakistan Air Force flight to Lahore he rushed to Munir's residence (Snelson "backed out" from this utterly improper conclave) and discussed in great detail the arguments and "suggested amended sections," indicated emergency powers the "C.J. had not noticed" and was given substantial insights into the Chief Justice's thinking of justifying the dissolution. Returning to Karachi "Snelson then carried me off to GG's house for a Cabinet meeting ... the GG, with applause, made a little speech which was obviously a speech of thanks to me"; perhaps, not entirely in jest due to the consequences, Jennings added "but as I understood not one word it might have been an order for my immediate arrest!" (March 28, 1955, B/XV/8, JP). The refrain "Would Sir Ivor Jennings be good enough to draft notes and the Order accordingly?" became a common one (Note by Snelson, March 30, 1955, ICS 125/BXV/4, JP). Nonetheless, in Court Munir did not give an easy ride as his collusion might have predicted. The Advocate-General, Fayaz Ali, for example, had clearly not read his Jennings for a master class in expedient precedents. This selection of exchanges in Court between the Chief Justice and Advocate-General gives a flavor.

AG: My first proposition is that the right of dissolving the legislative body in England is the prerogative right of the Crown.

CJ: Do you mean to suggest that the King of England has got the right to dissolve the Constituent Assembly of Pakistan?

CJ: Had the prerogative been exercised by any of the Dominion[s] independently of the Statutes? Can you give us an instance where this prerogative of dissolution was exercised by any one on behalf of [the] Dominion independently of the authority given to that functionary by the Act?

AG: I must say I have not been able to find a parallel but the principle is there ...

[13] Jennings also notes that the Sovereign would be justified in refusing assent to a policy "which subverted the democratic basis of the Constitution," ibid. Arguably in the 1954 it was the Crown, not any other institution, which was subverting the democratic principles of the Constitution.

CJ: Can you give us an instance where this right of prerogative was exercised in any Dominion by His Majesty the King independently of any Statute?
AG: Unfortunately, My Lords, there was no instance in which there was not a provision made for it . . .
CJ: Why should that obvious thing be missing from our Constitution?
CJ: But we are in Pakistan. Do not talk of English ideas or English institutions. (Summary of Proceedings Before the Federal Court, March 1955 in Pirzada 1995: 154–8)

Future Law Lord Kenneth Diplock QC, was brought in to defend the dissolution. Unlike the Advocate-General, Diplock was well prepared and "quoted authorities to 'make it clear that the power of the Crown to dissolve and convene representative Assemblies was extended to overseas colonies'" (Summary of Arguments of Mr Diplock in the Reference before the Federal Court in Pirzada 1995: 263).[14] No stretch of imagination is required to discern which "authority" he was getting these Commonwealth facts from as well as his line of argument. Nothing was off limits. Jennings, through Diplock, successfully questioned the validity of the Constituent Assembly on the grounds that it had failed in its functions of representing the people and presenting a constitution. He also in turn questioned the independence of Pakistan by arguing that the Queen's prerogatives still functioned despite not being used in Britain since the seventeenth century. The Chief Justice agreed and had stated previously that the Constituent Assembly "lived in a fool's paradise" if it thought it was the sovereign body of the state (*Federation of Pakistan* v. *Moulvi Tamisuddin Khan*. 1955. PLD 1955 FC 240). Instead the Court was convinced by Jennings' argument "there can never be a lacuna in the Constitution of an independent country under the Crown." He added, mischievously, that "the margin the powers of the Crown are deliciously vague, the draftsman's dream of the blanket clause that covers everything he has forgotten or cannot foresee" (Jennings 1957: 72). To this vacuum marched the Governor-General as the sole "properly constituted" authority in the land (Jennings 1957: 72). Salus Populi Suprema Lex was added in, which as we have seen the Chief Justice had secretly advised, to give further argument to the Governor-General taking on extraordinary powers in the absence of responsible advice or explicit statutory provision. Jennings' legal bravado consequently meant that all the laws of Assembly were invalid since they did not have the Royal Assent,

[14] Henceforth cited as Summary of Arguments.

which the Assembly never believed it needed since it did not see the Governor-General as part of the Assembly.

If this was not enough Diplock argued that "the statement of His Majesty's Government by which the Constituent Assembly was set up [sic] a particular manner, had no force of law nor the previous statements made by the Prime Minister of England about the Independence of India" and stated that the Constituent Assembly's claim to be a sovereign body and "perpetual" was nonsense and "the very negation of all democratic institutions" (Summary of Arguments in Pirzada 1995: 259–61). The very legality of Pakistan was thus put on trial. However, quick drafting from Jennings enabled his boss, the Governor-General, to re-validate the majority under emergency ordinance (McGrath 1996). Such dexterity did not disguise authoritarianism. Nonetheless, without shame, Jennings pronounced in his published account that "the British tradition for the Rule of Law has been firmly established in Pakistan. In the long run, clearly, it was to Pakistan's advantage to follow the straight and narrow path of legal rectitude, rather than the broad and attractive highway that might, in the end, reach a dictatorship" (Jennings 1957: 51). Pritt had many skirmishes with the Chief Justice including later where Munir alluded reproachfully to Pritt's political sympathies toward the Soviet Union (Summary of Arguments in Pirzada 1995: 278). Pritt sought to puncture the deception of using law to cover political acts.

> it [is] difficult to import the notion of prerogatives and the common law in the area of a Government and no amount of Latin phrases could justify the introduction of these principles in this context ... the argument of "salus populi" in the case of a lacuna was put forth only to give a legal force to a political conception. (Summary of Arguments in Pirzada 1995: 272, 275)

As Pritt argued, the fact that the Prime Minister, just nights before the Assembly was dissolved, felt emboldened to state that Pakistan would have a new constitution ready by Jinnah's birth anniversary, December 25, 1954, was hardly to be stated if it was not functioning properly. Instead the Assembly was tarred as "broken down" by the Governor-General's Ordinance (Pirzada 1995: 281). This argument was also used by the sole dissenting Justice A. R. Cornelius (Pirzada 1995: 361; PLD 1955 F.C.P: 506–7). Fellow counsel I. I. Chundrigar added that the Assembly "could commit suicide but could not be murdered" (Summary of Arguments in Pirzada 1995: 283). The Federal Court disagreed and found in favor of the Governor-General. Justice Cornelius dissented and in contrast to his fellow Federal justices saw no justification from the Commonwealth for the dissolution or value in the "lacuna" argument in the constitution for the use of the Royal Prerogative. Cornelius instead reflected that these cases revealed the "weakness" of law and of judges in Pakistan to uphold the rule of law thereby ushering in extraordinary law as ordinary for much of the country's subsequent existence (Lombardi 2010: 436–44).

The situation was taken further when the Governor-General and Law Minister, perhaps pushing for further advantage, asked for guidance on the constitutional position and whether further executive, legislative, and emergency powers could be usurped by the Crown over the state. Starkly the Chief Justice explained

> The situation ... is that after experimenting for more than seven years with a constitution which was imposed on this country, with the consent of its leaders, by a statute of the Parliament of the United Kingdom, called the Indian Independence Act, 1947, we have come to the brink of a chasm with only three alternatives before us:
> (i) to turn back the way we came by;
> (ii) to cross the gap by a legal bridge;
> (iii) to hurtle into the chasm beyond any hope of rescue. (*Report on the Special Reference* 1955)

Munir then proceeded to try and respect alternative (ii), but in fact followed alternative (iii). Drawing on the heavy transnational constitutional knowledge that common law judges then possessed he called upon several precedents from across South Africa, Southern Rhodesia, Colonial America, and the Australian states of Victoria and South Australia to justify the Crown power to "force" dissolution (*Report on the Special Reference* 1955). Almost four years before the famous 1958 *State* v. *Dosso and Another* that validated military rule by necessity, Munir established a lasting legacy to Pakistan's constitutional life with his evocation of the Law of Necessity.

> Having anxiously reflected over this problem I have come to the conclusion that the situation presented ... is governed by rules which are part of the common law of all civilised States and which every written constitution of civilised people takes for granted. This branch of law is, in the words of Lord Mansfield, the law of civil or State necessity.

Munir continued and emphasized his stark point:

> an act which would otherwise be illegal becomes legal if it is done *bona fide* under the stress of necessity, the necessity being referable to an intention to preserve the constitution, the State or the Society and to prevent it from

> dissolution, and affirms Chitty's statement that necessity knows no law and the maxim cited by Bracton that necessity makes lawful [that] which otherwise is not lawful. (*Report on the Special Reference* 1955)

The Chief Justice then treated the court to an array of English worthies for transnational consumption. In addition to Bracton and Chitty legal luminaries including Broom, Darling, Reading, Dicey, Hood Phillips and Maitland were joined in company of rulers Cromwell, Charles II, William and Mary, and James II to impress upon Pakistan the essential need and legitimacy of powers used by Ghulam Muhammad – despite such powers being unknown in Britain itself for almost 300 years (*Report on the Special Reference* 1955).

CONCLUSION

It is worth quoting at length the argument of Jennings' successor at Cambridge as the Downing Professor of the Laws of England, S. A. de Smith, who while never mentioning his near contemporary clearly has Jennings in mind when demeaning the position taken in Pakistan.

> What respectable legal arguments can be advanced for justifying the validity of conduct which appears manifestly unlawful? Ask the constitutional lawyer and the legal theorist. He will find the arguments. Into the dustbin with *Entick* v. *Carrington*. Into the law reports with Bracton, Grotius, Kelsen, the American civil war, salus populi suprema lex. Clubs shall be trumps, might right, and judges philosophers if not kings … In short, it was very important for the court not to come to a conclusion adverse to the Governor-General on the main issues. Fortunately it was possible for the court to come to a favourable conclusion, and by using rules of public law found in the books, albeit unfashionable books. Nor did the court have to justify its decision by treating the Governor-General as a successful revolutionary; instead, it was able to discern legal continuity by invoking the doctrine of necessity to bridge the gap between the law and the facts of political life. In 1958, as we shall see, this option was closed and the court was faced with undisguised revolution claiming the accolade of legitimacy. It is clear, then, that the leading Pakistani decision in 1955 was a not very well disguised act of political judgment. By the normal canons of construction, what the Governor-General had done was null and void. But the judges steered between Scylla and Charybdis and chose what seemed to them the least of evils. I must add that by accepting the principle of necessity as a justification for otherwise unlawful conduct they did not give the Executive carte blanche; for example, the principle did not invest the Governor-General with power to change the existing constitutional structure. Yet state necessity, civil necessity or

> what you will, is the unruliest of all horses, which can gallop away with constitutional law into the domain of political expediency. (Smith 1968: 94, 98)

Munir mournfully confessed on his retirement in 1960 "mental anguish caused to the Judges by these cases is beyond description and I repeat that no judiciary anywhere in the world had to pass through what may be described as a judicial torture . . . At moments like these public law is not to be found in the books; it lies elsewhere, viz, in the events that have happened." Ultimately he decided to side with the Governor-General since otherwise he was "quite sure that there would have been chaos in the country" (Chaudhri 1973: 20). Anil Kalhan argues that the Doctrine of Necessity, derived from Common Law, when transplanted to places like Pakistan, can be "used to validate extraconstitutional action, giving a judicial stamp of approval to . . . efforts to wrest control from democratic, legislative institutions" (Kalhan 2010: 102–3). Kalhan continues that colonial era emergency powers were more often than not crafted not to "establish legality" nor to "preserve legality," but instead to assert colonial executive power. Pakistan (and India) "inherited these understandings" in their independent constitutional set up (Kalhan 2010: 118). The crisis of 1954 as Anne Twomey argues "opened the door" of the "doctrine of necessity," which was to prove critical in the subsequent history of Pakistan, being relied upon as recently as 2007 by General Musharraf (Twomey 2016: 61). The situation further deteriorated after Jennings' time in Pakistan to a parlous state where as Siddique argues in his legal analysis of martial law that the courts were going "to fantastical extremes in order to validate llegal takeovers, adducing support from obscure and controversial jurisprudential sources" (Siddique 2006: 627). Newberg's study of judicial politics records the damaging consequences of this dramatic period in Pakistani history.

> By giving the Governor-General wide berth and offering precedents to uphold executive intervention in constitutional and legislative activities, the immediate consequences of the Federal Court rulings were detrimental for Pakistan's developing polity and particularly for legislative sovereignty. For the longer term, the court established a practice of striking unspoken bargains with those in power so that its rulings would be obeyed and those in power would not feel defied. For a higher purpose – stability, perhaps democracy – the illusion of judicial independence would overtake the reality of its partial domination by those it sought to restrain or influence. At a crucial time in Pakistan's history, the judiciary molded this interpretation of prudence into a precedent from which it would later find it hard to depart. (Newberg 2002: 68)

As Tahir Kamran argues Jennings "came and rescued those whose exit would have done Pakistan a world of good" (Kamran 2016: 109). A. G. Noorani, for one, excoriates Jennings in the strongest terms for breaches in confidentiality, impropriety, legal cherry-picking, giving "shocking" advice, and commanding fees seven times greater than those paid to the Federal Chief Justice. Jennings' role in the events following the dissolution of Pakistan's legislature is that of "a learned lawyer's gross misconduct" (Noorani 2008). As Pakistan's leading legal historian concluded, the "echoes" from the controversies and calamities of the constitutional and political crises that Jennings was directly involved in "can still be heard in current constitutional developments in Pakistan" (Khan 2001: 136). Ghulam Muhammad, ill and dying, was reluctantly pushed out of Government House not long after his "victory" in August 1955. The new Cabinet had I. I. Chundrigar as Law Minister – the same who had been defending the case of the Constituent Assembly in the Federal Court. Jennings records in his diary that the new Minister "politely sacked" him on 8 September. "I should be glad to be out of it . . . I have done all the interesting work, + the rest will be . . . unpleasant" (Diary, 8 September 1955, ICS 125, BXV/8, JP). The last entry for his Pakistan diary contains the following words: "everybody must be heartily sick of Constitution-making" (Diary 9 January 1956, ICS 125 B/XV/8, JP).

Looking at his actions from a Transnational Legal Order framework Jennings was decisively able as a legal-political actor to adopt Westminster legal forms and draw on the transnational body of Common Law and Royal Powers to selectively bring "order" to the "problem" of avoiding democracy in Pakistan (Halliday & Shaffer 2015: 475–6). The crisis, colonial heritage, and Westminster artifices created the "facilitating circumstances" and "precipitating conditions" in Pakistan to make detrimental norms for constitutional government (Halliday & Shaffer 2015: 32–37). Jennings as a transnational constitution-maker was instrumental in bringing transnational practices and precedents to bear on the national arena in Pakistan. This enabled national lawmakers to cite transnational practices from the Indian Empire, British Empire, and Commonwealth to justify controversial national actions such as the dissolution of the Constituent Assembly, that would have institutionalizing tendencies for Pakistani politics despite the dangers of "mismatch" in translating the law and practices (Halliday & Shaffer 2015: 522–41). The common law and Westminster-style government with its reliance on conventions and prerogatives without explicit constitutional codification is an illustrative example of how TLOs help in the "unmasking and unveiling of power" by not being limited to codified legal orders, but instead cover and "infuse" the behavioral and political nature of institutions and practices, as seen in Pakistan during this period when TLOs from the global common law were fashioned for national needs with near-explicit political objectives (Halliday & Shaffer 2015: 477–9). Expressing this sentiment classically through the Latin favored by many judicial officers in the sub-continent of that era, Chief Justice Munir stated in his judgment on the Governor-General's powers *Casus omissus et oblivioni datus dispositioni communis juris relinquitur* (a case unprovided for in a statute and given to oblivion must be disposed of according to common law). This situation allowed "analogies and first principles" to be interpreted differently since the "law books and precedents furnish no direct answer to the precise answer which … confronts the judiciary of Pakistan" (*Report on the Special Reference*: 1955). This created an opportunity for expedient national interpretation of transnational import. As Munir put it, words like "Crown," "Prerogative," and "King" were willfully introduced for the legal and political battles in the Pakistani courts from all corners of the common law world, and "are mere legal abstractions and do not in any manner imply the subordination of Pakistan to any outside power" (*Report on the Special Reference*: 1955).

Jennings considered the "Pakistan Formula" might prove useful, however, to other Westminster states engaged in state-building. To this end he provided it to the UK's Commonwealth Relations Office.

> Dear Sir Ivor, thank you very much. It is most kind of you to offer me a copy of your memorandum about the position in Pakistan and I should indeed be grateful if you would let me have it. It would be of the greatest interest to me personally, and I know that those at the top of the Commonwealth Relations Office in London would be equally interested in seeing the views of an acknowledged expert. I can assure you that we will all respect your confidence and see that no word about it gets back to the Government of Pakistan. (Sir Cecil Syers to Jennings, November 6, 1954, ICS 125, BXV/6, JP)

Jennings' job was over in Pakistan, but his legacy remains. Ivor Jennings' role in Pakistan shows the dangers that constitution-making can have and how transnational practice can easily be harnessed to lend legitimacy to actions beyond the original meaning. The Westminster style of government and the conventions that add "flesh" to it were particularly malleable to such habits. He directly and covertly helped establish precedents and principles to justify non-democratic actions and therefore sowed the seeds for detrimental constitutional practices that have congested the soil of Pakistan ever since.

REFERENCES

Bradley, A. W. 2016. "Sir William Ivor Jennings: A Centennial Paper." In *Constitution-Making in Asia – Decolonisation and State-Building in the Aftermath of the British Empire*, edited by H. Kumarasingham. London: Routledge.

Callard, Keith. 1958. *Pakistan – A Political Study*. London: George Allen and Unwin.

Chaudhri, Hussain Nizir. 1973. *Chief Justice Muhammad Munir – His Life, Writings and Judgements*. Lahore: Punjab Educational Press.

Choudhury, G. W. 1970. *Constitutional Development in Pakistan*, 2nd edition. London: Longman.

De Smith, S. A. 1961. "Westminster's Export Models: The Legal Framework of Responsible Government." *Journal of Commonwealth Political Studies* 1(1) : 2–16.

De Smith, S. A. 1968. "Constitutional Lawyers in Revolutionary Situations." *Western Ontario Law Review* 93.

Elkins, Zachary, Tom Ginsburg, and James Melton. 2013. "The Content of Authoritarian Constitutions." In *Constitutions in Authoritarian Regimes*, edited by Tom Ginsburg and Alberto Simpser. Cambridge: Cambridge University Press.

Federation of Pakistan v. *Moulvi Tamisuddin Khan*. 1955. PLD 1955 FC 240. [cited as PLD]

Ginsburg, Tom, Zachary Elkins, and Justin Blount. 2009. "Does the Process of Constitution-Making Matter?" *Annual Review of Law and Social Sciences* 5.

Gledhill, Alan. 1957. *Pakistan – The Development of Its Laws and Constitution*. London: Stevens and Sons.

Halliday, Terrence C. and Gregory Shaffer, eds. 2015. *Transnational Legal Orders*. Cambridge: Cambridge University Press.

Harding, Andrew. 2004. "The 'Westminster Model' Constitution Overseas: Transplantation, Adaption and Development in Commonwealth States." *Oxford University Commonwealth Law Journal (Winter)* 4(2): 143–66.

Jalal, Ayesha. 1985. "Inheriting the Raj: Jinnah and the Governor-Generalship Issue," *Modern Asian Studies* 19(1): 29–53.

Jalal, Ayesha. 1990. *The State of Martial Rule – The Origins of Pakistan's Political Economy of Defence*. Cambridge: Cambridge University Press.

Jennings, Ivor. 1957. *Constitutional Problems in Pakistan*. Cambridge: Cambridge University Press.

Jennings, Ivor. 1959a. *Cabinet Government*, 3rd edition. Cambridge: Cambridge University Press.

Jennings, Ivor. 1959b. *The Law and the Constitution*, 5th edition. London.

Jennings, Ivor. 1956. *The Approach to Self-Government*. Cambridge: Cambridge University Press.

Kalhan, Anil. 2010. "Constitution and 'Extraconstitution': Colonial Emergency Regimes in Postcolonial India and Pakistan." In *Emergency Powers in Asia – Exploring the Limits of Legality*, edited by Victor V. Ramraj and Arun K. Thiruvengadam. Cambridge: Cambridge University Press.

Kamran, Tahir. 2016. "Pakistan's First Decade: Democracy and Constitution – A Historical Appraisal of Centralisation". In *Constitution-Making in Asia – Decolonisation and State-Building in the Aftermath of the British Empire*, edited by H. Kumarasingham. London: Routledge.

Khan, Hamid. 2001. *Constitutional and Political History of Pakistan*. Karachi: Oxford University Press.

Khan, Maryam S. 2014. "Ethnic Federalism in Pakistan: Federal Design, Construction of Ethno-Linguistic Identity and Group Conflict." *Harvard Journal of Racial and Ethnic Justice* 30: 77–129.

Kumarasingham, H. 2013a. *A Political Legacy of the British Empire*. London: I.B. Tauris.

Kumarasingham, H. 2013b. "Exporting Executive Accountability? Westminster Legacies of Executive Power." *Parliamentary Affairs* 66(3): 579–96.

Kumarasingham, H., ed. 2015a. *Constitution-Maker: Selected Writings of Sir Ivor Jennings*. Cambridge: Cambridge University Press.

Kumarasingham, H., ed. 2015b. *The Road to Temple Trees – Sir Ivor Jennings and the Constitutional Development of Ceylon: Selected Writings*. Colombo: Centre for Policy Alternatives.

Kumarasingham, H. 2016. "Eastminster – Decolonisation and State-Building in British Asia." In *Constitution-Making in Asia – Decolonisation and State-Building in the Aftermath of the British Empire*, edited by H. Kumarasingham. London: Routledge.

Lombardi, Clark B. 2010. "Islamism as a Response to Emergency Rule in Pakistan: The Surprising Proposal of Justice A.R. Cornelius." In *Emergency Powers in Asia – Exploring the Limits of Legality*, edited by Victor V. Ramraj and Arun K. Thiruvengadam. Cambridge: Cambridge University Press.

McGrath, Allen. 1996. *The Destruction of Pakistan's Democracy*. Karachi: Oxford University Press.

Mackenzie, W. J. M. 1975. *Explorations in Government – Collected Papers 1951–1968*. London: Palgrave Macmillan.

McLean, Janet. 2012. *Searching for the State in British Legal Thought*. Cambridge: Cambridge University Press.

Madden, A. F. 1979. "'Not for Export': The Westminster Model of Government and British Colonial Practice." *Journal of Imperial and Commonwealth History* 8(1): 10–29.

Mahmud, Tayyab. 1993. "Praetorianism and Common Law in Post-Colonial Settings: Judicial Responses to Constitutional Breakdowns in Pakistan." *Utah Law Review* 1225–305.

Marshall, Geoffrey. 1957. *Parliamentary Sovereignty and the Commonwealth*. Oxford: Oxford University Press.
Newberg, Paula R. 2002. *Judging the State – Courts and Constitutional Politics in Pakistan*. Cambridge: Cambridge University Press.
Newman, Karl J. 1959. "Pakistan's Preventative Autocracy and Its Causes." *Pacific Affairs* 32(1): 18–33.
Noorani, A. G. 2008. "Court Martial: The Great Betrayal (Parts I and II)." *Dawn*. 27 October and 1 November.
Norris, Pippa. 2001. "The Twilight of Westminster? Electoral Reform and Its Consequences." *Political Studies* 49(4): 877–900.
Pirzada, S. S. 1995. *Dissolution of Constituent Assembly of Pakistan and the Legal Battles of Moulvi Tamizuddin Khan*. Karachi: Asia Law House.
Pritt, D. N. 1966. *The Autobiography of D.N. Pritt*, part III. London: Lawrence and Wishart.
Rajah, Jothie. 2015. "'Rule of Law' as Transnational Legal Order." In *Transnational Legal Orders*, edited by Terence C. Halliday and Gregory Shaffer. Cambridge: Cambridge University Press.
Report of the Indian Statutory Commission Report. 1930. Cmnd 3569. [cited as ISC Report]
Report on the Special Reference Made by His Excellency the Governor-General of Pakistan. 1955. [cited as Report on the Special Reference]
Sayeed, Khalid B. 1955. "The Governor-General of Pakistan." *Pakistan Horizon* 8(2): 330–9.
Sayeed, Khalid B. 1980. *Politics in Pakistan – The Nature and Direction of Change*. New York: Praeger.
Siddique, Osama. 2006. "The Jurisprudence of Dissolutions: Presidential Power to Dissolve Assemblies under the Pakistani Constitution and Its Discontents." *Arizona Journal of Comparative and International Law* 23(3): 615–722.
Simpson, A. W. Brian. 2001. *Human Rights and the End of Empire – Britain and the Genesis of the European Convention*. Oxford: Oxford University Press.
Sir Ivor Jennings Papers. 1928–1965. Institute of Commonwealth Studies (ICS125). University of London. [cited as JP]
The Round Table. 1954. "Crisis in Pakistan." *The Round Table*. 45(177): 44–50.
Twomey, Anne. 2016. "Discretionary Reserve Powers of Heads of State." In *Constitution-Making in Asia – Decolonisation and State-Building in the Aftermath of the British Empire*, edited by H. Kumarasingham. London: Routledge.
Zaidi, Z. H., ed. 1996. *Jinnah Papers*, vol. III. Islamabad: Quaid-I-Azam Papers Project/Government of Pakistan.

4

Constitutions in World Society: A New Measure of Human Rights

Colin J. Beck, John W. Meyer, Ralph I. Hosoki, and Gili S. Drori

INTRODUCTION

It is well known that constitutions, which are valorized as national statements of unity, values, and purpose, are not conceived of nor written by domestic actors alone. Constitution-making relies heavily on international legal traditions and archetypical imageries of the source and purpose of law (Arjomand 1992; Elkins, Ginsburg, & Simmons 2013; Go 2003; Law 2016; Law and Versteeg 2011; Resnik 2008). Beyond cultural constructions of law, it is also apparent that there exists a technical consulting class, exemplars of constitutions, international governmental organizations, and civil society actors who stand ready to assist with and even write these putatively sacred national documents (Elkins, Ginsburg, & Melton 2009; Halliday & Shaffer 2015). We thus argue that constitutions should be considered global-transnational documents as much as national ones.

Specifically, how constitutions treat legal rights reveals global-transnational imprints. Conceptions of rights have undergone a striking evolution across the centuries – from the naturally God-given to the rewards of citizenship in a polity, and now an inalienable part of individual humanity (Lauren 2003; Stacy 2009). A striking aspect of this development is the sanctification of personhood and a widely legitimate image of society built upon individuals rather than corporate groups (Frank & Meyer 2002; Meyer & Jepperson 2000). This has in no small part been accompanied and accomplished by the growth of what sociologists term "world society" – the network, discourses, and institutions of transnational actors and ideologies that fill the vacuum of a nonexistent global state (Meyer, Boli, et al. 1997). Human rights, once absent from law, now fill the conceptions and operations of nearly all aspects of nation-state institutions (Cole 2012; Elliott 2007; Koo & Ramirez 2009; Suárez 2007). From our perspective, human rights may, in fact, constitute a coherent transnational legal order (TLO) by itself (see Halliday & Shaffer 2015). Its expression in constitutions is thus as much a product of global norms as local actors.

Our previous work has documented global influences on the incorporation of human rights language in constitutions (Beck, Drori, & Meyer 2012). Here, we build on this idea and introduce a measure of constitutional human rights that incorporates the discourse on rights as well as specific legal provisions (see also Elkins, Ginsburg, & Simmons 2013). The measure is based on the Universal Declaration of Human Rights and cross-national, longitudinal data on constitutions. Our examination of this measure demonstrates that it is robust, as well as explanatory of variation in constitutional human rights. We first discuss the neo-institutional world society perspective on the development of human rights. Then, we introduce our new measurement of constitutional human rights and replicate our previous study to demonstrate its robustness. Our findings confirm that constitutions display striking world influences in both language and law, and can be fruitfully considered supranational documents.

HUMAN RIGHTS IN WORLD SOCIETY

The idea of universal human rights is quite old. Versions are found in ancient Greek, and ancient Chinese, thought (Risse & Meyer 2016). These ideas tend to be sketchy, bloodless, and little worked out: the philosophers focused much more on questions of rights and justice within the political community, not in an imagined human world. Notions of universal rights took on more meaning in western Christendom, with the understanding that everyone – women, children, and "savages" – had souls giving them special and potentially equal standing, sacralized and organized in a universal Church. Secularization with the Enlightenment turned the more transcendental soul into a person – real on more and more dimensions – and broke up the Church into partially-secular national-states with ultimate authority to be universally respected (e.g., Anderson 1991; Bendix 1978; Nettl 1968).

Thus the main focus, in the literature on rights, has been on the rights of citizens in national states, not conceptions of more universal human rights. Following Marshall (1964), a picture of constantly expanding ranges of citizenship rights arises. The expansion occurs on several dimensions. First, more and more citizenship rights are developed – from civil to political to socioeconomic, and now to psychological and cultural rights (Boli 1987; Frank & Meyer 2002; Go 2003; Thornhill 2008). Second, rights spread around the world in standardized ways (Anderson 1991; Meyer, Boli, et al. 1997). And third, citizenship rights increasingly are globalized: they come under the scrutiny of more and more supranational bodies, whose principles of soft law increasingly take on the appearances of rather hard law (e.g., in the European Union, but also many other structures).

All these changes refer to citizenship rights, though as we note above they are increasingly globalized. They appear with great and increasing regularity in national constitutions, which incorporate increasing ranges of them (Boli 1987), with increasing detail (e.g., Boli-Bennett & Meyer 1978 on the recognition of children). In some of the nineteenth-century constitutions – including the American one – rights are seen as prior to the national state, and rooted in some sort of natural or religious order. More commonly in later periods with the high period of the nation-state system, citizenship rights are seen as derived from the majesty of the state (Hooper 1988), with citizenship as the primary identity of the person.

Increasingly, after the late nineteenth century, explicitly supranational notions of human rights developed – and exploded later in the twentieth century: the story is well established (Lauren 2003; Stacy 2009). World War I was one trigger, and imagery of human rights over and above national citizenship were clearly part of the culture around the League of Nations. But the Great Depression, World War II, and the mass human destructions of the period, were all seen as reflections of the disasters of nationalism gone wild. Nuclear warfare, a Cold War, and a huge wave of decolonization reinforced the point. In some readings, the dominance of the radically liberal and individualist United States played an important role.

In any case, aggressive notions emerged that the individual human, not the national state, was the locus of universal rights. In the Atlantic Charter, imperialist Britain (and racist United States) celebrated rights principles neither of them would institutionalize at home: later on the Soviet Union joined them. And the ideas took hold in the world at large: so against some resistance from the great powers, the 1948 United Nations Declaration of Human rights appeared (Lauren 2003) and was dramatized in world attention.

Through the subsequent period, and to the present, the expansion of human rights norms in global society has been astonishing. Elliott (2007, 2011, 2014) tracks the numbers of international instruments that assert human rights – the growth has been rapid. Also expanding, he finds, are the ranges of rights asserted as universal human rights: political, social, cultural, religious, economic, and so on. Thus studies note the expansion of asserted human rights in education (Chabbott 2003; Suárez 2007), health (Inoue & Drori 2006), employment (Risse 2009), and many other areas.

The long history of growth in rights is depicted in a number of historical reviews (Lauren 2003; Stacy 2009), which tend to emphasize long-term continuity. Moyn (2010) takes issue with this perspective, emphasizing the discontinuity between citizenship rights as rooted in the nation-state and the human rights of recent decades as reflecting a dramatic transcendence of the state and re-asserting the universal bases of human rights. And indeed, there is a clear distinction between rights as defined in the positive law of national states and similar rights as seen as some sort of "natural law" based more universally. In our previous work, we noted that, in typical national constitutions, rights of citizenship take on clear legal forms, and are developed in legalized discussions, while human rights tend to be asserted more grandly in preambles and other depictions of national identity in universalized frames. Absent a world state organization, this seems inevitable: the identity-defining aspects of national constitutions refer to a wider moral order, while the positive laws and rights asserted treat the national-state itself as a basis.

Overall, there is a great deal of continuity in the substantive rights seen variously as nationally-based or as human rights. And there is an enormous expansion in such rights, worldwide, over a long period of time. But it is important to see the current re-grounding of these rights as overriding the former doctrines of national sovereignty as an important shift. The weakening of the primordial status attributed to the national state as core actor in human history is clearly linked to the expanded rights attributed to individuals. It is also linked to changes in the rights involved: as Elliott (2007, 2014) shows, the shift to modern human rights involves a shift in conceptions of rights from entitlements to empowerments. The human, apparently, is able to make a wider range of legitimate choices than is the citizen.

Further, the groups seen in the international instruments as entitled to pursue their own rights and the rights of others expand greatly over time. It is not simply the obligation of nation-state signatories to support universal rights: It is the obligation of all of us. It now, thus, becomes more and more legitimate for all sorts of groups to penetrate the sovereign boundary of a deviant national state in support of the rights of its citizens – now seen in their universal status as humans.

Beyond international treaties and other instruments, universal human rights expand in other arenas as well. Relevant international organizations (both governmental and especially non-governmental) have grown rapidly (Hafner-Burton 2013; Hafner-Burton, Tsutsui, & Meyer 2008; Tsutsui & Wotipka 2004; Wotipka & Tsutsui 2008). In Halliday and Shaffer's (2015) terms, human rights is a clear case of a transnational legal order, where norms, actors, and institutions align to promote a particular set of practices. Obviously, the expansion of global human rights norms vastly exceeds the capacity (and perhaps the desire) of extant social and political systems to implement them. It is well understood that national-states that support and adopt the relevant norms are often unlikely to implement them (Hafner-Burton, Tsutsui, & Meyer 2008; Hathaway 2002; Vreeland 2008). The term "decoupling" from sociological neo-institutional theory is often employed to describe the situation (Meyer 2010). However, the same line of theorizing suggests that widespread agreements on norms like human rights are likely to have diffuse long-term effects on all sorts of participants in world society, entirely over and above their limited short-term effects on adopting entities. An emergent literature looking for long-term and diffuse effects produces findings supportive of such ideas (Cole 2013; Cole & Ramirez 2013).

Questions of implementation entirely aside, it is entirely clear that the global human rights movement has had dramatic effects on the normative and policy frames of national states and other organizations. Human rights treaties are ratified around the world, and both public and private organizations incorporate them in their formal schemes and policies. All sorts of social movements arise, asserting their rights to assess events around the world (perhaps in countries protagonists could not find on their maps) in terms of human rights principles.

Our earlier study (Beck, Drori, & Meyer 2012) provided evidence on the penetration of global human rights norms into national constitutions over time, showing clear influences of these norms, especially in more recent periods. In the present study, we examine the situation with much better data, and much more sophisticated measurement.

One can theorize the situation from several points of view. More phenomenological institutionalisms suggest that nation-state identities, including constitutional structures, are themselves abstract models, and are built up and supported from frames in their environments (Meyer 2009; Meyer, Boli, et al. 1997). From this point of view, it is not surprising that a world cultural movement finds reflections in the identities claimed by subunits. More traditionally functionalist lines of thought see the expanded status of the human individual as a natural product of socio-economic development, and thus characterizes the current period. Extensions of such ideas might imagine generalizations of such effects in a period in world society in which goals of socioeconomic development are deeply institutionalized in world political and economic systems. But most versions of this general line of thought would predict great differences among countries differing in developmental status in their adoption of human right principles.

More realist institutionalisms might imagine world human rights norms as constructed in world power centers (obviously including the United States, but also its putative spin-offs in the World Bank and other structures), and as diffused through a variety of incentive structures. It is, however, difficult to imagine why raw centers of power would have such goals – dominating the world is not facilitated by widespread human rights norms, it would seem (see, e.g., Ritter 2015).

Theoretical issues aside, our goal here is less to examine any hypotheses about the issue than to examine, with improved data and measures, the strength of the impact of the global human rights system on national constitutional structures. We agree here with Ginsburg (Chapter two this volume) that constitutions represent a process through which different groups and actors advocate for particular norms and interests. In this sense, constitutions can be an expression of underlying global norms and transnational legal orders even as their very existence is transnationally normative. Constitutional documents are thus another vehicle for the spread and institutionalization of the cultural content of modern world society.

MEASURING HUMAN RIGHTS IN CONSTITUTIONS

Previous quantitative work on the appearance of rights in national constitutions has employed two different strategies. First, scholars have recognized that constitutions are discursive and symbolic documents as much as they are legal ones. To account for this, Law (2016) uses insights from computational linguistics to examine the preambles of constitutions as they tend to be expressions of national values, rather than merely law. More simply, Beck, Drori, and Meyer (2012) measure rights discourse by the number of times the phrase "human rights" is used within a document. A second strategy has been to examine the provisions of constitutions themselves. An early effort along these lines was undertaken by John Boli (1987; see also Boli-Bennett & Meyer 1978). More recently, data collected by Benedikt and Versteeg (2011) have been used to quantify rights within constitutions and their global spread (e.g., Law & Versteeg 2011) and Elkins, Ginsburg, and Simmons (2013) demonstrate that the Universal Declaration of Human Rights provided a menu of rights options available to constitution drafters.

Quantifying rights by symbolism and practicality are not mutually exclusive strategies. We thus construct a measure of human rights in constitutions that reflects both discursive and legal inclusions of human rights. To do so, however, what human rights actually are must be defined with care, particularly since numerous studies have documented the incorporation of older rights models – natural rights, citizen rights, etc. – into the sacred canopy of contemporary human rights frames (e.g., Beck, Drori, & Meyer 2012; Lauren 2003; Law & Versteeg 2011; Moyn 2010; Stacy 2009). Even without delving deeply into definitions of human rights, it is apparent that what constitutes a human right is global – that is broadly shared across the world – and transnational – existing outside above the laws of any one country. Global and transnational articulations of human rights are undertaken by international organizations, technical classes of legal experts, and civil society actors. While these actors interact in and influence a variety of domains, international governmental organizations are often taken to be key global-transnational sites of human rights production (Meyer, Boli, et al. 1997). We thus follow previous work by emphasizing the special role of the United Nations and its treaty regimes in the development of human rights (Cole 2005, 2009; Elkins, Ginsburg, & Simmons 2013; Elliott 2014; Hafner-Burton & Tsutsui 2005; Sandholtz 2015).

Among the articulations of human rights produced by the United Nations, the Universal Declaration of Human Rights has a special place. Not only is it the first explicit articulation of human rights for the post-World War II states system; it is also widely known and legitimated by actors of the global-transnational system. It is the most translated document in the modern world and provides the discursive and legal basis for international human rights law. As such, it provides a baseline description of what a human right is, even as subsequent treaties have extended and elaborated its protections.[1]

We match the discourse and provisions of the UDHR, including its preamble and articles, to data collected by the Comparative Constitutions Project (Elkins, Ginsburg, & Melton 2014). The CCP data, while not complete nor the only cross-national database of constitutions, provide a systematic coding of constitutional provisions over a lengthy period of time for the entire world. We are thus able to generate measures for over eight thousand country-year observations. Two coders examined the UDHR separately, identifying variables in the CCP data that matched the discourse of the Declaration as well as its specific provisions.[2] Sixty-five different variables in the CCP were identified as being present in the UDHR, which covers over 70 percent of the text of the

[1] Elkins, Ginsburg, and Simmons (2013) also use the UDHR to examine how treaty ratification affects constitutions.

[2] The CCP data includes codings of general statements such as "Does the constitution refer to the 'dignity of man' or 'human dignity'?" as well as specific law such as "Does the constitution provide for freedom of assembly?"

Declaration and 31 percent of variables that cover rights in the CCP.[3] This is in line with previous work that finds that measureable human rights, even as they have expanded, are still a subset of all possible rights (Beck, Drori, & Meyer 2012; Law & Versteeg 2011). Table 4.1 lists the variables and corresponding Declaration text identified.

The CCP variables are then combined into a sixty-five-point index of human rights discourse and law in national constitutions. A constitution is coded as having a right or phrase present if the dataset codes it affirmatively, including rights that are limited in some fashion. In the few cases of CCP codes of "other" requiring explanation, the right is treated as not being present. The resulting index covers 8,141 country-year observations from 1789 to 2013. The index ranges from zero – in 17 cases where no UDHR rights are found – to a high value of fifty-eight, with a mean score of twenty-five (SD = 12.63) over the entire time period.

Figure 4.1 presents the mean score by year on the UDHR index. Not surprisingly, the average global inclusion of human rights increases over time, with notable jumps after the Declaration's 1948 adoption and the collapse of communism in 1989. This suggests that the index is capturing the general expansion in human rights across the last two centuries, even when they had yet to be conceived as such.

Figure 4.2 shows the geographic spread of UDHR rights in 2013. The countries with the highest scores appear to be more peripheral states, such as in South America, Sub-Saharan Africa, and Eastern Europe. Older democracies, such as in North America, Western Europe, and the British Commonwealth have relatively lower scores. This may seem counterintuitive at first, but previous research has found that older, more established constitutions are less likely to incorporate human rights discourse even as they are amended (Beck, Drori, & Meyer 2012). Newer constitutions, particularly those of societies that are more susceptible to international influence, are more likely to adopt human rights talk. This pattern is borne out by consideration of the top and bottom ten countries on the UDHR scale (see Table 4.2). In 2013, Ecuador scores the highest, with fifty-eight of sixty-five possible human rights dimensions, and has a recent constitution from 2008. On the other hand, the Australian constitution has only six human rights indicators. Australia's constitution dates to 1901 and has only been amended eight times, most recently in 1977. The initial

[3] Of the text of the Declaration not covered, only two articles dealing with rights have no analogue in the CCP data (Articles 6 and 28). The number of possible CCP variables is calculated from its sections on voting, criminal procedure, rights, and education.

TABLE 4.1. *CCP Variables and UDHR Coverage*

Variable Name	Variable Description	UDHR Article(s)
ACHIGHED	Equal access to higher education	Article 26.1
ASSEM	Freedom of assembly	Article 20.1
ASSOC	Freedom of association	Article 20.1
ASYLUM	Provisions of stateless, refugees, or asylum	Article 14
CITREN	Right to renounce citizenship	Article 15.2
CIVIL	Meritocratic recruitment of civil service	Article 21.2
CRUELTY	Prohibits cruel, inhuman, or degrading treatment	Article 5
DEVLPERS	Right to individual self determination or personality	Article 22
DIGNITY	Refers to dignity of man or humans	Preamble; Article 1; Article 22; Article 23.3
DUEPROC	Due process	Article 10
EDCOMP	Compulsory education	Article 26.1
EDFREE	Free education	Article 26.1
EDUCATE	Provisions concerning education	Article 26
EQUAL	Equality before law, rights or non-discrimination	Article 7
EQUALGR_1	Equality of gender	Article 2
EQUALGR_3	Equality of country of origin	Article 2
EQUALGR_4	Equality of race	Article 2
EQUALGR_5	Equality of language	Article 2
EQUALGR_6	Equality of religion	Article 2
EQUALGR_10	Equality of color	Article 2
EQUALGR_11	Equality of creed/beliefs	Article 2
EQUALGR_12	Equality of social status	Article 2
EQUALGR_13	Equality of financial/property ownership	Article 2
EQUALGR_16	Equality of parentage	Article 2
EXPOST	Prohibits of ex post facto punishment	Article 11.2
EXPRESS	Freedom of expression or speech	Preamble, Article 19
FAIRTRI	Right to fair trial	Article 8, Article 10
FINSUP_1	General or financial support for elderly	Article 25.1
FINSUP_2	General or financial support for unemployed	Article 25.1
FINSUP_3	General or financial support for disabled	Article 25.1
FINSUP_4	General or financial support for children, orphans	Article 25.2
FNDFAM	Right to found a family	Article 16.1
FREEMOVE	Freedom of movement	Article 13
FREEREL	Freedom of religion	Article 18
HABCORP	Right to habeas corpus	Article 9
HEALTHHR	Right to health care	Article 25.1

TABLE 4.1. *(continued)*

Variable Name	Variable Description	UDHR Article(s)
INALRGHT	Certain rights are inalienable or inviolable	Preamble
INTPROP_1	Intellectual property rights for patents	Article 27.2
INTPROP_2	Intellectual property rights for copyrights	Article 27.2
INTPROP_3	Intellectual property rights for trademark	Article 27.2
INTPROP_4	Intellectual property rights general reference	Article 27.2
JOINTRDE	Right to form or join unions	Article 23.4
LESIURE	Right of rest or leisure	Article 24
LIBEL	Right of protection from libel	Article 12
LIFE	Right to life	Article 3
MARRIAGE	Right to marry	Article 16.1
MATEQUAL	Matrimonial equality	Article 16.1
OCCUPATE	Right to choose occupation	Article 23.1
OPINION	Freedom of opinion, thought, or conscience	Article 18
OVERTHRW	Right to overthrow government	Preamble
PRESINOC	Presumption of innocence	Article 11.1
PRESS	Freedom of the press	Article 19
PRIVACY	Right to privacy	Article 12
PROPRGHT	Right to own property	Article 17.1
PUBTRI	Generally requires public trials	Article 11.1
REMUNER	Right to just remuneration	Article 23.2, Article 23.3
RULELAW	General statement about rule of law	Preamble
SCIFREE	Right to enjoy benefits of scientific progress	Article 27.1
SHELTER	Right to shelter or housing	Article 25.1
SLAVE	Prohibits slavery, servitude or forced labor	Article 4
SOCECON	Uses words (socio-)economic rights	Article 22
SOCSEC	Refers to social security of society or nation	Article 22
STANDLIV	Right to standard of living	Article 25.1
TORTURE	Prohibits torture	Article 5
VOTEUN	Universal adult suffrage	Article 21.3

evidence thus suggests that the UDHR scale is capturing what other previous measures of human rights language in constitutions did.

The CCP data also provides the number of words present in the rights section of a constitution, which allows for consideration of the extent of overall rights discourse. Rights can be well articulated and extensively elaborated, or given only cursory attention. Over the entire sample, rights sections on average

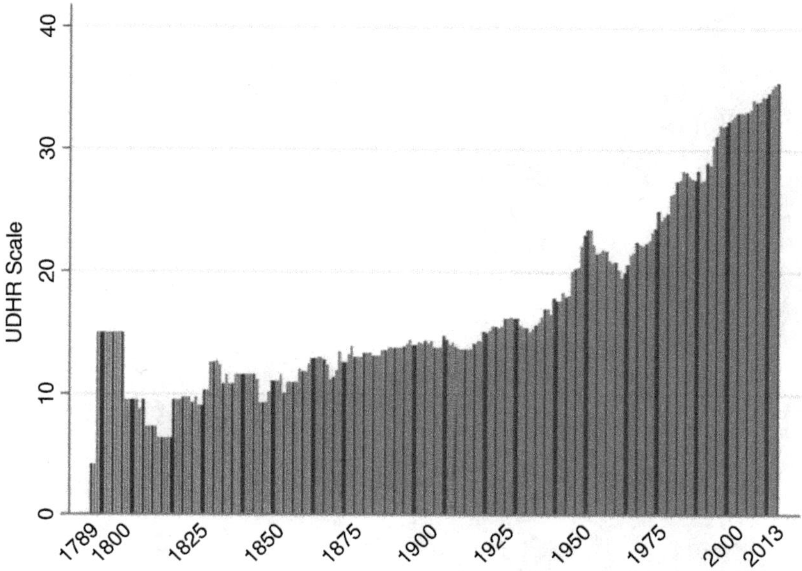

FIGURE 4.1: Average Human Rights in Constitutions by Year

are 2599 words, with a large standard deviation of 2528. This ranges from only forty-four words in a rights section as in the case of Thailand's 2006 constitution, to 15,799 words as in Mexico's current constitution. As with human rights, the number of words devoted to explaining rights expands over time. Throughout most of the nineteenth century, the average articulation of rights took less than a thousand words. By 2013, the average constitution devoted 3,624 words to rights. Geographically, in 2013, rights seem to be most extensively discussed in Latin America and least present in island states like Micronesia and Vanuatu, as well as non-democratic regimes like Bhutan, Kuwait, and Laos. The elaboration of rights in general is used below as the basis for comparison to global-transnational influences on human rights.

GLOBAL-TRANSNATIONAL INFLUENCES ON CONSTITUTIONAL HUMAN RIGHTS

A purpose of this study is to evaluate the robustness of a measure of constitutional human rights – the UDHR scale – and how it can be used to examine transnational influences on the constitution-making process. To do so, we build on our prior work on human rights language in constitutions (Beck, Drori, & Meyer 2012). This previous study examined the discourse of human rights in constitutions of the world in 2005 and found statistically significant

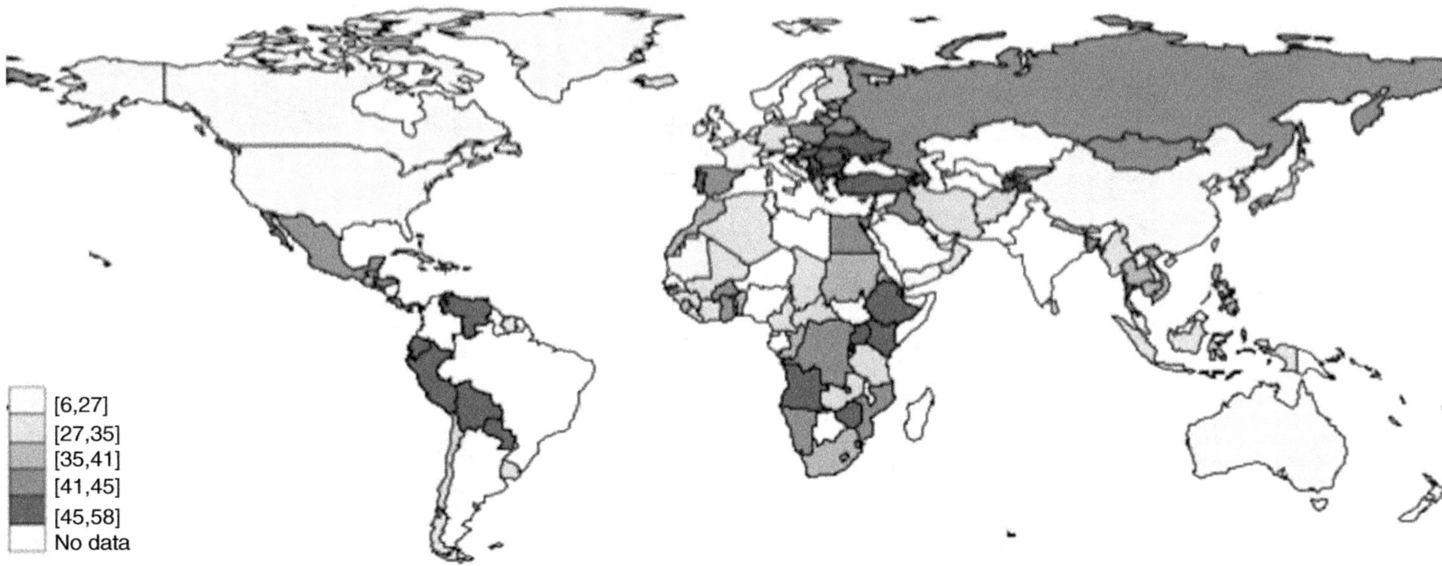

FIGURE 4.2: Geography of UDHR Scale in 2013

TABLE 4.2 *Top and Bottom Ten Countries by UDHR Scale, 2013*

Top 10		Bottom 10	
Country	UDHR Provisions	Country	UDHR Provisions
Ecuador	58	Liechtenstein	21
Venezuela	55	Monaco	21
Armenia	55	United States	21
Portugal	55	Luxembourg	18
Bolivia	55	Comoros	17
Serbia	54	Netherlands	16
Ethiopia	53	Singapore	14
Albania	51	Denmark	14
Angola	51	France	10
Azerbaijan	50	Australia	6
Turkey	50		
Ukraine	50		
World Mean	35		

support for the argument that the founding era of a constitution mattered for human rights inclusion above and beyond state-centered and international processes. In the remainder of the present study, we consider whether these results can be replicated using the new measure of human rights language and provisions drawn from the Comparative Constitutions Project dataset.

Cross-National Data on Countries and Constitutions in 2005

The primary dependent variable used is the UDHR index, described above. For secondary regression analyses, we use the number of words present in the rights section of a constitution as coded by the CCP. Controls and independent variables are drawn from Beck, Drori, and Meyer (2012), which contains further details about coding and measurement. Table 4.3 presents descriptive statistics for the variables included in regression analyses. All measures are as of 2005, including the dependent variables, which replicates the cross-sectional design of our earlier study.

In our analyses, we control for aspects common to cross-national research: population size; gross domestic product per capita; and international trade. In addition, qualitative consideration of constitutions suggests that a history of political violence may also affect the adoption of human rights. We also control for the length of constitution, as longer constitutions may be more likely to elaborate specific human rights, and the age of the last amendment – as more

TABLE 4.3 *Descriptive Statistics of Variables Used in Analysis, 2005*

Variable	Mean	S.D.	Min	Max
UDHR scale	35.69	10.80	6	55
Length of rights section	3221.17	2676.18	424	13404
Length in pages	65.60	106.12	11	1210
Years since amendment	8.55	7.81	1	53
Population (ln)	16.23	1.48	13.09	20.99
GDP per capita (log)	3.40	.73	2.01	4.82
Trade/GDP	90.22	48.72	26.65	448.28
History of political violence	.36	.48	0	1
Regime age in years	25.07	31.47	0	196
Regime democracy score	3.73	6.41	−10	10
Political terror scale score	2.62	.99	1	5
Post-communist	.19	.39	0	1
N of HR treaties signed	5.67	1.18	2	7
INGO memberships (log)	2.83	.44	1.53	3.61
Global HR instruments	82.50	47.16	0	147

frequently amended constitutions may be more likely to reflect contemporary understandings of rights. In addition to these controls, we present indicators for three sets of explanations on constitutional variation: regime characteristics, international linkages, and the extent of the global-transnational human rights field.

First, to assess regime-specific effects on constitutions, we include measures for the age of a regime, its level of democracy, the extent of its use of political terror, and whether or not the country is post-communist. For international linkages, we include two measures. As international law may influence constitutional law, we estimate the effect of the number of core human rights treaties signed as of 2005, and an indicator of the embeddedness of a country in world society more generally – international nongovernmental organization memberships within a society. World society scholars commonly capture national membership in the transnational system with this latter measure. Finally, our key independent variable reflects founding era effects in force at the time of a constitution's initial adoption – the global cumulative number of human rights instruments recognized by the United Nations (see Elliott 2011). The measure reflects not only international human rights law, but also transnational discourse and legitimation of human rights globally.

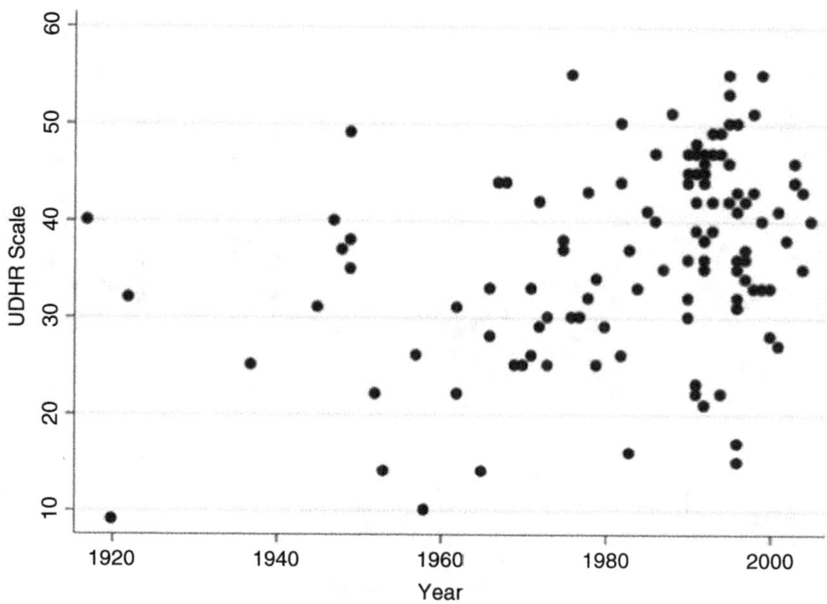

FIGURE 4.3: UDHR Scale and Year of Constitution

Results of Cross-National Analyses

Our primary argument is that constitutional human rights reflect global-transnational processes. As the transnational human rights regime and frame has grown in scope and legitimation, national law is more likely to incorporate understandings of the individual as the fundamental unit of society and personhood as sacred. We argue further that this process is unique to those rights conceived of as human rights. Thus, legal rights in general will not reflect the same transnational influences. The time in which a constitution is adopted is thus key – constitutions reflect the global-transnational environment at the time of their writing as much as national context.

Figures 4.3 and 4.4 present scatterplots of human rights language and provisions by the year of a constitution and the extent of the transnational human rights regime. For interpretability, the presentation is limited to constitutions written after 1914. Upon examination, it is clear that the number of UDHR provisions present in a constitution tracks time rather closely. More recent constitutions tend to have higher scores on the human rights index, and older ones lower. Not surprisingly, the relationship is statistically significant ($\beta = .46$, $p < .001$). The UDHR index also tracks the number of human right instruments at the time of writing (see Figure 4.4). This relationship is also

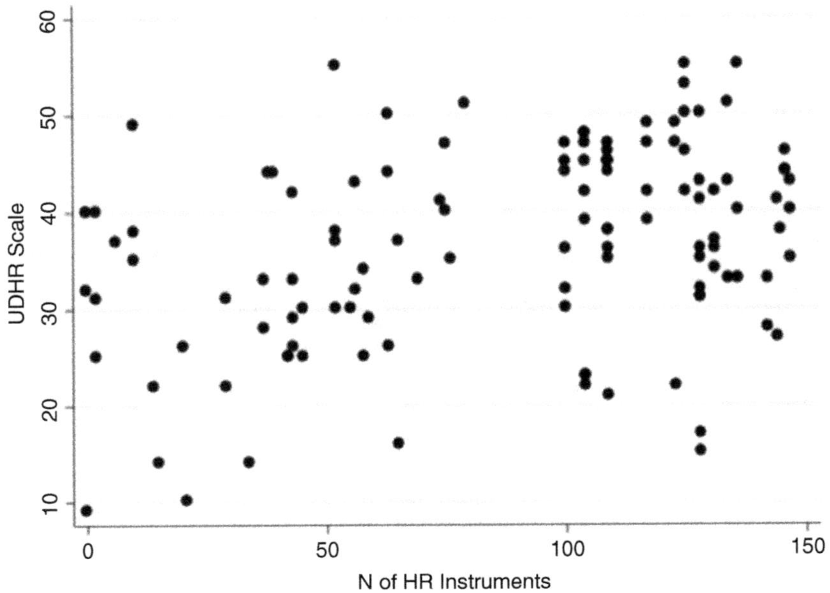

FIGURE 4.4: UDHR Scale and Human Rights Regime

statistically significant with a similar effect as the year of constitutional adoption ($\beta = .43, p < .001$).

In contrast, there is less of a relationship between the length of the rights section and the year of constitution and the transnational human rights environment. Figures 4.5 and 4.6 present scatterplots of the number of words devoted to rights in a constitution by year and number of human rights instruments. While there are increases in length along both axes, bivariate correlation shows that the relationships actually trend in a slight negative direction, and neither is statistically significant. In other words, the amount of attention paid to rights does not appear to be caused by founding era effects, unlike human rights.

To examine these trends systematically, we employ multivariate regression analyses (see Table 4.4). Model 1 in Table 4.4 presents the results from Beck, Drori, and Meyer (2012) that used human rights mentions in a constitution for comparison. Models 2 and 3 examine the new UDHR index of human rights and the number of words devoted to rights respectively. For each model, we present only the results of all independent variables and controls; partial models are available from the authors upon request. Given different configurations of missing cases for each dependent variable, the sample size differs across models.

TABLE 4.4 *Results of Multivariate Regression of Rights Measure, 2005*

	Model 1: Beck et al. 2012	Model 2: UDHR Scale	Model 3: Length of Rights Section
Length in pages	.008*	.065**	.015***
	(.004)	(.022)	(.002)
Years since amendment	−.037	−.085	.005
	(.019)	(.102)	(.007)
Population (ln)	.124	.774	.015
	(.107)	(.700)	(.059)
GDP per capita (log)	.271	.940	.111
	(.224)	(1.712)	(.122)
Trade/GDP	−.005	−.018	−.001
	(.003)	(.016)	(.001)
History of political violence	−.340	−1.858	−.039
	(.236)	(1.542)	(.119)
Regime age in years	−.014**	−.091*	−.004
	(.005)	(.039)	(.003)
Regime democracy score	.035	.097	.033**
	(.025)	(.143)	(.010)
Political terror scale score	.329*	.745	.008
	(.148)	(1.00)	(.088)
Postcommunist	.093	9.716***	.199
	(.283)	(1.733)	(.133)
N of HR treaties signed	.246*	1.630*	.151**
	(.114)	(.683)	(.051)
INGO memberships (log)	−.423	−3.616	−.160
	(.344)	(2.157)	(.193)
Global HR instruments	.010***	.049*	.001
	(.003)	(.021)	(.001)
Constant	−2.975	14.239	5.885***
	(1.869)	(13.831)	(.864)
R-squared	.125	.490	.048
N	143	122	113

In our 2012 study, we found that constitutional measures of human rights were negatively associated with regime age and positively associated with the length of a constitution, the use of political terror by a regime, the number of human rights treaties a country had signed, and the number of human rights instruments in existence at the time of a constitution's adoption (see Model 1, Table 4.4). The positive and statistically significant effect of the transnational

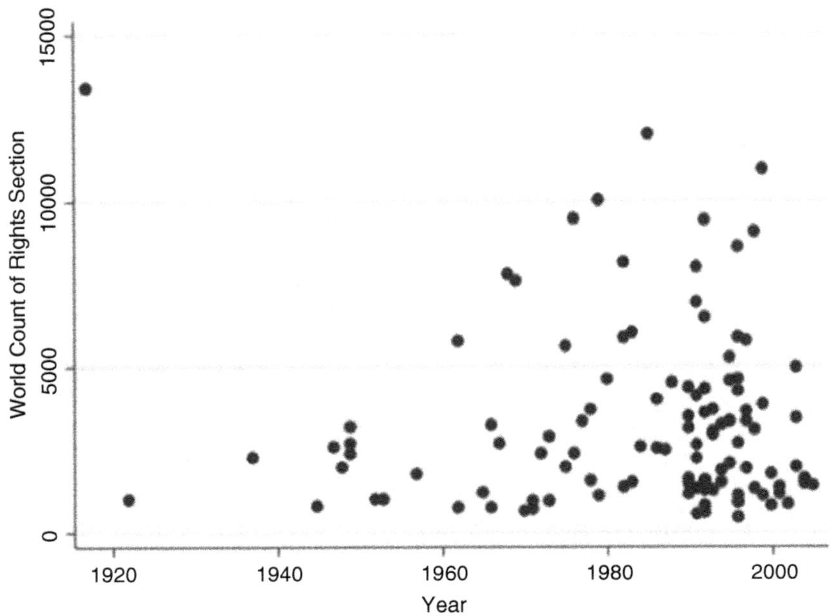

FIGURE 4.5: Rights Discourse and Year of Constitution

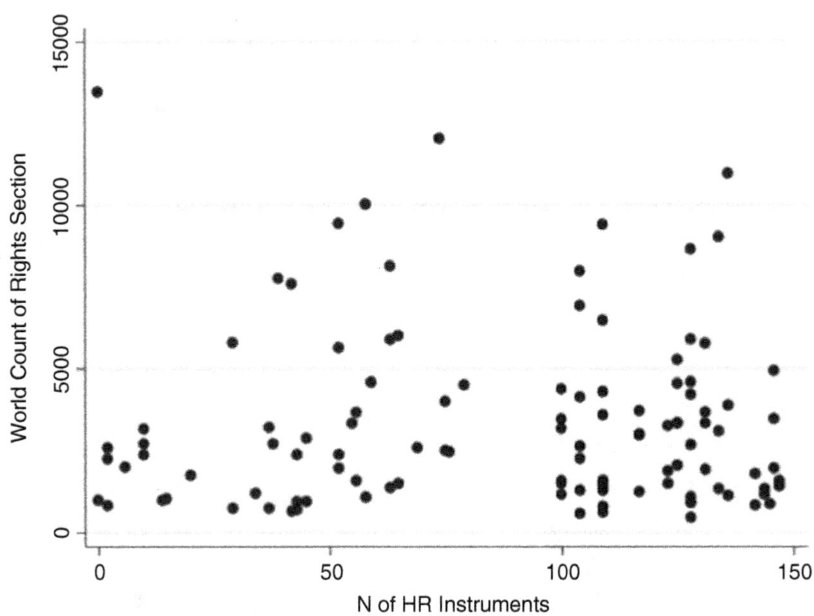

FIGURE 4.6: Rights Discourse and Human Rights Regime in Year Written

context and constitution's founding era held across all combinations of indicators.

For the current measure of human rights as articulated by the Universal Declaration of Human Rights, we find mostly similar effects. Model 2, Table 4.4 presents the results of ordinary least squares regression as the UDHR scale (which has a distribution approaching normality). Here, the inclusion of human rights language and legal provisions is again positively associated with the length of a constitution and the number of core human rights treaties signed. Also, similar to the earlier results, older regimes are less likely to incorporate UDHR rights. Most crucially, the number of human rights instruments globally at the time of writing is also positively and significantly associated with the inclusion of UDHR rights.

These results thus support our primary argument – that human rights in constitutions are driven by the transnational context. Further, that we replicate the findings of our previous study suggests quite strongly that both the old measure – number of mentions – and the present measure – UDHR provisions – of constitutional human rights are capturing an actual transnational dynamic of constitution-making.[4] The cross-validation also supports the use of the UDHR index for future work on human rights in constitutions.

There are two notable differences between the earlier study and the present results. First, for the UDHR scale, post-communism has a statistically significant and positive effect on the adoption of constitutional human rights. We do not find this surprising as our previous work suggested such a pattern, even if our multivariate analyses could not verify it. Second, the explanatory power of the UDHR index models is much greater than the discursive human rights measure employed in our previous paper. The amount of the variance explained in Model 1 is modest ($R^2 = .125$), while Model 2 explains a substantial portion of constitutional human rights language and law ($R^2 = .490$). These two differences suggest that the UDHR scale does a better job at capturing the interplay of human rights and the global environment than our previous measure. We thus conclude that the UDHR index is a robust measurement of human rights symbolism and legal authority in constitutions.

Finally, for comparison, Model 3 in Table 4.4 presents the results of multivariate analysis of the number of words in the rights section of constitutions. Here, we use zero-truncated negative binomial regression as there are no constitutions in 2005 without a rights section and there is notable positive skew in the dependent variable. The findings here are not dissimilar from our

[4] Unsurprisingly, the two measures are correlated ($\beta = .40$, $p < .001$).

previous secondary analyses of mentions of the word "right" in a constitution. In Model 3, unsurprisingly, the length of a constitution still matters, as does being a signatory of core human rights treaties and having a more democratic regime. Yet the cumulative number of instruments at time of adoption does not have a significant effect at all. Further, the variance explained by this model drops substantially (R^2 = .048).

In short, transnational dynamics do not mark rights in general as much as human rights specifically. Human rights are a distinctively global-transnational frame; one that is carried by global discourse, transnational institutions, and international actors, and embedded in national consciousness.

CONCLUSIONS

This study has two purposes: First, to present and test the validity of a measure of constitutional human rights discourse and law; and, second, to demonstrate how the inclusion of human rights in constitutions are driven by global-transnational as much as national characteristics and international linkages. We conclude, through comparison to our prior study, that the measure of constitutional human rights based on the Universal Declaration of Human Rights is robust and provides, in fact, a better way to examine human rights than discourse measures alone. Further, multivariate analyses confirm that constitutional law and language is affected by the transnational context at the time of its adoption. This contrasts to the articulation of civil and citizen rights more generally, where such world society influences are not found. In short, constitutions should be considered global-transnational documents as much as national ones.

This study thus extends a world society understanding of human rights. Rather than just a feature of international institutions and actors, world society scripts are present in domestic law and national symbolism. Constitutions are an institution of world society, much as previous work has found for ministries, educational systems, social movement activism, and other national features (e.g., Boli, Ramirez, & Meyer 1985; Inoue & Drori 2006; Meyer, Frank, et al. 1997; Schofer 2003; Schofer & Longhofer 2011; Suárez 2007; Tsutsui & Wotipka 2004). Our findings also suggest that legal scholarship that approaches constitutions as made in part by diffusion processes, legal archetypes, and international relationships is a fruitful area of inquiry (e.g., Elkins, Ginsburg, & Melton 2009; Elkins, Drori, & Meyer 2013; Goderis & Versteeg 2011; Law 2016; Law & Versteeg 2011).

The literature on transnational legal processes focuses on the recursive construction and diffusion of legal norms as well as the formation of transnational legal orders. Here, legal norms are institutionalized through transnational/global, national, and local normative settlement and alignment with a specific issue domain (Halliday & Shaffer 2015; Shaffer 2012). A transnational legal order view is particularly insightful as it theorizes the conditions and interrelationships (between various actors) that undergird the mechanisms of the emergence, persistence, strength, and demise of transnational legal norms which exogenously help shape even the most putatively "national" documents such as constitutions. Our findings here do not address the exact mechanisms by which the transnational legal order of human rights penetrates constitutional law. Rather, we document the conditions under which such penetration is more or less likely. Further conversation between global-transnational sociology and legal scholarship is likely to advance our understanding of both the transnational system and constitutions.

A logical extension of the work presented here is to consider whether international treaties, which have been found to have direct influences on national policy (Cole 2005; Cole & Ramirez 2013), may affect constitutional provisions themselves. The method of coding employed for the document that enshrined the modern discourse of human rights – the Universal Declaration of Human Rights – could be applied to the core human rights treaties recognized by the United Nations, or even all human rights instruments. As Elkins, Ginsburg, and Simmons (2013) find, signing the International Covenant on Civil and Political Rights leads to more constitutional human rights. This may also be the case for other human rights treaties. Second, as the analyses presented here are diagnostic and cross-sectional, there is room for further refinement and assessment of causal relationships. Future work can, and should, use an index of human rights provisions in a longitudinal fashion. Such work could confirm that constitutional human rights owe a debt to the culture of world society and its legitimation of the personhood of individuals.

REFERENCES

Anderson, Benedict Richard O'Gorman. 1991. *Imagined Communities: Reflections on the Origin and Spread of Nationalism*. London: Verso.

Arjomand, Saïd Amir. 1992. "Constitutions and the Struggle for Political Order: A Study in the Modernization of Political Traditions." *European Journal of Sociology/Archives Européennes de Sociologie* 33(1): 39–82.

Beck, Colin J., Gili S. Drori, and John W. Meyer. 2012. "World Influences on Human Rights Language in Constitutions: A Cross-National Study." *International Sociology* 27(4): 483–501.

Bendix, Reinhard. 1978. *Kings or People: Power and the Mandate to Rule.* Berkeley: University of California Press.

Boli, John. 1987. "Human Rights or State Expansion? Cross-National Definitions of Constitutional Rights, 1870–1970." Pp. 133–49 in *Institutional Structure: Constituting State, Society, and the Individual.* Thousand Oaks: Sage.

Boli, John, Francisco O. Ramirez, and John W. Meyer. 1985. "Explaining the Origins and Expansion of Mass Education." *Comparative Education Review* 29(2): 145–70.

Boli-Bennett, John and John W. Meyer. 1978. "The Ideology of Childhood and the State: Rules Distinguishing Children in National Constitutions, 1870–1970." *American Sociological Review* 43(6): 797–812.

Chabbott, Colette. 2003. *Constructing Education for Development: International Organizations and Education for All.* New York: Routledge.

Cole, Wade M. 2005. "Sovereignty Relinquished? Explaining Commitment to the International Human Rights Covenants, 1966–1999." *American Sociological Review* 70(3): 472–95.

Cole, Wade M. 2009. "Hard and Soft Commitments to Human Rights Treaties, 1966–2000." *Sociological Forum* 24(3): 563–88.

Cole, Wade M. 2012. "A Civil Religion for World Society: The Direct and Diffuse Effects of Human Rights Treaties, 1981–2007." *Sociological Forum* 27(4): 937–60.

Cole, Wade M. 2013. "Does Respect for Human Rights Vary Across 'Civilizations'? A Statistical Reexamination." *International Journal of Comparative Sociology* 20715213508767.

Cole, Wade M. and Francisco O. Ramirez. 2013. "Conditional Decoupling Assessing the Impact of National Human Rights Institutions, 1981 to 2004." *American Sociological Review* 3122413492762.

Elkins, Zachary, Tom Ginsburg, and James Melton. 2009. *The Endurance of National Constitutions.* Cambridge: Cambridge University Press.

Elkins, Zachary, Tom Ginsburg, and James Melton. 2014. "Characteristics of National Constitutions, Version 2.0." Retrieved (www.comparativeconstitutionsproject.org).

Elkins, Zachary, Tom Ginsburg, and Beth A. Simmons. 2013. "Getting to Rights: Treaty Ratification, Constitutional Convergence, and Human Rights Practice." *Harvard International Law Journal* 54(1): 61–95.

Elliott, Michael A. 2007. "Human Rights and the Triumph of the Individual in World Culture." *Cultural Sociology* 1(3): 343–63.

Elliott, Michael A. 2011. "The Institutional Expansion of Human Rights, 1863–2003: A Comprehensive Dataset of International Instruments." *Journal of Peace Research* 48(4): 537–46.

Elliott, Michael A. 2014. "The Institutionalization of Human Rights and Its Discontents: A World Cultural Perspective." *Cultural Sociology* 8(4): 407–25.

Frank, David John and John W. Meyer. 2002. "The Profusion of Individual Roles and Identities in the Postwar Period." *Sociological Theory* 20(1): 86–105.

Go, Julian. 2003. "A Globalizing Constitutionalism? Views from the Postcolony, 1945–2000." *International Sociology* 18(1): 71–95.

Goderis, Benedikt and Mila Versteeg. 2011. "The Transnational Origins of Constitutions: An Empirical Investigation." Pp. 4–5 in *Annual Conference on Empirical Legal Studies, Northwestern University, November*. Retrieved August 17, 2016 (www.law.uchicago.edu/files/files/Versteeg_April2011[2].pdf).

Hafner-Burton, Emilie. 2013. *Making Human Rights a Reality*. Princeton: Princeton University Press.

Hafner-Burton, Emilie M. and Kiyoteru Tsutsui. 2005. "Human Rights in a Globalizing World: The Paradox of Empty Promises." *American Journal of Sociology* 110(5): 1373–411.

Hafner-Burton, Emilie M., Kiyoteru Tsutsui, and John W. Meyer. 2008. "International Human Rights Law and the Politics of Legitimation." *International Sociology* 23(1): 115–41.

Halliday, Terence C. and Gregory Shaffer. 2015. *Transnational Legal Orders*. New York: Cambridge University Press.

Hathaway, Oona A. 2002. "Do Human Rights Treaties Make a Difference?" *The Yale Law Journal* 111(8): 1935–2042.

Hooper, Michael Kent. 1988. *The Relationship of College Education to Police Officer Job Performance*. Doctoral Dissertation, Claremont Graduate School.

Inoue, Keiko and Gili S. Drori. 2006. "The Global Institutionalization of Health as a Social Concern Organizational and Discursive Trends." *International Sociology* 21(2): 199–219.

Koo, Jeong-Woo and Francisco O. Ramirez. 2009. "National Incorporation of Global Human Rights: Worldwide Expansion of National Human Rights Institutions, 1966–2004." *Social Forces* 87(3): 1321–53.

Lauren, Paul Gordon. 2003. *The Evolution of International Human Rights: Visions Seen*. Philadelphia: University of Pennsylvania Press.

Law, David S. 2016. "Constitutional Archetypes." Texas Law Review. Retrieved August 17, 2016 (http://papers.ssrn.com/abstract=2732519).

Law, David S. and Mila Versteeg. 2011. "The Evolution and Ideology of Global Constitutionalism." *California Law Review* 99(5): 1163–257.

Marshall, Thomas H. 1964. *Class, Citizenship and Social Development*. Chicago: University of Chicago Press.

Meyer, John W. 2009. *World Society: The Writings of John W. Meyer: The Writings of John W. Meyer*, edited by G. Krücken and G. S. Drori. Oxford: Oxford University Press.

Meyer, John W. 2010. "World Society, Institutional Theories, and the Actor." *Annual Review of Sociology* 36: 1–20.

Meyer, John W., John Boli, George M. Thomas, and Francisco O. Ramirez. 1997. "World Society and the Nation-State." *American Journal of Sociology* 103(1): 44–81.

Meyer, John W., David John Frank, Ann Hironaka, Evan Schofer, and Nancy Brandon Tuma. 1997. "The Structuring of a World Environmental Regime, 1870–1990." *International Organization* 51(4): 623–51.

Meyer, John W. and Ronald L. Jepperson. 2000. "The 'Actors' of Modern Society: The Cultural Construction of Social Agency." *Sociological Theory* 18(1): 100.

Moyn, Samuel. 2010. *The Last Utopia: Human Rights in History*. Cambridge: Harvard University Press.

Nettl, J. P. 1968. "The State as a Conceptual Variable." *World Politics* 20(4): 559–92.

Resnik, Judith. 2008. "Law as Affiliation: 'Foreign' Law, Democratic Federalism, and the Sovereigntism of the Nation-State." *International Journal of Constitutional Law* 6(1): 33–66.

Risse, Mathias. 2009. "A Right to Work? A Right to Leisure? Labor Rights as Human Rights." *Law & Ethics of Human Rights* 3(1): 1–39.

Risse, Mathias and John W. Meyer. 2016. "Thinking about the World: Philosophy and Sociology." Retrieved (https://research.hks.harvard.edu/publications/getFile.aspx?Id=1255).

Ritter, Daniel. 2015. *The Iron Cage of Liberalism: International Politics and Unarmed Revolutions in the Middle East and North Africa*. Oxford: Oxford University Press.

Sandholtz, Wayne. 2015. "Domestic Law and Human Rights Treaty Commitments: The Convention against Torture." *Journal of Human Rights* 16: 25–43.

Schofer, Evan. 2003. "The Global Institutionalization of Geological Science, 1800 to 1990." *American Sociological Review* 68(5): 730–59.

Schofer, Evan and Wesley Longhofer. 2011. "The Structural Sources of Association." *American Journal of Sociology* 117(2): 539–85.

Shaffer, Gregory. 2012. "Transnational Legal Process and State Change." *Law & Social Inquiry* 37(2): 229–64.

Stacy, Helen. 2009. *Human Rights for the 21st Century: Sovereignty, Civil Society, Culture*. Stanford: Stanford University Press.

Suárez, David. 2007. "Education Professionals and the Construction of Human Rights Education." *Comparative Education Review* 51(1): 48–70.
Thornhill, Chris. 2008. "Towards a Historical Sociology of Constitutional Legitimacy." *Theory & Society* 37(2): 161–97.
Tsutsui, Kiyoteru and Christine Min Wotipka. 2004. "Global Civil Society and the International Human Rights Movement: Citizen Participation in Human Rights International Nongovernmental Organizations." *Social Forces* 83(2): 587–620.
Vreeland, James Raymond. 2008. "Political Institutions and Human Rights: Why Dictatorships Enter into the United Nations Convention Against Torture." *International Organization* 62(1): 65–101.
Wotipka, Christine Min and Kiyoteru Tsutsui. 2008. "Global Human Rights and State Sovereignty: State Ratification of International Human Rights Treaties, 1965–20011." *Sociological Forum* 23(4): 724–54.

5

Constitutional Dialects: The Language of Transnational Legal Orders

David S. Law*

What influences shape the drafting of constitutions, and to what extent? One way of tackling these questions is to analyze constitutions at the linguistic level. Just as literary language is rich with indications of influence, genre, and authorship, constitutional language contains telltale signs of the mix of influences at work. Conventional empirical research methods that rely on the manual coding of documents are poorly suited to studying subtle linguistic patterns. However, new methods from computational linguistics excel at identifying such patterns and enable us to measure how much of a text is associated with a particular topic, influence, or genre.

This chapter employs a technique known as topic modeling to analyze over two centuries worth of national constitutions, together with a selection of international human rights treaties, for telltale signs of various influences on constitutional drafting. The results suggest that certain hegemonic forces have left a profound impact on constitutional texts at the linguistic level. To be more specific, topic modeling identifies linguistic manifestations of four highly prevalent TLOs at the constitutional level: British colonialism, French colonialism, Spanish colonialism, and socialism. Each of these transnational legal orders is associated with a distinctive genre, or dialect, of constitutional language. Changes over time in the popularity of these constitutional dialects reflect the rise and fall of competing empires.**

* This chapter would not have been possible without the extensive cooperation and of Tom Ginsburg. I am grateful to all of the participants at the conference on Constitution-Making as Transnational Practice held at the UC Irvine School of Law, to my discussant, David John Frank, and to workshop participants at the University of Pennsylvania Law School for their constructive feedback.

** This chapter was made possible by a General Research Fund grant awarded by the Research Grants Council of Hong Kong (project number 17610717).

INTRODUCTION

What forces shape the content of constitutions, and to what extent? Ideology, colonialism, religion, geography, historical trends, local political circumstances, global political culture, and technical expertise: it is clear that the content of a constitution reflects the interaction of all of these forces and more (e.g., Klug 2000). The relative impact of these influences, however, can be difficult to gauge using traditional empirical techniques.

The standard way in which quantitative empirical scholars analyze large numbers of legal texts (including but not limited to constitutions) is to convert (or "code") the text into numerical data that can then be analyzed statistically. This process requires researchers to (1) devise a scheme for quantifying the content that they wish to analyze (a "coding scheme"), (2) scour the documents for the desired content, then (3) manually apply the coding scheme to the content that they find (the act of "coding") (Fischman & Law 2009, 156–66). This type of analysis has in recent years shed considerable light on a variety of questions about constitutions (Hirschl 2014: 267–81; Law 2010: 379) but, like any empirical method, has its limitations. In the process of coding language into numbers, the text itself is necessarily discarded – along with anything that falls outside the coding scheme. Consequently, traditional coding-based approaches are not well suited to studying phenomena that escape our awareness or cannot easily be coded by hand, such as subtle linguistic patterns.

These limitations can be problematic when it comes to the tasks of cataloguing and quantifying the impact of various influences on the content of constitutions. Constitutional language is not simply a transmission mechanism for legal rules and concepts of the type captured by manually coded data. It is also a medium of emphasis, tone, rhetoric, and style; it bears the semantic footprint of its author and the forces that have shaped its authorship. Just as an author's environment and literary diet shape her writing style, various influences on constitution-making manifest themselves in identifiable verbal patterns. Thus, a study of the influences on the content of constitutions would ideally take account of the actual language in its entirety. Systematic empirical analysis of constitutional language has long been stymied, however, by the fact it is difficult for human readers to discern subtle or complex linguistic patterns with accuracy and consistency across a large corpus of documents, such as the hundreds of constitutional texts that have been adopted over the last two centuries (Elkins, Ginsburg, & Melton 2009).

Recent innovations in the area of automated content analysis have made it possible to perform precisely this kind of analysis. These new methodologies, adopted from computational linguistics, excel at identifying and analyzing subtle, complex verbal patterns that are difficult, if not impossible, for human readers to capture reliably (Quinn et al. 2010). They enable us to decompose a text into its underlying linguistic patterns and measure, in quantitative terms, how much of the text is associated at the linguistic level with a particular topic, influence, or genre. Although automated content analysis has attracted interest for its obvious advantages of speed and consistency over manual techniques, its most profound advantage may be that it liberates us from reliance on potentially incomplete coding schemes. Instead of forcing us to analyze text through the filter of our preexisting conceptual categories, automated content analysis allows the text to speak for itself. When applied to constitutions, it can identify distinctive verbal patterns that are associated with familiar topics of discussion, such as federalism or parliamentarism. But it can also reveal subtle yet pervasive patterns that are indicative of competing genres or styles of constitution-writing.

This is precisely what automated analysis of the world's constitutions reveals. In this chapter, we employ a technique known as topic modeling to analyze over two centuries worth of national constitutions, together with a selection of international human rights treaties, for telltale signs of various influences on constitutional drafting. Our analysis indicates that certain transnational forces and influences – in particular, colonialism and socialism – have left a profound impact on constitutional texts at the linguistic level. Although it is widely recognized that processes of transnational legal ordering influence domestic constitution-making (e.g., Go 2003; McIntyre 2014; Son 2017), the extent to which they have shaped constitutions at the linguistic level over space and time is remarkable. These hegemonic projects infuse constitutional texts with distinctive linguistic patterns that are broad and deep enough to be characterized as competing constitutional genres or dialects. Each dialect is, in a literal sense, the constitutional language that can form the basis of a particular transnational legal order (TLO) (Halliday & Shaffer 2015).

To be more specific, automatic content analysis identifies highly prevalent linguistic manifestations of four TLOs at the constitutional level – namely, British colonialism, French colonialism, Spanish colonialism, and socialism. Each of these transnational legal orders is associated with a distinctive genre, or dialect, of constitutional language. Changes over time in the popularity of these constitutional dialects reflect the rise and fall of competing empires.

Part II of this chapter introduces the general notion of automated content analysis as well as the specific methodology of topic modeling. Part III applies this methodology to a large corpus of national constitutions and international human rights treaties. Estimation of a structural topic model suggests that constitutional texts can be broken down into a relatively small number of recurring verbal patterns, or "topics," consisting of words that tend to appear in conjunction with each other. Only some of the verbal patterns, however, correspond to substantive topics of constitutional design of the type that scholars are accustomed to studying. Instead, the most prevalent patterns are expressions of transnational hegemonic projects. The existence of these distinctive modes of expression reflects the fact that drafters think and write in ways that reflect the larger influences acting upon them, at both the conscious and unconscious levels.

Part IV describes how the prevalence of these dialects has changed over time. Unsurprisingly, their popularity rises and falls with the fortunes of the TLOs that spawn them. Part V explores the statistical relationship between the prevalence of each topic and the key variables of constitutional age and length, geographical region, and legal family. Consistent with expectations, the multivariate analysis suggests that the prevalence of each constitutional dialect over space and time tracks the influence of the corresponding constitutional TLO. The results support the view that the verbal content of national constitutions offers a quantifiable proxy for the relative influence of competing transnational forces and influences. Finally, the conclusion revisits the challenges raised by the analysis of translated texts and explains why our results cannot easily be dismissed as nothing more than artifacts of translation.

AUTOMATED CONTENT ANALYSIS AND TOPIC MODELING

Automated Content Analysis: What Is It, and Why Should We Use It?

The field of automated content analysis (ACA) is in its infancy but has the potential to revolutionize legal research and scholarship. Although legal scholars have yet to embrace ACA (Law 2016: 164) – especially as compared to scholars in other fields such as political science (e.g., Grimmer and Stewart 2013; Lucas et al. 2015; Roberts et al. 2014) – law as a field is especially ripe for applications of ACA (Dyevre 2015). Scholars, lawyers, and judges alike spend much of their time digesting and analyzing large volumes of text in the form of cases, constitutions, statutes, regulations, treaties, contracts, corporate filings, briefs, and so forth. ACA transforms these bread-and-butter tasks by enabling us to digest and analyze texts and documents at unprecedented speed and in novel ways.

There are two fundamental differences between ACA and conventional quantitative techniques for analyzing documents, both of which have far-reaching consequences. First, whereas conventional techniques require researchers to engage in a lengthy and potentially error-prone process of manually converting or "coding" text into numeric data that can then be analyzed using statistical techniques, ACA treats the text itself as the data (Grimmer & Stewart 2013). Exactly as its name suggests, automated content analysis automates the process of content analysis.

Second, whereas manually coded data relies on human understanding of what the text means, current ACA techniques rely on the identification and quantification of semantic patterns (such as the frequency with which certain words appear in conjunction with each other) that correspond to the concepts or topics of interest to the researcher. The computer does not understand the meaning or significance of the words that it encounters. It can tell you that the words "donald" and "trump" often appear in conjunction with each other, for example, or that these words are also positively correlated with the appearance of the words "republican," "putin," "russia," and "clinton," but it does not understand why these words appear together. It can, however, ascertain the probability with which certain words co-occur (such as "donald" and "trump" having a higher probability of co-occurrence than "donald" and "putin"), and it can identify clusters of words that co-occur so frequently that their presence likely signifies a distinctive topic of discussion.

Topic Modeling: Advantages and Drawbacks

The species of ACA known as topic modeling is usually billed as a technique for breaking down large bodies of text into their component topics. It relies on the fact that semantic patterns are a fairly good proxy for substantive topics (Quinn et al. 2010). Topic modeling conceptualizes (or models) a text corpus as consisting of a combination of "topics," where "topic" is a term of art that refers to a set of probabilities attached to a set of words. To give a simplified example, one topic might be defined by a 90 percent likelihood of "trump," together with an 85 percent likelihood of "donald" and a 60 percent likelihood of "russia," whereas another topic might be defined by an 80 percent likelihood of "trump," together with a 90 percent likelihood of "cards" and a 70 percent likelihood of "diamonds."

Topic modeling software breaks down a text corpus into its component topics by identifying patterns of word frequency and word co-occurrence. This approach means that the software need not (and indeed cannot) parse the meaning of the words that it encounters. Instead, it relies on the fact that one text frequently uses the words "donald," "trump," and "russia" in conjunction with each other, for example, whereas another text makes heavier use of a perhaps overlapping but nevertheless distinctive vocabulary, such as "trump," "cards," and "diamonds." On the basis of such differences in word usage, topic modeling attributes a different mix of topics to the first text than to the second. A key strength of topic modeling that flows from its reliance on patterns of word-occurrence is its ability to disambiguate words that appear in multiple topics (in this example, "trump") and assign them to the correct topics by taking into account the surrounding words (Law 2016, 204–6).

Topic modeling is known as an unsupervised, as opposed to supervised, method of ACA (Lucas et al. 2015). A supervised method is one in which the researcher furnishes the software with examples of the topics or patterns that he or she wishes to locate within a larger corpus of text (Lucas et al. 2015; Grimmer & Stewart 2013). The software then classifies or rates documents within the larger text corpus based on their similarity to the examples. With an unsupervised method such as topic modeling, by contrast, the researcher does not tell the software what patterns to seek. Instead, the software breaks down the text corpus into underlying, naturally occurring semantic patterns.

It is entirely possible that the "topics" identified by a topic model may not all correspond to "topics" in the layman's sense of the word. Topic modeling may identify "topics" that correspond not to substantive topics, but rather to other phenomena such as authorial style or emotional sentiment. There is therefore an element of surprise and discovery to unsupervised techniques such as topic modeling: because the researcher does not tell the software what to look for, the software may uncover unexpected yet meaningful verbal patterns. It is this element of serendipity that underlies the findings reported in this chapter.

The major drawbacks of topic modeling are, in many ways, the corollary of its strengths. First, the results are often difficult to interpret or, equivalently, open to multiple interpretations. Because unsupervised topic modeling is an inductive technique that identifies latent semantic patterns, not everything that emerges will be easy to interpret. Precisely because the researcher does not tell the software what patterns to seek, the researcher may not be able to recognize what the software finds.

Second, not everything that a topic model identifies is, is in fact, substantively meaningful or capable of interpretation. Because the computer cannot understand or interpret what it has found, the computer cannot distinguish topics that are meaningful from topics that are mere noise. But there is always some risk of mistaking verbal patterns for mere noise simply because we have failed to grasp their actual meaning or significance. The process is akin to panning for gold: one must search amidst the rocks and the dross for the occasional nuggets of useful material. What counts as useful or meaningful, however, depends on the interests and perceptiveness of the researcher. One scholar's garbage may be another scholar's gold. And we risk discarding diamonds simply because we were only on the lookout for gold.

Third, when a text corpus includes documents that have been translated from multiple languages, it is possible for translation-related idiosyncrasies to distort the results. If different translators prefer different terms for similar underlying ideas (e.g., "privacy" as opposed to "autonomy," or vice versa), multiple terms will appear in the text corpus in lieu of a single term. Fortunately, topic modeling is inherently robust against this type of translation error: as long as the various translations of the same term appear in similar contexts and are used interchangeably, they will tend to be lumped together into the same topic, precisely as they should be (Law 2016). Translation-induced distortion of topics is nevertheless a risk, however, especially to the extent that the vocabulary differences among topics are very subtle (which tends to happen as the number of topics increases) or certain translation quirks repeatedly co-occur, with the result that they resemble topics.

Although ACA is clearly no panacea for the challenges of quantitative empirical research on legal texts, it is likely to prove a useful and increasingly popular part of the methodological toolkit. For certain tasks and questions, it can greatly accelerate the research process. More importantly for present purposes, however, the unique characteristics of unsupervised ACA techniques such as topic modeling enable us to study patterns that might previously have been difficult to quantify or even eluded detection entirely. When applied to constitutions, for example, topic modeling unearths more than just substantive topics of a conventional variety. It also detects recurring linguistic patterns characteristic of various TLO models that even the drafters themselves may not necessarily have perceived.

A TOPIC MODEL OF CONSTITUTIONAL TEXTS

Data and Methodology

The raw material of our analysis is a corpus of 615 constitutional texts, drawn from a variety of sources and encompassing roughly two-thirds of all new or interim constitutions ever produced.[1] For purposes of facilitating comparison across documents that perform constitutional functions or serve as models for constitutional drafters, we also included a number of prominent international and regional human rights agreements – namely, the United Nations Declaration of Human Rights (UDHR), the International Covenant on

[1] Comparative Constitutions Project, Chronology of Constitutional Events, v. 1.2, April 2014.

Civil and Political Rights (ICCPR), the International Covenant on Economic, Social, and Cultural Rights (ICESCR), the European Convention on Human Rights (ECHR), the African Charter of Human and Peoples' Rights, the American Declaration of the Rights and Duties of Man, and the Charter of Civil Society for the Caribbean Community – bringing the total to 622 texts.

More than half of the texts are English translations of constitutions originally written in other languages. While roughly one-sixth of the total are official translations, a majority are taken from either Flanz and Blaustein's *Constitutions of the Countries of the World* or Hein Online's *World Constitutions Illustrated*. Although these translations are of relatively high quality thanks to the oversight and coordination exercised by the publishers and editors, they also introduce extraneous material (such as front matter, copyright references, and editorial and translation notes) that must be stripped from the documents prior to analysis. In the case of texts that have been digitized from poor-quality print documents, it is often also necessary to manually correct scanning errors (for example, if the scanning software mistakes "see" for "fee").

We use the STM package for R to estimate a structural topic model (Roberts et al. 2014). The package performs several additional steps to prepare the text corpus for analysis. One such step is stemming, which reduces words to their stems. In addition to simplifying the necessary computations, stemming sensibly ensures that conjugations of the same word, such as "vote" and "voting," or "right" and "rights," are not double-counted as unrelated concepts. The automated pre-processing eliminates extremely common and substantively uninteresting words such as articles and prepositions, as well as words that appear only once in the entire corpus and therefore cannot be analyzed in a meaningful way.

More controversially – but typical of the current generation of topic models – STM is insensitive to word order, meaning that the software draws no distinction between, for example, "man bites dog" and "dog bites man." The assumption that topics can be identified without paying attention to word order is known as the "bag of words" assumption. Although this assumption limits the granularity of the questions that can be explored at present using topic modeling, there are applications of topic modeling in which word order matters relatively little or not at all. Reassuringly, the assumption yields results similar to what human coders produce when faced with constitutional texts: most of the topics identified by the model correspond to recognizable concepts of the kind captured by expert coding schemes.

The main decision to be made when estimating a topic model is to settle upon the number of topics that the model should contain (or, in other words, the value of K, where K denotes the number of topics). In the context of a regression, certain combinations of variables will do a better job of explaining the variance in the dependent variable (or offer better goodness-of-fit) than other combinations of variables. Analogously, certain values of K will offer a better fit to the data (do a better job of explaining semantic variation within the text corpus) than other values. The STM package incorporates four diagnostic tests for evaluating the goodness-of-fit of competing models that substantially narrow down the range of plausible candidates (Law 2016).

Ultimately, however, there is no substitute for expert judgement as to what value of K yields topics that are substantively meaningful and lend themselves to interpretation. Because only the researcher can attach meaning to the topics identified, a model that defies interpretation by the researcher is not a useful model. The test of interpretability is all the more important where, as here, the quantitative diagnostics suggest more than one viable candidate.

In the present case, both a seven-topic model (K = 7) and a thirty-topic model (K = 30) score highly on at least one of the diagnostic tests and produce topics that lend themselves to substantive interpretation. Moreover, the results of the two models are generally consistent and highlight similar patterns. Neither model is clearly superior to the other for all intents and purposes. Just as different levels of magnification under a microscope will highlight different natural phenomena, different specifications of K will highlight different linguistic phenomena.[2] Because it divides the text into a larger number of topics, the thirty-topic model has the advantage of isolating less pervasive or more subtle patterns, but it also has a correspondingly greater tendency to produce topics that may not be genuinely distinct from each other. For the sake of brevity and simplicity, in this chapter focuses primarily on the seven-topic model except as indicated otherwise.

Results of the Topic Model

The output of a topic model poses an interpretive challenge. To illustrate the nature of this challenge, Table 5.1 reports the keyword output of the seven-topic model. For each topic, the middle column of each table identifies the

[2] For example, the greater granularity of the thirty-topic model makes possible the identification of distinctive variants or dialects of language relating to human rights that appear in national constitutions and transnational human rights treaties alike. The results of the thirty-topic model are reported and explored at greater length in Law (2018).

TABLE 5.1 *Keywords and Topic Labels (K = 7)*

Topic number and label (alternative label)	The 25 highest-probability words	The 25 words with the highest FREX scores
1: monarchy	shall, hous, council, member, state, section, king, repres, provinc, minist, govern, law, senat, provinci, act, case, one, elect, provis, paragraph, governor, bill, committe, provid, person	king, riksdag, regent, nepal, eireann, thailand, throne, canada, panchayat, quebec, royal, zanzibar, princ, thai, regenc, provinci, cameroon, kingdom, heir, oireachta, ontario, diplomaci, ife, seanad, mutandi
2: government branches (Central/ Eastern Europe)	articl, shall, law, republ, presid, nation, assembl, state, constitut, right, council, may, court, govern, minist, elect, member, public, deputi, citizen, within, power, case, author, one	azerbaijan, ukrain, seima, kenesh, jogorku, slovak, kyrgyz, turkey, poland, sejm, hluttaw, turkmenistan, mejli, lithuania, milli, khmer, jirga, croatia, congoles, serbia, kazakhstan, nakhichevan, loya, turkish, republ
3: federalism	feder, state, shall, articl, constitut, law, govern, may, union, provis, reserv, paragraph, court, project, compar, list, council, copyright, legisl, governor, part, nigeria, territori, offic, respect	feder, thenc, straight, thalweg, bundesrat, reichstag, laender, sabah, abuja, duma, sarawak, swiss, kadi, vienna, switzerland, landtag, palau, upstream, ruler, compar, saeima, uganda, confluenc, bavaria, burgomaster
4: parliament & judiciary	shall, constitut, court, parliament, presid, member, may, assembl, elect, offic, law, nation, provid, servic, govern, power, speaker, order, judg, day, provis, bill, justic, chief, year	speaker, pakistan, parliament, ghana, auditorgener, commenc, schedul, chief, cabinet, chairman, unless, nomin, zimbabw, immedi, write, deem, seychell, expenditur, court, seat, rhodesia, sit, affirm, assent, notwithstand
5: socialism	people, state, nation, right, organ, work, social, develop, public, establish, econom, administr, list, protect, must,	socialist, soviet, ssr, ussr, self-manag, china, monitor, hong, kong, moldavian, yuan, transpar, criteria, sociopolit,

(*continued*)

TABLE 5.1 (*continued*)

Topic number and label (alternative label)	The 25 highest-probability words	The 25 words with the highest FREX scores
	general, cultur, interest, committee, constitut, polit, will, system, activ, chapter	sector, ecuadoran, plurin, expand, mpr,[3] bosnia, mongol, structur, herzegovina, latvian, chinese
6: Latin America	shall, law, art, may, public, power, presid, nation, will, chamber, case, congress, execut, elect, year, republ, constitut, court, one, order, author, exercis, senat, establish, offic	dominican, spanish, salvador, nicaragua, nicaraguan, guatemalan, affin, consanguin, junta, spaniard, eepubl, panama, salvadorean, gratuit, colombia, peruvian, pure, colombian, honduran, delinqu, panamanian, directori, peso, jose, mexican
7: Commonwealth	person, offic, section, public, appoint, commiss, may, law, act, minist, subsect, provis, function, hous, author, purpos, case, appeal, member, reason, exercis, proceed, respect, right, prime	governor-general, subsection, guyana, fiji, lesotho, contravent, tobago, trinidad, advic, constru, belize, noth, commonwealth, sierra, reason, pursuanc, qualifi, appeal, offenc, commiss, jamaica, clerk, holder, bahama, kenya

twenty-five most frequent words (or the words that have the highest probability of appearing whenever the topic arises). A list of high-frequency words reveals much about a topic, but it does not reveal everything: a word such as "constitution," for example, appears so frequently across so many topics that it reveals relatively little about the character of any particular topic. It is therefore also essential to take into account the extent to which words are distinctive to a particular topic, which can be done by considering frequency-exclusivity ("FREX") scores (Airoldi & Bischof 2014). Whereas frequency refers to the frequency with which a word appears in a particular topic, exclusivity refers to the extent to which a word appears only in that topic and not in others. Words with high FREX scores are both relatively frequent within, and exclusive to, a

[3] The term "mpr" is an abbreviation for the Indonesian "Majelis Permusyawaratan Rakyat," or People's Consultative Assembly.

TABLE 5.2 *Topic Labels (K = 30)*

Topic number and label (alternative label)		
1: parliament	11: legislative rules	21: republic
2: legislative power	12: Latin America	22: provinces
3: municipalities	13: legal system	23: monarchy
4: civil service	14: socialism	24: generic rights
5: local government	15: judiciary	25: elections
6: officeholder	16: legislative chambers	26: foreign affairs
7: Commonwealth courts	17: public order	27: parliamentarism
8: governor-general (royal representative)	18: government powers	28: generic constitutional language
9: commissions and tribunals	19: territory	29: communism
10: social, economic, and cultural rights	20: federalism	30: Francophonie

particular topic. The twenty-five words with the highest FREX scores for each topic are reported in the right-hand column.

The verbal label attached to each topic in the left-hand column is not generated by the software but instead summarizes our understanding of the substantive nature or significance of the topic. In other words, whereas the *content* of each topic is an empirical finding driven purely by the methodology without any human intervention, the *label* affixed to the topic is a carefully considered, but contestable, product of judgement and interpretation.[4] In any model of this variety, some topics invariably prove harder to label than others: they may contain an abundance of relatively generic words, for example, or they may be difficult to distinguish in substantive terms from other topics. Fortunately, imprecise or controvertible labeling does not render the topics themselves illusory: the semantic patterns identified by the software are real, even if the labels attached to those patterns are subjective. Table 5.2 lists the labels that we devised for the topics generated by the thirty-topic model.[5]

[4] After forming an initial impression of each topic on the basis of the keywords reported in Tables 5.1 and 5.2, Tom Ginsburg and I examined a sample of actual constitutions containing a high proportion of the given topic to see the context in which the keywords were employed and to test our initial impressions of the topic's substantive significance. In this manner, each of us arrived independently at a tentative substantive interpretation of, and label for, each topic. Our tentative labels coincided between 30 percent and 50 percent of the time. Through discussion, we reconciled our interpretations and arrived at a mutually agreed label for each topic.

[5] Due to space constraints, the keyword output of the thirty-topic model is omitted from this chapter but can be found in Law (2018).

The Concept of Constitutional Dialects

Some, but not all, of the "topics" identified by the topic model resemble "topics" in the conventional sense. For the layman, the word "topic" carries with it strong connotations about what the methodology will discover when turned loose on a text corpus: it connotes a discussion of a substantive idea or concept. Reassuringly, both models yield numerous topics of this nature that are recognizable from the broader literature on constitutional design and diffusion, such as "federalism," "parliamentarism," and "monarchy."

Other "topics" identified by the topic model, however, do not resemble topics in the conventional sense. The technical explanation is simple enough. In the context of topic modeling, "topic" is a term of art that refers simply to a set of words that have a particular probability of appearing in conjunction with each other. Therefore, depending on what is being analyzed, some "topics" identified by the topic model may not be "topics" in the lay sense of the word. Instead, as in this case, they may be more reminiscent of genres or dialects, in the sense that they reflect distinctive ways of writing constitutions or linguistic palettes. The results of the topic model indicate that specific constitutions draw heavily on distinctive variants or subsets of the overall language of constitution-writing.

It would be a mistake to dismiss these semantic regularities we call dialects as lacking in substantive significance. Precisely because the semantically defined "topics" identified by the topic model do not correspond to the substantively defined "topics" ordinarily studied by scholars, the results of the topic model have the potential to reveal and highlight phenomena that conventional forms of empirical analysis can overlook. The resulting "topics" may not map neatly onto the parlance or concepts of the existing literature, but they are deeply revealing. They are indicative of a cognitive frame, a mindset, an intellectual and political legacy. In the words of the noted linguist Edward Sapir (1939: 232): "Language and our thought-grooves are inextricably interwoven, are, in a sense, one and the same." Likewise, the actual language found in a constitution reveals much about the framework in which its drafters operated.

A typical case of constitutional drafting situations involves a complex constellation of social, political, and historical forces that limit the choices that the drafters can plausibly make. Constitution-writers may consciously chafe against some of these limits and experience them as unwelcome constraints; other limits, however, may escape even the awareness of the drafters themselves. As expert users of specialized language, constitutional drafters are immersed within conceptual and intellectual frameworks that shape and constrain not only what they say, but also how they say it, in ways both conscious and unconscious. If we can identify the linguistic patterns that are the artifacts of these frameworks, we should in theory be able to identify the frameworks that generated them.

Automated analysis of the text corpus strongly suggests that at least some of these generative frameworks are TLO models.

Constitutional Language as the Language of Transnational Legal Orders

If the semantic structure of constitutions is any indication of the influences and concerns that drive constitution-writing, it would appear that constitution-writing is more a barometer of geopolitical hegemony and TLO influence than a technical, apolitical exercise in institutional design. On the whole, topics that are associated in some way with various transnational influences account for a larger proportion of the text corpus than topics associated with institutional design choices. The text corpus as a whole is dominated by semantic patterns that are, in essence, verbal markers of a hegemonic project, whether it be the Soviet Union's collection of satellite states or actual colonialism in the case of Britain, France, and Spain.

The results of the model suggest, for example, that more constitutional verbiage is spent on the verbal tics and tropes of British or French colonialism or Soviet domination than the finer points of foreign affairs or federalism. In the seven-topic model, all but two of the topics are proxies for some form of imperialism, such as British colonialism (the "Commonwealth" and "parliamentarism" topics), Spanish colonialism (the "Latin America" topic), and Soviet hegemony ("socialism"). The only two topics that lack any obvious facial connection to some hegemonic or imperialistic force are the "federalism" and generic "government" topics. The results of the thirty-topic model reinforce these conclusions: they include equivalents of all of the aforementioned topics, as well as additional markers of British[6] and Soviet[7] influence and a proxy for French colonialism.[8]

6 For this additional topic with strong overtones of British colonialism, the twenty-five highest probability words for this topic (in their stemmed form) are: shall, council, governor, hous, act, majesty, time, provinc, respect, order, law, may, member, new, general, said, senat, repres, canada, trinidad, tobago, provis, subject, provid, part. The twenty-five words with the highest FREX scores (again in stemmed form) are: turkey, quebec, canada, tobago, trinidad, turkish, papua, guinea, ontario, queen, equatorial, nova, hebrides, ireland, scotia, lieutenant, commonwealth, zealand, irish, greek, coast, brunswick, majesty, liberia, governor.

7 The twenty-five highest probability words for the additional topic associated with Soviet influence are (in stemmed form): state, republ, peopl, citizen, suprem, azerbaijan, deputi, right, council, soviet, organ, minist, elect, work, ssr, law, court, local, socialist, committe, activ, ussr, chairman, constitut, presidium. The twenty-five words with the highest FREX scores for this topic are: azerbaijan, soviet, ssr, ussr, presidium, seima, slovak, moldavian, turkmenistan, mejli, latvian, hural, romania, kazakhstan, nakhichevan, rumanian, fpri, mongol, lithuania, korea, milli, estonian, vietnam, dprk, china.

8 The telltale FREX words for this topic, to which we assigned the label "Francophonie," included the following: congolese, burundian, bureau, burundi, national, regulatory, domain, incompat, conseil, agenda, assur!, mandate!, magistratur!, text, togolese, round, congo, gabonese, armenian, transit, censure, modal, guarantcr, envoy, and unity.

In other words, the language of constitution-writing over the last two centuries has been, to a substantial degree and in a very literal sense, the language of a select handful of TLOs. This is neither surprising nor counter-intuitive. A constitution is a product of a particular moment in political time and world history. Constitution-writing is akin to a semantic seismograph: it registers the ideas and movements of a particular place and time. Because a constitution is a form of coagulated power, it bears the imprint of the powerful. And the transnational projects that have most extensively shaped the language used by constitution-writers have been powerful indeed.

The topic prevalence measures produced by the topic models offer a quantitative measure of the overall impact of various TLOs on constitutional semantics. Table 5.3 and Table 5.4 below report the average (mean and median) prevalence of each topic in each model, where prevalence is measured as the proportion of a constitution attributable to a particular topic and thus ranges from 0 to 1.0. The tables show that a hypothetical "average" constitution (average, in the sense of containing the mean proportion of each topic) would consist primarily of semantic content associated with a handful of hegemonic influences. According to the seven-topic model, for example, 58 percent of the semantic content of the "average" constitution is attributable to a hegemonic influence of some kind. Specifically, 18 percent is associated with British colonialism,[9] 27 percent is associated with Spanish colonialism,[10] and 13 percent is associated with socialism.

Similar patterns hold for the thirty-topic model. Increasing the number of topics in the model tends also to increase the number of topics associated with each TLO (or, put differently, the full impact of each TLO is more likely to be divided across multiple topics). While reasonable minds could disagree over exactly which topics ought to be associated with each TLO, a conservative estimate would be that the thirty-topic model associates at least 15 percent of the overall corpus with British colonialism,[11] at least 13 percent with Spanish colonialism,[12] 8 percent with French colonialism,[13] and 8 percent with socialism and communism.

9 This 18 percent figure, or 0.18 proportion, is the sum of the overall 0.10 mean prevalence of the "parliamentarism" topic and the overall 0.08 mean prevalence of the "Commonwealth" topic. See Table 5.3.

10 The 27 percent figure is simply the 0.27 mean prevalence of the "Latin America" topic. See Table 5.3.

11 This 15 percent figure is the sum of the mean prevalence of topics 1 ("parliament"), 6 ("officeholder"), 7 ("Commonwealth courts"), 8 ("governor-general"), 9 ("commissions and tribunals"), and 27 ("parliamentarism"). See Table 5.4.

12 The 13 percent figure is the sum of the mean prevalence of topics 12 ("Latin America"), 13 ("legal system"), and 26 ("foreign affairs"). See Table 5.4.

13 The 8 percent figure corresponds to the mean prevalence of the "Francophonie" topic. See Table 5.4.

TABLE 5.3 *Average Prevalence of All Topics in the K = 7 Model*

topic	1: monarchy	2: gov't branches	3: federalism	4: parliamentarism	5: socialism	6: Latin America	7: Commonwealth
mean	0.0823	0.2904	0.0428	0.1048	0.1306	0.2726	0.0766
median	0.0190	0.2033	0.0049	0.0353	0.0636	0.1232	0.0125

In reality, the average constitution does not contain an average amount of each topic. Instead, most constitutions tend to contain disproportionate amounts of certain topics. This is especially true for the topics that we characterize as constitutional dialects. Moreover, certain topics tend to be heavily correlated with each other. When we combine the highly skewed distribution of topic content with the fact that certain topics tend to be correlated with each other,[14] the resultant picture is one of clustering: constitutions do not consist of random mixtures of topics but instead tend to be dominated by clusters of related topics.[15] This clustering phenomenon is captured by the extent to which topics are correlated with each other. The more of a particular topic that appears in a document, the more that certain other topics will appear as well. These patterns of correlation are depicted in Figures 5.1 and 5.2.

Not only is there clustering of topics, but these clusters tend to exhibit a degree of internal coherence: most are associated with a TLO of an ideological or colonial variety. This tendency toward coherent clustering is most obvious in the case of the thirty-topic model simply because there are more topics and thus a greater number of possible correlations among topics. Toward the top left of Figure 5.2 can be found a particularly dense cluster of ten topics with heavily British and Commonwealth overtones. Several topics associated with Spanish colonialism are clustered toward the bottom right, while off to one side, the socialism and communism topics can be found in close proximity to one another. But coherent clusters are also evident in the seven-topic model. The correlation between the socialism and Central/Eastern Europe topics makes complete sense in light of the constitutions adopted in that region by the Soviet Union and its satellite states. Likewise, the monarchy, judiciary, and

[14] *See infra* Figure 5.1 and accompanying text.

[15] *See infra* Figure 5.1 and accompanying text (depicting graphically the clusters of correlated topics for both the seven-topic and thirty-topic models).

TABLE 5.4 *Average Prevalence of All Topics in the K = 30 Model*

topic	1: parliament	2: legis power	3: municipalities	4: civil service	5: local gov't	6: office-holder	7: Commonwealth courts	8: governor-general	9: comm'ns & tribunals	10: social, econ & cultural rights	11: legislative rules	12: Latin America	13: legal system	14: socialism	15: judiciary
mean	0.0097	0.04315	0.0253	0.0182	0.0102	0.0369	0.0194	0.0163	0.0358	0.0273	0.0560	0.0276	0.05392	0.03695	0.0544
median	0.0002	0.0015	0.0003	0.0009	5.53675E-05	0.0186	9.20065E-05	0.0001	0.0126	0.0112	0.0514	0.0014	0.0001	0.0013	0.0543

16: legis chambers	17: public order	18: gov't powers	19: territory	20: federalism	21: republic	22: provinces	23: monarchy	24: generic rights	25: elections	26: foreign affairs	27: parliamentarism	28: generic const language	29: communism	30: Francophonie
0.0178	0.0822	0.0436	0.0072	0.0119	0.0304	0.0109	0.0412	0.0343	0.0299	0.0517	0.0335	0.0149	0.0413	0.0773
3.7546 E-05	0.0675	0.0276	0.0001	0.0001	0.00666	0.0006	0.0004	0.0124	0.0124	0.0068	0.0024	0.0002	4.1837 E-05	0.0044

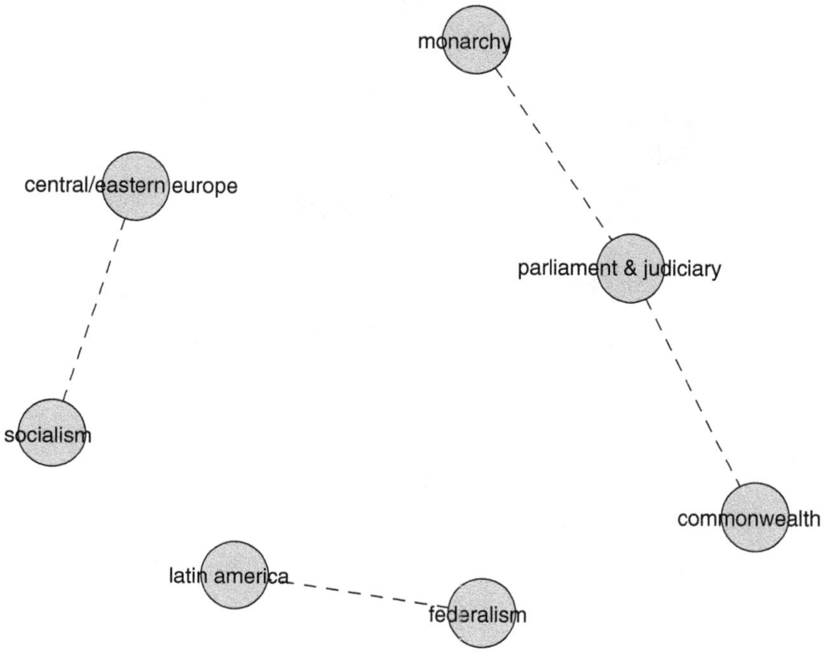

FIGURE 5.1: Topic Correlation Plot (K = 7)

Commonwealth topics form a coherent cluster: Commonwealth states are formally monarchies, while common law jurisdictions tend to accord a more substantial role to courts than civil law jurisdictions (Law 2016, 168).

These topic clusters correspond to constitutional dialects and are the semantic expression of two major hegemonic forces that have shaped the geopolitics of the last two centuries. The first is colonialism, which came in several varieties and peaked in semantic significance at different times depending on the colonial power at issue.[15] Different colonial dialects correspond to the influence of different colonial powers – namely, the British, the French, and the Spanish. The second is socialism, which reached its apogee in the 1970s thanks to a combination of Soviet influence and post-colonial constitution-writing but, even after the collapse of the Soviet Union, remains a significant semantic undercurrent due to the enduring if not growing popularity of social democracy and positive rights.[17]

16 *See infra* Figure 5.9–Figure 5.10 and accompanying text (tracing the average prevalence over time of the semantic topics associated with British and Spanish colonialism).

17 *See infra* Figure 5.8 and accompanying text (graphing the average prevalence over time of the "socialism" and "Central and Eastern Europe" topics).

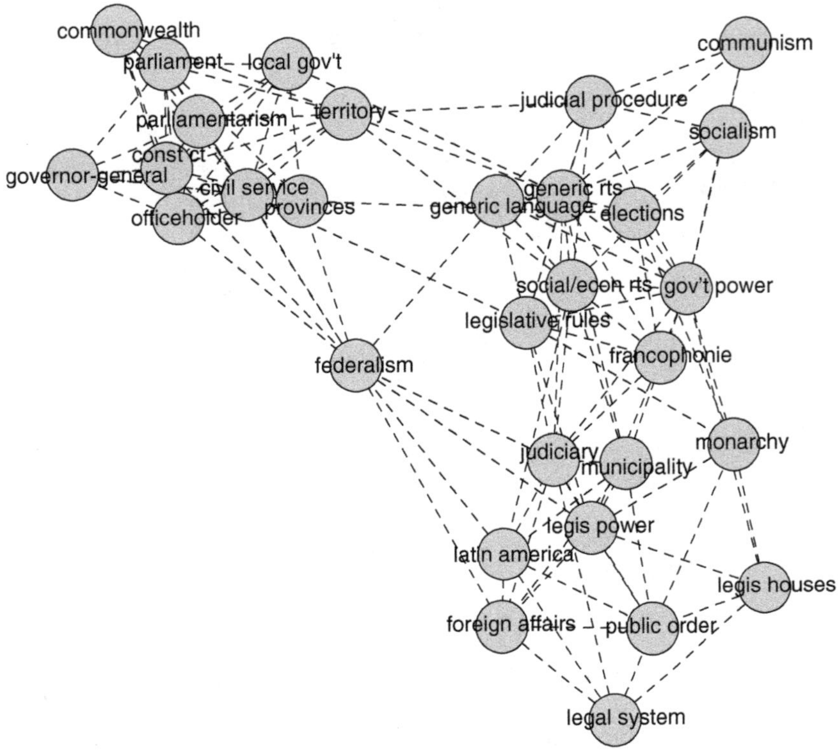

FIGURE 5.2: Topic Correlation Plot (K = 30)

The Colonial Dialects

First and foremost among the influences or constitutional dialects highlighted by both of the topic models is that of colonialism. It is no secret that Britain exerted a heavy influence on the drafting of not only the constitutions of its actual colonies, but also the constitutions of its former colonies upon attaining independence (MacIntyre 2014; Parkinson 2010; Ghai 1988). But it is not just the British who shaped constitutions in a distinctive colonial mold.

Consider the topic in the thirty-topic model named after "la Francophonie," the French counterpart to the Commonwealth. Members of *la Francophonie* are known for sharing certain elements of public law (Reyntjens 1986; Yan & Saura 2015). Our analysis suggests that they share a constitutional idiom as well. This topic made up an outsized proportion of the constitutions of former French colonies in Africa. Not only do all fifteen of the constitutions with the highest concentrations of this topic belong to former French colonies, but this topic by itself accounts for over half of their verbal

TABLE 5.5 *Constitutions Containing the Highest Proportion of "Francophonie" Topic (K = 30)*

Constitution	Year	Proportion of "francophonie" topic
Guinea	2010	0.5914
Niger	1989	0.5841
Senegal	2001	0.5633
Comoros	1996	0.5591
Central African Republic	1994	0.5505
Madagascar	2010	0.5334
Mali	1992	0.5308
Chad	1996	0.5201
Burkina Faso	1960	0.5150
Central African Republic	2004	0.5147
Niger	2010	0.5099
Guinea	1990	0.5069
Gabon	1975	0.5037
Mali	1968	0.5032
Congo	2001	0.5028

content. Moreover, high concentrations of this semantic topic appear in post-independence constitutions as well as colonial-era constitutions. From a linguistic perspective, many of these now-independent states possess constitutions that are semantically more "Francophonie" than the French constitution itself, which contains only the thirty-third highest proportion of this topic. In sum, the topic model suggests the existence of a Francophonie genre of constitution-drafting that is both pervasive and durable. Figure 5.3 depicts graphically the high-frequency words associated with this topic (with the size of each word reflecting its frequency relative to the other words in the cloud),[18] while Table 5.5 lists the constitutions that contain the highest proportions of the topic.

The semantic footprint of British colonialism on constitution-writing is even greater than that of French colonialism.[19] It is so profound that it can justifiably be said, from a linguistic perspective, to amount to a distinctive

18 The word cloud conveys the same information as the middle column of Table 5.1, but in graphical form.

19 This differential is consistent with what we know from colonial history. Many British colonies accepted constitutions in the course of negotiations over independence at Lancaster House in London. French decolonization, by contrast, was much more haphazard and hence less coordinated; many former French colonies adopted their own texts and amended them soon thereafter (Parkinson 2010).

FIGURE 5.3: High-Frequency Words Associated with "Francophonie" Topic (K = 30)

genre of constitution-writing. In the seven-topic model, the topics labeled "Commonwealth" and "parliament and judiciary" capture this genre. These topics are difficult to distinguish from each other for the simple reason that they are largely fungible manifestations of the same constitutional dialect: they are better understood not as substantive topics, but rather as boilerplate language characteristic of a particular genre of constitution. The size of their collective footprint, meanwhile, reflects deep and broad linguistic similarity across Commonwealth constitutions. Table 5.6 lists the constitutions that contain the highest proportion of these two topics: combined, they account for over 98 percent of the verbal content of a multitude of Commonwealth constitutions in Africa and the Caribbean. Figures 5.4 and 5.5 below depict the vocabulary most frequently associated with these topics.

A Commonwealth constitutional dialect or genre is evident in the thirty-topic model as well. By its very nature, a thirty-topic model divides the same corpus of text into more topics than a seven-topic model. The result is an increase in the number of topics associated with British colonization, all of

FIGURE 5.4: High-Frequency Words Associated with "Parliament and Judiciary" Topic (K = 7)

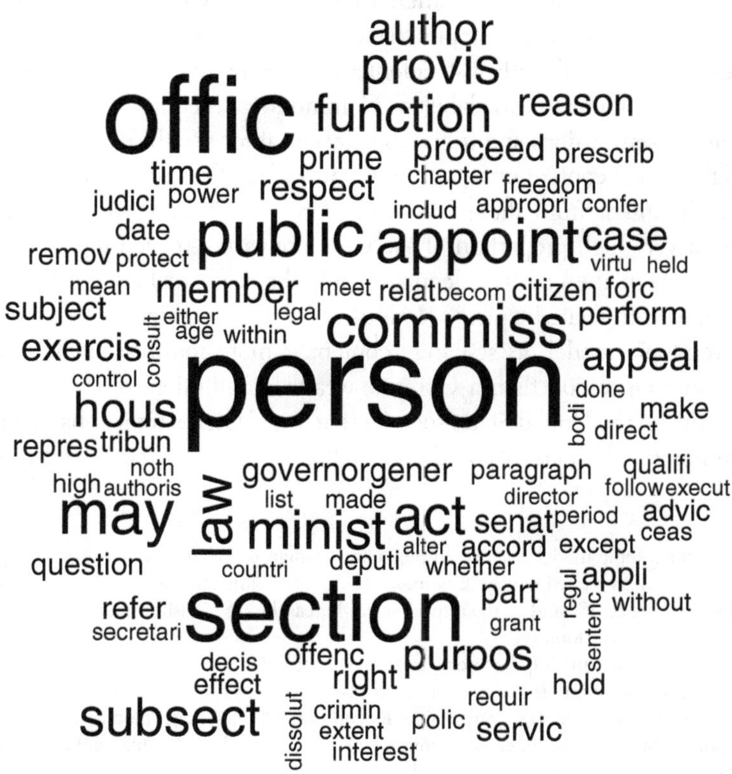

FIGURE 5.5: High-Frequency Words Associated with "Commonwealth" Topic (K = 7)

TABLE 5.6 *Constitutions Containing the Highest Proportion of Commonwealth-Related Topics (K = 7)*

Constitution	Year	Proportion of "Commonwealth" topic	Proportion of "parliament & judiciary" topic	TOTAL
Botswana	1966	0.4335	0.5626	0.9961
Tanzania	1961	0.3572	0.6369	0.9941
Malawi	1964	0.3426	0.6509	0.9932
Gambia	1970	0.4067	0.5846	0.9913
Mauritius	1968	0.3715	0.6185	0.9901
Dominica	1978	0.3436	0.6462	0.9899
Sierra Leone	1961	0.3063	0.6826	0.9889
Saint Lucia	1978	0.3095	0.6787	0.9883
Saint Vincent & Grenadines	1979	0.3031	0.6839	0.9870
Grenada	1974	0.3065	0.6740	0.9805

which are correlated with each other. Table 5.7 lists the constitutions with the highest concentrations of the topics that collectively define this genre. Each list is, once again, a parade of British colonies past and present. By themselves, just three of the six topics – those labeled "Commonwealth courts," "parliamentarism," and "commissions and tribunals" – account for two-thirds to three-quarters of the verbal content of numerous Commonwealth constitutions.

Notably absent from these lists is the US Constitution, which does not contain a very high proportion of the Commonwealth-related topics. Out of the 622 texts in the corpus, it contains only the 129th highest proportion of Commonwealth-related topics.[20] (Indeed, if we were to judge by the results of the seven-topic model, its semantic content is more reminiscent of a Latin American constitution than a Commonwealth constitution.[21]) The relatively low ranking of the United States suggests that this cluster of topics characterizes a Commonwealth model of constitutional drafting, as opposed to a model for all

20 In the thirty-topic model, the overall mean and median prevalence of the most widespread Commonwealth-related topics ("Commonwealth," "parliamentarism," and "commissions & tribunals") are 0.0887 and 0.0190 respectively, whereas the US Constitution contains a 0.0791 proportion of these topics.

21 In the seven-topic model, the mean and median prevalence of the Commonwealth topic across all constitutions are 0.077 and 0.0125 respectively, but this topic accounts for only a 0.0417 proportion of the US Constitution. By contrast, the US Constitution contains a 0.4488 proportion of the "Latin American" topic, which is significantly higher than either the overall mean of 0.2726 or the overall median of 0.1232 for this topic.

TABLE 5.7 *Constitutions Containing the Highest Proportion of Commonwealth-Related Topics* (K = 30)

Topic 1 ("parliament")	Year	Proportion	Topic 6 ("officeholder")	Year	Proportion	Topic 7 ("Commonwealth courts")	Year	Proportion
Zimbabwe	1965	0.1673	Tuvalu	1978	0.2037	Malawi	1964	0.2917
Zimbabwe	1969	0.1457	Tanzania	1961	0.2018	Lesotho	1966	0.2865
Nauru	1968	0.1410	Kiribati	1979	0.1987	Saint Vincent & Grenadines	1979	0.27509
Tuvalu	1986	0.1389	Zambia	1964	0.1980	Swaziland	1968	0.2674
Hungary	2011	0.1334	Mauritius	1968	0.1971	Mauritius	1968	0.2660
Papua New Guinea	1975	0.1237	Solomon Islands	1978	0.1967	Botswana	1966	0.2649
Bangladesh	1972	0.1073	Malawi	1964	0.1943	Grenada	1974	0.2647
Tanzania	1977	0.0970	Guyana	1966	0.1936	Lesotho	1993	0.2619
Vanuatu	1980	0.0908	Zambia	1973	0.1892	Tuvalu	1978	0.2619
Vanuatu	1979	0.0893	Fiji	1970	0.1889	Kiribati	1979	0.2612

Topic 8 ("governor-general")	Year	Proportion	Topic 9 ("commissions & tribunals")	Year	Proportion	Topic 27 ("parliamentarism")	Year	Proportion
Canada	1791	0.8926	Gambia	1970	0.1908	Saint Lucia	1978	0.3457
New Zealand	1852	0.8525	Zambia	1964	0.1896	Jamaica	1962	0.3426
Canada	1867	0.8394	Dominica	1978	0.1892	Fiji	1970	0.3394
Canada	2011	0.7792	Tanzania	1962	0.1886	Grenada	1974	0.3375
Australia	1901	0.4875	Pakistan	1973	0.1820	Tanzania	1961	0.3329
Ireland	1922	0.3542	Lesotho	1983	0.1819	Trinidad & Tobago	1962	0.3311
Sri Lanka	1946	0.3381	Botswana	1966	0.1814	Antigua & Barbuda	1981	0.3276
Sri Lanka	1931	0.3077	Zambia	1973	0.1811	Barbados	1966	0.3267
Ghana	1954	0.3032	Ghana	1966	0.1798	Saint Vincent & Grenadines	1979	0.3232
Cyprus	1960	0.2314	Sierra Leone	1978	0.1791	Fiji	1990	0.3226

TABLE 5.8 *Constitutions Containing the Highest Proportion of "Latin America" Topic (K = 7)*

Constitution	Year	Proportion
Peru	1822	0.9261
Peru	1856	0.9229
Peru	1823	0.9206
Peru	1826	0.9194
Peru	1828	0.9160
Bolivia	1826	0.9102
Honduras	1894	0.9099
El Salvador	1880	0.9088
El Salvador	1883	0.9081
El Salvador	1872	0.9076
Bolivia	1851	0.9013
El Salvador	1871	0.9011
Venezuela	1858	0.8990
Nicaragua	1858	0.8971
Bolivia	1831	0.8966

common law jurisdictions or the English-speaking world as a whole. The evidence points toward a Commonwealth model of constitutionalism writ large – one that is characterized by not only (1) innovative forms of "soft" or dialogic judicial review (Gardbaum 2013), and (2) rights protections of a primarily negative and liberal variety (Law & Versteeg 2011), but also (3) constitutional texts that are permeated at the linguistic level by distinctive semantic patterns.

Like British colonialism, Spanish colonialism has left a profound mark on the way in which constitutions are written. Former Spanish colonies in Latin America exhibit a linguistically distinctive model of constitution-writing. As its label suggests, the "Latin America" topic in the seven-topic model is found in very high concentrations in nineteenth-century constitutions throughout Latin America. As shown in Table 5.8, this topic alone counts for 90 percent or more of the linguistic content of various constitutions dating back to the 1800s and belonging to Peru, Bolivia, Honduras, El Salvador, Venezuela, and Nicaragua. Indeed, the fifty constitutions containing the highest proportion of this topic all belong to Latin American countries that won their independence from Spain.[22] This semantic similarity is unsurprising in light of the substantive similarity that Latin American constitutions exhibit with respect to such

22 Likewise, 88 of the 100 constitutions with the highest proportion of this topic are former Spanish colonies. The remainder all belong to former French or Portuguese colonies, such as

matters as the extent of executive power, the number of rights enumerated, and the overall level of detail (Law & Ginsburg 2018). Viewed together, these findings suggest that language is indicative of content (and vice versa), and that it is indeed plausible to treat linguistic patterns as a proxy for substantive content (as topic models tend to do).

The results of the thirty-topic model suggest that the constitutional dialect found in the former Spanish colonies has evolved in distinctive stages over time. Much as it does with the British colonial dialect, the thirty-topic model identifies a cluster of topics that are associated with Spanish colonization and correlated with each other. This cluster appears toward the bottom-right of Figure 5.2: Most of the topics in this cluster are significantly correlated with the Spanish legal family, the Latin American region, or both. Within this cluster, certain topics are virtually synonymous with Latin American constitutions, including not only the topic labeled "Latin America" (topic 12), but also those labeled "legal system" (topic 13) and "foreign affairs" (topic 26).[23]

Each of these topics is further associated with a particular historical period. As Table 5.9 shows, the constitutions with the highest proportion of topic 13 ("legal system") date back to the early nineteenth century. By contrast, those with the highest proportion of topic 26 ("foreign affairs") are from the late nineteenth century and early twentieth century, while those with the highest proportion of topic 12 ("Latin America") are predominantly twentieth-century constitutions. The change in the average prevalence of these three topics over time is illustrated in Figure 5.11. The most reasonable inference is that the substantive coverage of Latin American constitutions has shifted over time. The notion of different generations or eras of Latin American constitutions is wholly consistent with what we already know about constitutional drafting practices – namely, that there are secular as well as geographical trends in constitution-writing. The concerns and preoccupations of constitution-writers change over time: matters of urgency in the nineteenth century may seem obsolete or moot in the twentieth century, while the critical challenges of today may have been unimaginable in times past (Elkins, Ginsburg, & Melton 2009: 86).

Haiti (fifty-first) and Brazil (fifty-eighth), with the sole exception of Ethiopia's 1931 constitution.

23 Topic 17 ("public order") might also be included in this core group as well: four of the ten constitutions with the highest proportion of the "public order" topic, and fourteen of the top twenty, are Latin American (with various iterations of the French, Icelandic, and Haitian constitutions occupying the other six places).

TABLE 5.9 *Constitutions Containing the Highest Proportion of Spanish Colonial Topics (K = 30)*

Topic 13 ("legal system")	Year	Proportion	Topic 26 ("foreign affairs")	Year	Proportion	Topic 12 ("Latin America")	Year	Proportion
Peru	1823	0.5903	Colombia	1863	0.3144	Venezuela	1931	0.4312
Chile	1823	0.5630	Nicaragua	1911	0.2823	Venezuela	1929	0.4292
Peru	1826	0.5464	Colombia	1853	0.2811	Venezuela	1928	0.4046
Paraguay	1813	0.5319	Venezuela	1891	0.2784	Venezuela	1901	0.3474
Dominican Republic	1821	0.5317	Paraguay	1870	0.2766	Dominican Republic	1934	0.2782
Peru	1828	0.5210	Honduras	1894	0.2744	El Salvador	1824	0.2576
Bolivia	1826	0.5143	Honduras	1904	0.2737	Dominican Republic	2010	0.2507
Spain	1845	0.5061	Venezuela	1874	0.2718	Venezuela	1925	0.2465
Bolivia	1831	0.4956	Venezuela	1922	0.2678	Venezuela	1909	0.2454
Chile	1833	0.4946	Honduras	1880	0.2674	Venezuela	1914	0.2445
Peru	1822	0.4873	Argentina	1853	0.2670	Venezuela	1922	0.2429
Chile	1828	0.4767	Venezuela	1914	0.2660	Dominican Republic	1942	0.2381
Peru	1839	0.4757	Colombia	1858	0.2655	Venezuela	1891	0.2306
Mexico	1836	0.4678	Venezuela	1881	0.2613	Dominican Republic	1963	0.2135
France	1802	0.4663	Nicaragua	1905	0.2580	Panama	1940	0.2134

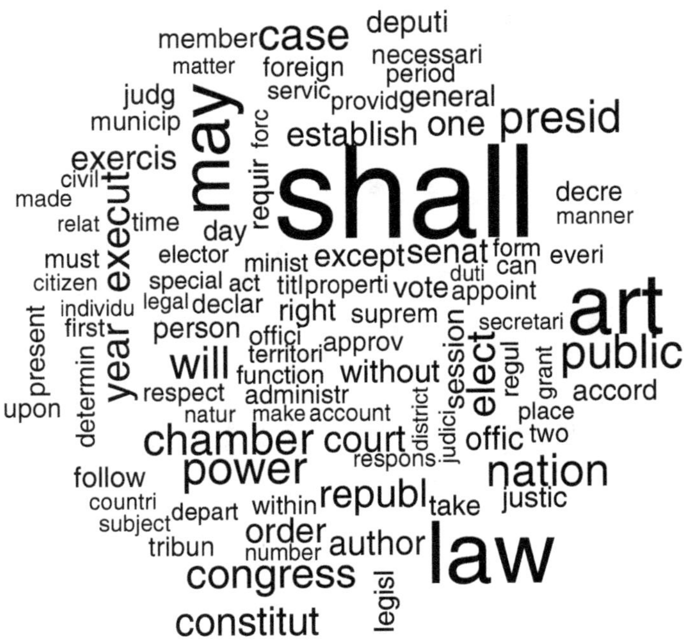

FIGURE 5.6: High-Frequency Words Associated with "Latin America" Topic (K = 7)

The Socialist Dialect

Scholars have long categorized socialist states as possessing their own legal tradition that is distinct from both the common law and civil law traditions (David & Brierly 1985; Glenn 2014). Our analysis suggests that part and parcel of this socialist legal tradition is a distinctive constitutional idiom or dialect. At the highest level of abstraction, this genre is characterized by a broad conception of state power and a close identification of the state with the people. At the intermediate level upon which constitutional scholarship tends to focus – trademarks of this genre include a lengthy preamble that offers an ideologically charged history of the state and an emphasis on social and economic rights as opposed to civil rights and political freedoms (Law 2016: 169–74; Law & Versteeg 2011: 1224–6).

The results of the topic model add to our understanding of this constitutional genre by highlighting its characteristics at the most granular level – namely, word choice. A distinctive vocabulary or constitutional dialect can be added to the list of the socialist genre's identifying features. Figure 5.7 highlights the keywords of this vocabulary, while Table 5.10 identifies the

FIGURE 5.7: High-Frequency Words Associated with "Socialism" Topic (K = 7)

constitutions with the highest proportions of the "socialism" topic in the seven-topic model. All belong to either Soviet-era or present-day socialist regimes. The thirty-topic model splits this dialect across two topics, which we name "socialism" and "communism"; the latter makes greater use of explicitly Soviet terminology, but the reality is that the two topics are difficult to distinguish and are best understood as manifestations of the same underlying idiom. Once again, the constitutions with the highest proportions of these topics belong to socialist states, as indicated in Table 5.11.

TABLE 5.10 *Constitutions Containing the Highest Proportion of "Socialism" Topic (K = 7)*

Constitution	Year	Proportion
Burkina Faso	1988	0.5790
Mozambique	1975	0.5568
Serbia	1974	0.5515
Cambodia	1976	0.5404
China	1949	0.4766
Angola	1975	0.4246
Guinea-Bissau	1973	0.3999
China	1975	0.3969
Cambodia	1981	0.3877
Guinea	1984	0.3817

TABLE 5.11 *Constitutions Containing the Highest Proportion of "Socialism" and "Communism" Topics (K = 30)*

Topic 14 ("socialism")	Year	Proportion	Topic 29 ("communism")	Year	Proportion
Burkina Faso	1988	0.5790	Latvia	1940	0.8221
Mozambique	1975	0.5568	Russia	1936	0.7680
Serbia	1974	0.5515	Moldova	1978	0.7453
Cambodia	1976	0.5404	Estonia	1978	0.7450
China	1949	0.4766	Russia	1977	0.7147
Angola	1975	0.4246	Mongolia	1940	0.6750
Guinea-Bissau	1973	0.3999	Mongolia	1960	0.6093
China	1975	0.3969	North Korea	1948	0.5851
Cambodia	1981	0.3877	Romania	1952	0.5686
Guinea	1984	0.3817	Latvia	1919	0.5237

THE RISE AND FALL OF CONSTITUTIONAL DIALECTS AND TRANSNATIONAL LEGAL ORDERS

The global popularity of these constitutional dialects changes over time in ways that reflect the power and influence of the underlying transnational legal orders. In the case of the socialist dialect, the prevalence of this species of constitutional language in new constitutions serves as a proxy for the rise and

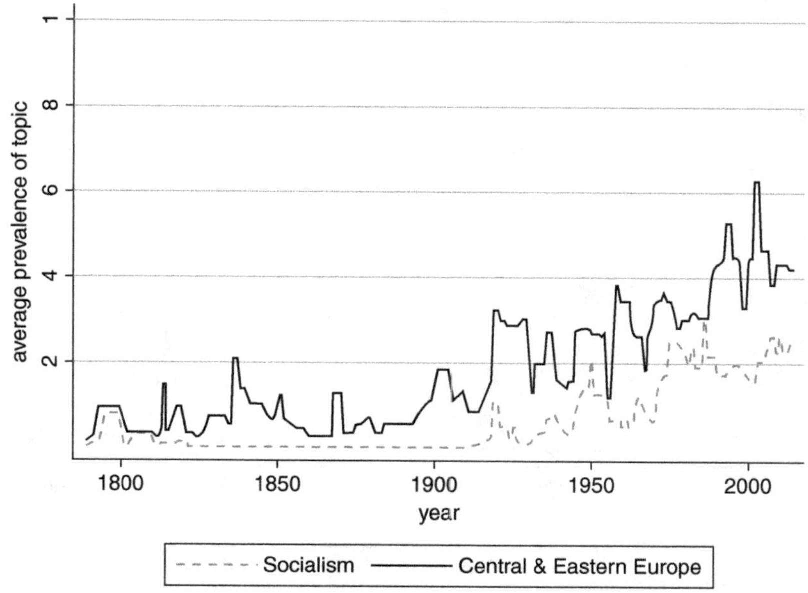

FIGURE 5.8: Average Prevalence in New Constitutions of "Socialism" and "Central and Eastern Europe" Topics (K = 7)

fall of the Soviet Union. As seen in Figure 5.8,[24] the two topics associated with the socialist dialect in the seven-topic model (namely, the socialism and Central and Eastern Europe topics) exhibit the same trends in popularity beginning with the Russian revolution of 1917 and the ensuing adoption of the first Soviet Constitution in 1919.

The fact that the socialist dialect declines in prevalence after the fall of the Berlin Wall in 1989 and the collapse of the Soviet Bloc is unsurprising. The decline is not steep, however, and the socialist topics thereafter experience a partial comeback. Possible explanations for this rebound include the rise of socialist discourse in other parts of the world (such as the Bolivarian constitutions in Latin America; see King 2013) and the strong tendency toward constitutional inertia, meaning that constitutions within the same country exhibit a high degree of continuity (Elkins, Ginsburg, & Melton 2009). Whatever the cause, the enduring prevalence of the socialist dialect, even in newly adopted

[24] Figure 5.8 through Figure 5.11 depict five-year rolling averages of topic prevalence in new constitutions. Thus, for example, the point in Figure 5.8 corresponding to the year 1930 is actually the average prevalence of the Central and Eastern Europe topic across all constitutions adopted from 1928 through 1932. A five-year rolling average was used because the number of new constitutions can vary considerably from one year to the next, and the small number adopted in a lean year may be highly unrepresentative.

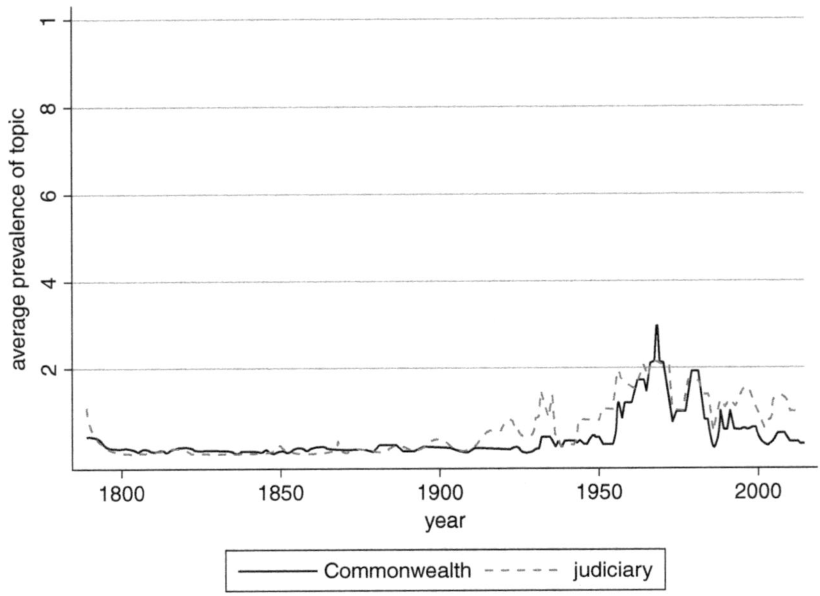

FIGURE 5.9: Average Prevalence in New Constitutions of "Commonwealth" and "Judiciary" Topics (K = 7)

constitutions, is consistent with previous empirical findings that statism remains a robust theme of constitutional preambles and bills of rights alike (Law 2016; Law & Versteeg 2011).

The rise of the colonial dialects, by contrast, corresponds to the unwinding and aftermath of colonialism rather than its peak. As Figure 5.9 shows, the Commonwealth constitutional dialect emerges from the post-war wave of constitution-making that marked the independence of Britain's former colonies and diminishes as that wave of constitution-making activity subsides. Part of this dialect is captured by the topic labeled "judiciary," which reflects the emphasis that Commonwealth constitutions have historically placed upon the role of the courts (Law 2016: 168). From the end of the twentieth century onward, the prevalence of the Commonwealth topic declines in tandem with the prominence of the Commonwealth in global affairs. The judiciary topic, however, remains more robust in popularity and begins to take on a life of its own independent of the Commonwealth genre that spawned it. The resilience of the judiciary topic is unsurprising in light of the tremendous growth in judicial power or "judicialization of politics" that occurred over the course of the late twentieth century (Law 2010: 384–7; Tate & Vallinder 2005).

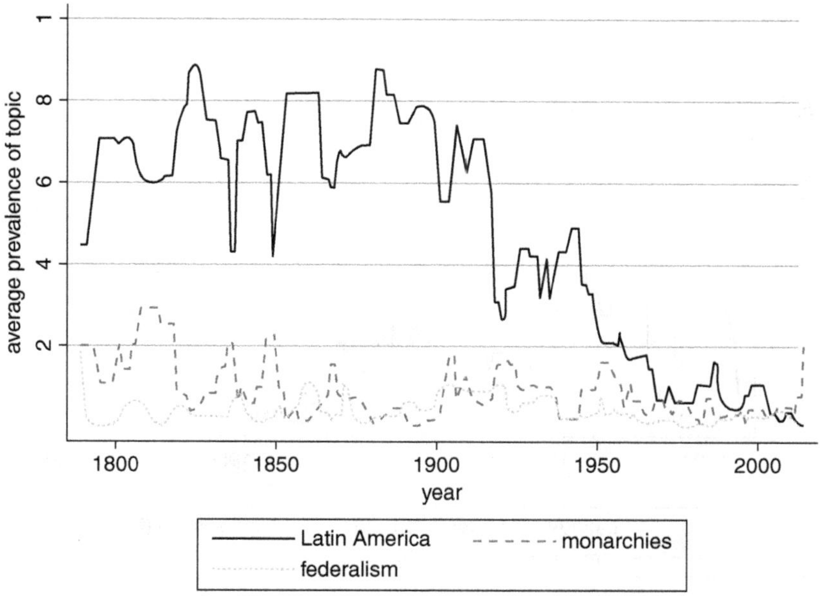

FIGURE 5.10: Average Prevalence in New Constitutions of "Latin America," "Federalism," and "Monarchy" Topics (K = 7)

A similar story can be told of the Spanish colonial dialect. For the most part, constitution-making in Spain's former colonies occurred not under the direction and tutelage of the colonial power, but instead after they gained their independence in the early 1800s. The trajectory over time of the Latin America topic in the seven-topic model matches this story. As Figure 5.10 shows, the average prevalence of this topic in new constitutions rises over the early nineteenth century, hits its peak around the quarter-century mark, and remains near peak levels for much of the remainder of the century. Thus, much like the Commonwealth dialect, the rise of the Spanish colonial dialect marks not the heyday of an empire, but rather its demise and its legacy.

The subsequent sharp decline in the prevalence of this topic over the twentieth century, also depicted in Figure 5.10, mirrors the declining relative importance of Latin America to the evolution of constitution-writing. Latin America was the home of the plurality of constitutions drafted in the nineteenth century, which reflects the region's pairing of relatively old nation-states with relatively unstable politics (Elkins, Ginsburg, & Melton 2009: 24–8). However, as new nation-states and new constitutions proliferated in other parts of the world over the course of the twentieth century (Elkins, Ginsburg, & Melton 2009: 41), Latin American constitutions came

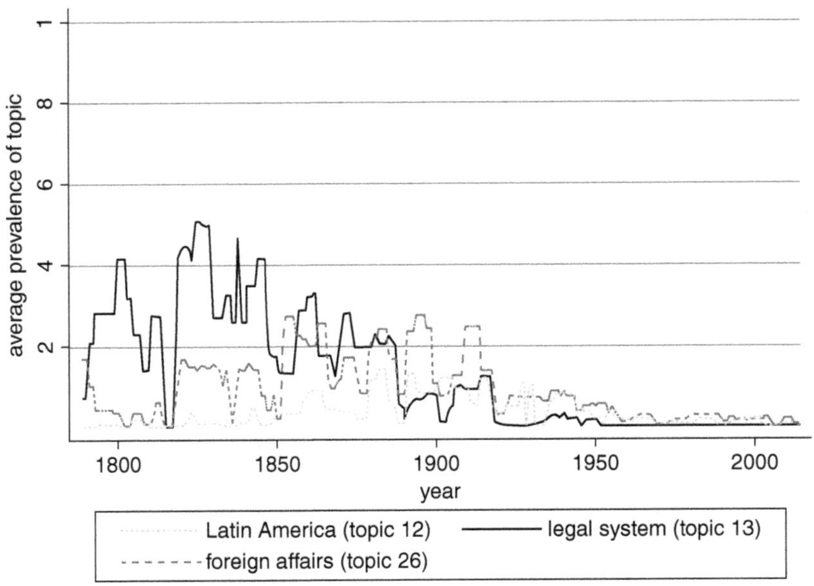

FIGURE 5.11: Average Prevalence in New Constitutions of "Latin America," "Legal System," and "Foreign Affairs" Topics (K = 30)

to account for a declining proportion of a rapidly expanding text corpus, while constitution-makers in other parts of the world faced a growing number of other examples on which they could draw instead.

At the same time as the Spanish colonial dialect declined in overall prevalence, it also changed in composition. The thirty-topic model enables us to disaggregate the Spanish colonial dialect into a larger number of narrower topics that exhibit different popularity trends over time. Doing so reveals evidence that the substantive preoccupations of Latin American constitution-writers evolved over time. Figure 5.11 depicts the average prevalence in new constitutions of the three topics most closely associated with the Spanish colonial dialect – namely, the "legal system," "foreign affairs," and "Latin America" topics – while Table 5.9 identifies the specific constitutions with the highest concentrations of each topic.

Over the second half of the nineteenth century, the "foreign affairs" topic supplants the "legal system" topic as the backbone of the Spanish colonial dialect. The prevalence of the "legal system" topic in newly adopted constitutions peaks in 1823 and is in clear decline by the mid-century mark. Conversely, the "foreign affairs" topic spikes at the mid-century mark, hits its peak in 1863, and continues to reach similar levels into the early 1900s. One possible explanation for this shift might be that post-colonial Latin America as a whole underwent developmental phases, and that constitution-writing practices throughout the region reflected and responded to the distinctive challenges and imperatives of each phase. It is plausible, for example, that in the immediate aftermath of independence, these new nations focused out of necessity on building their legal systems and other basic internal capacities but, after several decades of existence, found it advisable to pay greater attention to external relations.

The "foreign affairs" topic, in turn, peters out after World War I and is eventually overtaken by the generic "Latin America" topic, which begins to grow in the late 1800s and does not peak until 1929. Table 5.9 confirms this impression: the constitutions with the highest proportion of the "Latin America" topic are predominantly twentieth-century constitutions. Lacking any obvious substantive focus, this topic might best be understood as generic boilerplate language characteristic of constitution-writing in Latin America from the late nineteenth century onward. The post-World War II decline in the prevalence of the generic "Latin America" topic can be explained by the global surge in constitution-writing that that shifted the global mix of constitutional texts away from Latin America (Elkins, Ginsburg, & Melton 2009: 41).

PREDICTORS OF TOPIC PREVALENCE

Covariate analysis offers further evidence both that certain topics do in fact correspond to hegemonic influences, and that these influences have a statistically significant effect on constitutional semantics. A covariate is roughly analogous to a predictor variable in a regression analysis: it is a variable containing information about each document in the corpus. In the present case, for example, potential covariates include the age and length of each constitutional text. An advantage of the STM software over other currently available implementations of topic modeling is that it includes support for analyzing the effect of covariates. STM is capable of estimating the effect of each covariate on both *topic content* (namely, the presence or absence of specific words within each topic) and *topic prevalence* (namely, the proportion of each document that belongs to each topic). Moreover, much like a regression model, STM estimates the effect of each covariate controlling for the other covariates in the model.

Because the covariates are data about the documents – or, in other words, data about the data – the data on the covariates is a form of metadata. For all of the constitutional texts in the corpus, we collected metadata on four variables: the age of the constitution (measured in years), the length of the constitution (measured in words), the geographical region to which the constitution belongs,[25] and the legal family to which the state adopting the constitution belongs.[26] Both the seven-topic and thirty-topic models incorporated these four covariates as predictors of topic prevalence.[27]

As expected, each of the covariates is a statistically significant predictor of the prevalence of a variety of topics. For the seven-topic model, Appendix I identifies the covariates that are correlated with the prevalence of the topic in a statistically significant way and reports whether the correlation is positive or negative.[28] The results of the seven-topic model show, for example, that the monarchy and federalism topics are positively correlated with constitutional age (meaning that discussion of monarchy and federalism is more prevalent in older constitutions), whereas socialism is negatively correlated with constitutional age (which is unsurprising, given that socialism largely postdates the nineteenth century). Constitutional length is also a statistically significant

25 Constitutions were assigned to one of nine geographical categories: Central and Eastern Europe; East Asia; Latin America; the Middle East and North Africa; Oceania; South Asia; Sub-Saharan Africa; Western Europe, Canada, and the United States; and an "international" category for the seven international and regional human rights instruments included in the corpus. Central and Eastern Europe is not listed in Appendix I because it is the default or baseline category against which the effect of other categories is measured.

26 We defined a legal family as consisting of (1) countries that were ever colonized, together with (2) the state by which they were colonized. We also included separate legal families for (3) Islamic legal systems, and (4) international documents (namely, the seven international and regional human rights agreements that we included in the corpus). In those cases in which a country's legal system has been influenced by multiple foreign systems, we attempted to ascertain, by agreement between the authors, which foreign system was most influential. Any orphan country that was never colonized or occupied by another country, did not model its own legal system on that of another country, and did not fall in the Islamic category was coded as constituting its own legal family. The net result was a total of eighteen legal families or groupings: American; Belgian; British; Chinese; Danish; Dutch; French; German; Hungarian; Italian; Japanese; Portuguese; Russian; Scandinavian (other than Danish); Spanish; Turkish; Islamic; and international. The American legal family is not listed in Appendix I because it is the default or baseline category against which the effect of other categories is measured.

27 For data-related and computational reasons, STM can be used to estimate the effect of categorical variables, but not continuous variables, on topic content (meaning the specific words and probabilities thereof associated with each topic) as well as topic prevalence (meaning the proportion of each text associated with a particular topic). Two of our four covariates (age and length) are continuous rather than categorical. Accordingly, the analysis in this article does not dwell on the effect of the covariates on topic content. The approximate content of each topic is conveyed by the lists of high-frequency and FREX words in Table 5.1.

28 The thirty-topic model yielded consistent results that are not reported here for reasons of space but can be found in Law (2018).

predictor of certain topics: discussion of the federalism, parliamentarism, and Commonwealth topics is more prevalent in longer constitutions, whereas discussion of socialism is not.

These findings are largely consistent with prior research and expectations. For example, the correlation between length and the Commonwealth topic confirms previous empirical research to the effect that constitutional drafting in common law countries tends to be more verbose, while the relationship between length and the federalism topic seems consistent with the notion that federal constitutions require institutionally complex elaboration of governmental structures (Ginsburg 2010). The results of the covariate analysis tend also to confirm the validity of our topic labels. The constitutional prevalence of the parliamentarism and Commonwealth topics is positively correlated with membership in the British legal family, for instance, while the "Latin America" topic is positively correlated with both membership in the Spanish legal family and the Latin America geographical region.[29]

CONCLUSION

The verbal building blocks of a constitution are not just conceptual or functional in nature. They are also ideological, historical, political, and transnational. Constitutional drafting is at least as much a manifestation of ideological and political hegemony as it is a technical exercise in institutional design. The influence of transnational forces such as European colonialism and Soviet hegemony on constitution-writing manifests itself at the semantic level in ways that can be difficult for conventional empirical analysis to capture. Even in their current early iterations, automated content analysis techniques such as topic modeling offer a way of capturing the impact of such forces on the actual language used by constitutional drafters. And if there is anything that legal scholars ought to appreciate, it is surely the importance of wording and language.

[29] In the unreported thirty-topic model, the prevalence of the Francophonie topic is positively correlated with the Sub-Saharan Africa region (as it ought to be, given the abundance of former French colonies in Africa) and membership in the Belgian and French legal families. Also as expected, the communism topic is more prevalent in the constitutions of countries from the Central and Eastern European region, and from the Chinese and Russian legal families. The communism topic is also positively correlated with membership in the Japanese legal family. This correlation is attributable to the fact that North Korea is coded as belonging to this small family due to the period of Japanese occupation of the Korean peninsula. However, given the subsequent heavy influence of Soviet law, North Korea might be better classified as belonging to the Russian legal family.

The application of topic modeling to the study of constitutions is far from foolproof. For example, as noted previously, our conclusions are complicated by the possibility that some of the verbal patterns identified by the model may be partly or wholly attributable to translation-related quirks or idiosyncrasies. Certain topics – such as those associated with British, French, and Spanish colonialism – are also tied to specific languages. In such cases, it becomes difficult to tell whether the distinctive verbal patterns associated with a topic reflect drafting choices or translation choices. To the extent that the topics reflect translation choices rather than drafting idiom or substantive content, our quantitative estimates of the impact of TLOs on constitutional drafting will be imprecise.

Nevertheless, it seems unlikely that our overall finding of pervasive TLO influence on constitutional language reflects nothing more than the vagaries of translation. First, not all of the transnational legal orders highlighted by the topic models are associated with a specific language. Socialism is not language-specific, yet it emerged as a significant influence on constitution-writing over the course of the twentieth century. If decades of socialism have influenced constitutional language, it is hard to believe that centuries of European colonialism have not.

Second, many of the patterns of semantic similarity uncovered by the topic model do not track language of authorship and cannot easily be attributed to translation. For example, the US Constitution hardly resembles the constitutions of other former British colonies from a semantic perspective, even though they are written in the same language. Rather, according to the results of the seven-topic model, it more closely resembles the constitutions of Latin America,[30] which is entirely consistent with the region's history of heavy textual borrowing from the United States (e.g., Billias 2011; Rosenkrantz 2003). Indeed, the US Constitution contains a higher proportion of the Latin American dialect than the constitution of Spain itself,[31] which does not strongly resemble those of its former colonies notwithstanding their use of a common tongue.[32] Such results are obviously driven not by translation, but

30 See supra notes 20–21 and accompanying text.

31 Only a 0.3365 proportion of Spain's current constitution (adopted in 1978) consists of the "Latin America" topic, as compared to a 0.4488 proportion of the US Constitution.

32 In the seven-topic model, Spain's current constitution (adopted in 1978) contains only a 0.3365 proportion of the Latin American topic. Out of a total of 622 texts, it contains only the 215th highest proportion of this topic and trails numerous constitutions translated from other languages (including Albania, Iceland, and Cambodia, to name just a few non-Spanish examples). Likewise, in the thirty-topic model, the Spanish constitution contains a 0.0355 proportion of the Latin American topic and ranks 139th out of 622 (behind the constitutions of Afghanistan, Somalia, and Turkey, among many others).

rather by other factors such as geographical grouping and the degree of constitutional imposition on the part of the mother country.

It should come as no surprise that transnational legal orders shape the content of constitutions. What may come as a surprise, however, is the sheer magnitude of their impact, as measured by their linguistic footprint. In many cases, our model associates a majority of the constitution's verbal content with a particular topic. Topics this dominant are not mere topics in any conventional sense. They are tantamount, instead, to constitutional dialects or genres of constitution-writing. They double as the linguistic markers of competing transnational legal orders, and their prevalence captures the rise and fall of empires.

APPENDIX I

Covariates Correlated with Each Topic in the Seven-Topic Model

Reference category for the region covariate: Central and Eastern Europe[33]
Reference category for the legal family covariate: American legal family

topic	covariate	estimated effect of covariate	level of statistical significance	effect of covariate on topic prevalence
1: monarchy	region: East Asia	1.74E-01	$p < 0.01$	positive
	region: Middle East/N. Africa	8.18E-02	$p < 0.05$	positive
	region: South Asia	1.46E-01	$p < 0.05$	positive
	region: W. Europe/ US/Canada	9.65E-02	$p < 0.05$	positive
	age	9.16E-04	$p < 0.01$	positive

(*continued*)

[33] Because region and legal family are categorical variables, their effect can only be assessed relative to a baseline or reference category. In the case of legal family, the reference category is the American legal family (meaning the United States and other countries whose legal systems were most heavily influenced by the United States), while the reference category in the case of region is Central and Eastern Europe. Thus, for example, for topic 29 ("communism"), all of the listed regions are negatively correlated with this topic, while Central and Eastern Europe is not listed. The way to interpret these findings is that, compared to the reference category (Central and Eastern Europe), all of the other regions were characterized by lower levels of the "communism" topic.

(*continued*)

topic	covariate	estimated effect of covariate	level of statistical significance	effect of covariate on topic prevalence
	legal family: Chinese	−1.76E-01	$p < 0.05$	negative
	legal family: Islamic	1.55E-01	$p < 0.05$	positive
	legal family: Japanese	−1.83E-01	$p < 0.05$	negative
2: government branches	region: East Asia	−2.77E-01	$p < 0.01$	negative
	region: Latin America	−2.94E-01	$p < 0.01$	negative
	region: Oceania	−2.11E-01	$p < 0.01$	negative
	region: South Asia	−1.95E-01	$p < 0.01$	negative
	region: Sub-Saharan Africa	−7.71E-02	$p < 0.10$	negative
	region: W. Europe/ US/Canada	−1.68E-01	$p < 0.01$	negative
	age	V1.98E-03	$p < 0.01$	negative
	length	−5.27E-06	$p < 0.01$	negative
	legal family: Belgian	1.36E-01	$p < 0.10$	positive
	legal family: Danish	−1.74E-01	$p < 0.10$	negative
	legal family: French	1.38E-01	$p < 0.05$	positive
	legal family: British	−1.39E-01	$p < 0.05$	negative
	legal family: Dutch	1.92E-01	$p < 0.05$	positive
3: federalism	region: East Asia	9.74E-02	$p < 0.01$	positive
	region: Latin America	9.00E-02	$p < 0.01$	positive
	region: South Asia	7.47E-02	$p < 0.10$	positive
	region: Sub-Saharan Africa	7.21E-02	$p < 0.05$	positive
	region: W. Europe/ US/Canada	9.55E-02	$p < 0.01$	positive
	age	2.35E-04	$p < 0.10$	positive
	length	1.36E-06	$p < 0.10$	positive
	legal family: Belgian	−1.21E-01	$p < 0.05$	negative
	legal family: Chinese	−1.42E-01	$p < 0.05$	negative

(*continued*)

(*continued*)

topic	covariate	estimated effect of covariate	level of statistical significance	effect of covariate on topic prevalence
	legal family: Danish	−1.21E-01	$p < 0.10$	negative
	legal family: Spanish	−8.63E-02	$p < 0.10$	negative
	legal family: French	−1.09E-01	$p < 0.05$	negative
	legal family: British	−9.78E-02	$p < 0.05$	negative
	legal family: international	−1.27E-01	$p < 0.10$	negative
	legal family: Dutch	−1.52E-01	$p < 0.05$	negative
	legal family: Scandinavian	−1.59E-01	$p < 0.05$	negative
4: parliamentarism	region: East Asia	8.66E-02	$p < 0.01$	positive
	region: Oceania	1.46E-01	$p < 0.01$	positive
	region: South Asia	1.93E-01	$p < 0.01$	positive
	region: Sub-Saharan Africa	9.49E-02	$p < 0.01$	positive
	length	2.43E-06	$p < 0.01$	positive
	legal family: Belgian	−1.35E-01	$p < 0.01$	negative
	legal family: Chinese	−9.67E-02	$p < 0.10$	negative
	legal family: Spanish	−9.78E-02	$p < 0.05$	negative
	legal family: French	−8.78E-02	$p < 0.05$	negative
	legal family: British	1.06E-01	$p < 0.05$	positive
	legal family: Italian	−1.03E-01	$p < 0.05$	negative
	legal family: Portuguese	−1.33E-01	$p < 0.01$	negative
5: socialism	region: Latin America	−1.59E-01	$p < 0.01$	negative
	region: Middle East/N. Africa	−1.20E-01	$p < 0.01$	negative
	region: Oceania	−1.77E-01	$p < 0.01$	negative
	region: South Asia	−1.43E-01	$p < 0.05$	negative
	region: Sub-Saharan Africa	−1.51E-01	$p < 0.01$	negative
	region: W. Europe/US/Canada	−1.15E-01	$p < 0.01$	negative

(*continued*)

(*continued*)

topic	covariate	estimated effect of covariate	level of statistical significance	effect of covariate on topic prevalence
	age	−1.36E-03	$p < 0.01$	negative
	legal family: Chinese	3.39E-01	$p < 0.01$	positive
	legal family: Spanish	1.22E-01	$p < 0.05$	positive
	legal family: international	3.06E-01	$p < 0.01$	positive
	legal family: Japanese	2.05E-01	$p < 0.05$	positive
	legal family: Dutch	1.46E-01	$p < 0.10$	positive
	legal family: Portuguese	2.33E-01	$p < 0.01$	positive
6: Latin America	region: Latin America	2.53E-01	$p < 0.01$	positive
	age	2.07E-03	$p < 0.01$	positive
	length	− 1.34E-06	$p < 0.05$	negative
	legal family: Belgian	1.10E-01	$p < 0.10$	positive
	legal family: Spanish	1.88E-01	$p < 0.01$	positive
	legal family: international	−1.58E-01	$p < 0.10$	negative
	legal family: Italian	2.06E-01	$p < 0.05$	positive
7: Commonwealth	region: Latin America	9.70E-02	$p < 0.01$	positive
	region: Middle East/N. Africa	−4.59E-02	$p < 0.10$	negative
	region: Oceania	1.50E-01	$p < 0.01$	positive
	region: South Asia	−8.91E-02	$p < 0.05$	negative
	region: Sub-Saharan Africa	5.74E-02	$p < 0.05$	positive
	length	3.39E-06	$p < 0.01$	positive
	legal family: Spanish	−9.57E-02	$p < 0.05$	negative
	legal family: British	1.86E-01	$p < 0.01$	positive
	legal family: Portuguese	−8.09E-02	$p < 0.05$	negative

REFERENCES

Airoldi, Edoardo M. and Jonathan M. Bischof. 2014. *A Poisson Convolution Model for Characterizing Topical Content with Word Frequency and Exclusivity*, arXiv:1206. 4631 [CS]. Available at https://arxiv.org/pdf/1206.46 31.pdf.

Beck, Colin et al. 2012. World Influences on Human Rights Language in Constitutions: A Cross-National Study. *International Sociology* 27: 483–501.

Billias, George Athan. 2011. *American Constitutionalism Heard Round the World, 1776–1989: A Global Perspective*. New York: NYU Press.

Böckenforde, Markus and Daniel Sabsay. 2012. "Supranational Organizations and Their Impact on National Constitutions." Pp. 469–83 in *Routledge Handbook of Constitutional Law*, edited by Mark Tushnet et al. New York: Routledge.

David, René and John E.C. Brierley. 1985. *Major Legal Systems in the World Today: An Introduction to the Comparative Study of Law*. London: Stevens & Sons.

Dyevre, Arthur. 2015. *The Promise and Pitfalls of Automated Text-Scaling Techniques for the Analysis of Judicial Opinions* (April 10, 2015). Available at https://ssrn.com/abstract=2626370 or http://dx.doi.org/10.2139/ssrn.2626370.

Elkins, Zachary, Tom Ginsburg and James Melton. 2009. *The Endurance of National Constitutions*. New York: Cambridge University Press.

Fischman, Joshua B. and David S. Law. 2009. What Is Judicial Ideology, and How Should We Measure It? *Washington University Journal of Law and Policy* 29: 133–214.

Gardbaum, Stephen. 2013. *The New Commonwealth Model of Constitutionalism: Theory and Practice*. New York: Cambridge University Press.

Ghai, Yash. 1988. "Constitution Making and Decolonisation." Pp. 1–46 in *Law, Politics and Government in the Pacific Island States*, edited by Yash Ghai. Suva: University of the South Pacific, Institute of Pacific Studies.

Ginsburg, Tom. 2010. "Constitutional Specificity, Unwritten Understandings and Constitutional Agreement." Pp. 69–94 in *Constitutional Topography: Values and Constitutions*, edited by Andras Sajo and Renata Utz. The Hague: Eleven Publishing.

Glendon, Mary Ann. 1991. *Rights Talk: The Impoverishment of Political Discourse*. Cambridge: Harvard University Press.

Glenn, H. Patrick. 2014. *Legal Traditions of the World: Sustainable Diversity in Law*, 5th edition. Oxford: Oxford University Press.

Go, Julian. 2003. "A Globalizing Constituionalism? Views from the Postcolony 1945–2000." *International Sociology* 18: 71–95.

Grimmer, Justin and Brandon M. Stewart. 2013. "Text as Data: The Promise and Pitfalls of Automatic Content Analysis Methods for Political Texts." *Political Analysis* 21: 267–97.

Halliday, Terence C. and Gregory Shaffer, eds. 2015. *Transnational Legal Orders*. Cambridge: Cambridge University Press.

Harding, Andrew. 2013. *The Constitution of Malaysia: A Contextual Analysis*. Oxford: Hart Publishing.

Hirschl, Ran. 2004. *Towards Juristocracy*. Cambridge: Harvard University Press.

Hirschl, Ran. 2013. "From Comparative Constitutional Law to Comparative Constitutional Studies." *International Journal of Constitutional Law* 13: 1–xx.

Hirschl, Ran. 2014. *Comparative Matters: The Renaissance of Comparative Constitutional Law*. Oxford: Oxford University Press.

King, Gary, Robert Keohane, and Sidney Verba. 1995. *Designing Social Inquiry*. Princeton: Princeton University Press.

King, Phoebe. 2013. "Neo-Bolivarian Constitutional Design." In *The Social and Political Foundations of Constitutionalism*, edited by Denis Galligan and Mila Versteeg. New York: Cambridge University Press.

Klug, Heinz. 2000. *Constituting Democracy: Law, Globalism and South Africa's Political Reconstruction*. Cambridge: Cambridge University Press.

Law, David S. 2010. "Constitutions." Pp. 376–98 in *Oxford Handbook of Empirical Legal Research*, edited by Peter Cane and Herbert M. Kritzer. Oxford: Oxford University Press.

Law, David S. 2016. "Constitutional Archetypes." *Texas Law Review* 95: 153–243.

Law, David S. 2018. "The Global Language of Human Rights: A Computational Linguistic Analysis." *Law & Ethics of Human Rights* 12(1): 111–50.

Law, David S. and Tom Ginsburg. 2018. "Constitutional Drafting in Latin America: A Quantitative Perspective." In *Constitutionalism in the Americas*, edited by Daniel Bonilla Maldonado and Colin Crawford. Cheltenham: Edward Elgar Publishing.

Law, David S. & Mila Versteeg. 2011. "The Evolution and Ideology of Global Constitutionalism." *California Law Review* 99: 1163–257.

Lucas, Christopher, Richard A. Nielsen, Margaret E. Roberts, and Brandon M. Stewart. 2015. "Computer-Assisted Text Analysis for Comparative Politics." *Political Analysis* 23: 254

Mazzone, Jason. 2005. "The Creation of a Constitutional Culture." *Tulsa Law Review* 40: 671–98.

McIntyre, David W. 2014. *Winding Up the British Empire in the Pacific Islands*. New York: Oxford University Press.

Moyn, Samuel. 2010. *The Last Utopia: Human Rights in History*. Cambridge: Harvard University Press.

Parkinson, Charles O. H. 2010. *Bills of Rights and Decolonization: The Emergence of Domestic Human Rights Instruments in Britain's Overseas Territories*. New York: Oxford University Press.

Quinn, Kevin, Burt L. Monroe, Michael Colaresi, Michael H. Crespin, and Dragomir R. Radley. 2010. "How to Analyze Political Attention with Minimal Assumptions and Costs." *American Journal of Political Science* 54: 209–28.

Reyntjens, Filip. 1986. "Recent Developments in the Public Law of Francophone African States." *Journal of African Law* 35: 75–90.

Roberts, Margaret E., Brandon M. Stewart, Dustin Tingley, Christopher Lucas, Jetson Leder-Luis, Shana Kushner Gadarian, Bethany Albertson, and David G. Rand. 2014. "Structural Topic Models for Open-Ended Survey Responses." *American Journal of Political Science* 58: 1064–82.

Rosenkrantz, Carlos F. 2003. "Against Borrowings and Other Nonauthoritative Uses of Foreign Law." *International Journal of Constitutional Law* 1: 269–95.

Sapir, Edward. 1939. *Language: An Introduction to the Substance of Speech*. New York: Harcourt Brace.

Scheppele, Kim Lane. 2004. "Constitutional Ethnography: An Introduction." *Law and Society Review* 38: 389–406.

Son, Bui Ngoc. 2017. "The Global Origins of Vietnam's Constitutions: Text in Context." *University of Illinois Law Review* 2017: 525–62.

Tate, C. Neal and Thorsten Vallinder. 2005. *The Global Expansion of Judicial Power*. New York: NYU Press.

Yan, Léopold Mu Si and Bruno Saura. 2015. "Decolonization, Language, and Identity: The Francophone Islands of the Pacific." *Contemporary Pacific* 27: 325–35.

6

Transnational Constitution-Making: The Contribution of the Venice Commission on Law and Democracy

Paul Craig*

This chapter examines the contribution to transnational constitution-making of the European Commission for Democracy through Law, better known as the Venice Commission. It is part of the Council of Europe, but much less understood than the European Court of Human Rights, ECtHR, notwithstanding the existing literature (Bartole 2000; Bartole 2014; Buquicchio & Garrone 1998; Buquicchio & Durr 2008; Buquicchio 2009; Buquicchio & Granata-Menghini 2013; de Visser 2015; Hoffmann-Riem 2014). The chapter therefore seeks to explicate and evaluate. It begins by explicating the organizational foundations of the Venice Commission, followed by analysis of its remit and role. The focus then shifts to triggering and working methodology.

The remainder of the chapter is concerned with evaluation of the Commission's role in relation to constitution-making broadly conceived, the analysis being situated within the literature concerning transnational legal orders (TLOs) (Halliday & Shaffer 2015). There is an overview of the central elements of TLO theory, the reasons why the Venice Commission can be conceptualized within this theoretical frame, and its distinctive contribution to constitution-making. *TLOs are increasingly prevalent across diverse fields, including that concerned with constitutions, democracy, human rights and the rule of law. It renders it all the more important that we reflect hard on the impact of TLOs.* The chapter therefore considers implementation by the addressee of

* Note: I am the alternate UK representative on the Venice Commission, but this chapter contains my personal view. I am grateful for comments from the participants at a conference at the Law School, UC Irvine, and subsequently from Gregory Shaffer, Terence C. Halliday and Tom Ginsburg. An earlier version of this chapter was published in *UC Irvine Journal of International, Transnational, and Comparative Law*. It included discussion of the process rights afforded to the state that is the subject of a Venice Commission opinion, and the substantive criteria that the Commission brings to bear when producing its opinions. That material has been omitted from this chapter, since the focus of this book is rather different. It has been replaced by more extensive discussion of impact.

the opinion, and the impact of the Venice Commission working in conjunction with other organizations that fall within the same TLO, insofar as they are also concerned with protection for democracy, the rule of law, and human rights. The chapter concludes with discussion of the broader impact of the Commission through sharing best practice and cooperation.

FOUNDATIONS AND ORGANIZATION

The impetus for the creation of the Venice Commission came from Antonio La Pergola, Italy's minister for European affairs, who, in the late 1980s, raised the possibility of a body that would monitor respect for democracy and the rule of law. The communist regime in Poland fell in 1989, followed by the fall of the Berlin Wall in November 1989, and the ousting of communist governments in Czechoslovakia, Romania, Bulgaria, and Albania in the ensuing two years. La Pergola organized a conference in Venice in January 1990 in which members of the Council of Europe participated, complemented by observers from some central and east European countries. It was the catalyst for creation of the Venice Commission,[1] the original agreement being for two years.[2] Membership was initially confined to states that were party to the Council of Europe.

The current statute dates from 2002, and it enabled states that were not parties to the Council of Europe to become members of the Venice Commission,[3] which now has sixty-one member states, comprising the *forty-seven Council of Europe member states*, plus *fourteen other countries*.[4] It is funded from a budget to which the participating states contribute, which has to be agreed by the Committee of Ministers.[5] Its permanent secretariat, which provides assistance to the Commission,[6] is located in Strasbourg at the headquarters of the Council of Europe. Plenary sessions are held in Venice four

1 Mr. La Pergola's founding role is mentioned in his obituary, viewable in the list of Venice Commission events that took place in 2007. See: www.venice.coe.int/webforms/events/.

2 The Council of Europe's Committee of Ministers established the Venice Commission with Res. 90(6) adopted May 10, 1990, which contained the original statute of the Venice Commission.

3 Resolution Res. (2002) 3 Adopting the Revised Statute of the European Commission for democracy through Law, CDL (2002) 27.

4 Algeria, Brazil, Chile, Costa Rica, Israel, Kazakhstan, the Republic of Korea, Kosovo, Kyrgyzstan, Morocco, Mexico, Peru, Tunisia, and the USA. It is for the Committee of Ministers of the Council of Europe to invite a non-member state to join the Venice Commission, Revised Statute (n. 3) Art. 2.5.

5 Revised Statute (n. 3) Art. 6.1.

6 *Ibid.*, Art. 8; Revised Rules of Procedure, CDL-AD(2015)044, Art. 7.

times a year, with the secretariat preparing the agenda and supporting materials,[7] which are normally distributed two weeks before the plenary.[8] The Commission of the European Union participates in the plenary sessions of the Venice Commission. So too does the Organization for Security and Cooperation in Europe, OSCE,[9] and the OSCE office for Democratic Institutions and Human Rights, ODIHR,[10] which also participates in sub-Commissions of the Venice Commission.

The Venice Commission elects, for two years renewable, a Bureau, composed of the President, three Vice-Presidents, and four other members.[11] The President presides over the Commission's work and represents it.[12] There are sub-commissions dealing with fundamental rights, federal states and regional states, international law, protection of minorities, the judiciary, democratic institutions, working methods, Latin America, the Mediterranean Basin, the rule of law, and gender equality. Opinions and reports are discussed by the relevant sub-Commission before consideration by the plenary.[13] There is, in addition, a joint Council on Constitutional Justice, and a Council on Democratic Elections, which are discussed below. There is also a Scientific Council, composed of the President and Vice-Presidents of the Commission; the Chairs of the Sub-Commissions; and members who direct research centers on Constitutional, International, or Human Rights Law. It prepares restatements of Commission doctrine in specific areas; takes stock of implementation of Commission opinions and reports; proposes the studies that should be undertaken; and provides rapporteurs with material for the preparation of opinions and reports.[14]

Membership of the Venice Commission is regulated by Article 2 of the statute. It stipulates that the Commission shall be composed of "independent experts who have achieved eminence through their experience in democratic institutions or by their contribution to the enhancement of law and political science."[15] The members of the Commission serve in their individual capacity

7 Revised Rules of Procedure (n. 6) Art. 8.1.

8 *Ibid.*, Art. 9.1.

9 OSCE decisions adopted by the plenary session of the Venice Commission, as well as an overview of the OSCE's human rights mission, can be found at the organization's website: www.osce.org/.

10 Details of the ODIHR's work with the Venice Commission can be found in the organization's 2017 annual report, viewable at www.osce.org/odihr.

11 Revised Statute (n. 3) Art. 4.

12 Revised Rules of Procedure (n. 6) Art. 6. Gianni Buquicchio has been President since December 2009.

13 Guidelines Related to the Working Methods of the Commission, CDL-AD(2010)034, II.D.

14 *Ibid.*, II.C; Revised Rules of Procedure (n. 6) Art. 17a.

15 Revised Statute (n. 3) Art. 2.1.

and "shall not receive or accept any instructions."[16] They are appointed by their respective countries, and hold office for four years, renewable.[17] The individual members are professors of public law and international law, national judges, practicing lawyers, members of national parliaments, and civil servants. Representatives of the Committee of Ministers, the Parliamentary Assembly of the Council of Europe, the Congress of Local and Regional Authorities of Europe, and the Giunta of the Regione Veneto may attend the sessions of the Commission.[18] The European Union is "entitled" to participate in the work of the Commission,[19] and the Committee of Ministers is empowered to authorize the Commission to invite international organizations to participate in its work.[20] It is open to the Venice Commission to use consultants to facilitate attainment of its objectives.[21]

REMIT AND ROLE

The Venice Commission's role is elaborated in Article 1.1 of the statute, which mandates that it is to fulfil the following objectives: strengthen the understanding of the legal systems of the participating states, with a view to bringing them closer; promote the rule of law and democracy; and examine the problems raised by the working of democratic institutions and their reinforcement and development. Article 1.2 instructs the Venice Commission to give priority to work concerning the constitutional, legislative, and administrative principles and techniques, which serve the efficiency of democratic institutions and their strengthening, as well as the rule of law; fundamental rights and freedoms; and the contribution of local and regional self-government to the enhancement of democracy. The reality is that the Venice Commission works in three broad areas.

Democratic Institutions and Fundamental Rights

The first concerns democratic institutions and fundamental rights, which includes:[22] the relations between the different branches of state power;

16 *Ibid.*, Art. 2.1.
17 *Ibid.*, Arts. 2.2–2.3.
18 *Ibid.*, Art. 2.4.
19 *Ibid.*, Art. 2.6.
20 *Ibid.*, Art. 2.7.
21 *Ibid.*, Art. 5.
22 An overview of the Venice Commission's goals for democratic institutions can be found at www.venice.coe.int/WebForms/pages/?p=01_Const_Assistance&lang=EN.

inter-institutional cooperation; the rule of law; judicial reform; protection of fundamental rights; protection of minorities; emergency powers; parliamentary immunity; ombudsman institutions; decentralization; federalism and regionalization; and the interplay between international law and human rights.

Constitutional reform is central to the Venice Commission's work, including the drafting of constitutions and constitutional amendments, and legislation of a constitutional nature. The Venice Commission is also concerned with the functioning of political institutions, the balance of power between the main state organs, and the legal framework of national judicial systems. Opinions on fundamental rights constitute a significant part of the Commission's workload, the paradigm being whether a state's law relating to a fundamental right, such as speech, is consistent with European and international standards.

Constitutional Justice

The second area in which the Venice Commission works is constitutional justice.[23] From its early years, it facilitated dialogue between constitutional courts, as manifest by the creation in 1992 of a documentation center to foster mutual exchange of information between the courts, and to inform the public about their decisions. The Commission established a network of liaison officers with constitutional courts. They contribute three times per annum to the Bulletin on Constitutional Case-Law and the Commission database CODICES.[24] There is a facility, the "Venice Forum," which fosters information exchange between the courts on current issues.

Cooperation between the constitutional courts and the Venice Commission was institutionalized post-2002, through the Joint Council on Constitutional Justice (JCCJ).[25] The JCCJ is co-chaired, one being a member of the Commission, the other being a liaison officer elected by the liaison officers during a meeting of the JCCJ.[26] The Venice Commission invites Constitutional Courts and courts of equivalent jurisdiction in its Member States, Associate Member States, Observer States, and States with Special Co-operation Status (South Africa, Palestine) to participate in the JCCJ. Courts from other States can be invited to JCCJ meetings as special guests.

23 An overview of the Venice Commission's goals regarding constitutional justice can be found at www.venice.coe.int/WebForms/pages/?p=01_Constitutional_Justice&lang=EN.

24 The cases uploaded by the commission can be found at www.codices.coe.int/NXT/gateway.dll?f=templates&fn=default.htm.

25 Revised Statute (n. 3) Art. 3.4.

26 Revised Rules of Procedure (n. 12) Art. 18.

The JCCJ is thus the steering body for cooperation between the Venice Commission and the Constitutional Courts. It has responsibility for publication of the Bulletin on Constitutional Case-Law,[27] which, since 1993, contains summaries of the most important decisions submitted by the constitutional courts of circa fifty countries, the European Court of Human Rights, ECtHR, and the Court of Justice of the European Union, CJEU. The JCCJ also oversees the CODICES database, which is updated three times per year. It contains circa 4000 summaries that are also published in the Bulletin, and the full texts of approximately 5000 decisions. The Bulletin and CODICES make data available from countries whose constitutional decisions would not otherwise be readily available. This facilitates research, and offers a resource to constitutional courts as to how endemic problems have been dealt with elsewhere, thereby fostering trans-constitutional exchange of ideas. The JCCJ annual meeting will be followed by a conference on a topic of current interest concerning constitutional justice.

Elections, Referendums, and Political Parties

The third area in which the Venice Commission is active concerns elections,[28] including referendums and political parties.[29] The electoral work is undertaken under the auspices of the Council for Democratic Elections (CDE) which is a tripartite body composed of members of the Venice Commission, the Parliamentary Assembly of the Council of Europe (PACE), and the Congress of Local and Regional Authorities of the Council of Europe. The CDE and Commission cooperate with OSCE/ODIHR. CDE opinions are subject to approval by the plenary of the Venice Commission in the same way as those on other topics.

The Council for Democratic Elections proffers advice and gives opinions on electoral legislation. The Venice Commission has adopted approximately 120 opinions and issued sixty texts of a general character on elections, referendums, and political parties. Considerable attention has been devoted to codes of good electoral practice, analogous documents concerning referendums, and guidelines that relate to political parties.[30] The Commission also

27 A description of the bulletin, as well as copies of the bulletin dating back to 2000, can be found at www.venice.coe.int/WebForms/pages/?p=02_02_Bulletins.

28 An overview of the Venice Commission's goals and efforts regarding elections can be found at www.venice.coe.int/WebForms/pages/?p=01_Elections_and_Referendums&lang=EN.

29 Details about the Venice Commission's goals and efforts regarding political parties specifically can be found at the following site: www.venice.coe.int/WebForms/pages/?p=02_parties.

30 See, e.g., Code of Good Practice in Electoral Matters, CDL-AD(2002)23 rev; Code of Good Practice on Referendums, CDL-AD(2007)008; Guidelines on Political Party Regulation by

organizes the annual European Conference of Electoral Management Bodies, provides training for those involved in electoral work, and participates in some electoral observation missions.[31]

The Specific and the General

The Venice Commission's work is an admixture of opinions concerning particular countries, and general studies that draw, inter alia, on these to furnish more general guidance on particular fundamental rights or political parties, with the hope that these can assist legislators, public authorities, the judiciary, and the like.[32] Closely related to the general studies are the compilations of extracts from opinions adopted by the Venice Commission in particular areas.[33] The objective is to provide an overview of doctrine in the particular area, as a reference resource for drafters of constitutions and of legislation.[34]

Such compilations facilitate the task of Venice Commission members when preparing an opinion on a particular country, helping to ensure consistency of treatment between countries. They are structured thematically and are regularly updated. Thus to take the compilation concerning freedom of association by way of example, the principal thematic headings are: definition of freedom of association; national and international frame of reference; content of freedom of association; expression of freedom of association; legal status and registration of an association; dissolution of an association; non-governmental organizations; and religious or belief organizations.[35]

OSCE/ODIHR, CDL-AD(2010)024; Code of Good Practice in the Field of Political Parties, CDL-AD(2009)021.

31 These efforts are described in more detail at the following site: www.venice.coe.int/WebForms/pages/?p=02_seminars.

32 See, e.g., Guidelines for Legislative Reviews of Laws relating to Religion or Belief, CDL(2004)061; OSCE/ODIHR – Venice Commission Guidelines on Freedom of Peaceful Assembly, 2nd ed, CDL-AD(2010)020; Venice Commission – OSCE/ODIHR Joint Guidelines on Freedom of Association, CDL-AD(2014)046; Report on the Implementation of International Human Rights Treaties in Domestic Law and the Role of the Courts, CDL-AD(2014)036.

33 These compilations, as well as a brief description of their purpose, can be found at www.venice.coe.int/WebForms/pages/?p=04_Compilations&lang=EN.

34 See, e.g., Compilation of Venice Commission Opinions concerning Freedom of Association, CDL-PI(2014)004; Compilation of Venice Commission Opinions concerning Constitutional Provisions for Amending Constitutions, CDL-PI(2015)023; Compilation of Venice Commission Opinions and Reports concerning Political Parties, CDL-PI(2016)003; Compilation of Venice Commission opinions and Reports concerning Gender Equality, CDL-PI(2016)007.

35 Compilation of Venice Commission Opinions concerning Freedom of Association (n. 34).

TRIGGERING AND METHODOLOGY

Triggering the Venice Commission

The Venice Commission has power to produce reports on its own initiative. Article 3.1 states that without prejudice to the competence of the organs of the Council of Europe, the "Commission may carry out research on its own initiative and, where appropriate, may prepare studies and draft guidelines, laws and international agreements." Any proposal from the Commission can then be discussed and adopted by the statutory organs of the Council of Europe.

Article 3.2 lists the institutions/states that can request an opinion from the Venice Commission, on a subject that falls within its mandate.

> The Commission may supply, within its mandate, opinions upon request submitted by the Committee of Ministers, the Parliamentary Assembly, the Congress of Local and Regional Authorities of Europe, the Secretary General, or by a state or international organization or body participating in the work of the Commission.
>
> Where an opinion is requested by a state on a matter regarding another state, the Commission shall inform the state concerned and, unless the two states are in agreement, submit the issue to the Committee of Ministers.

The reality is that most opinions are triggered by requests from a state party to the Venice Commission. It may seek help in drafting a constitution or changes thereto, or it may request assistance because it has learned that a national law is in some way deficient, or not fit for purpose. The reference may also be explicable because of some intra-institutional tension within the referring state, whereby the request becomes part of some larger struggle between executive and legislature, or between rival political parties. The request from the state means in effect the current governing party, and the Venice Commission does not formally inquire as to the intrastate political forces that precipitated the reference. These forces will, however, invariably become apparent when the working group begins its inquiry, aided by documentation provided by the secretariat, and further information in this respect will be forthcoming when the Commission undertakes its site visit, during which it will talk to a wide range of parties, official and unofficial.

It might, in a more cynical vein, be felt that state referrals serve as window dressing, helping the state to buttress its democratic credentials when it has no intention to implement the recommendations. The Venice Commission has no formal enforcement mechanism, but we should nonetheless be cautious about this argument. There may be a plethora of reasons why it proves difficult to effectuate Commission recommendations, many of which are consistent with good faith motivation for the initial request for help. It is, moreover, doubtful whether a "rational state actor" would act in this way. It sounds simple. The state takes the democratic plaudits from asking the Commission for help, while avoiding the costs, since it has no intention to comply with the opinion. Matters are more complex. The reference to the Commission inevitably lets the genie out of the bottle. The "defective law" is revealed, thoroughly analyzed, and there will be a site visit to the country, in which the working group talk to official and non-official players alike. The outcome of all this is not predictable when the state makes the request for assistance, and any "benefits" it secures from willingness to make the referral would be significantly outweighed by the "costs" when it becomes apparent that it had no interest in implementing the opinion.

It is clear from Article 3.2 that the Venice Commission can also be triggered by other bodies. The Parliamentary Assembly for the Council of Europe is the source of many such requests. There are, inevitably, differences in the "tone and feel" of an opinion that has not been requested by the state, more especially where it does not want such scrutiny, and the relationship between the Commission and the state can be more adversarial in such instances.

The Venice Commission's expertise can, in addition, be triggered by a state that is not a member by making a request to the Committee of Ministers.[36] It can also provide amicus curiae opinions, not on the constitutionality of the act concerned, but on comparative constitutional and international law issues, at the request of a constitutional court, or the ECtHR.[37]

Working Methodology of the Venice Commission

The way in which opinions are prepared is determined by the Guidelines on Working Methods,[38] and by practice that has evolved over time. When a reference has been made to the Venice Commission, a working group, normally between four and six, is then established. These are the rapporteurs,

[36] Revised Statute (n. 3) Art. 3.3.

[37] See, e.g., Amicus Curiae Brief on the case Santiago Bryson de la Barra et al (on crimes against humanity) for the Constitutional Court of Peru, CDL-AD(2011)041; Amicus Curiae Brief for the Constitutional Court of Georgia on the non ultra petita rule in criminal cases, CDL-AD (2015)016; Republic of Moldova – Amicus Curiae Brief for the Constitutional Court on the Right of Recourse by the State against Judges, CDL-AD(2016)015.

[38] See Section II, Part E of the document: www.venice.coe.int/WebForms/pages/?p=01_founding_documents&lang=EN.

who are national members of the Venice Commission.[39] They are chosen for their expertise over the subject matter, and their availability to contribute within the timeframe. The temporal dimension is important in this respect, the reality being that for a plethora of reasons most Venice Commission opinions have to be produced within tight time lines.[40] The rapporteurs are assisted by a member of the secretariat.[41] The secretariat proposes the time schedule for preparation of the draft opinion or study, and provides the rapporteurs with information concerning the background of the request, the national legislation, the applicable standards, and previous Commission work that is relevant.[42]

The draft opinion will be produced by the rapporteurs, in conjunction with the member of the secretariat. The rapporteurs are sent the preceding material, which is translated into English or French. In the paradigm situation all rapporteurs on the working group write an individual report on the issues raised by the request for an opinion. There is normally no direct collaboration between the individual rapporteurs, although it is possible for the working group to meet between Commission sessions.[43] The member of the secretariat then produces a draft opinion, which draws on the views of the individual rapporteurs. This is circulated to the working group, who can suggest amendments. The proposed amendments are circulated to the working group, and a consensus is reached on the draft opinion that represents the view of the working group as a whole. In some cases the procedure is different. Thus where the subject matter is large, as with the drafting of a constitution, then the individual rapporteurs may be assigned specific issues. The reports from the rapporteurs will be collated by the member of the secretariat, and the draft opinion will be circulated to all rapporteurs, who can suggest amendments to the draft text.

The draft opinion thus produced will analyze the issue against the backdrop of the relevant standards, the content of which will be considered below. It is normal for there to be a site visit to the country. This might not occur where there has already been extensive discourse between the Commission and the

[39] Any member of the Commission may indicate an interest in becoming a member of a particular working group, provided that he or she is in a position to participate within the relevant time-frame, Guidelines Related to the Working Methods of the Commission (n. 13) II.E.

[40] *Ibid.*, II.E., which provides that "the rapporteurs will present their observations and text proposals in due time to enable the Secretariat to prepare a draft (consolidated) opinion within the time limit previously agreed upon."

[41] *Ibid.*, II.E.

[42] *Ibid.*, II.G.

[43] *Ibid.*, II.E.

state when the opinion was being drafted, or because the state does not allow the Commission to enter its territory. The Commission has no right to enter a state without its consent, and there can be difficulties where the Commission has been triggered by a request from a body other than the state itself, although the reality is that even in such instances the state normally does allow the Commission to visit.

The site visit serves two related purposes. It provides an opportunity for the state to have "voice" and proffer observations in response to questions posed by the working group. The questions focus on issues that the group regards as problematic from the work that it has undertaken thus far. The site visit also enables the working group to make contact with civil society and other interested stakeholders. This may be especially important where the reference to the Venice Commission was made by a body other than the state. However even where the reference has been made by the state, the site visit provides an opportunity for "voice" to non-governmental bodies who will often bring perspectives to bear that complement, supplement, or contradict those of the official state entities.

The final draft opinion is prepared after the site visit. It is sent to all Commission members two weeks before the plenary session,[44] including the representatives of the state that is the subject of the report, who will normally receive it slightly earlier than the other members of the Commission.[45] Such opinions may be considered by a sub-Commission, which meets the day before the plenary session. There can be discussion between the rapporteurs and the state prior to the plenary. The final draft opinion is then presented to the plenary session by one of the rapporteurs. This is followed by opportunity for comment by the state that is the subject of the report. The comments may concern the factual accuracy of the opinion; the state may contest the working group's interpretation of its law, or its compatibility with international standards; or the state may query the specific recommendations. When the state has voiced its view at the plenary the floor is then open for any other member of the plenary to comment.

How much discussion takes place at the plenary perforce varies. At one end of the spectrum there is the opinion requested by the state, which is content with the recommendations, more especially because it discussed the issues during the site visit and subsequent thereto. In such instances discussion at the

44 *Ibid.*, II.E.

45 When the national situation so requires, the President, in consultation with the Bureau, may authorize that the rapporteurs' opinion that has not yet been adopted can be sent to the national authorities prior to its adoption at the plenary, *Ibid.*, II.E.

plenary is brief. At the other end of the spectrum there can be opinions that originate from references by bodies other than the state, where the state is not happy with the scrutiny or with the opinion, notwithstanding that it had the opportunities for voice adumbrated above. In such instances discussion can be more protracted and heated. There are of course intermediate positions along this spectrum.

It should, moreover, be emphasized that discourse continues throughout the process. Thus if the plenary discussion reveals contestable issues that had not been fully recognized hitherto, the rapporteurs may acknowledge a point, and the final draft opinion is accepted subject to its being addressed. The rapporteurs will then meet on the day of the plenary, draft an amendment to the relevant point, which is circulated to the plenary. The opinion is made public when it has been adopted by the plenary, and is then available on the Commission website. The dialogic nature of the process is captured by this statement on the Commission website.[46]

> The Commission does not seek to impose the solutions set out in its opinions. Rather, it adopts a non-directive approach based on dialogue and shares member states' experience and practices. For this reason, a working group visits the country concerned to meet the various stakeholders and to assess the situation as objectively as possible. The authorities are also able to submit comments on the draft opinions to the Commission.

THE VENICE COMMISSION, TRANSNATIONAL LEGAL ORDERS, AND CONSTITUTION-MAKING

Transnational Legal Orders

The discussion thus far has been concerned principally with explication. The focus now shifts to evaluation, which is framed within the emerging literature on transnational legal orders, TLOs. The core ideas underlying this literature are set out by Ginsburg, Halliday, and Shaffer in the introduction to this volume. TLOs are defined by Terence C. Halliday and Gregory Shaffer as "a collection of formalized legal norms and associated organizations and actors that authoritatively order the understanding and practice of law across national jurisdictions" (Halliday & Shaffer 2015b: 5). The term associated organization is construed broadly to include any organization or social

46 The website provides an overview of the opinion-generating process in detail, listing those who can request an opinion and providing a step-by-step account of how an opinion is prepared: www.venice.coe.int/WebForms/pages/?p=01_activities&lang=EN.

formation, so too is the term actor, which includes collective actors and individuals whose activities span national boundaries.

The concept of order within TLO thought is conceived of in terms of shared social norms and institutions that orient social expectations, communication, and behavior. Much social ordering is achieved through law, and "this ordering becomes authoritative when the legal norms become accepted and institutionalized across national jurisdictions" (Halliday & Shaffer 2015b: 8) whereby the normative orientation of those applying the law is changed and their behavior affected.

A TLO is legal "when it involves international or transnational legal organizations or networks, directly or indirectly engages multiple national and local legal institutions, and assumes a recognizable legal form" (Halliday & Shaffer 2015b: 11). The resulting transnational legal norms "may reflect pre-existing national ones, such as those of powerful nation-states, or they may reflect norms developed by private parties and networks through bottom-up processes" such that trans-national organizations and networks are "part of the process of the legal norms' formation, conveyance, and potential institutionalization" (Halliday and Shaffer 2015b: 12). For Halliday and Shaffer the legal dimension of TLOs does not, however, require a "single hierarchy of norms, nor is it always formally binding; nor is it invariably backed by coercion" (Halliday & Shaffer 2015b: 18).

A legal order thus defined is transnational insofar as it orders social relationships in some way that transcends the nation state. It is clear, moreover, that "TLOs span legal orders that vary in their geographic scope, from bilateral and plurilateral agreements to private transnational codes to regional governance bodies to global regulatory ordering" (Halliday & Shaffer 2015b: 18–19). They can evolve over time, there may be more than one TLO that covers a particular substantive area, and there may be contestation between TLOs that cover the same area, or where the coverage of TLOs overlaps (Halliday & Shaffer 2015b: 30).

There can be various catalysts for the creation of TLOs. There might be a disjunction between national regulation and global markets in the light of changes in economic interdependence; the driving force might be technological change; or it might be the ascendancy of certain political ideals that are regarded as central for state legitimacy, such that states employ TLOs to advance such ideals. Transnational theory is recursive, in the sense that it integrates the study of law production and law implementation within a single frame, assessing how "the production and implementation of transnational legal norms among international, transnational, national, and local lawmakers and law practitioners dynamically and recursively affect each other" (Halliday & Shaffer 2015b: 38).

The Venice Commission and Transnational Legal Orders

The study of TLOs provides a helpful frame for consideration of the Venice Commission, which plays an important transnational role in the dispersion of legal norms concerning democracy, human rights, and the rule of law. This is readily apparent from three related perspectives: function, membership, and values.

Function

The Commission's origins were adumbrated above, becoming part of the Council of Europe (CoE), following the initiative from Antonio La Pergola. This enhanced the role of both institutional actors, since they performed complementary functions. The Council of Europe was already part of a TLO that fostered human rights and the rule of law, most prominently through the ECtHR. The Strasbourg Court, in common with other judicial institutions, was primarily concerned with fire-fighting, dealing with particular adjudicative problems when cases were brought to the Court, although its judgments could have some effect on shaping state behavior ex ante. The Venice Commission offered the Council of Europe the opportunity for more generalized intervention ex ante, whereby the Commission could give opinions on constitutions, legislation, and the like, with the objective of fire prevention, thereby helping to avoid problems concerning human rights and the rule of law arising within a state, or suggesting ways in which they could be addressed through reform of the constitution or law that was the source of the problem.

From the perspective of the nascent Venice Commission the institutional home within the Council of Europe was equally beneficial, not only because the Commission could tap into CoE institutional resources, but also because the association meant that the Venice Commission did not have to build its legitimacy from scratch. It was not just another organization among many seeking to promote human rights.

The agreement whereby the Venice Commission became part of the CoE thereby strengthened both players. It provided the Council of Europe with the opportunity, through the Venice Commission, for shaping the post-communist political order, providing advice on the establishment of more liberal democratic regimes within the relevant states. This was regarded both as an intrinsic good, and was also perceived more instrumentally as a way of strengthening the polities that had hitherto been communist regimes.

Membership

The relationship between the CoE and the Venice Commission also enhanced this TLO because of membership. The Commission did not actively have to solicit states to become members, since it could tap directly into the existing membership of the CoE. This provided the initial core of Commission members, and also fueled its expansion as ex-Communist states joined the CoE during the 1990s. It increased the immediate client base, and did so through the addition of states that were most likely to call on the Commission for assistance, since they sought help to ensure that their constitutions and laws were more in accord with a liberal democratic ordering.

It should also be acknowledged that there are states that are members of the Venice Commission, such as Russia, which are unlikely to request assistance and are likely to resist inquiries when they are triggered by an institutional player. It begs the question as to why they remain within the Council of Europe, since it is this that provides the linkage with membership of the Commission. The answer to that broader question takes us beyond the scope of this paper. Suffice it to say for the present that viewed from the perspective of the rational state actor, Russia must believe that the legitimacy gains of membership outweigh the costs in terms of challenges to Russian laws through the ECtHR, and through the Venice Commission, although there are signs that it wishes to limit as far as possible the impact of both arms of the CoE while still remaining a member.[47]

Membership expanded further post-2002, whereby states that were not party to the CoE were allowed to become members of the Commission. The revised statute allowing for non-CoE members to join the Commission was driven initially by the desire of such states to become full members, but not surprisingly this was pushing at an open door as far as the Commission was concerned, since the expanded membership enhanced its status. The reasons why such states sought membership are eclectic, ranging from the straightforward desire to tap into Commission expertise when framing constitutions and laws, to the legitimacy gains for the state by becoming a full member. The rationale was different yet again in the case of the USA, since neither of the preceding reasons have much purchase in explaining its transition from observer status, to full member. This was probably driven more by the desire to lend support to

47 Russian Federation – Final Opinion on the Amendments to the Federal Constitutional Law on the Constitutional Court, CDL-AD(2016)016-e.

an organization that was perceived to be a force for the maintenance of liberal democratic ordering and stability in Europe and beyond, which would be in accord with more general precepts of US foreign policy.

The Commission membership of sixty-one states is diverse, and this has augmented the recursive nature of the Commission's modus operandi. The Commission, as will be seen more fully below, utilizes a blend of hard and soft law when writing opinions. The very diversity of membership, which is replicated within working groups, highlights the need for plurality in the application of Commission values, and serves as a constant reminder of the need to be cognizant of local circumstance when applying such values.

There is a further dimension to membership that enhanced this TLO with respect to democracy, human rights, and the rule of law. The Commission membership rules institutionalize cooperation with other prominent institutional actors that form part of this TLO, most notably the European Commission and OSCE/ODIHR, while leaving it open for the Venice Commission to liaise on a more ad hoc basis with other organizations. Liaison between the Venice Commission and the European Commission has been especially prominent in relation to rule of law problems that have arisen in EU countries, such as Hungary and Poland, while cooperation with OSCE/ODIHR is common, most especially in the context of elections.

Values

The values advanced by the CoE and the Venice Commission are democracy, human rights, and the rule of law. The Commission plays an important role in this TLO. It is, drawing on Halliday and Shaffer, one of the associated organizations that authoritatively order the understanding and practice of law across national jurisdictions within this domain. There are many other organizations that make important contributions to the TLO concerned with human rights and the rule of law, but the Commission's contribution is nonetheless distinctive and flows from its institutional structure.

Its membership of two representatives from each state, combined with the institutional support of the secretariat, means that it is capable of responding to numerous requests for assistance at any one point in time. The institutional capacity to accept multiple requests for assistance that require detailed evaluation of national constitutions and laws within a tight timeframe enables the Commission to make a distinctive contribution to this area. This is further enhanced by the diversity of membership, which means that those with expertise and cultural understanding can be combined on the same panel. This has in turn facilitated the development of databases, compilations, and the like, which furnish guidance on particular areas such as speech, association, assembly, and good electoral practice. The authority of the formalized legal norms within this area is thereby enhanced. Implementation is, as we shall see below, not perfect. There can, moreover, be contestation as to the "correct" application of such values in a particular instance, but much of this occurs within the frame of the underlying values that are central to this TLO.

There is, however, as Kim Lane Scheppele has cogently argued (Chapter seven this volume), increased evidence of states seeking to cloak themselves with the garb of constitutionalism, while seeking to undermine it from within. This in itself provides interesting evidence about the evolution of TLOs, as the established TLO within the relevant area is challenged, with the possible emergence of a rival TLO. The Venice Commission nonetheless exemplifies the following principle (Halliday & Shaffer 2015b: 59).

> It is a demonstrable premise of constructivist theory in international relations scholarship that the ability of an international organization to promulgate norms that are widely adopted by nation-states across the world is likely to increase the power of those international organizations themselves. That is to say, the transnational propagators of legal norms become more than the sum of the interests of nation-states – they become emergent actors in their own right and thus come to exert organizational interests that cannot be reduced to an amalgam of their constituent state delegations.

The Venice Commission and Constitutions

There are at least four "sedimentary" layers that can be discerned in the study of constitutions: the making and terms of the constitution itself; constitutional amendment; legislation that impacts directly or indirectly on the meaning and application of the constitutional terms; and constitutional practice, whether in the form of institutional conventions, or perceptions of the constitution by the people. Constitution-making broadly conceived is an important part of the Venice Commission's work,[48] and this is attested to by the large number of opinions that have dealt with this issue.[49] The Commission's work in this area is dependent on a reference being made by the relevant state, or another institution that is entitled to do so, and this will determine the scope of the

48 An overview of the Venice Commission's approach to constitutional issues, as well as its opinions on recent constitutional reforms, can be found at www.venice.coe.int/WebForms/pages/?p=02_Reforms&lang=EN.

49 See the constitutional reform decisions listed on the Venice Commission's website: www.venice.coe.int/webforms/documents/?topic=4&year=all.

opinion. Commission opinions have addressed three out of the four aspects of constitutions set out above.

First, there are opinions that concern the drafting and terms of the constitution, or significant parts thereof. This is exemplified by Commission opinions on Tunisia,[50] Iceland,[51] Bosnia and Hercegovina,[52] Hungary,[53] Moldova,[54] and Armenia.[55] While the scope of the Commission opinions differed in these cases, they exemplify its role in advising on the constitution as a whole, or in proffering advice on parts that were central to the constitutional schema of that particular country.

Second, there are a large number of opinions dealing with constitutional amendment. The process of constitutional reform is often complex and lengthy. In some countries it has spanned several years, with changes wrought through constitutional amendment. The catalyst for such amendment varies. In some instances it is the realization that the initial constitutional design is imperfect; in others it is the result of new political configurations that wish to reshape the country's institutional and constitutional architecture; in yet other instances, the motives may be darker, such that current majorities seek to reinforce their power through constitutional amendment designed, for example, to limit the power of the judiciary (Scheppele, Chapter seven this volume). An overview of the Commission's many opinions can be gleaned from its compilation on constitutional amendments,[56] and its conceptual approach to constitutional amendment is evident in a separate report on the topic.[57]

Third, there is an even larger group of opinions concerned with legislation that fleshes out constitutional provisions. It is not fortuitous that the Commission website on constitutional reform lists, inter alia, the following issues:[58] checks and balances between powers and the principle of inter-institutional cooperation; delegation of legislative powers; judicial reform;

[50] Opinion on the Final Draft Constitution of the Republic of Tunisia, CDL-AD(2013)032-e.

[51] Opinion on the Draft New Constitution of Iceland, CDL-AD(2013)010-e.

[52] Opinions on the constitutional regime of Bosnia and Herzegovina, CDL-INF(1998)015-e.

[53] Opinion on the new Constitution of Hungary, CDL-AD(2011)016-e.

[54] Cooperation between the Venice Commission and the Republic of Moldova on Constitutional Reform, CDL-INF(2001)003-e.

[55] First Opinion on the Draft Amendments to the Constitution (Chapters 1 to 7 and 10) of the Republic of Armenia, CDL-AD(2015)037-e.

[56] Compilation of Venice Commission Opinions concerning Constitutional Provisions for Amending the Constitution, CDL-PI(2015)023.

[57] Report on Constitutional Amendment, CDL-AD(2010)001.

[58] See the "Key Topics" portion of the Venice Commission's site on constitutional reforms (cited above in n. 48) www.venice.coe.int/WebForms/pages/?p=02_Reforms&lang=EN.

guarantees for the rule of law and fundamental rights and freedoms; electoral systems; and issues related to local self-government and decentralization. It might be felt that we should demarcate the constitution, its making and its provisions, from all else. The influences that shape the making of the constitution and the content of its provisions are clearly central. Counting how many constitutions contain provisions of a particular kind is of some help, albeit limited. It is nonetheless normatively and pragmatically mistaken to draw a rigid line between the constitution and legislation that is designed to fill out the meaning of its provisions, and it is misguided to elide the existence of the same provision in many constitutions with equivalence of application.

Constitutional legislation is in many respects the lifeblood of the constitution. Other things being equal, the thinner the constitution and the more abstract its provisions, the greater the role for constitutional legislation and adjudication to imbue the terms with more concrete meaning. Such legislation is nonetheless important in all constitutions, although its incidence may vary. The constitution may contain noble provisions concerning free and fair elections, but the reality can only be tested by examination of the detailed electoral legislation that puts flesh on these constitutional bones. There may be laudable constitutional guarantees for political parties, only for these to be heavily circumscribed by legislation that defines the qualifications for a political party to appear on the ballot. The force of constitutional protections for free speech may be qualified by legislative rules related to association. The need to be mindful of the link between constitutional terms and consequent legislation is important in relation to many other issues commonly found in constitutions, such as principles concerning equality, the judiciary, and the like, which are then articulated in more detail in, or are affected by, legislation. The importance of this linkage is repeatedly attested to by Commission opinions.

Fourth, and finally, there is constitutional practice, which may take various forms. There may be institutional conventions, or perceptions of the constitution by the people. There may be practice by the relevant players, which either undermines the formal constitutional norms, or imbues them with greater force than they would otherwise have as judged by their formal text. There may be events that test the ambit of formal constitutional provisions, with the resolution of the contestation casting the constitutional norms in a somewhat different light than hitherto.

This can be exemplified by the Venice Commission investigation into elections to the Russian Duma.[59] The inquiry, which was triggered by the

59 Opinion on the Federal Law on the election of the Deputies of the State Duma of the Russian Federation adopted by the Council for Democratic Elections at its 40th meeting (Venice,

Parliamentary Assembly for the Council of Europe, considered the compatibility of the Russian electoral rules with Venice Commission principles. The inquiry neatly exemplifies the interrelationship between the sedimentary layers. Some electoral principles were contained in the Russian constitution, but these were fleshed out by a constitutional statute, stretching to 140 pages, which regulated in great detail all features of the electoral process. The Russian statute was in turn interpreted against the backdrop of Venice Commission codes concerning matters such as good electoral practice, regulation of political parties, and participation of minorities in elections. These codes were the result of Venice Commission deliberations from previous inquiries. They were symbiotic, drawing on experience and best practice from various countries, combined with considerations of first principle, with the expectation that the code thus formulated would influence future constitutional development at state level. The Russian statute was not perfect, and the Venice Commission report revealed shortcomings as adjudged by the preceding criteria. The statute, nonetheless, contained much that was sophisticated and thoughtful in terms of ensuring fair and free elections. The real problem was constitutional practice or malpractice, which undermined in subtle ways attainment of the legislative objectives. The Venice Commission could not magically cure such malaise, but the problem was very much seen as coming within the Venice Commission's brief. The report provided the occasion for frank discourse concerning the interrelation between formal articles of the constitution, amendments thereto, constitutional statutes, and constitutional practice.

It is instructive to relate the preceding discussion back to that concerning TLOs. It would be possible to conceive of a TLO that was solely concerned with the making and terms of constitutions. We would then identify the "collection of formalized legal norms and associated organizations and actors that authoritatively order the understanding and practice of law across national jurisdictions" (Halliday and Shaffer 2015b: 5) in this respect. The reality is that a TLO thus conceived would miss much if it excluded the second, third or fourth dimension articulated above. Nor would this sit easily with the emphasis placed on national law in TLO discourse and on the recursive nature of TLO theory, which accords prominence to the way in which "the production and implementation of transnational legal norms among international, transnational, national, and local lawmakers and law practitioners dynamically and recursively affect each other" (Halliday &

March 15, 2012) and by the Venice Commission at its 90th Plenary Session (Venice, March 16–17, 2012), CDL-AD(2012)002.

Shaffer 2015b: 38). A distinctive contribution made by the Commission to constitutional study is that it provides a window onto the interaction between the constitution, amendment thereto, and constitutional legislation, through the many Commission opinions that exemplify this relationship.

THE VENICE COMMISSION AND COMPLIANCE

We have already seen that classic coercive enforcement is not a condition precedent for the existence of a TLO, or for an organization to be regarded as part thereof. The extent of compliance is nonetheless important, since it is a factor that affects the extent to which the TLO's legal norms can be said authoritatively to order the understanding and practice of law across national jurisdictions.

Compliance and the Addressee: An Initial Estimation

The data on the impact of Venice Commission opinions on the addressees is regrettably thin, since there is no systematic method through which the Commission is cognizant of the extent to which its recommendations have been followed, notwithstanding space allotted on the plenary agenda for follow-up on previously adopted opinions. The data may, somewhat paradoxically, become apparent if the state becomes a repeat player in relation to the same issue. This does not alter the fact that systematic compliance data is not readily available. This problem could be alleviated relatively simply if the following suggestion were to be acted upon (Hoffmann-Riem 2014: 589 n.44).

> At a minimum, those states that initiate requests to the VC on their own could be obligated to report, *inter alia*, about the implementation of recommendations in a systematic, comprehensive, and reliable manner. The same could also be asked from member states when requests are initiated by other authorities, such as the Parliamentary Assembly. Moreover, the members appointed to the VC by member states could be tasked with helping the Secretariat document and evaluate implementation efforts and making themselves available to the *plenum* for further questions

This is a sensible proposal. There will, to be sure, be instances where states prove recalcitrant and fail to provide the requisite information, testimony to the fact that the world is imperfect, and that the Commission has no enforcement mechanism. The proposal nonetheless embodies a clear obligation, and failure to comply will be indicative of prima facie non-compliance, and thereby facilitate further inquiry. The very fact that there are differences of view as to implementation rates bears testimony to the importance of securing better information in this regard.

Thus on one view implementation is the norm when states request a reference. This view has been voiced by Pieter van Dijk (van Dijk 2007: 188). It has been echoed by Buquicchio and Granata-Menghini, who state that "when the opinion requests come from the interested States themselves, it is the rule that they are followed, in part or in full" (Buquicchio & Granata-Menghini 2013: 250). By way of contrast Hoffmann-Riem regarded that assessment as "probably too optimistic" (Hoffmann-Riem 2014: 589), based on analysis of data concerning implementation from a sample of opinions between 2009 and mid-way through 2012. He concluded that in some instances states did not take up the recommendations, although this was in part explicable because "the project submitted for review – including in reaction to the criticism by the VC – was abandoned or had yet to be completed," while "in other cases, the project was pursued without taking up the VC's suggestions, or at least the majority of them" (Hoffmann-Riem 2014: 589). Hoffmann-Riem, however, also found evidence that other opinions had been fully or partially implemented. There can, moreover, be a temporal element to implementation: recommendations that have been ignored by the incumbent government may be taken up by a later government (Buquicchio & Granata-Menghini 2013: 248).

Hoffmann-Riem identifies factors that affect compliance, which accord with basic intuition in this regard. The most significant factor is whether the state requested the opinion, or whether it was thrust on the state through request for Commission intervention by an institutional player. Compliance is significantly less likely in the latter instance than the former. This is more especially so when one adds in the power of the relevant state, and the nature of the opinions requested by the institutional intervener. This is exemplified by the five opinions concerning Russia produced by the Commission in 2012 at the behest of the Parliamentary Assembly of the Council of Europe. Not only was the target state very powerful, but the opinions focused on high-profile laws relating to elections to the State Duma,[60] political parties,[61] assembly,[62] combating of extremism,[63] and the Russian Federal Security Service.[64] It was

60 Opinion on the Federal Law on the election of the Deputies of the State Duma of the Russian Federation, CDL-AD(2012)002. I was one of the rapporteurs on this opinion.

61 Opinion on the law on political parties of the Russian Federation, CDL-AD(2012)003.

62 Opinion on the Federal Law no. 54-FZ of 19 June 2004 on assemblies, meetings, demonstrations, marches and picketing of the Russian Federation, CDL-AD(2012)007.

63 Opinion on the Federal Law on Combating Extremist Activity of the Russian Federation, CDL-AD(2012)016.

64 Opinion on the Federal Law on the Federal Security Service (FSB) of the Russian Federation, CDL-AD(2012)015.

scarcely surprising that Russia was resistant to change in these areas. The reality was nonetheless that Russia consented, after some delay, to site visits for the separate reports, and engaged with the reports when they went through the Commission decision-making process, culminating in heated exchanges at the plenary session.

There are, as Hoffmann-Riem notes, other factors that play into compliance. Thus there is the extent to which the Venice Commission opinion draws support from other institutional players, such as the Commission of the European Union, where the state that is the subject of the opinion has reason not to offend that other institution. A factor that inclines in the other direction is the extent to which the state cares about the critique. Where the state remains authoritarian, with little appetite for change and little incentive to seek the imprimatur of more liberal states, then the opinion is likely to fall on stony ground.[65]

Limits as to the impact of opinions are explicable in part at least by the fact that the Commission "can analyse and compare the texts of norms and suggest changes, but it has no direct influence on the basic conditions that drive practical application of norms in the state concerned" (Hoffmann-Riem 2014: 589). This point is important and has wider resonance for the limits of transnational impact on national constitutions. Lawyers naturally focus, initially at least, on text, and the provenance thereof. We ask whether there is evidence that a country's constitution was shaped by other constitutions. We inquire as to causality in this respect. We debate about the relative importance of indigenous influence and foreign input. This is an important part of the story, but it can only ever be part thereof, for the reason identified by Hoffmann-Riem. Thus even where there is formal implementation of Venice Commission opinions, substantive implementation will necessarily depend on a broad range of societal factors that affect reception of such norms in that state. These include, inter alia, the prevailing governmental culture, the bureaucratic willingness/capacity to apply the relevant provisions, the independence of the judiciary, and access to court.

Compliance and the Addressee: TLOs and Interlocking Organizations

The preceding discussion has focused on the factors that most immediately affect compliance by the addressee of the Venice Commission opinions. It is nonetheless important to place the issue into the broader framework of TLO

65 See, e.g., Joint opinion on the law on mass events of the Republic of Belarus, CDL-AD (2012)006.

thought, and reflect thereby on what this tells us about this body of scholarship. There are three factors that are pertinent in this respect.

Compliance, TLOs, and Interlocking Organizations

It is important to recall the definition of TLOs as "a collection of formalized legal norms and associated organizations and actors that authoritatively order the understanding and practice of law across national jurisdictions" (Halliday & Shaffer 2015b: 5). We have seen that the term associated organization is construed broadly to include any organization or social formation. This is true also of the term actor, which includes collective actors and individuals whose activities span national boundaries.

Viewed from this perspective, the Venice Commission is but one of the associated organizations that seeks to foster respect for democracy, the rule of law, and human rights. The organizations that constitute a TLO can not only be associated in the loose sense that they respectively foster adherence to the relevant values. They can also work more closely to deal with challenges to those values, an idea which is captured by the term interlock as it is used within this section. The possibilities for compliance are enhanced, because the two organizations join forces to tackle the problem. It can therefore be artificial to consider the impact of an organization on a problem where the reality is that two or more associated organizations have attempted to tackle it. The immediate catalyst for the involvement of the organizations can differ, but this does undermine the commonality of their shared purpose. This does not, however, guarantee success in dealing with difficult situations.

This can be exemplified by the efforts made by the EU and the Venice Commission in relation to problems with the rule of law and human rights that have arisen in Hungary, Poland, and Romania (von Bogdandy et al. 2012; Canor 2013; von Bogdandy & Sonnevend 2015; Kochenov & Pech 2015; Jakab & Kochenov 2016; Closa & Kochenov 2016). Three rationales for EU intervention are evident in the Commission's 2014 paper.[66]

First, compliance with the rule of law was a prerequisite for the protection of all fundamental values listed in Article 2 TEU, these being respect for human dignity, freedom, democracy, equality, and human rights. Second, such compliance was also a prerequisite for upholding all rights and obligations derived from the Treaties and from international law. Third, and more specifically, it was required to ensure the mutual trust on which the area of freedom, security, and justice was grounded. If there were concerns as to the

[66] Commission Communication on Article 7 of the Treaty on European Union – Respect for and promotion of the values on which the Union is based, COM(2003) 606 final, 4–5.

rule of law in a particular EU country, as manifested in the integrity of its judicial system, then this would undermine the trust that was a necessary precondition for such mutual recognition to operate.

Article 7 TEU authorizes EU action where there is a clear and persistent risk of a serious breach by a Member State of Article 2 TEU, which can lead to suspension of Treaty rights, including voting rights in the Council. The Commission believed that a new regulatory mechanism was nonetheless needed, because a systemic threat to the rule of law in Member States could not be effectively addressed by Article 7, which was too limited: the preventive mechanism in Article 7(1) could be activated only in case of a "clear risk of a serious breach," while the sanctioning mechanism of Article 7(2) TEU could only be used for cases of "serious and persistent breach by a Member State" of the values in Article 2 TEU. The new framework embodied a three stage process: assessment, recommendation, and follow up, and was used for the first time against Poland.[67]

The catalyst for Venice Commission involvement was the referral of constitutional issues relating to Hungary and Poland, which focused in particular on rule of law problems concerning the independence of the regimes for constitutional adjudication in the respective countries. It is common for the Venice Commission to deliver more than one opinion where the initial investigation revealed serious problems, the object being to determine whether the problems have been alleviated in the intervening period. This is evident in relation to Hungary,[68] Romania,[69] and Poland.[70] These detailed studies furnished empirical foundation for the EU's rule of law concerns with respect to these countries. The Venice Commission opinions also contained detailed recommendations for alleviating the problems that were identified. The symbiotic nature of the organizational interchange was further

67 Rule of law in Poland: Commission starts dialogue, January 13, 2016, http://ec.europa.eu/news/2016/01/20160113_en.htm.

68 See, e.g., Opinion on the new Constitution of Hungary, CDL-AD(2011)016; Opinion on Act CLXII of 2011 on the Legal Status and Remuneration of Judges and Act CLXI of 2011 on the Organisation and Administration of Courts of Hungary, CDL-AD(2012)001; Opinion on Act CLI of 2011 on the Constitutional Court of Hungary, CDL-AD(2012)009; Opinion on the Cardinal Acts on the Judiciary that were amended following the adoption of Opinion CDL-AD(2012)001 on Hungary, CDL-AD(2012)020; Opinion on the Fourth Amendment to the Fundamental Law of Hungary, CDL-AD(2013)012.

69 See, e.g., Opinion on the Two Draft Laws amending Law NO. 47/1992 on the Organisation and Functioning of the Constitutional Court of Romania, CDL-AD(2006)006; Opinion on the Draft Law on the Review of the Constitution of Romania, CDL-AD(2014)010.

70 See, e.g., Opinion on amendments to the Act of 25 June 2015 on the Constitutional Tribunal of Poland, CDL-AD(2015)001e; Poland – Opinion on the Act on the Constitutional Tribunal, CDL-AD(2016)026.

emphasized by the fact that the EU regularly participated in Venice Commission sessions, paying particular attention to opinions about EU Member States.

Compliance, TLOs, Competence, and Legitimacy

There are, however, limits to the competence of the organizations within any TLO, which perforce constrain their impact. The Commission's 2014 initiative was challenged by the Council legal service, which argued that it lacked a legal basis in the Treaties. This view was, in turn, persuasively contested (Besselink 2016). The Council backed away from the advice of its legal service, endorsed the approach in the Commission 2014 paper, and evinced a willingness to outsource this task to the Commission. The rationale is not hard to divine, since a lesson from governance within nation states is that the executive may be willing to outsource regulatory power where it can thereby avoid the "heat" that is attendant on the task.

The reality is that the EU is caught in a dilemma, which has implications for the legitimacy of its intervention. The EU feels, on the one hand, that it should do something about the problem, which is felt to be partly its responsibility. It is argued that the state withstood scrutiny under the Copenhagen criteria on accession,[71] and that the EU should therefore bear responsibility for what happened thereafter, even if the relevant problem could not have been detected, or did not exist, earlier. There are, on the other hand, limits as to what the EU can do. If there are serious systemic failures in relation to the rule of law within a Member State, which are grounded in deep rooted socio-political problems, then there will perforce be limits to what can be done by the EU.

The Venice Commission is also constrained, albeit in different ways. It has no formal enforcement mechanism, nor does it have the competence to engage in more wide-ranging or free-standing critique of the socio-political arrangements within a particular state, even if those are in reality the root cause of the problems revealed in a Venice Commission opinion. It can advert to such problems by way of background, but the focus of the opinion is nonetheless on the particular rule of law problem that the Venice Commission is asked to investigate. It can also express disquiet by way of follow-up to an earlier opinion, as exemplified by the statements made by the President of the Venice Commission in relation to Poland, expressing concern

[71] The Copenhagen criteria require aspirant accession states to have, inter alia, stable institutions guaranteeing democracy, the rule of law, human rights, and respect for and protection of minorities.

as to the worsening situation with respect to the position of the Constitutional Tribunal.[72]

There are, moreover, constraints on further interaction between the EU and the Venice Commission in this area. A proposal for addressing the preceding problems has been that the Copenhagen criteria should be relevant post-accession, thereby meeting the critique that the EU currently subjects aspirant states to more searching scrutiny on such matters than it does those in the club. The post-accession criteria would operate via a scoreboard to which all states would be subject, thereby reducing the sense that a particular state was being singled out for scrutiny. This would facilitate early detection, allowing problems to be nipped in the bud before they developed into something more serious.

There are issues concerning the efficacy of such an approach, and also about the institution that should apply the post-accession Copenhagen criteria. It has been suggested that this might be done by the Venice Commission. There would be no doubt as to its independence, nor would it be susceptible to pressure from an EU Member State or EU institution. There are, nonetheless, practical and political difficulties with this option. In practical terms, the ongoing monitoring would involve the Venice Commission in extra work, which would require further personnel, and it would entail a significant shift in the focus of its work. In political terms, the problems are greater, since it would mean subjecting the EU Member States and the EU institutions to scrutiny for compliance with fundamental rights and the rule of law by an external institution. It is questionable whether the EU institutions would be willing to accept this, and it is equally questionable whether the CJEU would tolerate it.

Compliance, TLOs, and the Challenge to Global Values

There is a further aspect to compliance, which is relevant to the problems discussed in this section. Exigencies of space preclude detailed treatment, but it should nonetheless be mentioned.

We adverted earlier to Kim Lane Scheppele's important contribution (Chapter seven this volume), where she pointed to increased evidence of states seeking to cloak themselves with the garb of constitutionalism, while seeking to undermine it from within. The current rise of populism has potentially far-reaching implications for the very values that TLOs such as the Venice Commission seek to preserve. There is a fine line between a state

[72] The President's statements can be accessed here: www.venice.coe.int/webforms/events/?id=2352.

cloaking itself in the garb of constitutionalism, while undermining it from within, and a state that more directly challenges the content and interpretation of the liberal values that we traditionally associate with constitutionalism.

The anti-globalization evident in populist movements not only has an economic, but also an ethical and moral dimension, whereby the values that inhere in the liberal constitutional order are increasingly challenged, thereby also posing challenges to the TLOs that embrace constitutionalism and rule of law values. The fact that the authority of TLOs can ebb and flow over time, in response to endogenous and exogenous variables, should come as no surprise. It is indeed recognized within TLO theory. It remains to be seen how far-reaching the current challenge is.

THE VENICE COMMISSION AND IMPACT: SHARING BEST PRACTICE AND COOPERATION

Assessment of the Commission's impact should not, however, be confined solely to consideration of whether the state implements the opinion addressed to it. From its very inception the Venice Commission has operated on a broader front, more especially so in relation to countries making the transition to more liberal democratic regimes. The Commission has always recognized that change will not happen overnight, but that it can also be fostered through other activities, including training of personnel, seminars, engagement with judges and conferences. The Venice Commission has initiatives across all these areas, and although it is difficult to assess their precise impact, it would be misguided to ignore or undervalue such initiatives.[73] These initiatives are also significant in relation to countries that are not formally members of the Commission. It has developed programs with Central Asia, the Southern Mediterranean, and Latin America.

Thus in Central Asia[74] the Venice Commission developed projects, some of which involved particular countries, others of which were regional, in relation to issues such as constitutional assistance, constitutional justice, reform of the judiciary, and electoral legislation and practice. The bilateral dimension can be exemplified by cooperation, whereby the Commission furnished the newly created Constitutional Chamber of Kyrgyzstan with assistance in the field of constitutional justice. The Chamber requested such assistance in order to

73 See, e.g., the various initiatives listed on the front page of the Venice Commission website, www.venice.coe.int/webforms/events/.

74 Descriptions of both regional and country-specific projects in Central Asia can be found at www.venice.coe.int/WebForms/pages/?p=03_Central_asia&lang=EN.

better understand international standards and best international practice, since it had no experience in the field of constitutional justice hitherto. The regional dimension to such cooperation is exemplified by the 2009 rule of law initiative, run jointly with the EU, which was aimed at the five Central Asian countries, Kazakhstan, Kyrgyzstan, Tajikistan, Turkmenistan, and Uzbekistan. The objectives of the program were, inter alia, to strengthen the rule of law and separation of powers; enhance the independence of the judiciary; assist in reform of the public prosecutorial function; facilitate integration of international law into national law; reform electoral law and administration; and assist in the training of judges and officials.

The Venice Commission activities in the Southern Mediterranean region focused on provision of assistance and advice to Arab countries even before the Arab Spring, with close contacts established with Morocco and Tunisia. This can, as in the context of Central Asia, take the form of bilateral exchange, or regional support. The former is exemplified by Commission support, following a request from Morocco in 2014 for assistance in the preparation of two organic laws concerning the High Judicial Council and the Status of Judges. A good example of the regional dimension is the University for Democracy (UniDem) Campus for the Southern Mediterranean Countries.[75] The program ran from 2015 to 2017, with seminars on good governance, the rule of law, and fundamental rights for high-level civil servants of the region.

The theme of sharing best practice and cooperation is also apparent in relations between the Commission and countries in Latin America. Some countries from this region, such as Brazil, Chile, Mexico, and Peru, are members, and Commission initiatives designed to foster best practice in areas such as democratic transition, constitution-building, constitutional justice, and electoral legislation have been especially prevalent in relation to such countries. Such initiatives have been fostered by the sub-Commission on Latin America. The sharing of best practice is not, however, confined to states that are members of the Commission. There have been further conferences involving in excess of twenty countries from Latin America and Europe, which dealt with matters such as individual access to constitutional justice, and implementation of human rights treaties at domestic level. Moreover, in 2013, the first meeting of the sub-Commission on Latin America outside Venice took place in Mexico City in 2013, and was attended by states that were not members of the Venice Commission.

75 An overview of the UniDem project can be found at www.venice.coe.int/WebForms/pages/?p=03_CampusUniDem&lang=EN. The summary specifically calls the seminars "regional."

CONCLUSION

There will be no attempt to summarize the entirety of the preceding argument. Suffice it to say the following. We should be cautious about extremes, more particularly so where they relate to the evaluation of the transnational impact of a particular institution on national constitution-making broadly conceived. There are dangers of overestimation, imagining a transformative effect that cannot readily be sustained on the facts.

The preceding discussion has sought to explicate and evaluate the work of the Venice Commission, and its impact on transnational constitution-making broadly conceived. The very fact that there is an institution, which is independent and can draw on the legal expertise of highly qualified members in order to proffer advice to countries concerning the compatibility of their constitutions and laws with the precepts of democracy, human rights, and the rule of law is a force for the good. It should, moreover, be emphasized that the Venice Commission is not simply a transnational institution compelling states to comply with a set of norms from above. There is, in addition, a powerful recursive dynamic, whereby the local and national are brought to bear, influencing the elaboration of transnational norms such as opinions and guidelines.

The very fact that membership of the Venice Commission encompasses all states that are party to the Council of Europe, and some that are not, helps to ensure the very plurality and respect for cultural difference that is necessary when engaged in the provision of such opinions. The very fact that the Venice Commission has been asked for advice outside the traditional European arena, in Africa, Asia, and Latin America, attests to the salience of the principles that it espouses, notwithstanding differences in traditions and values in different parts of the world.

There will inevitably be instances where there will be contestation as to the content of a particular opinion. Thus was it ever so in this domain. It should nonetheless also be recognized that transnational contribution to national constitutions can take various forms, from aid in the drafting of the constitution itself to advice on laws concerning human rights, and from measures to safeguard the independence of the judiciary to those designed to secure free and fair elections. The very fact that the Venice Commission can operate across this range has enhanced its impact.

REFERENCES

Bartole, Sergio. 2000. "Final Remarks: The Role of the Venice Commission." *Review of Central and East European Law* 26(3): 351–63.

Bartole, Sergio. 2014. "International Constitutionalism and Conditionality, The Experience of the Venice Commission." Associazone dei Italiana Costituzionalisti (4/2014).

Buquicchio, Gianni and Pierre Garrone. 1998. "L'harmonisation du droit constitutionnel européen: La contribution de la Commission européenne pour la démocratie par le droit." *Uniform Law Review/Revue de Droit Uniforme* 3(3): 323–38.

Besselink, Leonard. 2016. "The Bite, the Bark and the Howl: Article 7 and the Rule of Law Initiatives." In *The Enforcement of EU Law and Values: Methods against Defiance*, edited by András Jakab and Dimitry Kochenov. Oxford: Oxford University Press.

Buquicchio, Gianni. 2009. Vingt ans avec Antonio La Pergola pour le développement de la démocratie. Pp. 29–38 in *Liber amicorum Antonio La Pergola*, edited by Pieter van Dijk and Simona Granata-Menghini. Lund: Juristförlaget I.

Buquicchio, Gianni and Schnutz Durr. 2008. "The Venice Commission's Action in Africa." Pp. 165–74 in *Essays in Honour of Ergun Ozbudun* Vol. 2, edited by S. Yazici, G. Kemal, and E. Goztepe. Ankara: Yetkin.

Buquicchio, Gianni and Simona Granata-Menghini. 2013. "The Venice Commission Twenty Years on, Challenges met, but Challenges Ahead." Pp. 241–54 in *Fundamental Rights and Principles, Liber Amicorum Pieter van Dijk*, edited by Marjolein van Roosmalen, Ben Vermeulen, Fried van Hoof, and Marten Oosting. Cambridge: Intersentia.

Canor, Iris. 2013. "My Brother's Keeper? Horizontal Solange: 'An Ever Closer *Distrust* among the Peoples of Europe.'" *Common Market Law Review* 50(2): 383–421.

Closa, Carlos and Dimitry Kochenov, eds. 2016. *Reinforcing Rule of Law Oversight in the European Union*. Cambridge: Cambridge University Press.

de Visser, Martje. 2015. "A Critical Assessment of the Role of the Venice Commission in the Processes of Domestic Constitutional Reform." *American Journal of Comparative Law* 63(4): 1–35.

Halliday, Terence C. and Gregory Shaffer, ed. 2015a. *Transnational Legal Orders*. New York: Cambridge University Press.

Halliday, Terence C. and Gregory Shaffer. 2015b. "Transnational Legal Orders." Pp. 1–70 in *Transnational Legal Orders*, edited by Terence. C. Halliday and Gregory Shaffer. New York: Cambridge University Press.

Hoffmann-Riem, Wolfgang. 2014. "The Venice Commission of the Council of Europe – Standards and Impact." *European Journal of International Law* 25(2): 579–97.

Jakab, András and Dimitry Kochenov, eds. 2016. *The Enforcement of EU Law and Values: Methods against Defiance*. Oxford: Oxford University Press.

Kochenov, Dimitry and Laurent Pech. 2015. "Monitoring and Enforcement of the Rule of Law in the EU: Rhetoric and Reality." *European Constitutional Law Review* 11(3): 512–40.

van Dijk, Pieter. 2007. "The Venice Commission on Certain Aspects of the European Convention of Human Rights, *Ratione Personae*." Pp. 183 et seq in *Human Rights, Democracy and the Rule of Law: Liber Amicorum Luzius Wildhaber*, edited by S. Breitenmoser et al. Zurich: Nomos.

von Bogdandy, Armin, Matthias Kottmann, Carlino Antpöhler, Johanna Dickschen, simon Hentrel, and Maja Smrkolj. 2012. "Reverse Solange – Protecting the essence of fundamental rights against EU Member States." *Common Market Law Review* 49(2): 489–519.

von Bogdandy, Armin and Pál Sonnevend, eds. 2015. *Constitutional Crisis in the European Constitutional Area: Theory, Law and Politics in Hungary and Romania*. Oxford: Hart Publishing.

7

Autocracy under Cover of the Transnational Legal Order

Kim Lane Scheppele

INTRODUCTION

In the middle of 1989, Francis Fukuyama famously pronounced "the end of history" (Fukuyama 1989). It was an exaggeration even then, but it has become a cautionary tale now. As he wrote, one state after another in Eastern Europe was throwing off its Soviet past and hurtling toward a liberal constitutional-democratic future. Following two "waves" of prior democratization in Southern Europe and Latin America (Linz and Stepan 1996b), the changes in Eastern Europe heralded a world in which liberal constitutionalized democracies became the international norm. As one newly liberated people after another became able to chart their own futures, they seemed to converge on a common model of governance: Update as Liberal, Democratic, Constitutional.

Of course, we all knew then – and we know better now – that history never stops. At any given historical moment, it is all too easy to imagine that we stand at the end of a grand narrative that has led to us, to here and to now, when of course later developments will change that narrative so that our present moment is but a way-station on the way to a different ending (which will itself in turn be provisional). Premature conclusions like "the end of history" are routine but almost always wrong.

That said, the general theoretical frameworks for understanding the history through which we are passing sometimes get stuck at particular moments. Constitutional consultants are still in the grips of the "end of history" narrative. Globe-trotting academics (for the players, see Widner 2008; and for skepticism, see Tushnet 2008), international organizations (with the UN, World Bank, and the Venice Commission leading among them), rule-of-law development programs (see Kleinfeld 2012) and designed-for-purpose NGOs (like Interpeace and International IDEA) have gone into the constitutional consulting business and themselves constitute the key players in a transnational network peddling norms. Constitutional consultants often seem optimistically fixed in the 1990s when the protection of human rights, rule of law, checked and balanced powers, powerful independent judiciaries, open states engaged in transnational cooperation, liberalized economies, and internal and external peace – along with many other things – were universal goals that all could be counted upon to share. As International IDEA, one of the most influential constitutional-consulting organizations proclaims in its 2018 mission statement: "We believe that democracy is a universal human aspiration" (International IDEA 2018).

If the "end of history" once stood for the universal appeal of constitutional democratic government, then we are no longer in that moment. In fact, not only has history not ended, but it now seems to be speeding up. As my colleague David Bell has noted, history appears to accelerate when one major event becomes the reason for others – and so a key historical trigger can generate cascades of good news or cascades of bad news all at once. Bell quotes a probably apocryphal remark by Lenin: "there are decades where nothing happens, and weeks where decades happen" (Bell 2016). And democratic states have been having too many decade-like weeks of late, as one former democracy after another has fallen under the sway of a populist leader. While this cascade started with relatively newer democracies, the Brexit vote and the election of Donald Trump signal that even long-standing democracies are not immune from trouble. Elites across many once-secure constitutional democracies are now urgently discussing topics like how one knows when democracy has died (Levitsky and Ziblatt 2018).

These pessimistic conversations about the fate of democracy are not just reacting to transient headlines or individual countries. Each year between 2006 and 2017, more countries declined than improved on various Freedom House measures of democratic performance (Freedom House 2018). For the first time in 2015, Freedom House lowered the status of a country, Hungary, from a "consolidated" democracy to a "partially consolidated" one (Freedom House 2015: 8), despite the fact that the very definition of a consolidated democracy was that democracy was the "only game in town" and had no ideologically attractive competitors (Linz and Stepan 1996a). In 2018, Freedom House lowered a candidate country of the European Union, Turkey, from "partly free" to "not free," (Freedom House 2018) even as the EU has continued to act as if Turkey were a normal interlocutor and as NATO keeps Turkey firmly within its ranks despite the fact that the NATO treaty preamble commits its signatories "to safeguard the freedom, common heritage and civilisation of their peoples, founded on the principles of democracy, individual liberty and the rule of law."

While the validity of Freedom House's indicators has been contested, even critics of the Freedom House view of the world can see that democracy is in global crisis (Schmitter 2015). At a minimum, there has been a growth in the number of countries that are hard to classify one way or another as democracies or autocracies (Diamond 2015: 142) as well as a record number of democracies declining quickly into something else (Freedom House 2018).

Among the casualties in the shrinking democratic ecosystem are a number of once relatively clear liberal, constitutional democratic states that have now fallen victim to ideological decay. Even in Western Europe and the United States, a recent survey documents that growing numbers of citizens are so disillusioned with democracy that many are open to other alternatives – raising the possibility that even established liberal, constitutional democracies may "de-consolidate" (Foa and Mounk 2016). Liberal, democratic constitutionalism is – to borrow the language of marketing – a damaged brand. If the end of history was supposed to represent the moment when liberal, democratic constitutionalism triumphed across the world and was so normatively powerful that no state that had achieved it would ever renege on its pledges, then the end of history is clearly over.

How can we reconcile the fact that democracies are in decline and yet the constitutional consulting community soldiers on as usual with its universalizing aspirations? As I will argue in this chapter, the constitutional consulting community has created a particular form of "transnational legal order" that has allowed the new autocrats to escape detection – and even to thrive.

CONSTITUTIONALISM AS A TRANSNATIONAL LEGAL ORDER

Democratic decline started to occur after the international constitutional consulting community had already clearly met the trademark standards of a transnational legal order (TLO): "a collection of formalized legal norms and associated organizations and actors that authoritatively order the understanding and practice of law across national jurisdictions" (Halliday & Shaffer 2015: 5). As we will see, the norms were defined by varieties of "liberal" and "democratic" legal forms, and the institutions and actors clustered around the "rule of law industry" (Kleinfeld 2012). One can see the constitutional consulting community most clearly at work when constitutions are being written.

It may seem odd that constitution writing – the process most implicated in the creation of national identity – would have become routinely infused with transnational influence just before liberal and democratic constitutionalism began crumbling as a normative model. First, it is a puzzle how most national (and often nationalistic) of legal exercises could have come under the influence of a TLO in the first place. And then it is a puzzle how some formerly liberal constitutional democracies could escape the normative pull of liberal and democratic constitutionalism while the TLO still remains formally in place. To see how we got to this odd moment, it helps to look back at how the constitutionalist TLO was established.

During the Cold War, before the present international consensus had sedimented into a TLO, the international struggle over governance models was polarized. At that time, there were different ideological options advocated as normatively justifiable on each side of the conflict. Communism and people's democracies were held out as both a development strategy and a route to social justice on one side. Capitalism and "real" democracies were offered as a route to prosperity and freedom on the other. Both the USSR and the US believed that winning hearts and minds was a legitimate tool of both war and diplomacy, so the battle between the two models was in fact often waged in normative terms (Osgood 2002; Zheng, Liu, & Szonyi 2010). The Cold War was, at the constitutional level, precisely a conflict over which of these two normative models would win.

Today's constitutionalism TLO has its origins in the effort to bring transnational advice to newly decolonized states in the 1960s and 1970s on the Western side of the Cold War divide. Experts awash in money from the "West" appeared in the developing world to show local politicians how to set up their newly independent governments. (The same, of course, was happening in the "East" but under a different rapid development model that died at the end of the Cold War.) These Western experts attempted and failed to bring democratic governance to newly de-colonialized states when they simply transplanted Western models to these radically different places without taking local cultures, histories, and norms into account (Schönteich 2013). After a number of the key players in this effort acknowledged that they had done little good for all of their effort and money, a major rethink of the Western development project brought local context back into the picture.

The new "rule of law movement" that was born in the 1980s and that became universalized after the end of the Cold War therefore took a different tack. Instead of inserting whole institutions and laws from model democracies into newly developing democratic states, consultants would encourage local stakeholders to take the lead (Kleinfeld 2012). After all, democracy would be reinforced by having the local democratically-endorsed leaders out in front of the process. Moreover, the rule of law community had by that time learned that not all democracies were exactly the same in any event, so local knowledge was considered essential for constitutional drafting to create a product capable of surviving in the particular context.

With this change of emphasis from universal to local knowledge, the transnational rule of law consultant was transformed from the "man with the plan" to one of many advisors who could offer ideas – but could no longer make or even leverage key decisions – in the process of local legal change (Dezalay & Garth 2001). Consultants had to learn to be modest because they knew only cosmopolitan ideas and did not have the local knowledge on which the acceptance of these cosmopolitan ideas depended. The constitutional consultants knew that models from "advanced" democracies could not just be transplanted without more, but instead had to be adapted to a particular site using local knowledge that the transnational experts did not have.

To acknowledge that local knowledge was now a central ingredient in all rule of law projects, the transnational experts took their "self-denying expertise" as a badge of honor, demonstrating they were really democrats at heart because they were no longer trying to override the legitimate local stakeholders in the democratization project by appearing to know it all. This denial of relevant knowledge to carry out rule of law reform generated what Deval Desai has termed "expert ignorance":

> Expert ignorance refers to experts, such as rule of law reformers, for whom it is a legitimate professional position to deny that they know anything about the object of their expertise, thereby placing [local] observers in the difficult position of either projecting their fantasies onto these experts or cohabiting with them in their ignorance. (Desai 2017: 1)

Since the new rule of law reformers were now supposed to turn to their local interlocutors for the knowledge of context, the local political heritage, and details of the specific terrain, the external reformers could merely offer for local reformers' consideration a set of options that the reformers might take up and use. Local leaders were therefore given a set of choices rather than a one-size-fits-all model. Experts became the global equivalent of roving salesmen, peddling wares from a global marketplace that could be taken up (or not) by local consumers.

To cast this more dramatically: Rule of law advisors from the constitutionalist TLO started as gardeners, transplanting seedlings from democratic soil to soil that aspired to democracy. The seedlings died when the soil didn't sustain them. Rule of law advisors then transformed themselves into itinerant merchants, offering the world's knowledge to those they visited, but leaving the choice and adaptation of this knowledge to the locals who knew the terrain.

Experts now explain variations in the standard models (parliamentarism versus presidentialism, federalism versus unitary state, diffuse versus concentrated judicial review) and then leave the choice of system to the locals. But if this is how constitutional and rule of law advising works these days, how can it be the subject of a TLO?

To sustain a TLO, one needs two components: Actors and norms. The actors and organizations are easy to identify. The demand for constitutional advice has created a supply of specialized constitutional consultants, bringing to governments undergoing constitutional change knowledge of how to set up a constitutional democracy along liberal lines. Built-for-purpose NGOs like International IDEA and Interpeace work hand-in-hand with dedicated divisions of the United Nations and other international organizations like the Venice Commission of the Council of Europe (Craig, Chapter six) as well as national and international bar associations, to compile knowledge about successful governance initiatives in order to package and present this cosmopolitan knowledge to local leaders who might put it to good use. The "rule of law community" (Kleinfeld 2012) is full of institutions and actors who travel the world consulting on how to bring good constitutions and rule of law to places in need of both.

As for norms, the constitutional consulting community gives lip-service to the idea that each constitution has to be designed for a specific time and space, but it still shows signs of having been born in the heady moment at the end of the Cold War when the protection of human rights, rule of law, checked and balanced powers, powerful independent judiciaries, open states engaged in transnational cooperation, liberalized economies, and internal and external peace – along with many other things – were suddenly universal goals that all could be counted upon to share. Two of the most important institutions in this new TLO are the networked UN programs that provide constitutional consulting advice and International IDEA which provides handbooks on many different aspects of constitutional drafting to guide local drafters. Documents produced by both show how much agreement there is within the TLO community on the norms to be promoted in advising on draft constitutions.

Within the UN, no fewer than five different departments work on constitutional drafting assistance: Department of Peacekeeping Operations, the Office of the High Commissioner for Human Rights, the UN Development Programme, the United Nations Children's Fund, and UN Women, in addition to specific country missions.[1] They are instructed in the twin pillars of

[1] For the UN newsletter, which one suspects is at least as much for internal coordination as for public consumption, see http://peacemaker.un.org/Constitutions/Newsletter.

local ownership of constitution-making and the need for the process to stay within the red lines set out by the international community.

Both pulls are visible in the UN General Secretary's office Guidance Note that explains the common mission of the various UN agencies engaged in constitutional consulting. First it reminds them that the local consumers of expert constitutional knowledge should remain in control of these processes:

> The UN should recognize that constitution-making is a sovereign national process, and that to successful the process must be nationally owned and led. The UN should be particularly sensitive to the need to provide advice and options without causing national actors to fear that UN or other international assistance could lead to a foreign imposed constitution. Any assistance will need to stem from national and transitional authorities' requests. The options and advice provided must be carefully tailored to the local context, recognizing there is no "one size fits all" constitutional model or process, and that national ownership should include official actors, political parties, civil society and the general public. (United Nations General Secretary 2009)

And yet, as one would expect in a TLO which offers not only helpful actors but also clear norms, the UN is not neutral among different constitutional visions, strongly preferring particular models to others and instructing the various UN agencies to ensure that local constitutional drafters understand their obligations under international law:

> The UN should consistently promote compliance of constitutions with international human rights and other norms and standards. Thus, it should speak out when a draft constitution does not comply with these standards, especially as they relate to the administration of justice, transitional justice, electoral systems and a range of other constitutional issues. The UN should be the advocate of the standards it has helped to develop. Accordingly, the UN should engage national actors in a dialogue over substantive issues, and explain the country's obligations under international law and the ways in which they could be met in the constitution. The UN should address the rights that have been established under international law for groups that may be subjected to marginalization and discrimination in the country, including women, children, minorities, indigenous peoples, refugees, and stateless and displaced persons. For example, the principle of equality between men and women should be embedded in constitutions, and states should be encouraged to consider special provisions on children recognizing their status as subjects of human rights. (United Nations General Secretary 2009)

Countries that accept UN advising assistance may be forgiven for thinking that the choice of constitutional model is all theirs – except when it isn't.

International IDEA also accepts the new rule of law model in which constitutional experts recognize the pluralism of possible legitimate models and defer to local knowledge, encourage local buy-in, and accept local choices as an exemplar of democratic decision-making in action. As an International IDEA mission statement proclaims:

> [Democracy] comes in multiple forms. These forms are in constant evolution. There is no single and universally applicable model of democracy. There is no end point in improving democracy. Fundamentally, democracy is a system in which the government is controlled by the people and citizens are considered equals in the exercise of that control. Beyond the basic tenets of citizens' choice and citizens' political equality, the critical choices are best made and the quality of democracy is best gauged by those directly concerned: the citizens themselves. We systematically nurture an open and pluralistic understanding of democracy. This is respectful of the national context, and is in line with our non-prescriptive and non-intrusive approach, as well as with the priorities set by national actors. (International IDEA 2018)

But International IDEA shares with the UN the idea that local variation has its limits. International IDEA's key handbook on constitution-building states:

> Democracy as a normative framework requires constitution builders to support and guarantee civil and political rights. Since rights are indivisible, there are many rights recognized as economic, social, cultural or collective whose recognition completes political rights and makes it possible to realize them. In the context of diversity . . . effective constitutional protection that is broad and equal across all categories of people is not possible except on the basis of a right to equality and non-discrimination. Human rights allow the constitutional dismantling of unjustifiable inequality. The human rights of women, children and people living with disabilities are examples of rights that cut across cultures and identity groups, and which should be guaranteed because of the vulnerabilities faced by these groups, which are sharpened by violent conflict and deep division. (International IDEA 2013: 28)

From these examples of mission statements taken from some of the key players in the transnational dimension of the TLO, one can see what the broader *substantive* normative ordering of the TLO looks like. Experts within the TLO itself must stand back and let local leaders make the major choices, with expert knowledge remaining firmly in the background. But the TLO also has some red lines that cannot be crossed, red lines that are provided by international human rights norms, among others. Other chapters in this volume provide further evidence that a set of transnational institutions has developed norms that now preside over the birth of almost every new constitution world-wide. There are even job notices for experts to work on specific constitutions[2] and the practice has started to sprout its own normative justifications (e.g. Agné 2012).

However, after the transnational consolidation of liberal, democratic, and constitutional norms around constitution-writing produced a TLO that was institutionalized inside many countries, more and more national governments began moving away from a sincere defense of these norms. Instead, they adopted nationalist and nationalistic constitutional ideologies, cut loose from these global models. The trend has continued already for more than ten years and shows little signs of reversing. The transnational legal order may have been present at the creation of many of these constitutions, but its norms are often now honored in the breach.

HONORING THE TRANSNATIONAL LEGAL ORDER IN THE BREACH

We can count among the ranks of countries that were once liberal, constitutional democracies an increasing number of states that can be better described as "legalistic autocracies" (Scheppele 2018; Corrales 2015). Legalistic autocracies are suspended between democracy and dictatorship with features of both. In legalistic autocracies, ambitious leaders are swept to power with (often large) plebiscitary mandates and they seek to govern under the appearance of law, but often outside a framework of separated and checked powers that is the hallmark of a liberal state. As we will see, many of these new legalistic autocracies have invested a great deal in constitutional legitimation – often by drafting new constitutions, even as they deny the most important elements

[2] A recent job ad for the United Nations Development Program at https://jobs.undp.org/cj_view_job.cfm?cur_job_id=41268 said the following:

"The United Nations support constitution-making making processes throughout the world. Several UN entities, including UNDP, UN Department of Political Affairs, UN Women, UN Department of Peacekeeping Operations, and OHCHR are collaborating to respond to the growing demand of UN agencies, member states and other partners who are frequently called upon to field constitutional experts to support UN Missions, UN Country Teams and Governments. Such constitutional advice and support is required in various settings ... UNDP and DPA are now soliciting highly-qualified experts and experienced consultants (individuals, not firms) to be considered for inclusion in a new UN Constitution Experts' Database, which will be used to rapidly identify and deploy constitutional expertise in support of constitutional processes."

of *liberal* constitutionalism: Limitation of public power by law, the exercise of public power in a transparent and accountable manner, the importance of checks and balances in the design of the state, the unconditional and non-discriminatory protection of rights. This careful attention to constitutional form while hollowing out liberal constitutional content is what marks legalistic autocracies as a special category among competitive authoritarian regimes (Levitsky and Way 2010).[3]

Perhaps ironically, however, the weakening of the normative grip that liberal and democratic constitutionalism held on these processes is a sign of the success of the transnational legal order. We can see it in the *way* that constitutional norms are being skirted in backsliding states, which often go to great lengths to appear *as if* they still value liberal, constitutional, and democratic norms even while they undermine them in practice. In the world of the legalistic autocrats, hypocrisy now guides the creation of new forms of government, as leaders bent on consolidating power do so wielding the shield of constitutionalism and acting in the name of democracy while they concentrate inordinate and unchecked powers in very few hands. As Francois de La Rochefoucauld famously observed, "Hypocrisy is the tribute that vice pays to virtue."

Successful hypocrisy is not easy to accomplish. Learning how to hide under constitutional cover while attacking constitutionalism's inner normative core requires some fancy legal maneuvering. The aspiring legalistic autocrat needs to assemble a constitutional toolkit that provides the right tools for the job. Advisors to such legalistic autocrats know that their job is to pick from the set of comparative constitutional practices advocated by constitutional TLO experts not the constitutional best practices but instead the *constitutional worst practices.* Constitutional worst practices pass constitutional muster somewhere and therefore are hard to criticize without being accused of double standards, but they assist in undermining the functioning of sincere constitutionalism in the place to which they have been moved.

But note how the new constitutionalism TLO lends itself to being undermined in this way. Under the old constitutional consulting practices, the institutions of the TLO recommended particular solutions for particular

3 Competitive authoritarian governments hold nominally competitive elections on a decidedly non-level playing field; they uphold civil liberties most of the time, but not always. They are structured primarily to keep the governing forces in power. As I will elaborate below, a legalistic autocracy is also a hybrid regime in which there are nominally competitive elections which the opposition parties are highly unlikely to win. But legalistic autocracies make a big show of constitutionalism along with a public display of legalism, making them a particular subset of competitive authoritarian regimes.

places. Those solutions might not have worked, but at least they passed constitutional muster or else they wouldn't have been recommended. Now, however, under the assumption that local knowledge is always necessary to make constitutionalist practices work, the advisors of the TLO present local leaders with a *variety* of alternatives that they could adopt, all of which are – almost by definition – *not* normatively equal. If local leaders are always given choices so that they take ownership by selecting from the set, then they have a big playing field on which to play. Putting together a composite of acceptable alternatives in ways that consolidate power without allowing it to rotate turns out to be quite possible. Every constitutional democratic state has its embarrassing practices that, nonetheless, don't undermine the integrity of democratic constitutionalism as a whole. But in the hands of the legalistic autocrats, these practices can accumulate into a toxic composite.

Take one example: Germany – usually a model of constitutionalist propriety – has an election system featuring highly unequal district sizes for the single-member districts that elect representatives to the Bundestag. The German election law formally permits district size deviation of up to 25 percent and doesn't require redistricting until the variation reaches 33 percent (ACE 2012), despite the fact that the European Commission for Democracy through Law (the Venice Commission) recommends that district sizes vary by no more than 10 percent (European Commission for Democracy through Law, 2002) and the German Federal Constitutional Court has on multiple occasions found the election law to be in violation of the constitutional requirement of equal suffrage (Kommers & Miller 2012: 249–54). As it turns out, the disproportionate effects of skewed district sizes are minimized because half of the representatives in the Bundestag are elected on party lists, and the method of calculating the allocation of seats from party lists restores proportional representation (ACE 2012). But the huge deviation from international norms on district size and the standing violation of Constitutional Court decisions on point is a huge embarrassment to German constitutional lawyers.

If Germany tolerates a particular legal practice, however, how can it be wrong for another country to copy their system? The Hungarian government of Viktor Orbán amended his inherited constitution almost immediately after taking office in 2010, cutting the number of parliamentary seats in half. This required redistricting the whole country and, in the end, the new district sizes varied by up to 25 percent (Scheppele 2014a: Part II), the exact variation tolerated in the German system. The political opposition and a number of international organizations were convinced that there had been gerrymandering (OSCE/ODIHR 2014). But what could be wrong with the Hungarian system if the Germans had done the same thing?[4]

Putting together a complex constitutional system that passes muster as an agglomeration of worst practices requires expertise, however. Even though there is a constitutional consulting consensus that now underwrites the constitutionalism TLO, experts working for these new legalistic autocrats are recommending and road-testing constitutional worst practices. These practices permit constitutional values to be undermined even as acceptable (or tolerable) constitutional forms are preserved. If creating responsive, transparent, human-rights respecting, constitutionalist governments has become the goal of the "do-gooding" international community operating within the TLO, then use of the same constitutional tactics for anti-constitutional purposes had come to be valorized by their "do-badding" opponents.

I should say at the outset that by using the language of "best practices" and "worst practices," "do-gooders," and "do-badders," I don't mean immediately to engage only the normative argument – at least not before I get a descriptive account of what is going on out on the table. Instead, I want to point out that the current constitutional consulting consensus that has been incorporated into the TLO has naturalized a particular normative model (liberal, constitutional, democratic) that can be easily turned on its head by legalistic autocrats who give lip service to constitutionalism and democracy but have no truck with liberalism. These new legalistic autocrats talk the talk of constitutionalism while not walking the walk, which means that they run afoul of the dominant normative consensus in practice while often appearing to honor it in theory. They can do this because the practical realization of constitutionalism occurs in an uneven landscape in which even "good" countries, constitutionally speaking, continue to support "bad" practices, as our example of the German election law shows. If the transnational legal order has codified a normative consensus, then these new do-badding challengers want to appear to sign onto it, while simultaneously undermining what makes the consensus valuable. They can do so by searching the constitutional landscape for worst practices that exist in other imperfect liberal, constitutional democracies and using those practices as models for their own new constitutional orders. The landscape on which this contest plays out is normative through and through because the TLO has normative goals that the legalistic autocrats

[4] Hungary's election system was constructed à la carte from the election systems of a number of different European states. While Hungary has an election system most formally similar to Germany's and it used German standards for redistricting, it used the Italian system for "winner compensation" on the party list side of the calculation, which made the Hungarian system one of the most disproportionate in Europe (Scheppele 2014: Part III).

seek to evade through adopting the worst practices of compliant states, worst practices that often appear among the wares that the constitutional consultants peddle in their role as iterant idea merchants.

Perhaps ironically, the countries I will discuss in this chapter – Hungary, Poland, Russia, Venezuela, Ecuador, Turkey – passed through liberal, democratic constitutionalism as they emerged from the dictatorships that once overtly undermined such values. In developing their first "post-horror" constitutions (Scheppele 2009),[5] many of these countries' transitional leaders embraced the TLO model along with international assistance that helped them to create their first liberal-democratic constitutions in the first place. Many of these countries were the star pupils for the end-of-history narrative when they rode the early waves of international constitution-building assistance. The legalistic autocracies that we will be examining are not engaged in the *first* constitution-making efforts after the fall of the prior dictatorships, but rather are promoting second or later constitutional revisions after constitutional democratic liberalism had already been introduced. This is why these countries often go under the label of "backsliders" because they once had – or at least appeared to have – liberal, democratic constitutions. Just as the transitional democrats embraced the normative model that rejected the history of dictatorship, so too the legalistic autocrats reject liberalism because they believe it has failed.[6] Because of the international consensus, however, legalistic autocrats want to appear to be in the normative mainstream while they go off in their own directions. How do these new autocrats do what they do? They learn from constitutional imperfections and worst practices elsewhere.

The international network that has grown and sustained the consensus around liberal, democratic constitutionalism as well as the efforts by the new autocrats to undermine these principles aids and abets the legalistic autocrats by giving them new ideas to use for toxic ends. To see the terrain on which the legalistic autocrats are playing, we first need to learn how the "end of history" – where there was global normative consensus on the desirability of the liberal, democratic, constitutionalist model – ended.

5 "Post-horror" constitutions are the ones that follow dictatorships that were pervasive violators of human rights.

6 I have long argued that we should think about constitutional creation not as the building of bright futures, but instead as the rejection of immediate pasts (Scheppele 2003; Scheppele 2008). The current widespread rejection of liberalism by the new legalistic autocrats is another example of this general tendency.

THE RISE OF THE LEGALISTIC AUTOCRATS

If we look at the state of governance around the world in recent decades, there is some good news to go along with the bad news about the declining number of democracies in good standing. The *ways* that democracies are being undermined are changing for the better.

If there is now a dominant liberal, democratic constitutional consensus that characterizes the do-gooders in the world, a consensus forged by the TLO, then how do those who want to topple or radically change this consensus proceed? How do "do-badders" counter the "do-gooders" in normative terms? The do-badders do not all agree on an alternative model. As a result, they cannot unite to put forward a new normative vision of governance. Instead, they are united in adopting a similar tactic for hiding behind elections and constitutions: first, they come to power in democratic elections and then they pull up the constitutional ladder after themselves so that no one else can win the next election, or the one after that.

We can see these kinder, gentler tactics in the way that liberal, constitutional, democratic governments are now toppled. The most frequent way to oust an existing government during the Cold War used to be by coup (for coups sponsored by the CIA, see Stuster 2013; for coups sponsored by the KGB, see David 1986). But the good news for those who believe the normative model of the TLO is that coups aren't what they used to be. The number of successful coups peaked in the early 1960s at the height of the Cold War and has been declining ever since, until there was a small uptick again after 2000 (Bermeo 2016). Perhaps more crucial, however, is the sharp decline in what Nancy Bermeo has called the "open-ended coup" (Bermeo 2016) and what Ozan Varol has called the "democratic coup d'état" (2012). Open-ended coups or democratic coups d'état used to bring down governments in one fell swoop with devastating consequences for democratic governance and for the rights of those living in the country. But these have now become rare.

Over the last several decades since the end of the Cold War, we have seen a rise in what Bermeo calls "promissory coups" or gradual "executive aggrandizement" instead. According to Bermeo, promissory coups are disruptions in the democratic order carried out in the name of improving the democracy itself. The new leader (or old leader with new powers) claims to be ridding the democracy of its enemies, not undermining democracy as such. He may even promise to create a better democratic state in the future, hence the term "promissory coup." Alternatively, one now sees in democratically backsliding states a gradual accumulation of executive power under an existing constitution, rather than a complete break with a prior constitutional order. In these less devastating breakdowns of prior governments, the new leaders are typically affirmed through elections (though sometimes with a little help from strategic manipulation). Democracy may be battered, but it still lives. And the coup leaders pledge fealty to their electorates and to governing by constitution. The new democratic backsliders are not like the old-fashioned government-topplers. They often give lip-service to the very democratic values that their activity actively undermines.

As we will see, however, an important subset of the leaders of these new kinder, gentler coups works under constitutional cover. These legalistic autocrats do not usually overthrow constitutions in a sharply illegal way, but they accompany their takeover with constitutional amendments, invocations of constitutional emergency clauses, or sometimes even wholly new constitutions. They portray themselves as leaders dedicated to constitutional order. They, too, seek legitimacy through the (sometimes stuffed) ballot box. As with Bermeo's and Varol's modern-day coup-leaders, these constitutional autocrats purport to share the values of constitutional democracy even as they shake those values to the core.

Compared with a half-century ago at the height of the Cold War, then, the political events that cause democratic decline now are less radical and aim at a less sharp break with the dominant normative order of liberal, democratic constitutionalism. Backsliding is a less drastic and harmful form of democratic decay than a radical overthrow.

What accounts for the change? If there weren't such a consensus about what counts as a legitimate government these days, we would not see so many leaders with questionable motives attempting to justify themselves in the name of constitutional democracy. If there weren't such a consensus about the need for a democratic pedigree of a national leader, we would not see elections occurring nearly everywhere in the world. In short, the TLO itself may be responsible for the kinder, gentler face of coups these days.

How do we know that the TLO is having these effects? Governments that are overthrown without constitutional niceties are sanctioned. For example, the government of Pervez Musharraf, who seized power in a military coup in Pakistan in 1999, was widely sanctioned despite the fact that his government had a great deal of popular support and he promised to restore democracy as soon as possible (Goldberg 1999). But governments that operate within constitutional parameters – even when those constitutions are radically altered – do not attract such harsh global reactions and even pass as democracies in good standing. International practice clearly demonstrates a preference for the kinder, gentler coup, especially if there is no radical break with the prior regime. No wonder that "constitutional coups" are now the preferred method of consolidating and wielding power! In the next section, we will test this by looking at a set of legalistic autocrats and their constitutional reforms to see whether leaders who stay within constitutional tracks are sanctioned less than those who do not.

Against this overwhelming normative pressure coming from the constitutionalism TLO, then, what's a twenty-first century aspiring dictator to do? It is clear that someone who would like to seize power without running into international trouble should make an effort to keep up appearances by continuing to hold elections and by maintaining or writing new constitutions. Such budding dictators should even (sometimes) promote liberalism, even if only in soundbites. But if a budding dictator hollows out these constitutional forms so that they do not work as advertised, but the constitutional forms still exist, this is much harder to check. When constitutional forms are followed, change on the ground does not ring alarm bells – at least not loudly or quickly.

Winning elections and hiding illiberal change behind liberal-sounding constitutions is not a strategy used by all do-badders. For example, the most obvious governments that shun liberal, constitutional democracy are portrayed as nationally specific deviations from global norms with their own distinctive (and therefore non-transmittable) local cultures. China, for example, has never gone in for constitutionalism, nor have the Islamic world's most important challengers to Western hegemony: Saudi Arabia, the Gulf States, and Iran (Garver 2006; Brown 2001). Liberal, democratic constitutionalism is simply not on their maps; they offer no international normative alternative but instead rely on their distinctive national or religious traditions for normative support. They are not challengers to transnational legal order; they have simply opted out of it by claiming a form of exceptionalism.

From our standpoint, the more interesting do-badders are the new crop of legalistic autocrats who take the constitutionalist TLO seriously enough to try to hide behind it. These legalistic autocrats come to power in countries that had in place liberal, democratic constitutional governance, however flawed. These leaders try to maintain that democratic and constitutional façade while they undermine its values. They are often acting in ideological terms, but these are not ideologies that explicitly attack the normative value of democratic and constitutional government. Legalistic autocrats have a variety of home-cooked reasons for opposing the parts of the transnational legal order even as they don't challenge the democratic and constitutionalist hegemony of the constitutionalist TLO.

For example, some legalistic autocrats are opposed to the unipolar world that emerged after 1989 in which the United States and its allies dominated the framework for global governance. These autocrats believe that the lack of competition for leadership in the global community has worked to the disadvantage of countries that do not always play along. For example, while Russia started out as one of the end-of-history cheerleaders, the painful collapse of the Russian economy under neoliberal reform and the visible corruption of the new governing elite soured the public on liberal constitutionalism (Kotkin 2001). Moreover, the fall from being a superpower to being an ordinary middle-sized economy and the accompanying decline in influence in international affairs was more than the new Russian leadership and its battered public could tolerate (Gaidar 2007). Under the leadership of Vladimir Putin, Russia turned its back on liberalism and set its sights on building up state strength that could protect it from second-class status. But however challenging Putin's actions have been to the hegemony of the "West"[7] in international terms, Putin never abandoned the public commitment to democracy and constitutionalism at home. Within Russia, Putin consolidated power within a constitutional footprint and continued to have regular (if flawed) elections. He governs – as he always reminds us – as a democratically elected leader who promised and delivered on "the dictatorship of the law," which was the slogan of his first presidential campaign (Gel'man 2000).

Other countries departed from the end-of-history narrative by opposing neoliberal economic policy in the name of restoring a vibrant new vision for the left. Leaders like Hugo Chávez (followed by Nicolás Maduro) in Venezuela and Rafael Correa in Ecuador developed policies that were intended to free their countries from the grip of neoliberal international financial institutions to send their states on the path of socialism (Elner 2012). But both Chávez and Correa wrote new constitutions rather than proceed without one or operating openly as dictators. And both proceeded to legitimate themselves (and in Chávez's case, his successor) through winning elections. They may have challenged neoliberalism but they did not challenge the need for electoral mandates or constitutional legitimacy.

Still other countries that blew past the end of history narrative did so for religious reasons. Mohamed Morsi's brief Muslim Brotherhood government

7 The "West" is no longer a description of a place, but instead a description of an ideology. This ideology is characterized by a self-conscious dedication to a particular political trajectory that began with the late-eighteenth century revolutions and that has since followed a path toward expanding the democratic franchise, increasing the respect for rights, developing governance systems that constrain the power of executives, and engaging in liberal internationalism. In short, it is the "end of history" that is now institutionalized in the TLO. This path is obviously not hard-wired into a country's history, nor is it necessarily followed in a linear fashion. And the creation of a liberal, democratic constitutional order is not – as we will see – an irreversible achievement.

in Egypt and Recep Tayyip Erdoğan's entrenched AKP government in Turkey claimed popular support on the basis of restoring Islam to public life (Ramadan 2011). Both Morsi and Erdogan radically transformed the constitutions they inherited, and made much of their constitutional transformations – as much for being constitutional as for being transformations. Here, too, election victories sealed their legitimacy and their constitutional reforms sealed their accumulated power (Trofimov 2016).

Another siren-call to depart from the end-of-history narrative has come from nationalists. Viktor Orbán in Hungary and Jaroslav Kaczyński in Poland rode waves of popular discontent to overwhelming election victories by campaigning against the globalizing elites that had preceded them and by promising pride in national sovereignty free of meddling external influences. To seal the deal, Orbán enacted a new constitution while Kaczyński has so far not had the parliamentary supermajority to do so – but he clearly aspires to constitutional change nonetheless. (As I write, the Polish government has started discussing a possible referendum to enact a new constitution and Orbán has announced after his third successive electoral victory that he, too, may preside over yet another constitutional drafting process.) Both claim their personal legitimacy derives from their ability to win elections and their normative legitimacy derives from their ability to speak in the name of nationalist constitutional principles.

As this list indicates, the motivations for challenging some aspects of hegemony of the "West" on the part of the legalistic autocrats are many. But each of these countries that challenges particular facets of the hegemonic control of the end-of-history narrative also sees itself as crucially tied to democratic constitutionalism at the same time. While all these leaders have struck out on their own in some ways, they also wanted to legitimate their rule through democratic and constitutional (if not liberal) form. It is this apparent public support of the constitutionalist transnational legal order on the part of its biggest challengers that shows that liberal, democratic, constitutional government is the only legitimate (and legitimizing) game in town.

CONSTITUTIONAL COUPS AND CONSTITUTIONAL COVER

How can we understand these new legalistic autocrats who challenge aspects of the global order[8] while maintaining a public commitment to democracy and constitutional government? I have called these new constitution-

[8] The "global order" is broader than any particular transnational legal order and includes a set of organizing practices that go beyond law.

respecting, democracy-maintaining revolutions against prior liberal governments "constitutional coups":

> A constitutional coup is constitutional because there is no break in legality, never a moment when a government does something formally illegal to attain its desired goals. It is nonetheless a coup because the end result turns the prior constitutional order on its head without a legitimating process to confirm the changes. Through a series of perfectly legal moves the constitutionally devious leaders of a state can achieve a substantively anti-constitutional result, including, in the extreme case, transforming a state in plain sight from a constitutional democracy to an autocracy, all the while appearing to honor the constitution. (Scheppele 2014c: 51)

Constitutional coups gut the prior democratic, liberal, constitutionalist ideology of state by keeping constitutional and democratic forms while removing the liberal content (Corrales 2015).

The script for doing so is now familiar. First, an aspiring power-hungry leader wins a domestic election, sometimes as freely and fairly as the country's preexisting election laws permit, but sometimes with a little help from electoral manipulation. Sometimes this leader takes advantage of a national or international crisis to do so. Armed with an electoral mandate and speaking in its name, the budding autocrat then undertakes constitutional or other major institutional changes to consolidate power quickly before the bloom is off the electoral rose, to so speak. These constitutional moves are sometimes accomplished through drafting wholly new constitutions; sometimes constitutional amendments suffice. Sometimes the aspiring autocrat amends ordinary laws to change structural features of key institutions. Sometimes capturing the appointments process for particular offices is enough to achieve the desired aims. Whichever path is taken, the targets to be neutralized are clear: the independent judiciary, particularly constitutional courts (where they exist); the pluralistic media; independent bodies of state, particularly the transparency and accountability institutions; and civil society, particularly the organizations controlled by the political opposition. All of this has to be done under cover of law and in the name of a democratic mandate. This is no easy trick.

In what follows, I will sample from the tactics used to consolidate power within constitutional boundaries used by some of the most visible and successful constitutional legalistic autocrats, including Vladimir Putin of Russia, Hugo Chávez in Venezuela, Rafael Correa in Ecuador, Recep Tayyib Erdoğan in Turkey, Viktor Orbán in Hungary, and Jaroslav Kaczyński in Poland. By examining these cases, we can see not only how each of these leaders consolidated their power in constitutional terms, but also how the "international community" (that is, the TLO) reacted to these developments.

All of the changes that I will discuss happened in plain sight, especially for people who pay attention to comparative constitutional law and who therefore know how to analyze legal changes beyond press releases and political speeches. The fact that some of these tactics spread from place to place could easily have been a function of the constitutional advisers in one country picking up from public sources what they have seen in other places, or it could have been constitutional advisers moving from place to place. But the spread of constitutional worst practices suggests that there is a toolkit in use that provides handy fixes for overly liberal systems while maintaining the façade of democratic constitutionalism, especially if other autocrats get away with the particular fix first without being criticized by the community that constitutes the TLO.

Presidents Chávez in Venezuela and Correa in Ecuador used their first term in office to rewrite their national constitutions. Later, Prime Minister Viktor Orbán of Hungary did the same. While Vladimir Putin contemplated rewriting the Russian constitution in his first term of office to move the country from a presidential to parliamentary system, ultimately he decided against it,[9] but he consolidated powers in other ways. Recep Tayyib Erdoğan in Turkey has rewritten the constitution to move from parliamentarism to presidentialism, concentrating power in new super-presidency through series of constitutional amendments (Watmough, Öztürk, Tittensor and Yilmaz, 2017). Jaroslav Kaczyński in Poland aspires to change the constitution, but has moved forward with unconstitutional legislation in the absence of a constitutional majority in parliament. To get away with it, he disabled the Constitutional Council so that it cannot nullify the unconstitutional laws. We will look at each of these cases in detail.

Hugo Chávez was elected president of Venezuela in 1998 with the rallying cry that the country was in crisis and needed a new constitution. He won the

9 I know this because I worked as a researcher at the Russian Constitutional Court in 2003, where some staffers had seen a draft constitution produced by the Presidential Administration at Putin's request. The reason for the constitutional rewrite was the eventual problem of term limits that would bite in 2008. In a parliamentary system, prime ministers do not typically have term limits because it is assumed that they are accountable to parliaments that will hold them in check. But, in the political context of Russia at the time, there was really only one well-organized party and that party would invariably support Putin. In the end, Putin opted to swap places with his prime minister for one term, during which time the constitution was amended to increase the length of the presidency from four to six years. My sources who said that a draft of a new constitution was in circulation within the presidential administration were confirmed by others who heard the same whispers in Russian elite political circles (Colton and Skach 2005).

election by a narrow margin but won a referendum to start a new constitution-making process with an overwhelming vote: 81 percent approved, though on a low turnout (Brewer-Carías 2010). He designed the rules for election of representatives to a constituent assembly in a way that gave his party 95 percent of the seats in the assembly with 60 percent of the popular vote (Landau 2013). The new constitution that resulted from a convention full of "Chávistas" (as Chávez supporters were called) gave Chávez everything he wanted. It established a strong presidency and eliminated the Senate which had been an important constraint on executive power before that time. It gave the president the power to call referenda to recall specific legislators, which handed the president a Sword of Damocles to hang over the head of any legislator who resisted his programs. It banned funding for political parties, weakening the opposition. And it gave the president the power to propose constitutional amendments, giving him effective control over any future constitutional change (Corrales 2015). The sum total of the changes greatly strengthened the power of the president.

Were any of these changes outside of the constitutional consensus typical of the TLO? Not really. Many democracies in good standing have no upper house of parliament (Constitution Unit 1998), so eliminating the Venezuelan Senate – while a radical move in the local context – could not be deemed to have removed an essential element of constitutional design[10] Ditto on the recall of specific legislators. While it may be a bit unusual to give the power to call a recall referendum to the president, citizen recall of legislators through referenda is explicitly contemplated in the advice given by the gold standard of constitutional advising, International IDEA (International IDEA 2008: Chapter 5).[11] Many countries, including the United States, have little or no public funding for political parties, so this cannot be a core normative principle of constitutionalism (International IDEA 2014a).[12] In addition, many countries require presidential approval (if not always initiation) of constitutional amendments (International IDEA 2014b), though this is more common in presidential and hyper-presidential systems, which have their own problems. But given all of this, what could be wrong with Chávez's constitution?

10 Mario Renzi's proposed constitutional reforms in Italy included a radical weakening of the Italian Senate, a move that has been praised in TLO circles for making Italy more governable (Clementi 2016). But these reforms were defeated in a referendum and Renzi stepped down (Kirchgaessner and Guiffrida 2016).

11 In addition to Venezuela, the constitutions of Ecuador, Ethiopia, Peru, Taiwan also contain such mechanisms.

12 International IDEA's handbook shows the massive variation in funding schemes. This means that, while some approaches can count as best practices, others are worst practices and yet cannot be fully condemned because they are in use in some reasonable democracies.

Take these major changes one by one, and they may not represent constitutional best practices, but they are not disqualifying ones. Most of the criticism of the Chávez experiment in transforming the Venezuelan democratic project has been ideological instead of constitutional (Gargarella 2012).

International criticism was far more pronounced when Chávez proposed constitutional amendments in 2007 that would have extended the presidential term from six to seven years and would have removed term limits so that he could run for president indefinitely. The amendments would also have given the president direction of the central bank and more control over regional governors as well as banning foreign funding of NGOs. The amendments were narrowly defeated and Chávez accepted the defeat – for a while. In 2009, he brought back the abolition of presidential term limits in another constitutional amendment package, this time combined with the abolition of term limits for members of the parliament, regional governors, and local officials. That set of amendments passed.

Blowing past term limits, however, is a TLO no-no. In fact, removing term limits is one of those few points of consensus about specific constitutional structures in the TLO (International IDEA, 2015b). It is virtually always taken as a sign that a current national executive intends to abuse his power when the abolition of term limits comes up. But while the practice is generally condemned, it is also widely practiced (Ginsburg, Melton, & Elkins 2011). By the time that Chávez got constitutional permission to keep running for office, however, he was cut down by cancer instead.

Modeling himself explicitly on Chávez in tailoring a constitution to a new legalistic autocracy, Rafael Correa "came to office with the view that winning the presidency was, at best, a prelude to a more profound struggle for political power one that would involve confronting rivals both within the state and in society at large" (Conaghan 2008: 46–7). He called for a new constitution in Ecuador as soon as he was elected president in 2006 with a 73 percent approval rating.

Emphasizing his democratic mandate, Correa proclaimed that he was leading a "citizens' revolution":

> During the campaign we were clearly aware that what we were proposing was a revolution, understood as a radical and rapid change in the existing structures of Ecuadorean society, in order to change the bourgeois state into a truly popular one. Faced with the delegitimization of the political class, which no longer represented anyone except itself, we said to ourselves that it was we citizens who had to reveal its inadequacies. So we decided to call it a citizens' revolution, a revolt of indignant citizens. (Correa 2012)

Correa governed as a plebiscitary president, using "direct, unmediated appeals to public opinion in order to govern 'over the heads' of other institutions, especially legislatures . . . With the public's overwhelming approval, he rendered Congress totally irrelevant" (Conaghan 2008: 47).

Against this background, Correa's new constitution was approved in a referendum in 2008 with 64 percent public support. It mixed "hyperpresidentialism with an expanded list of rights" (Conaghan 2008). The 1998 constitution that the Correa constitution replaced already had expansive presidential powers, which were maintained. The Correa constitution, like the Chávez constitution, put the power to call national referenda into the president's hands, which enabled him to continue his plebiscitary presidency. In addition, Correa was given the power to veto not just whole laws, but also parts of laws, which gave him the power to hand-pick just which parts of the legislature's work he would endorse (Conaghan 2016). The 2008 constitution allowed Correa to run for reelection once, something that the 1998 constitution did not permit.

Did the new Ecuadorian constitution run afoul of international norms? As an International IDEA publication noted in a formula that showed how well Correa skirted the edge of the transnational constitutional consensus: "It is important to note that while President Correa may not be a political tyrant, he is not exactly a liberal democrat either" (International IDEA 2015b). Strong presidents had been the norm in Latin America; it would be hard for the "international community" to condemn the practice when strong presidencies did not automatically turn all Latin American presidents into dictators, and where the US model constantly acted as a counter-example (Landau 2015; Mainwaring and Shugart 1997).

Gaining the power to bypass the legislature by calling national referenda is also not an unusual practice, so it is hard to condemn in general.[13] The line-

[13] But International IDEA has been skeptical of executives calling referenda especially in Latin America:

"Executives have also initiated referendums in order to demonstrate popular support for a specific political decision. Governments often claim that this is their main or only reason for organizing a referendum, whereas the true motivation may be (and often is) provided by political and tactical considerations. Such political and tactical reasons for initiating referendums have been criticized from a democratic point of view because here the referendum instrument has been used not in order to strengthen popular sovereignty and increase political equality but rather to bypass popular control and maintain or even extend the authority of the executive. Both democratic and authoritarian governments can initiate referendums, which may contribute to the stability and efficiency of the regime. Thus, a large number of referendums held in Latin America have been called by the executive branch ... Some referendums called by the executive in Latin America were attempts to legitimize authoritarian regimes, but such attempts have not always been successful" (International IDEA 2008: 49).

item veto, which was crucial in Ecuador in moving power from the parliament to the president, is something that has been sought for years by the US President and is not unheard of elsewhere. As International IDEA noted, "[T]he line-item veto has become common in US states (about 90 per cent of US states allow governors to exercise a line-item veto) and at the national level in Latin America (e.g. Argentina, art. 83; Brazil, art. 66; Paraguay, art. 208)" (International IDEA 2015b). How could that common tool be criticized?

Though Correa was not attacked by the TLO for his new constitution, when Correa approached the end of his second term in office under this new constitution, he sought to amend it to allow himself to run again in 2017. The National Assembly agreed but 80 percent of the public told pollsters that they did not approve of the change. The National Assembly then modified the constitutional amendment to make reelection indefinite only starting after the next election, to which the amendment would not apply and, conceding the point, Correa said he would not run for the presidency again. In the subsequent election, Correa's loyalist Lenín Moreno ran and won. But Correa and Moreno feuded constantly; in the end Moreno called a referendum that would amend the constitution to institute an absolute ban on a president ever returning after he had served two terms, even after a break. The Ecuadorian public passed the referendum by a two-to-one margin and Correa is now blocked from running again (Associated Press, February 5, 2018). So far, the constitutional limits are holding.

The abolition of term limits is one of those red lines that virtually always raises international concern. For example, the International IDEA blog expressed concern about the Latin American trend toward throwing out term limits to benefit current incumbents, calling out Chávez and Correa in particular (Landau, July 21, 2015). The *Journal of Democracy* published an article analyzing the effects of the removal of presidential term limits, showing that it was often a tool of autocrats in training (Corrales and Penfold 2014). One wonders whether the abolition of term limits in both Venezuela and Ecuador was saved for a constitutional amendment after the original constitution was drafted to make it less visible to international audiences and to make the autocratic tendencies of the new constitutions less clear. Both Chávez and Correa saw little criticism of their constitutional overhauls, until they touched the question of presidential terms.

Viktor Orbán, Hungary's prime minister, also opted for constitutional revolution, having won 53 percent of the vote in 2010 which, under Hungary's disproportionate election law, awarded his Fidesz party 67 percent of the seats in the Parliament Under the constitution Orbán inherited, a single two-thirds vote of the Parliament could change anything in the constitution, so his party won the possibility of changing the constitution at will. Even though constitutional reform was not mentioned during the election campaign, Orbán's Fidesz government quickly embarked on an ambitious and immediate program of constitutional change for which it needed – and for which it accepted – no input from other parties. It first promulgated a "Statement of National Cooperation" that was to be compulsorily displayed in public buildings (Hungarian Government 2010) that laid out the nationalist template to follow.

In its first year in office, the new Fidesz government amended the constitution it inherited twelve times before pushing through the Parliament a new constitution (the "Fundamental Law") one year into its term. The amendments of the old constitution facilitated the concentration of power in the hands of the party by changing the way constitutional judges were nominated to give the Fidesz government complete control over appointments and by cutting the size of the Parliament in half so that electoral reform could begin immediately. These amendments also removed the obstacles to drafting a new constitution by removing from the constitution the clause that required a four-fifths majority, which the government did not have, to agree to procedures for writing a new constitution. Both the amendments to the old constitution and the new constitution were adopted with the votes of only the governing party (Bánkuti, Halmai, & Scheppele 2012).

The new constitutional order reorganized many of the state's standing bodies, including the Constitutional Court, Supreme Court, ordinary judiciary, National Council of Judges, Media Council, Budget Council, National Bank, Election Commission, and Ombudsmen's Offices (Bánkuti, Halmai, & Scheppele 2012). These reorganizations were frequently accompanied by the removal before the completion of their terms of incumbent officials in the predecessor institutions and by the extension of the terms of office for the new Fidesz-backed officials who replaced them in the new institutions. While the constitution retained unicameral parliamentarism, at least on paper, the new constitutional order shifted power strongly toward the prime minister.

Given the plasticity of constitutional norms in the TLO about state structures, however, the general reorganization of the structural constitution was not generally criticized by international bodies. Instead, international critics focused on the procedure used to enact the constitution, which had been non-transparent, excluded the political opposition, and was done in a mad rush.

The new Fundamental Law was reviewed by the European Commission for Democracy through Law (the Venice Commission)[14] which opined: "It is regrettable that the constitution-making process, including the drafting and the final adoption of the new Constitution, has been affected by a lack of transparency, shortcomings in the dialogue between the majority and the opposition, the insufficient opportunities for an adequate public debate, and a very tight timeframe" (Venice Commission 2011b: Paragraph 144). The US State Department also noted with concern in its 2012 Human Rights Report that "[t]he government [of Hungary] used its two-thirds parliamentary majority to implement constitutional reform, the speed and extent of which raised concerns that checks and balances were eroding" and called attention to "little or no minority consultation in many cases" (US Department of State 2012: Executive Summary). The European Parliament also condemned the one-sided and strictly majoritarian nature of the Hungarian constitutional drafting process (European Parliament 2011: Paragraph E).

But almost no one criticized most of the substance of the new constitution. They could not; Hungary had violated few existing international norms. The Venice Commission's opinion on the new constitution made a few gentle suggestions; the constitution should be less detailed on economic policy and more detailed on the structure of the judiciary, for example. Had the government chosen to leave out a bill of rights or to overtly deny the independence of the judiciary, then that would have been an issue. De facto independence of the judiciary and the actual realization of rights was another matter, beyond the reach of the constitutional consultant. But since the constitution gave lip service to all the right values, except in the bombastic nationalist preamble, which the Venice Commission was inclined to downplay,[15] Hungary passed its new-constitution check-up with (almost) flying colors. Simply rearranging familiar institutional forms so that they concentrated power in the hands of the prime minister was harder to challenge because it was harder to demonstrate.

Constitutional democracies in good standing come in all kinds of shapes and flavors. It would be hard to pick out a feature of any well-drafted constitution that did not have some close relatives elsewhere. And Hungary had a well-

[14] The Venice Commission might be considered a core institution of the constitutional TLO as it provides expertise in drafting new constitutions, evaluations of major new laws, and assessments of the compliance of national constitutions and legislation with international norms.

[15] "The relevance of the Preamble for the Constitution's interpretation and some potentially problematic statements and terms contained therein … gave reason to question and would call for adequate clarification by the Hungarian authorities" (Venice Commission 2011: Para. 149).

drafted constitution, which the government defended by pointing to all of the other countries that had this form of judicial review, or that form of parliamentary system, or some distinctive form of appointments process to independent agencies. Was unicameral government a problem? No, because even within the EU there are many unicameral parliaments. Was removing the *actio popularis* petition from the Constitutional Court's jurisdiction a problem? No, because Hungary was the only country in Europe that ever had such an option in the first place.[16] Was having the President of the Republic elected by the parliament a problem? No, because that was the system Hungary had when Parliament was admitted, with no objections, to the EU. The government's experts who drafted the constitution had done their homework in comparative law and knew that there were always unobjectionable examples of each individual point in the constitution to be used against critics who challenged it. Despite international criticism of the process, the government of Hungary emerged relatively unscathed in international perspective on the content of the constitution itself, albeit with strongly consolidated power. Hungary's new constitution passed TLO muster.

With Putin's and Erdoğan's proposals for constitutional change – only the latter of which was finally enacted – we see strategic choices of political system to match the particular configuration of support on the ground. Putin entertained the idea of moving from presidentialism to parliamentarism and Erdoğan was able to accomplish a switch the other way around. Each was designed to ensure its respective leader a long time in power. In principle, nothing is wrong with either presidentialism or parliamentarism so it is hard for the international community to criticize either system, or even the switch from one to another.[17] It is the motivation for switching that raises eyebrows but motivation is hard to prove. But it is also a testament to the strength of the TLO's norms that the apparently easier option – simply abolishing term limits in Russia, for example, or rigging elections in Turkey – was considered more costly as it would make these leaders' ambitions completely clear.

In 2003, Vladimir Putin (or perhaps more accurately, people in the close circle of his presidential administration) contemplated switching from

[16] That said, the Venice Commission noted that the *actio popularis* petition had served an important function in Hungarian democracy and they regretted its demise. But they could not insist that Hungary retain it: "The Venice Commission would like to stress that the availability of an *actio popularis* in matters of constitutionality cannot be regarded as a European standard" (Venice Commission 2011a: Paragraph 57).

[17] For a long time, presidentialism was condemned for its dictatorial tendencies (Linz, 1990). But that criticism has since softened with new evidence from Latin America (Mainwaring and Shugart, 1997).

a presidential to a parliamentary system in order to evade the term limits that would bite in 2008. In a parliamentary system, prime ministers do not typically have term limits because it is assumed that they are accountable to parliaments that will hold them in check. In the political context of Russia at the time, there was really only one well-organized political party, United Russia, and that party would invariably support Putin given that he controlled the fates of all individual party members. Critics also darkly guessed that Putin would never allow another party to gain that level of power but those criticisms almost always came from political analysts who were critical of Putin's challenges to a unipolar world and not from institutions that were part of the TLO. Parliamentarism seemed a safe system for keeping Putin in power for the foreseeable future because it was inconceivable at the time that Putin would ever lose his parliamentary majority. But a move to parliamentarism would have been just fine with the TLO.

In the end, Putin declined the constitutional reform and opted to swap places with his prime minister for one term, during which time the constitution was amended to increase the length of the presidency from four to six years (Pan 2008). The move to lengthen presidential terms was immediately seen by foreign critics as guaranteeing Putin the opportunity to be czar for life (*The Economist*, November 8, 2008). When Putin ran for president again after his one-term time-out, he became eligible to stay in office for twelve years with only one reelection, which occurred easily in the absence of meaningful competition.

The increased length of the term of the Russian president was taken as a sign of constitutional dictatorship by Putin's political critics. But what could be wrong with lengthening the term of office, a Russian constitutional expert might ask? France had an independently elected president with a seven-year term for nearly a half century without falling into dictatorship![18] Indeed France's super-long super-presidency had been criticized for a long time, which did not prevent France from being considered a constitutional democracy in good standing (Knight 2001). Surely, Russia's six-year presidency was within reasonable international legal limits. International criticism was directed at Putin and what observers thought he was up to, not to the constitutional system as such.

We see the opposite move in Turkey, where Recep Tayyib Erdoğan has steadily consolidated power over the last decade, finally ending in a dictatorship that Freedom House has judged in 2018 to be "not free." He

[18] The 1958 constitution established the seven-year presidency, which was amended in 2000 to shorten the term to five years (Duhamel 2000).

originally rode an electoral wave to victory, as his AKP party won the parliamentary elections in 2003, the first overtly Islamist party to do so.[19] For his first six years in office, he supported legal reforms that enabled Turkey to comply with Council of Europe human rights norms for the first time as he steered his country toward joining the EU (Scharfe 2015). But when the European door slammed in his face, he took his country in a different direction: toward more centralized control. As he began to worry that his electoral support might not last forever, he opted for presidentialism over parliamentarism.

Toward that end, Erdoğan was able to first amend the constitution to make the presidency a directly elected office, replacing the then-existing system in which the Parliament elected the president. Since presidentialism is a widely accepted political system and direct election of presidents seems even more democratic than parliamentary election, it was hard for the "international community" to challenge the proposal as such.

But international criticism started when Erdoğan pushed through a package of constitutional amendments in 2010, strengthening the power of the presidency at the expense of the Constitutional Court. The AKP President Abdullah Gül referred the constitutional package to the people – where the AKP Prime Minister Erdoğan was able to win 58 percent support for the thirty new provisions, affecting twenty-three articles of the constitution (Ciddi 2011). Some provisions strengthened rights – notably the rights of families, children, workers, and women who wear the headscarf – and also removed the special privileges of the military. But other provisions gutted the judicial checks on the executive branch. Under the constitutional amendments, the Constitutional Court was enlarged from eleven to eighteen judges and the president was given the power to name fourteen of the eighteen judges. The Supreme Board of Judges and Prosecutors – a body that handles judicial and prosecutorial appointments, promotions, disciplinary procedures, and dismissals – was expanded as well, giving the president more control over those who would select the ordinary judges and prosecutors.

Reaction to these constitutional changes from the international community was mixed. The EU welcomed the new rights provisions and abstained from comment on the rest. While some constitutional experts attacked Erdoğan for packing the Constitutional Court (Halmai 2012), others contextualized the changes in the local political context by noting that the Constitutional Court had repeatedly struck down AKP legislation on the basis of constitutional secularism that the public no longer supported (Bali 2013). Those opposed

[19] I should say that it was the first Islamist party to be *allowed* to do so. All of the previous religious parties had been dissolved by party bans (Kogacioglu 2004).

to court-packing worried about executive infringement on judicial independence while those in favor of the changes argued that the court had blocked democratic change for decades and needed to be reformed. In short, the debate was joined over how to balance constitutionalism and democracy, both staples of intra-TLO debate.

After the constitutional amendments, Erdoğan's AKP party won a huge electoral victory in 2011, so a multi-party constitutional drafting committee was formed to write a new constitution, something all parties had agreed was desirable given that the 1982 constitution still in effect had been written under military supervision after the last coup. But even though there was agreement across the political spectrum on many aspects of the change, the process foundered over the issue of presidentialism:

> AKP proposals for a stronger presidency or even a full presidential system were viewed as unacceptable by the opposition as a whole. The opposition parties knew that a powerful presidency would suit Erdoğan's personal political ambitions perfectly, and it is largely for this reason that the constitutional reform process slowed to a halt and finally collapsed at the end of 2013. (Scharfe 2015)

Erdoğan was so confident that he would eventually be able to remake the presidency into the strongest position in the constitutional order that he ran for president and won in 2014 before all of his desired powers had been transferred to that office. In anticipation of the enlarged presidency, he even built an enlarged presidential palace (with 1,100 rooms), but he was blocked in gaining the power he sought in the constitution itself because he lacked a constitutional majority in the parliament. Worse yet for him, he lost his simple parliamentary majority with the June 2015 election, but he quickly found a way around that temporary setback. He called a snap election for November 2015 and won back his parliamentary majority though with not quite enough seats to pass a new constitution (Önis 2016). He again tried to push constitutional reform again in a multi-party process, but failed (Özsov 2016).

With the attempted coup in July 2016 and Erdoğan's subsequent announcement that he would push constitutional reform again, the path was cleared for Erdoğan to finally succeed in his presidential ambitions and govern like a dictator. With the country on edge after the coup and Erdoğan's hard crackdown on every sign of dissidence or opposition, a constitutional referendum giving unlimited powers to the president passed in April 2017 (Shaheen 2017). Erdoğan wasted no time in consolidating all state power, marginalizing the parliament, crushing the judiciary, jailing his opponents, and ending democracy in Turkey. By that time, criticism from the TLO community was too late.

Jaroslav Kaczyński of Poland's Law and Justice (PiS) party has been heavily criticized by the TLO community because he has acted without the shield of constitutional protection. Since the 2015 election of PiS candidates first to the presidency of Poland and then to a majority of seats in the Parliament a constitutional revolution has begun there as well. The leader of the revolution is Kaczyński, the head of PiS and formally an MP in the Parliament but he has no formal state position that reflects his influence. Both President Andrzej Duda and then-Prime Minster Beata Szydło openly deferred to him while he operated from the shadows of the constitutional order without having an official role.

Without the constitutional majority to change the constitution legally, Kaczyński is leading what experts have described as a constitutional coup d'état (Sadurski 2016). Statutes in blatant violation of the existing constitution were being passed by the PiS majority in the Parliament. Then, when the Constitutional Tribunal struck them down, the government refused to publish the decisions of the Court and claimed that therefore the decisions had no legal effect. Poland represents a classic case of the overt do-badder operating without the benefit of constitutional cover. And not surprisingly, the international community came down on Poland hard.

The Venice Commission issued a highly critical opinion backing the Constitutional Tribunal's efforts to restore constitutionalism (Venice Commission 2016). For good measure, the Council of Europe Human Rights Commissioner chimed in too (Muižnieks 2016). The European Commission, which had been rather muted in response to the Hungarian constitutional revolution (Scheppele 2014c), suddenly sprang into action, invoking its "rule of law framework" in January 2016 (European Commission 2016a), pressuring Poland through the following two years before issuing a "reasoned opinion" to the Council of Ministers, urging activation of the warning mechanism in Article 7 of the Treaty on European Union against Poland (European Commission, 2017). The Commission demanded that the Polish government honor the decisions of the Constitutional Court and stop tinkering with the judiciary. In short, when the Polish government acted illegally under its own law and refused to keep up appearances under the TLO, the international community united quickly in its condemnation of Poland.

From these examples – Venezuela under Chávez, Ecuador under Correa, Hungary under Orbán, Russia under Putin, Turkey under Erdoğan, and Poland under Kaczyński – we can see that there is a TLO in place that generally approves when change occurs pursuant to democratic elections and in constitutional form, almost no matter what the content. But we can also see that changing the structural provisions of constitutions so as to consolidate power in the hands of an all-powerful executive is hard for the TLO to identify and criticize because most of the rules and institutions used for this consolidation will be included in the set of options that are on offer from the TLO as its consultants roam the world instructing on constitutional possibilities. Apart from the disapproval of extending the constitutionally permissible time that presidents can stay in office or overtly engaging in court-packing, no other methods of concentrating power generate sustained criticism because some other constitutional-democratic state in good standing can always be found to demonstrate that this particular institutional form can be used without danger. Of course, abandoning all pretense of constitutional government by overtly violating the existing constitution generates intense criticism. Stealthy attacks under cover of constitutionalism pass the TLO unnoticed.

It is important to note that the TLO has a consensus over rights and how they must be observed, but the new legalistic autocrats are not usually engaged in massive rights violations until very late in the process of constitutional consolidation when they have already won. Instead of touching rights, budding autocrats are typically seeking to gain unlimited power by removing checks and balances. But hollowing liberal constitutions out from the inside through concentrating power and preventing its rotation is outside the field of vision in the TLO except in extreme cases, and only then after the damage has been done.

When legalistic autocrats step out from under constitutional cover, however, we see the transnational institutions of the TLO start to attack. With Erdoğan's use of emergency powers in Turkey to finally seize all power, and with Kaczyński overtly violating the constitution in Poland, international criticism has been fast, sharp, and overwhelming. No wonder the others have tried to appear to follow the norms of the TLO!

TOWARD SELF-SUSTAINING DEMOCRACY

What are TLO entrepreneurs and their state champions to do when other states fall from normative grace? On one hand, the very existence of a TLO means that there is substantial normative consensus about the normative shape of a particular area of law that is institutionalized at transnational, national, and local levels. But on the other hand, the consensus may not be very sharp as it applies to concrete examples on the ground. The vague positive ideas that float around a TLO may have attracted consensus only because they are vague. This would not be the only time that law has had an attraction in theory that it was unable to cash out in practice. As Karl Llewellyn famously said to the first-year law students at Columbia Law School when he gave the lectures that turned into *The Bramble Bush*: "You have come here to embark upon the study of the law . . . [A]round [the law] I take it, there floats a pleasant haze. If it were not pleasant, you would not be here. Perhaps you would not, if there were no haze" (Llewellyn 1930: 3).

The transnational legal order around constitutions is also full of pleasant haze as it attempts to encourage liberal and democratic constitutions with all of the good things they promise. There is clear international agreement that a government that breaks its own constitution deserves criticism; the (relatively) swift reaction to the Polish government's activity when it passed unconstitutional laws and then tried to muzzle the Constitutional Tribunal when it said so, or the criticism of the Turkish government for calling a state of emergency and engaging in a massive purge of all critics, shows as much. It is also clear that certain particular tactics, in particular removing presidential term limits or engaging in overt court-packing, also generate some push back from the TLO.

But legalistic autocrats these days are cleverer than the guardians of the liberal constitutionalist TLO. They recognize that the world's constitutions are full of worst practices just as they are full of best practices. Very long terms of presidential office have graced constitutions that have passed TLO muster. So have other executive-enhancing practices like authorizing executive line-item vetoes, allowing presidents to call referenda to bypass legislative proposals, and assigning the president the ability to appoint judges to a peak court. In each case, there are other perfectly reasonable democracies that have those constitutional arrangements, which makes it hard for the TLO community to criticize these practices. Thus, the consensus seems to be that unless all – or even most – uses of a particular constitutional practice lead to dictatorship, then a state can escape with only mild condemnation at most.

If the TLO around constitutionalism is to have any traction at stopping the decline of liberal, democratic, constitutional systems, it will need better diagnostics to tell when a constitutional system is in trouble and more consensus over what norms are to be enforced. Of course, if such a consensus were easy, it would have been reached already. I think that making progress on this point requires changing the frame.

We might start by changing the method that institutions within the TLO use. The constitutionalist TLO-consulting community loves checklists. If we browse through the main activities of some of the key transnational institutions at the core of the TLO, we find that they have divided up good governance through constitutionalism into a number of manageable pieces, each of which gets separate treatment. Go to the International IDEA website and one must immediately choose whether to focus on one branch of government or another, and within each branch, one must further concentrate on specific issues to get advice.[20] Separate pieces written by different teams of authors cover one part of the state at a time: how to design a sensible legislature, build an independent judiciary, and work out whether decentralized government is a good thing in the particular location. But nothing puts the pieces together into a coherent whole. Consult the National Democratic Institute website, in the democratic governance section, and one is immediately directed to various specific issues. For example, one can get advice on legislative committee structures, the role of the speaker and so on but nothing on the overall need for legislative checks on executive power. The United Nations Development Program's Guidance Note on Constitutional Drafting Processes deals primarily with getting the right process in place for drafting constitutions and says little about substance (United Nations Development Program 2014). One has to look up advice for each particular issue one by one – how to draw election districts, how to include more women in legislatures, how to set up the internal management of the judiciary, or how to write a constitution – without in the end going back to some coherent vision of what a constitution should do once all of the parts are in place and interacting.

Even the gold standard institution providing constitutionalist advice, the Venice Commission, deals with one issue at a time, usually one law at a time. When the Hungarian constitutional consolidation was proceeding apace, for example, the Venice Commission sent a team first to assess pieces of the draft constitution, then the new constitution as a whole, then particular constitutional amendments. While that made a certain amount of sense since they constituted a sequence, other more specialized evaluations were being organized along the way as one-off assessments. So there were separate teams to review the media law (twice), the reorganization of the judiciary (twice), the reorganization of the Constitutional Court, the new election law, the new law on ethnic minorities, the new law on religious organizations, the new law

20 International IDEA's Practical Guide to Constitution Building advertises its own flexibility. As the guide explains, one can download the whole book or one can download each chapter separately. Chapters focus on human rights, executive branch, legislative branch, judiciary, and decentralization (federalism). One chapter deals with "cross-cutting issues" and references political principles (like the role of religion in the state). Each chapter is written by a different team of authors and, while they are not flat-out contradictory, they also do not work together to create a systemic picture of constitutionalism as such (International IDEA, 2013).

reorganizing the prosecutor's office, the new freedom of information act, and so on. To its credit, the Venice Commission itself assigned one particular set of experts to the general constitutional revisions (in three stages) so there was continuity within a single subject matter. The Venice Commission did the same for repeat analyses of a particular area where the job had to be done twice because of amendments that were alleged not to have met the first set of criticisms (with regard to the media and judiciary, in particular). That said, the Venice Commission teams were clearly limited by their mandate (and the translations available to them) to review one law at a time. Because different experts worked on different aspects of the constitutional consolidation of power, no particular team got to see everything. Each individual assessment swam in its own lane, so to speak, unable to take account of everything else happening in the pool. While each team of Venice Commission experts did an excellent job on their particular topic, no one in the end assessed what the set of changes did as a whole.

Constitutional governance is a huge area with many different specialized nooks and crannies. But the structure of normative assessment of constitutional government – parceled out across experts in election law, experts on media laws, experts on the judiciary or on legislatures or on human rights – allows important things to fall between the cracks. This can lead to disasters because constitutional provisions have important interaction effects. Whether rule A works well will depend on what rule B is. But if rule A is assessed by one team and rule B is assessed by another, no one has responsibility for spotting the fatal interaction between the two.

Take one of most famously consequential interaction effects in the history of constitutional drafting. In the Weimar Constitution of inter-war Germany, Article 25 permitted the President of the Republic to dissolve the Parliament, though only one time for any one reason. Elections had to be held within sixty days after a parliamentary dissolution. This was a perfectly reasonable rule, especially in Weimar Germany where it was hard to form stable parliaments. Unworkable parliaments could be dissolved and the electorate would be asked to create a new mandate. That made good democratic sense. So, a constitutional consultant with a checklist should say: Check! Good rule!

But then in that same constitution, Article 48 gave the President the power to declare a state of emergency "in case public safety is seriously threatened or disturbed." Such an awesome power should have a check, according to best practices, and Article 48 had one. The President had to inform the Parliament immediately about the state of emergency and the Parliament could order a halt to the emergency if it did not agree that the emergency was warranted.

The constitutional consultant with the checklist would again say: Check! Good rule!

As history now tells us, there was a problem when the two rules were used together. President Hindenburg first dissolved the Parliament under Article 25 at his Chancellor's urging. And then, before elections could be held, he once again took his Chancellor's advice and invoked Article 48. (Of course now, we know the problem: the Chancellor at the time was one Adolf Hitler, but contemporary constitutional consultants only look at the form and not at the personalities.) Both actions were completely constitutional on the surface, but once the Parliament was dissolved legally under Article 25 it was no longer around to object to the emergency measures taken under Article 48. While each article taken alone could pass constitutional muster since those powers exist in many constitutions and the Weimar Constitution possessed the requisite checks on their exercise, the interaction between the two was fatal to the republic and to the constitutional order. And far beyond Germany.

A checklist approach to constitutions cannot spot these interaction effects. I think that this is the main reason why the key institutions of the TLO have been slow to react to the rise of legalistic autocracies. Legalistic autocrats are, after all, elected. That satisfies the basic premise that governments are democratic. The legalistic autocrat will often follow the rules laid down in achieving constitutional change by using the existing amendment procedure (Orbán and Erdoğan) or by calling a new constitutional convention according to the established rules (Chávez and Correa). That seems to satisfy the good governance checklist that the methods of constitutional change used are themselves constitutional. The constitutional changes will generally consist of a package of new rules and institutional design elements in which each one individually can be found somewhere in a perfectly reasonable constitution, as we have seen. Abolition of presidential term limits and expanding the number of judges on a peak court in order to be able to pack it are among the few exceptions that set off flashing lights at the TLO. But the interaction effects that result from combining reasonable individual rules can nonetheless be fatal.

Bad interaction effects in otherwise reasonable constitutions can sneak in accidentally, but they can also be inserted into constitutions deliberately by clever legalistic autocrats. I have called this the Frankenstate problem:

> Victor Frankenstein's monster – nameless in Mary Shelley's novel – was assembled from various component parts of once recognizably reasonable bodies. However, he went on to look and act a monster. The Frankenstate,

> too, is composed from various perfectly reasonable pieces, and its monstrous quality comes from the horrible way that those pieces interact when stitched together. (Scheppele 2013: 560)

In fact, one bad interaction effect brought down Hungary's 1989–90 constitution in 2011. Fearing that many small parties would make it impossible to form stable parliamentary majorities, the drafters of Hungary's 1990 election law gave the party winning a plurality extra seats to boost their chances of achieving a stable majority. At the same time, knowing that the 1989–90 constitution had been written quickly, the constitutional framers did not want to entrench it too deeply. As a result, they kept the constitutional amendment rule, left over from the communist constitution, that any provision could be changed by a single two-thirds votes of the Parliament. Both fears proved unfounded: Hungary quickly settled on a stable party structure that, by 2010, meant that there were two dominant parties and the 1989–90 constitution came to be taken for granted as a functioning document that worked well. When the disproportionate election law therefore brought a legalistic autocrat to power in 2010 with a two-thirds constitutional majority, the stage was set for autocratic takeover.

The TLO community of states and transnational actors needs to rethink its constitutional standards. It is impossible to imagine agreeing on detailed one-size-fits-all constitutional institutions across the board (a model election code, a precisely constructed legislature) given the diversity of reasonably well-functioning democratic and constitutional governments in the world, but it may be possible to develop holistic standards that look at what happens when various constitutional provisions interact. Such standards would not rely on getting into the weeds on every single aspect of constitutional design. A holistic standard should focus the TLO community's attention on what really matters about liberal, democratic constitutionalism: That it does not self-destruct.

I would argue, then, for a new normative standard by which to assess constitutional systems of government: a liberal, constitutional democracy must be *self-sustaining*. Both constitutions and democracies are open-ended experiments in self-governance. If the principles underlying both constitutionalism and democracy are to be honored, one political generation should not be able remove the possibility of self-governance from future generations. The requirement that the overall effect of constitutional change cannot be to prevent one's successors from governing themselves also goes a long way toward realizing the liberal promise of democratic constitutionalism.

The Weimar Constitution was not self-sustaining – because emergency powers that were invoked when the Parliament was dissolved led to dictatorship. The present Hungarian constitution is not self-sustaining – because the current election law will not allow any other party to win except the current governing party. The weaknesses of the Venezuelan constitution are becoming clear after President Chávez's successor, Nicolás Maduro, refused to accept the results of a parliamentary election in which his party lost as it grappled with an economic crisis. Maduro's state of emergency declaration, rejected by the Parliament, was then upheld by the very court his predecessor packed. Constitutional experts see few ways to require Maduro to govern with a Parliament dominated by his opponents (Sanchez 2016). The Chávez constitution ultimately concentrated so many powers in the hands of the President that no parliamentary election can dislodge him.

Of course, it is not always so clear whether constitutions have built-in harmful interaction effects until a weakness reveals itself. All the more reason to develop expertise about these legalistic autocracies and the tricks they have learned already while thinking through how to train experts to spot interaction effects. We are seeing the rise of Frankenstates because right now the legalistic autocrats are cleverer than their TLO assessors.

If we start from the principle that liberal constitutional democracies should be self-sustaining, at least we know what to look for. If the TLO consulting community is in the business of assessing and articulating the normative bona fides of constitutions around the world, it would be better off having constitutional generalists look at whole systems and how the parts function together rather than simply sending election specialists off for one mission and experts in legislative committee structures or judicial selections processes off on another. Specific advice like that is useful, of course, if one already has a functioning liberal, constitutional, democratic system or leaders who sincerely want to create one. But ultimately the experts who look at one isolated area – election law or the structure of the cabinet – cannot really tell much about self-sustainability of the liberal, democratic constitutional order. Until experts learn to see a constitution as a system and ask whether the system can last to allow the next generation (or the next electorate) to make its own choices about how it wants to be governed, we will see the number of liberal, constitutional democracies shrink as the end of history itself comes to a crashing end.

REFERENCES

Abramowitz, Michael J. 2018. "Freedom in the World 2018: Democracy in Crisis." *Freedom House*. Available from: https://freedomhouse.org/sites/default/files/FH_FITW_Report_2018_Final_SinglePage.pdf.

ACE: The Electoral Knowledge Network. 2012. "Germany: Delimiting Districts in a Mixed Member Proportional Electoral System." Available from: http://aceproject.org/ace-en/topics/bd/annex/bdy/bdy_de.

Associated Press. 2018. "Ecuador Votes to Limit President's Terms in Blow to Rafeal Correa." *The Guardian*, February 5, 2018. Available from: www.theguardian.com/world/2018/feb/05/ecuador-votes-to-limit-presidents-terms-in-blow-to-rafael-correa.

Bâli, Asli. 2013. "Courts and Constitutional Transition: Lessons from the Turkish Case." *International Journal of Constitutional Law* 11: 666–701.

Bánkuti, Miklós, Gábor Halmai, and Kim Lane Scheppele. 2012. "Hungary's Illiberal Turn: Dismantling the Constitution." *Journal of Democracy* 21 (3): 138–45.

Bell, David A. 2016. "The Theory behind a Very Bad Year (and It's Only Half Over)." *Foreign Policy* (20 July). Available from: https://foreignpolicy.com/2016/07/20/why-decades-do-happen-in-weeks-brexit-coup-turkey-trump-isis/.

Bermeo, Nancy. 2016. "On Democratic Backsliding." *Journal of Democracy* 27 (1): 5–19.

Brown, Nathan. 2001. *Constitutions in a Non-Constitutional World: Arab Basic Laws and the Prospects for Accountable Governance*. Albany: SUNY Press.

Brewer-Carías, Allan R. 2010. "The 1999 Venezuelan Constitution-Making Process as an Instrument for Framing the Development of an Authoritarian Political Regime." In *Framing the State in Times of Political Transition*, edited by Laurel Miller with Louis Aucoin, Washington, DC: US Institute for Peace Press: 505–31. Available from: www.usip.org/sites/default/files/Framing%20the%20State/Chapter19_Framing.pdf.

Ciddi, Sinan. 2011. "Turkey's September 12, 2010 Referendum." MERIA Journal 15 (4) (December). Available from www.rubincenter.org/2011/12/turkey%E2%80%99s-september-12–2010-referendum/.

Clementi, Francesco. 2016. "Italian Constitutional Reforms: Toward Stable and Efficient Government." *Constitution.Net* (23 June). Available from www.constitutionnet.org/news/italian-constitutional-reforms-towards-stable-and-efficient-government.

Colton, Timothy and Cindy Skach. 2005. "The Russian Predicament." *Journal of Democracy* 16 (3): 113–26.

Conaghan, Catherine M. 2008. "Ecuador: Correa's Plebiscitary Presidency." *Journal of Democracy* 19 (2): 46–60.

Conaghan, Catherine M. 2016. "Ecuador under Correa." *Journal of Democracy* 27 (3): 109–18.

The Constitution Unit. 1998. "Checks and Balances in Single-Chamber Parliaments: A Comparative Analysis." Available from: www.ucl.ac.uk/spp/publications/unit-publications/24.pdf.

Corrales, Javier. 2015. "Autocratic Legalism in Venezuela." *Journal of Democracy* 26 (2): 37–51.

Corrales, Javier and Michael Penfold. 2014. "Manipulating Term Limits in Latin America." *Journal of Democracy* 25 (4): 157–68.

Correa, Rafael. 2012. "Ecuador's Path." *New Left Review* 77: 90 (September–October).

David, Steven R. 1986. "Soviet Involvement in Third World Coups." *International Security* 11 (1): 3–36 (Summer).

Desai, Deval. 2017. "Ignorance/Power: Expert Ignorance and the Performance and Practice of Rule of Law Reform." SJD Dissertation, Harvard Law School.

Dezalay, Yves and Bryant Garth. 2001. "The Import and Export of Law and Legal Institutions." Pp. 241–56 in *Adapting Legal Cultures*, edited by David Nelken and Johannes Feest. Oxford: Hart Publishing.

Diamond, Larry. 2015. "Facing up to Democratic Recession." *Journal of Democracy* 26 (1): 141–55.

Duhamel, Olivier. 2000. "France's New Five-Year Presidential Term." *Brookings Institute*. March 1, 2000. Available from: www.brookings.edu/articles/frances-new-five-year-presidential-term/.

The Economist. 2008. "On Putin's Terms." November 8, 2008. Available from www.economist.com/node/12622987.

Ellner, Stephen. 2012. "The Distinguishing Features of Latin America's New Left in Power: The Governments of Hugo Chavez, Evo Morales, and Rafael Correa." *Latin American Perspectives*. January 17, 2012. Available from: https://venezuelanalysis.com/analysis/6754.

European Commission. 2016a. "Fact Sheet: College Orientation Debate on Recent Developments in Poland and the Rule of Law Framework: Questions & Answers." January 13, 2016. Available from: http://europa.eu/rapid/press-release_MEMO-16-62_en.htm.

European Commission. 2017. "Reasoned Proposal in Accordance with Article 7 (1)of the Treat on European Union Regarding the Rule of Law in Poland." December 20, 2017. Available from: ec.europa.eu/newsroom/just/document.cfm?doc_id=49108.

European Commission for Democracy Through Law, "Code of Good Practice in Electoral Matters: Guidelines and Explanatory Report." *Council of Europe*, October 2002, www.venice.coe.int/webforms/documents/?pdf=CDL-AD(2002)023-e (accessed 11 November 2018).

European Parliament. 2011. Resolution of 5 July 2011 on the Revised Hungarian Constitution, P7_TA(2011)0315.

European Parliament. 2013. Resolution of 3 July 2013 on the Situation of Fundamental Rights: Standards and Practices in Hungary (pursuant to the European Parliament Resolution of 16 February 2012) (2012/2130 (INI)), P7_TA(2013)0315.

Foa, Roberto Stefan and Yascha Mounk. 2016. "The Democratic Disconnect." *Journal of Democracy* 27 (3): 5–17.

Fukuyama, Francis. 1989. "The End of History?" *National Interest* 16 (Summer): 3–18.

Gaidar, Yegor. 2007. *Collapse of an Empire: Lessons for Modern Russia.* Washington, DC: Brookings Institute Press.

Gargarella, Roberto. 2012. "Neo-Constitutionalism in Twenty-First Century Venezuela: Participatory Democracy, Deconcentrated Decentralization or Centralized Populism?" Pp. 163–82 in *New Constitutionalism in Latin America: Promises and Practices*, edited by Detlef Nolte and Almut Schilling-Vacaflor. New York: Ashgate.

Garver, John W. 2006. *China and Iran: Ancient Partners in a Post-Imperial World.* Seattle: University of Washington Press.

Gel'man, Vladimir. 2000. "Dictatorship of the Law: Neither Dictatorship Nor Rule of Law." PONARS Policy Memo 146, European University at St. Petersburg. Available from: www.ponarseurasia.org/sites/default/files/policy-memos-pdf/pm_0146.pdf.

Ginsburg, Tom, James Melton, and Zachary Elkins. 2011. "On the Evasion of Executive Term Limits." *William and Mary Law Review* 52 (6): 1807–72.

Goldberg, Suzanne. 1999. "Musharraf Seeks to Soften Coup Image." *The Guardian*. October 16, 1999. Available from: www.theguardian.com/world/1999/oct/16/pakistan.suzannegoldenberg.

Habdank-Kołaczkowska, Sylvana. 2015. "Nations in Transit 2015: Democracy on the Defensive in Europe and Eurasia." *Freedom House*. Available from: https://freedomhouse.org/sites/default/files/FH_NIT2015_06.06.15_FINAL.pdf.

Halliday, Terrence and Gregory Shaffer, eds. 2015. *Transnational Legal Orders in Transnational Legal Orders*. New York: Cambridge University Press.

Halmai, Gábor 2012. "Unconstitutional Constitutional Amendments: Constitutional Courts as Guardians of the Constitution?" *Constellations* 19 (2): 182–203.

Hungarian Parliament 2010. Government Resolution 1/2010 (VI. 16.), Proclamation of the Parliament, 1140/2010. (VII. 2.).

International IDEA. 2008. "Direct Democracy Handbook." Available from: www.idea.int/sites/default/files/publications/direct-democracy-the-international-idea-handbook.pdf.

International IDEA. 2013. "Practical Guide to Constitution Building." Available from: www.idea.int/sites/default/files/publications/a-practical-guide-to-constitution-building.pdf.

International IDEA. 2014a. "Funding of Political Parties and Election Campaigns: A Handbook on Political Finance." Available from www.idea.int/publications/catalogue/funding-political-parties-and-election-campaigns-handbook-political-finance.

International IDEA. 2014b. "Constitutional Amendment Procedures, September." Available from: www.idea.int/cbp/loader.cfm?csModule=security/getfile&pageid=65937.

International IDEA. 2015a. "To Go or Not to Go? Debates about Constitutional Term Limits, Chapter VI of the Annual Review of Constitution-Building Processes 2014." Available from: www.idea.int/publications/annual-review-of-cbp-2014/upload/annual-review-of-cbp-2014-c6.pdf.

International IDEA. 2015b. "Presidential Veto Powers, May." Available from: www.idea.int/cbp/loader.cfm?csModule=security/getfile&pageid=69562.

International IDEA. 2018. "Mission and Values." Available from: www.idea.int/about-us/mission-values.

Kirchgaessner, Stephanie and Angela Guiffrida. 2016. "Italian PM Matteo Renzi Resigns after Referendum Defeat." *The Guardian*. December, 5 2016.

Kleinfeld, Rachel. 2012. *Advancing the Rule of Law Abroad: Next Generation Reform*. Washington, DC: Carnegie Endowment for International Peace.

Knight, Louise. 2001. *Presidentialism in Contemporary France: De Gaulle and Mitterrand*. PhD thesis (unpublished manuscript), University of Warwick. On file at http://wrap.warwick.ac.uk/66773/.

Kogacioglu, Dicle. 2004. "Progress, Unity, and Democracy: Dissolving Political Parties in Turkey." *Law and Society Review* 38 (3): 433–62.

Kommers, Donald and Russell Miller. 2012. *The Jurisprudence of the Federal Constitutional Court of Germany*, 3rd edition. Durham: Duke University Press.

Kotkin, Stephen. 2001. *Armageddon Averted: The Soviet Collapse 1970–2000*. New York: Oxford University Press.

Landau, David. 2013. "Constitution-Making Gone Wrong." *Alabama Law Review* 64 (5): 923–80.

Landau, David. 2015. "Term Limit Manipulation across Latin America and What Constitutional Design Could Do about It." *Constitution.net*. July 21, 2015. Available from: www.constitutionnet.org/news/term-limits-manipulation-across-latin-america-and-what-constitutional-design-could-do-about-it.

Levitsky, Steven and Lucan Way. 2010. *Competitive Authoritarianism: Hybrid Regimes after the Cold War*. New York: Cambridge University Press.

Levitsky, Steven and Daniel Ziblatt. 2018. *How Democracies Die*. New York: Crown Publishing Group.

Linz, Juan. 1990. "The Perils of Presidentialism." *Journal of Democracy* 1 (1): 51–69.

Linz, Juan and Alfred Stepan. 1996a. "Toward Consolidated Democracies." *Journal of Democracy* 7 (2): 14–33.

Linz, Juan and Alfred Stepan. 1996b. *Problems of Democratic Transition and Consolidation: Southern Europe, South America, and Post-Communist Europe*. Baltimore: Johns Hopkins University Press.

Llewlleyn, Karl. 1930. *The Bramble Bush: On Our Law and Its Study*. Dobbs Ferry: Oceana Books.

Mainwaring, Scott and Matthew S. Shugart. 1997. "Juan Linz, Presidentialism, and Democracy: A Critical Appraisal." *Comparative Politics* 29 (4): 449–71.

Muižnieks, Nils. 2016. Report by Nils Muiznieks, Commissioner for Human Rights of the Council of Europe, following His Visit to Poland from 9 to 12 February 2016, CommDH(2016)23, 15 June 2016, Strasbourg. Available from: https://wcd.coe.int/ViewDoc.jsp?p=&Ref=CommDH(2016)23&Language=lanEnglish&Ver=original&direct=true.

Önis, Ziya. 2016. "Turkey's Two Elections: The AKP Comes Back." *Journal of Democracy* 27 (2): 141–54.

Organization for Security and Cooperation in Europe/Office of Democratic Institutions and Human Rights 2014. Hungary Parliamentary Elections 6 April 2014 Limited Election Observation Mission Final Report, Warsaw, 11 July 2014. Available from: www.osce.org/odihr/elections/hungary/121098?download=true.

Osgood, Kenneth A. 2002. "Hearts and Minds: The Unconventional Cold War." *Journal of Cold War Studies* 4 (2): 85–107.

Özsoy, Şule. 2016. "Erdoğan's Long-Standing Struggle for a Turkish Type of Presidential System." *Presidential Power Blog*. February 23, 2016. Available from: http://presidential-power.com/?p=4495.

Pan, Philip P. 2008. "Russia's Medvedev Signs Constitutional Amendment to Lengthen Presidential Terms." *Washington Post*. December 30, 2008. Available from: www.washingtonpost.com/wp-dyn/content/article/2008/12/30/AR2008123000839.html.

Ramadan, Tariq. 2011. "Democratic Turkey Is the Template for Egypt's Muslim Brotherhood." *New Perspectives Quarterly* 28 (2): 42–5.

Sadurski, Wojciech. 2016. What Is Going on in Poland Is an Attack Against Democracy. Interview with Wojciech Sadurski and Maximillian Steinbeis, *Verfassungsblog*. July 15, 2016. Available from: http://verfassungsblog.de/what-is-going-on-in-poland-is-an-attack-against-democracy/.

Sanchez, Maria Isabel. 2016. "Venezuela: Opposition Vows All Means, Including Constitutional Amendment, to Oust Maduro." *Constitution. Net*. March 9, 2016. Available from: www.constitutionnet.org/news/vene

zuela-opposition-vows-all-means-including-constitutional-amendment-oust-maduro.

Scharfe, Patrick. 2015. "Erdoğan's Presidential Dreams, Turkey's Constitutional Politics." *Origins* 8 (5). February 2015. Available from: http://origins.osu.edu/article/erdo-s- presidential-dreams-turkey-s-constitutional-politics.

Scheppele, Kim Lane. 2003. "Aspirational and Aversive Constitutionalism: The Case for Studying Cross-Constitutional Influence through Negative Models." *International Journal of Constitutional Law* 1 (2): 296–324.

Scheppele, Kim Lane. 2008. "A Constitution between Past and Future." *William & Mary Law Review* 49 (4): 1377–407.

Scheppele, Kim Lane. 2009. "Constitutional Interpretation after Regimes of Horror." Pp. 233–58 in *Legal Institutions and Collective Memories*, edited by Susanne Karstedt. Oxford: Hart Publishing.

Scheppele, Kim Lane. 2013. "The Rule of Law and the *Frankenstate*: Why Governance Checklists Do Not Work." *Governance* 26: 559–62.

Scheppele, Kim Lane. 2014a. "An Election in Question Part II: Writing the Rules to Win: The Basic Structure." On Paul Krugman's, *Conscience of a Liberal Blog*. February 28, 2014. Available from: http://krugman.blogs.nytimes.com/2014/02/28/hungary-an-election-in-question-part-2/.

Scheppele, Kim Lane. 2014b. "An Election in Question Part III: Compensating the Winners." On Paul Krugman's, *Conscience of a Liberal Blog*. February 28, 2014. Available from: http://krugman.blogs.nytimes.com/2014/02/28/hungary-an-election-in-question-part-3/.

Scheppele, Kim Lane. 2014c. "Constitutional Coups and Judicial Review: How Transnational Institutions Can Strengthen Peak Courts at Times of Crisis (with Special Reference to Hungary)." *Journal of Transnational Law and Contemporary Problems* 23: 51–117.

Scheppele, Kim Lane. 2018. "Autocratic Legalism." *University of Chicago Law Review* 85: 545–83.

Schmitter, Philippe. 2015. "Crisis and Transition but Not Decline." *Journal of Democracy* 26 (1): 32–44.

Schönteich, Martin. 2013. "The Rule of Law Movement: A Review of Its Origins, Evolution and Ambitions." Pp. 27–46 in *Promoting the Rule of Law: A Practitioner's Guide to Key Issues and Developments*, edited by Lelia Mooney. Chicago: American Bar Association Book Publishing.

Shaheen, Kareem. 2017. "Erdoğan Claims Victory in Turkish Constitutional Referendum." *The Guardian*. April 16, 2017. Available from: www.theguardian.com/world/2017/apr/16/erdogan-claims-victory-in-turkish-constitutional-referendum.

Stuster, Diana. 2013. "Mapped: The 7 Governments the U.S. Has Overthrown." *Foreign Policy*. August 20, 2013. Available from: http://foreignpolicy.com/2013/08/20/mapped-the-7-governments-the-u-s-has-overthrown/.

Trofimov, Yaroslav. 2016. "Turkey's Erdogan Avoids the Fate of Egypt's Morsi." *Wall Street Journal*. July 17, 2016. Available from: www.wsj.com/articles/turkeys-erdogan-avoids-fate-of-egypts-morsi-1468672547.

Tushnet, Mark. 2008. "Some Skepticism about Normative Constitutional Advice." *William & Mary Law Review* 49 (4): 1473–95.

United Nations Development Program. 2014. UNDP Guidance Note on Constitution-Making Support. Available from: www.onu.cl/onu/wp-content/uploads/2016/06/Constitution-Making-Support-Guidance-Note.pdf.

United Nations General Secretary. 2009. Guidance Note of the Secretary-General: United Nations Assistance to Constitution-Making Processes. Available from: www.un.org/ruleoflaw/blog/document/guidance-note-of-the-secretary-general-united-nations-assistance-to-constitution-making-processes/.

US Department of State. 2012. "Human Rights Report: Hungary 2012."

Varol, Ozan. 2012. "The Democratic Coup d'État." *Harvard International Law Journal* 53 (2): 292–356.

Venice Commission. 2002. Code of Good Practice in Electoral Matters: Guidelines and Explanatory Report, Adopted by the Venice Commission at Its 52nd Session, Venice 18–19 October 2002, Opinion No. 190/2002, CDL – AD (2002) 23 rev. Available from: www.venice.coe.int/webforms/documents/CDL-AD(2002)023rev-e.aspx.

Venice Commission. 2011a. Opinion on Three Legal Questions Arising in the Process of Drafting the New Constitution of Hungary, Adopted by the Venice Commission at Its 86th Plenary Session, Venice 25–26 March 2011, Opinion no. 614/2011, CDL-AD(2011)001. Available from: www.venice.coe.int/webforms/documents/?pdf=CDL-AD(2011)001-e.

Venice Commission. 2011b. Opinion on the New Constitution of Hungary, Adopted by the Venice Commission at Its 87th Plenary Session, Venice 17–18 June 2011, Opinion no. 621/2011, CDL-AD(2011)016. Available from: www.venice.coe.int/webforms/documents/CDL-AD(2011)016-E.aspx.

Venice Commission. 2016. Opinion on Amendments to the Act of 25 June 2015 on the Constitutional Tribunal of Poland, adopted by the Venice Commission at Its 106th Plenary Session, Venice, 11–12 March 2016, Opinion no. 833/2015, CDL-AD(2016)001-e. Available from: www.venice.coe.int/webforms/documents/?pdf=CDL-AD(2016)001-e.

Watmough, Simon P., Ahmet Erdi Öztürk, David Tittensor, and Ihsan Yilmaz. 2017. "Turkey's Constitutional Referendum: Experts Express Fear for a Divided Country." *The Conversation*. April 16, 2017.

Available from https://theconversation.com/turkeys-constitutional-referendum-experts-express-fear-for-a-divided-country-76289.
Widner, Jennifer. 2008. "Constitution Writing in Post-Conflict Settings: An Overview." *William & Mary Law Review* 49 (4): 1513–41.
Zheng, Yangwen, Hong Liu, and Michael Szonyi. 2010. *The Cold War in Asia: The Battle for Hearts and Minds*. Boston: Brill.

8

Democratic Erosion and Constitution-Making Moments: The Role of Transnational Legal Norms

David E. Landau

Recent scholarship has brought into focus the downside risks of constitution-making moments. Ideally, constitution-making would help to establish or rejuvenate a democratic order. But across a range of recent cases, constitution-making has helped to erode democracy or to increase political tension, rather than strengthening the democratic order and bridging political and social divisions. Would-be authoritarian actors and movements can use a number of different devices to undermine democracy, including the tools of constitutional change (Landau 2013a). Replacement of the existing constitution may be a particularly efficient way for powerful actors to entrench themselves, to weaken institutions intended to check their power and protect minority rights, and to marginalize political opposition groups.

There are several well-studied recent examples. In both Venezuela and Ecuador, powerful presidents (Hugo Chavez and Rafael Correa) rewrote constitutions shortly after taking office and used the constitution-making process as a way to weaken opposition groups and undermine democracy (Brewer-Carias 2010; Landau 2013b). In both cases, the constitution-making process excluded the opposition and the resulting constitution strengthened presidential power while weakening the power of other institutions. Similarly, in Hungary, the Fidesz party used its two-thirds majority in Parliament to replace the existing constitution, after having previously passed a series of amendments designed to weaken the judiciary and otherwise undermine checks on its power (Bánkuti, Halmai, & Scheppele 2012; Scheppele, Chapter seven this volume). The resulting constitution has again been criticized for entrenching the ruling party and weakening institutions designed to limit its power.

As many scholars have pointed out, there now exists what can be viewed as a transnational legal order (TLO) (Halliday & Shaffer 2015a) reinforcing the creation of liberal-democratic norms during constitution-making processes

(Levitsky & Way 2010). This TLO emphasizes certain "core" features that regimes should have: particularly free and fair elections, a bill of rights, and institutions designed to hold governments accountable and protect individual rights, particularly a constitutional court (Dixon & Landau 2015). As Scheppele points out (this volume), modern authoritarianism often works by adopting constitutional texts that formally comply with these rules, but through a combination of formal and informal norms, in practice sidestep them. My argument here is that the nature of domestic constitution-making moments, as well as the dominant theory of constitution-making, deepens these risks. In other words, during constitution-making moments both weaknesses in the way the TLO interacts with local political conditions, and internal incoherencies in the international TLO itself, reduce its effectiveness during constitution-making moments (Halliday & Shaffer 2015a: 42–6).

First, constitution-making usually takes place during periods of crisis or transition at which domestic institutions have broken down or become broadly illegitimate; powerful leaders can take advantage of the resulting vacuums to consolidate power in a durable way. A legal/conceptual problem compounds this issue: leading theories of constitution-making hold that it can properly take place outside of the existing constitutional order, via institutions that cannot be controlled by existing institutions. Thus, not only does constitution-making usually take place at moments of domestic institutional weakness, but actors can plausibly wield transnational legal theories of constitution-making that undermine domestic institutions even further. Even where risks of democratic erosion do not materialize, the resulting uncertainty in even the basic legal framework can lead to a constitution-making environment that exacerbates rather than lessens social and political tension. That is, while the TLO places some regulations on the content of constitution-making, it leaves the process of constitution-making largely unfettered.

The frequent absence of domestic legal constraint during constitution-making moments may create a *prima facie* case for a strengthened TLO that would deal more specifically with the process of constitution-making in order to protect liberal democracy. However, achieving effective international involvement as a solution to abusive constitution-making seems much easier said than done. Strong international norms governing constitution-making do not exist, may never exist, and perhaps should not exist. Other approaches at the international or regional level are similarly either inchoate or flawed. As a first step, the goal of this chapter is to survey the range of possibilities and their potential for development, recognizing both the potential utility and drawbacks of each approach. In general, the weaknesses of the liberal democratic TLO at the moment of constitution-making stem from an insufficient grappling with the highly politically-charged nature of the moment. That is, they are either too legalistic to deal effectively with the concerns of such a moment, or simply unwilling to become involved in what is seen as a moment of domestic political sovereignty.

Part I of this chapter frames the problem of constraint at the domestic level during constitution-making processes. While acknowledging that the issue is not universal, it argues that the absence of effective constraint from domestic institutions is a common one, and that this absence is associated with a range of longer-term problems including the erosion of democracy and the increase in political tension associated with "failed" constitution-making. Part II considers the strengths and drawbacks of four distinct models through which a TLO dealing more specifically with constitution-making is either incipient or could be constructed: Democracy clauses requiring that states abide by their own domestic mechanisms of constitutional change, international norms directly governing the procedure or substance of constitution-making, international organizations or NGOs wielding "best practices," and review of constitution-making processes and texts by advisory bodies at the supranational level. Part III concludes by arguing that since the problem of abusive constitution-making is particularly difficult to solve at either the domestic or international levels, the most feasible approach involves making some use of all of these distinct tools while recognizing each of their limitations. More broadly, it involves achieving a more successful integration of the legal regulation of the TLO with attentiveness to political contexts and concerns.

CONSTITUTION-MAKING AND DOMESTIC INSTITUTIONS

This part argues that constitution-making moments often occur during unique moments of stress and weakness for the domestic institutional order, and indeed themselves can tend to contribute significantly to this stress on existing institutions. The first section argues that constitution-making, whether undertaken during periods of regime transition or within a democratic regime, are often associated with deep crises that render existing institutions weak, illegitimate, or both. This breakdown in institutional order makes it more difficult for transnational norms promoting liberal democracy to constrain at the domestic level. But as the second section points out, the prevailing conception of constitution-making (which itself can be viewed as a meta-TLO) itself is part of the problem: dominant legal theories of constitution-making envision constitution-making as an act by "the people" outside of existing constitutional and legal constraints. The effect of these dynamics is to make constitution-making an activity that is particularly difficult to regulate at the domestic level.

As the third section notes, this absence of effective domestic constraint can have very problematic consequences for the end result of constitution-making.

Political Dynamics of Constitution-Making

The political environment in which constitution-making is most commonly undertaken is one where existing institutions are either eroded, have collapsed completely, or are badly tainted by association with the prior regime. As Elster notes, the normal situation in which constitution-making occurs is not where things are going well, but instead where some deep crisis necessitates the creation of a new constitution (Elster 1995). This is of course not inevitable: Chile represents an ongoing case of a country seeking to rewrite its constitution during periods of relative institutional normalcy. And even where a crisis is occurring, as for example recently in Iceland, political institutions may maintain sufficient force to block or shape the constitution-making process (Landemore 2015). But very often, the crisis that spurs constitution-making will also have undermined domestic political institutions.

This is easiest to see in cases of constitution-making during regime transition. Some recent instances of constitution-making have occurred after the fall of authoritarian regimes, and as a part of a transition process that would supposedly end in a democratic order. In these instances, the problem is that all of the old institutions – courts, legislatures, bureaucrats, the military, etc. – may be tainted by association with the existing regime. In some cases, they may also have collapsed or been gravely weakened through the dynamics preceding and contemporaneous with the transition process. Scholarship suggests various ways in which actors might work around this problem. Arato, for example, suggests a model of roundtable talks followed by temporary constitutions that structure the transition process (Arato 2000). This model essentially makes use of authoritarian-era institutions and constitutions (as often occurred in Eastern Europe), but breathes new life into them through the results of the roundtable talks, and gradually phases out old for new institutions. The institutions created by the new temporary constitution should have more authority to restrain constitution-makers than would the institutions associated with the old authoritarian regime.

But in many transitional cases, the preconditions for roundtable talks may not be met: contending forces affiliated with both the old and new orders may not agree on the basic contours of the process. In those conditions, the ability of the authoritarian-era institutions to shape constitution-making may be very problematic. In Egypt, for example, the military and the courts, holdovers from the old order, tried to play a significant role in restraining constitution-making that was controlled by two newly-constituted institutions, the Parliament and the presidency (Stilt 2012). As examples, the military sought to insert substantive principles into the process (with which any final constitution would need to comply), and the courts issued significant decisions governing the composition of the Constituent Assembly and dissolving it when it did not meet constitutional and legal requirements. Ideally, the judiciary would be seen as an impartial arbitrator. But in the Egyptian case, they were viewed as allies of interests associated with the old order (as well as promoters of their own corporatist interests), which hampered their ability to impose legitimate constraints on the constitution-making process.

Often overlooked is the similarity between transitional and democratic constitution-making with respect to the weak or tainted nature of existing institutions. Democratic constitutional replacement also tends to occur in moments where institutions have either collapsed, been gravely weakened, or lost legitimacy. The Andean region of Latin America – Colombia, Ecuador, Venezuela, and Bolivia – offers a recent example. Since 1991, a period in which each of these countries has been consistently democratic, all four of them have adopted new constitutions (twice in the case of Ecuador). In all of the cases, constitution-making was conducted in an environment of political crisis, in which existing political institutions were seen as at least partly accountable. In Colombia in 1991, Venezuela in 1999, and Bolivia (beginning in 2006 and ending in 2009), constitution-making broadly took place as part of the end of "pacted" regimes or power-sharing arrangements between rival parties (Brewer-Carias 2010; Cepeda-Espinosa 2004; Gamarra 2008). In all cases (although to varying degrees), these political arrangements were once seen as working fairly well, but in recent years have been viewed as increasingly corrupt as well as incapable of channeling social demands and divergent social forces and the providing public goods like stability and growth. In Ecuador, both the 1998 and 2008 constitutions were preceded by periods of extraordinary political instability in which, for example, democratically-elected presidents were irregularly removed and could not complete their terms (Conaghan 2008).

By the time constitution-making was undertaken in all of these cases, and again to varying degrees, the legitimacy of many existing political institutions was thus suspect in all of them. In some, such as Colombia in 1991, ordinary political institutions maintained some ability to influence the constitution-making process (although the Constituent Assembly would eventually revoke the mandate of the existing Congress). In others, like Venezuela, the old order had basically collapsed by the time constitution-making occurred. After Hugo Chavez won the presidency in 1998, he faced opposition control (from the residuals of the old pacted regime) of most other institutions in the country (the Congress, the Supreme Court, and most local governments, for example). But these institutions were able to exercise virtually no influence over the constitution-making process, which was entirely controlled by Chavez's forces. Indeed, as explained in more detail below, these opposition-controlled institutions were eventually shut down or cleansed by the Chavez-controlled Assembly. Similar dynamics occurred in Ecuador in 2008, where the newly-ascendant President Correa and his allies were able to argue that the existing institutional order was a large part of the national problem and needed to be swept away. The broad point, then, is that in democratic constitution-making as in transitional constitution-making, the institutional order is often very weak.

Conceptual Dynamics of Constitution-Making

Beyond the fact that institutions during constitution-making are often weak, tainted, or both, theories of constitution-making themselves also often contribute to making it a process that is difficult to restrain. The leading theory of constitution-making, building off of Sieyes and Schmitt, is built around "constituent power" (Colon-Rios 2012; Tushnet 2015). The basic idea here is that "the people" retain the ultimate power to remake their institutional order. In writing a constitution, they delegate some of their power to "constituted powers," or ordinary political institutions. These institutions have the power to make ordinary political decisions and even to carry out exercises of constitutional change that fall short of constitutional replacement, for example by using textual mechanisms for amendment. All of these acts are restrained by the existing constitutional order. But the ultimate act of constitutional replacement can be done by "the people" at any time, and can take place outside of the existing constitutional order.

The basic theory of constituent power has some ramifications for the design of constitution-making processes. Since constitution-making is supposed to take place outside of the normal institutional rules, specialized bodies like Constituent Assemblies may make more sense as constitution-makers than ordinary institutions like legislatures. Moreover, these specialized institutions are not bound by the rules and restraints put on them by other political institutions, but instead can define their own operating rules and competencies. They cannot be regulated by the existing constitutional rules or the existing institutional order. Indeed, since the Constituent Assembly, once constituted, represents the sovereign power of the people, it can limit or shut down the power of other institutions at will.

Some recent constitution-making experiences in the Andes represent a fairly clear illustration of the constituent power approach. In Colombia (1991), Venezuela (1999), and Ecuador (2008), political actors evoked the constituent power theory to remake the institutional order. In all of these cases, designers followed processes for constitutional replacement that were outside of the existing constitutional order (Cameron & Sharpe 2010). In each case, presidents called referenda on whether specialized Constituent Assemblies should be called to rewrite constitutions. The Assemblies, once constituted, were not bound by any limitations that may have been placed on them by the existing institutional order. And indeed, in all three cases they shut down ordinary institutions so they could be remade or reconstituted.

The Venezuelan case is perhaps emblematic: the newly elected President Hugo Chavez (who was the driving force behind the Assembly), went before it and laid down his mandate, stating that he would only continue in office if ratified by the Assembly (which of course he was, overwhelmingly) (Brewer-Carias 2010). The Assembly then used its "original constituent power" to limit the power and composition of the Congress, shut down the Supreme Court, and remove hostile local and union officials. It also issued legislation directly. But Constituent Assemblies across all three countries worked under similar dynamics. The only real difference was the political context – Colombian constitution-making was extratextual but based on a broad consensus between political forces, while constitution-making in both Ecuador and Venezuela was dominated by unilateral political forces associated with newly-elected presidents in each case.[1]

Constitution-making under "constituent power" theories tends to make restraint at the domestic level problematic. The reasons are obvious: if constitution-making occurs outside rather than inside existing constitutional frameworks, then existing political institutions may have limited or no ability to restrain constitution-making bodies. Indeed, the Constituent Assembly can plausibly claim an ability to shut down any institution that interferes with its decisions. As much recent work has argued, this may raise the risk of majoritarian constitution-making, where a text is imposed by a bare majority on minority groups. Or it may allow for abusive constitution-making by a powerful individual or party claiming to act on behalf of the people (Landau 2013b). That constitution-maker, able to unilaterally remake the constitution, may be able to entrench themselves in power and weaken

[1] For example, the Colombian Assembly also revoked the mandate of the legislature and called for new elections, and the Ecuadorian Assembly revoked the mandate of various institutions.

institutions intended to check their power. The result may be a regime that is less than fully democratic.

The risk of this outcome is not a result of stepping outside of the existing institutional order as such, which can indeed be either useful or necessary for successful constitution-making. In transition cases, there may be little or no existing institutional order to fall back on, or restrained constitution-making may require bargains with actors that are too tainted by affiliation with the authoritarian regime. Even in democratic cases, constituent power theory can provide a useful exit in situations where the existing institutional order threatens to freeze or block important changes – both Colombia and Venezuela, which were pacted regimes that had run their course, offer plausible examples (Segura & Bejarano 2004). More recently, Iceland offers a plausible example of a case where a political elite blocked a needed constitutional replacement, and constitution-makers thus may have been better off proceeding via extra-constitutional rather than constitutional channels (Landemore 2015). The exit function of constitution-making via constituent power theory can be a true advantage.

The problem instead may be that once constitution-makers step outside of the existing political order, there is no other obvious source of restraint. Political leaders may choose, or be forced because of circumstances, to form multi-party agreements or act by relative consensus. The 1991 Constituent Assembly in Colombia offers an example: the process took place outside of the existing constitutional framework but was governed by a multi-party pact between major political forces (Cepeda-Espinosa 2004). In contrast, in the Venezuelan and Ecuadorian cases powerful political actors – in both cases the president – largely acted unilaterally and marginalized opposition political forces.

Theorists have discussed various ways in which restraint might exist within a constituent power framework. One possibility is to allow political actors to step outside of the existing constitutional framework but to allow or require regulation by existing political institutions. This has been the tradition, for example, in many of the US states, where limited Constituent Assemblies governed by rules set by legislatures have been fairly common (Partlett 2014). Another possibility is to have courts or other domestic institutions use the theoretical construct of "constituent power" to limit abusive exercises of constitution-making. Not just any act of power is plausibly in the name of "the people." Courts might step in, for example, to verify that sufficient support exists to call an Assembly, or to ensure that the process itself reflects a sufficient level of consensus. The Venezuelan Supreme Court attempted mild restrictions along these lines, although with little success (Landau & Dixon 2015; Braver 2016). Suffice it to say that in comparative terms, restrictions along either line appear to be fairly difficult to impose on constitution-making processes, even if they are theoretically possible. The theory tends to marginalize existing political institutions (as noted above), and it may provide relatively little guidance as to what levels of support are necessary for constitution-making. For example, it may not be able to easily adjudicate between a majoritarian and a consensus-based constitution-making process, since either kind of process can plausibly claim to represent "popular will."

Constituent power theory is not, of course, the only way in which recent constitution-making has occurred. Rather than being carried out outside of the existing constitutional order, constitution-making sometimes occurs inside that order, and is restrained by the existing constitutional text. Some constitutions, for example, contain replacement clauses that govern the process by which new constitutions can be made: some acts of constitution-making turn to these clauses and in other cases, political actors get together and agree on changes to the existing constitution that will govern a foreseen act of new constitution-making. Such replacement clauses can be very useful. However, even where replacement clauses exist, the lure of constituent power theory can exercise an influence on constitution-making.

The example of Bolivia is an interesting one in this respect. There a president installed a replacement clause in 2004, during a deep political crisis, which essentially required a special congressional law approved by two-thirds of the Congress to trigger and regulate a constitution-making process by Constituent Assembly (Lehoucq 2008). A short time but two crisis-laden presidencies later, President Evo Morales took power at the head of an insurgent political party backed by indigenous movements and other traditionally-excluded groups. Morales sought constitutional replacement, as did broad sectors of the opposition. The two sides initially agreed on a special law to regulate the process, which among other things called for a two-thirds vote in the resulting Constituent Assembly to approve any constitutional draft. But as the process dragged on, battles erupted between the allies of President Morales (who had a majority but lacked a two-thirds supermajority in the Assembly), and the opposition. The former insisted that the Assembly had "original constituent power" and thus could adopt rules and procedures that differed from those found in the congressional enabling law, while the latter argued that the process was a regulated one that must be carried out within existing constitutional and legal rules. The result was a process in which the rules influenced the text but were constantly in danger of being bent or ignored (Landau 2013a). A constitution was finally adopted after a difficult three-year process, with the final draft hammered out by negotiations in the Congress.

The constituent power doctrine has in recent years been particularly influential in the Andes, but the threat of "constituent power" or similar discourses to regulated constitution-making processes appears to be a global phenomenon. Take two examples of constitution-making during political transition. In Russia, the legislature and high courts likewise attempted to regulate a constitution-making process that would be carried out within existing constitutional rules. But President Yeltsin eventually won, using the results of a referendum to lift the process out of these ordinary institutions and placing it instead in a Constituent Assembly appointed by him (Partlett 2012). Critics of the Russian process have argued that the resulting constitution helped shaped Russia into a hybrid regime that was less than fully democratic.

Similarly and more recently, the Egyptian constitution-making process in 2012 emerged at times as a battle between the military and the courts, which sought to place the constitution-making process under the regulation of the existing constitution and ordinary laws (by for example imposing "constitutional principles" on the process and by dissolving the Assembly when the judiciary determined it had been improperly conformed), and the majoritarian political forces surrounding President Mohamed Morsi, who argued that the sweeping electoral mandate of them and their allies should legitimate the process. The Morsi side eventually pushed through the constitution using "constituent power" logic: it immunized the work of the Assembly from any judicial challenges, enabling to finish the draft. But of course the Morsi government was shortly thereafter removed in a coup (Brown 2013). The point here is not to evaluate any particular constitution-making process: in some of these cases the end result was at least passable (as in Bolivia), while in others the dynamic was plausibly disastrous (as in Egypt). The point instead is that even in a supposedly "regulated" constitution-making process, the importance of transnational ideas about constituent power can destabilize them.

One final point is also worth noting: even where replacement clauses exist and are adhered to, they may do relatively little to ensure that the values one would want to achieve in a constitution-making process are met. That is, regulation is far from assurance that a constitution-making process is a "good" one. Take the example of Hungary. During the transition to democracy, parties used the amendment rules found in the old, communist-era constitution: a two-thirds majority. The new constitutional text was thought to be temporary, however, and to exist only until a wholly new constitution could be written. In 1995, the parliament added a clause requiring that the permanent constitution be approved by a four-fifths vote, although that clause was supposed to have a sunset date.[2] The Fidesz party won over two-thirds of seats with just over a majority of votes in 2009; this vote total gave them the ability to amend the constitution unilaterally. Using their supermajority, they amended many parts of the constitution, including provisions dealing with judicial power. They also repealed the four-fifths clause, and then used a two-thirds vote to completely replace the existing constitution with a new one in 2011 (Arato 2010).

Depending on the legal status of the four-fifths clause, of course, the legitimacy of this process could be contested. (It makes little conceptual sense to allow legislative actors to remove a more entrenched provision with a lesser vote.) But even assuming Fidesz acted properly, the two-thirds clause would have failed to ensure that the process was consensual and deliberative. The scholarly consensus instead is that the text was rushed through parliament unilaterally with virtually no debate and no participation or input from opposition groups (Bánkuti, Galmai, & Scheppele 2012). One problem with replacement clauses is that they may have very different effects depending on the exact contours of the political system. A threshold that might require broad consensus in some political environments (such as where fragmentation is high and parties are fluid, which was the case shortly after the Hungarian transition), might work very differently in other political contexts where one political party is able to gain broad power. The insensitivity of some replacement clauses to changes in political context might make them particularly problematic as time passes (Dixon & Landau 2015).

Problems Caused by an Absence of Domestic Institutional Constraint

The link between process and outcome is notoriously difficult to draw with respect to constitution-making, even for basic variables like levels of public participation and inclusion (Ginsburg, Elkins, & Blount 2009; Negretto 2012). The ability to draw causal inferences of the effect of a particular constitution-making process is plagued both by problems of endogeneity (the constitution-making process is not randomly selected, but is likely to reflect preexisting patterns of political support) and context-dependence (the effect of any particular design choice is likely to depend heavily on many other features of the political and social context). Nonetheless, the absence of effective domestic constraints appears to be associated with two kinds of problems across a range of cases. These problems are not inevitable: In some cases despite the absence

[2] There is some debate about the legal status of the sunset provision (Arato 2010).

of legal regulation, the parties may agree on the process or otherwise reach a good outcome. But they appear to be common enough to warrant concern.

The first potential problem is unilateral control of constitution-making processes by particular individuals or parties, which can lead to "abusive" forms of constitution-making that undermine democracy. Much recent work, drawn from a range of sources including Venezuela, Russia, and Hungary, has argued that unilateral domination of the constitution-making process can undermine an existing or nascent democratic order. The hegemonic actor who controls that process may be able to shape the constitutional text so that they are more difficult to dislodge, tilting the playing field in any future elections. They may also be able to weaken or pack control institutions that are designed to limit their power and to protect the rights of minority groups. Finally, constitution-making may act as a critical juncture that allows ascendant political actors to weaken the power of their political opponents by rapidly removing them from institutional power bases. Put simply, in certain political contexts unrestrained constitution-making raises significant risks of democratic erosion.

A second problem is related to an increased risk of political and social conflict because of an absence of clear ground rules. During moments of ordinary political contestation, contending actors may disagree on their particular programs but agree on which channels and methods may be used to seek power, as well as which institutions are charged with making decisions in the event of political disagreement. A peculiar feature of constitution-making can be to weaken or eliminate the institutions that normally channel these disagreements. Given that constitution-making also normally takes place in an atmosphere of political crisis, the inability to agree even on basic ground rules can heighten tensions between competing groups.

The Bolivian case referred to above offers one example of such a dynamic. At the outset of the constitution-making process in Bolivia, there were significant tensions between the forces of the new President Morales and the opposition. These tensions were based on region, ethnicity, centralization versus decentralization, and economics, among other issues (Lehouqc 2008). But both sides agreed on the need for a new constitution, and their goals may not have been so distinct as to make agreement impossible. The process of constitution-making was greatly inflamed by disputes about whether the Constituent Assembly had original constituent power, who would get to determine its rules, and how these rules should be interpreted. The process ended up heightening political tension between the two groups rather than enabling compromise. Indeed, at one point the tension became so significant that the process broke down completely over a peripheral but emotional issue: A proposal to move the capital to Sucre, where the Constituent Assembly was sitting (Landau 2013a: 955). Similarly, in Egypt, debates about the basic parameters of the process, and particularly whether the Assembly was subject to legal control from the judiciary, inflamed disputes between competing groups and plausibly made it more difficult for the political parties who held a democratic majority to compromise with elements of the old regime and democratic minorities (Brown 2013).

To a significant degree, these consequences could be ascribed to weaknesses within the liberal-democratic constitutional TLO. As Scheppele has noted, modern hybrid regimes often take advantage of ambiguities in that dominant legal order, or interaction effects between different kinds of norms, to write constitutions that formally comply with its substantive norms – they contain bills of rights and constitutional courts, for example – but in practice allow a significant degree of authoritarianism (Scheppele 2013; Scheppele, Chapter seven this volume). And as noted above, the conception of constitution-making within that TLO itself contributes by framing the process of constitution-making as primarily unregulated. Would-be authoritarian actors exploit these gaps to undertake projects of democratic erosion.

It is worth considering the extent to which these challenges themselves constitute alternative projects of transnational legal ordering, or in other words attempts to *contest* the dominant liberal-democratic constitutional TLO rather than merely to exploit its cracks (Halliday & Shaffer 2015b: 490–2). There is clearly borrowing, at least within regional clusters: The recent Polish experience drew on the earlier Hungarian one, and the Venezuelan constitution-making process influenced the processes in Ecuador and Bolivia, as well as constitutional developments in parts of Central America. The Andean cases have also developed an ideology that is critical of some tenets of liberal democracy (although which continue to work in some ways within a liberal paradigm) (Cameron & Sharpe 2010). For example, at times they have downplayed ideas like the separation of powers and the enjoyment of certain rights in service of goals like the overcoming of historically entrenched patterns of inequality. Chavez also attempted to construct alternative international institutions to spread these projects. The Eastern European cases suggest less ideological and institutional construction and more exploitation of gaps in the European Union and Council of Europe. The Andean Bolivarian project has weakened at the international and domestic level following the death of Chavez. While it is probably right to say that these practices form more or less open challenges to the liberal-democratic TLO, there is not enough conceptual definition or organization for them to be called alternative constitutional TLOs at anything beyond an incipient stage.

CONSTITUTION-MAKING AND INTERNATIONAL LAW: A CRITICAL REVIEW OF APPROACHES

The prior part argued that domestic institutions are particularly weak during constitution-making moments, which naturally raises the question of whether a TLO could be constructed or strengthened in order to focus more directly on the process of constitution-making. This part surveys existing approaches that might help provide such support. It considers several different possibilities: (1) "democracy clauses" that police whether a state has followed its own rules; (2) international norms governing the procedure or substance of constitution-making; (3) international organizations and NGOs carrying best practices; and (4) advisory institutions at the international level. The analysis concludes that each of these approaches may have some promise at limiting abusive acts of constitution-making, but that all also have serious pitfalls. In some cases, the construction of stronger transnational orderings would likely prove ineffective; in other cases, it could actually promote perverse consequences. In the end, international legal actors may achieve the best results from an approach that seeks modest gains from several different models. Such an attempt might fall short of a true transnational legal order regulating constitution-making, but would more clearly resemble a set of roughly defined tools to ward off abusive practices case by case.

Democracy Clauses and Legality

Perhaps the most straightforward approach would be an institutional order seeking to ensure that domestic actors follow their own rules. This approach has several advantages. Most importantly, it is most consonant with what already exists at the international level: several regional organizations, including Latin America and Africa, have democracy clauses (Piccone 2005). These are normally tied to the constitutionality of action taken. The Latin American clause, found in article 20 of the Inter-American Democratic Charter, allows for the suspension of member states in the event of an "unconstitutional alteration of the constitutional regime that seriously impairs the democratic order in a member state." Similarly, article 25 of the African Charter on Democracy, Elections, and Governance calls for suspension in the event of an "unconstitutional change of government," and the Commonwealth nations similarly commit to action after an "unconstitutional overthrow of a democratically elected government." Thus, many regions have a clause that requires that certain fundamental actions – changes in regime or governance – be handled in a constitutional manner.[3]

[3] The Andean Community and Mercosur also include similar clauses (Piccone 2005: 108–9).

This kind of approach is also consonant with some proposals for bringing fundamental issues of domestic constitutional governance into the international realm. The ex-Tunisian President Moncef Marzouki's 2014 proposal to the United Nations for an International Constitutional Court, for example, referred to "abuse" of political power by domestic actors and the prevention of "illegitimate, bogus elections." The suggestion is that at least a large part of the Court's work would be in preventing political leaders from taking actions that violated their own domestic rules.

The normative attractiveness of such an approach stems from the fact that it does not require international actors to construct a set of procedural or substantive norms, but instead simply requires that countries abide by whatever rules they have already set. In that sense, it seeks to close the gap between the way national leaders say they will behave and the way they actually behave. However, at least when it comes to constitution-making, the normative attractiveness of the model is often overcome by two crippling problems: (1) the difficulty of figuring out when a country has violated its own constitutional rules; and (2) the potential irrelevance of whether a country has followed its settled rules on this question.

The first problem is a general one that afflicts any act of what Jackson and Dixon call "extraterritorial constitutional interpretation" (Jackson & Dixon 2013). While sometimes judging the constitutionality of an act may be fairly easy (take a military coup as the paradigmatic example), very often it requires difficult issues in judgement. In those cases, actors tend to accept the decisions of final constitutional interpreters such as high courts not because they are definitely correct, but simply because of their procedural position. External interpreters lack the formal procedural authority to act as final constitutional interpreters. They also may lack necessary knowledge about the rules and legal culture of a system in which they were not trained and have not practiced.

These problems tend to be particularly acute in exercises of constitutional change and constitution-making. The reasons why were reviewed in the prior Part. Constitutional texts often say little or nothing about their own replacement. And whether they are silent or not, political leaders may be able to use constituent power doctrine to carry out an act of constitution-making outside of the existing constitutional framework. Whether a given act of constitution-making is thus "legal" or "constitutional" will often involve highly contestable theoretical judgments about the scope of the constituent power doctrine in a given context.

An example from Honduras may be helpful to make this more concrete. In 2009, then-President Manuel Zelaya announced that he would seek a process of constitutional replacement of the existing 1982 constitution.

Zelaya sought a plebiscite, which he later renamed a "nonbinding poll," on whether to move forward with the replacement of the existing constitution (Feldman, Landau, Sheppard, & Rosa-Suazo 2011). Since Zelaya did not enjoy congressional support, he tried to move forward unilaterally. The results of the poll would be counted by the National Institute of Statistics (not the Electoral Courts as with ordinary elections) and used to leverage the Congress into approving binding steps to move toward a possible Constituent Assembly.

The administrative, electoral, and civil courts all issued decisions at different points holding that Zelaya could not move forward with the non-binding poll. Their core reasoning was that Zelaya lacked the authority to go forward with a non-binding poll, since such an instrument did not exist under Honduran law. Critics outside of the courts, which included virtually all of the domestic political class, also made a much broader argument: That although he was not explicit on the point, Zelaya was actually trying to change the country's one-term limit found in article 239 of the Honduran constitution, which was textually unamendable under article 374 by any means. They therefore argued that the entire process of constitutional replacement was unconstitutional regardless of what route would be taken. After Zelaya nonetheless moved forward with preparations, high military officials came to his house in the morning several days before the poll and put him on a plane to Costa Rica. The Congress met later that day and named the president of Congress as the new national president; Zelaya was never restored to power.

The Organization of American States (OAS) activated the democracy clause in response to the military coup removing Zelaya, suspending Honduras from the organization for two years as a result.[4] Some analysts have argued that the OAS also should have utilized or threatened to activate the democracy clause in response to the actions of President Zelaya before the coup (Human Rights Foundation 2010). One problem, though, is that while it

[4] The removal triggered a non-trivial debate about the legality of the actions of the military and the Congress as well as about the actions of Zelaya. Those who supported the removal of Zelaya made various arguments: they argued that an arrest warrant for the president had already been issued by the Supreme Court, which is explicitly given the power to try, suspend, and remove the president under the Honduran constitution, and that the military was a proper entity to serve that warrant given the president's stature. They also argued that the president violated a special constitutional provision, article 239, stating that anyone seeking to change the country's strict one-term presidential term limit would "immediately cease to occupy their respective posts." While I was part of a team that rejected these arguments during the Truth and Reconciliation process, the fact that they could be made shows that even judging the constitutionality of military coups – the classic form of extraconstitutional act – may not always be simple (Dixon & Jackson 2013).

was reasonable to suppose that Zelaya's actions may have posed a threat of democratic erosion, it was more difficult to determine whether his actions were "constitutional" or "unconstitutional." The sequence of events proposed by Zelaya to carry out constitutional replacement was somewhat similar to that which had been proposed and carried out in Colombia in 1991, although under very different political conditions: A non-binding poll carried out outside of the legal order, followed by a binding referendum, followed by a Constituent Assembly (Segura & Bejarano 2004). Whether preexisting legal authority was necessary for each of these steps is a very difficult legal question. Even more difficult is the underlying question of whether the "unamendable" one-term limit could be removed or rewritten via constitutional replacement. It is certainly plausible to argue that the petrified clause could not be changed via the textual mechanisms of constitutional amendment, but making it untouchable even by Constituent Assembly, effectively cutting off any route of change, is a different thing.[5]

This leaves one key argument: Zelaya's actions were different from those of other contexts where extra-constitutional mechanisms were used – like Venezuela, Colombia, and Ecuador – because the courts in those other countries either approved the mechanisms or were silent, while the Honduran courts issued several orders for Zelaya to stand down. These judicial orders are certainly relevant, but they do not make the problem of extraterritorial constitutional interpretation go away, even where relevant judgments have been issued (often courts will simply avoid weighing in). The problem in the Honduran case is that virtually the entire judiciary was aligned with other members of the political elite and against Zelaya. Indeed, after the coup, the president of the Supreme Court gave interviews to the national and international press defending it, and the Court issued several decisions legitimating the coup under Honduran constitutional law. At least in circumstances like those, which are fairly common during moments of constitution-making, the international community cannot simply accept the verdict of the domestic courts as the last word on the matter. They are participants, not simply arbitrators.

Even putting aside the difficulties with extraterritorial constitutional interpretation during moments of constitution-making, there is a separate problem:

[5] The complexities of the interpretation of the petrified clause were made clear several years later – in a 2015 decision, the Honduran Supreme Court held that the one-term limit, as well as the clause making it unamendable by any means, were themselves unconstitutional and it excised them from the constitutional text. Among other arguments, the Court found that the petrified clause threatened to prevent any peaceful mechanism of constitutional change (Landau 2015).

Whether a system follows its own rules may be basically orthogonal to the underlying procedural values that one would want to promote. The dangers to democracy that are posed by a process of constitutional replacement may not depend precisely on whether or not that process is "legal" under the existing constitutional order. Insisting on legality may in some cases be used as a tool to block a desirable process, while in other cases adherence to the formal procedural rules may do little to ensure such a process. Even a relatively close monitoring of legality or constitutionality may thus do little to improve outcomes.

The Colombian case offers a good example: as already noted, in 1991 the political elite used extra-textual means to replace the 1886 constitution, since the existing text contained no provision whatsoever allowing for such an Assembly. Indeed, in a prior case from the 1970s the Supreme Court had struck down an attempt to delegate certain powers of constitutional change to such an Assembly, holding that the method of constitutional change found in the constitution (basically approval by congress in two separate sessions by first a simple and then an absolute majority) was exclusive (Cajas 2008: 59–72). In the lead-up to the Constituent Assembly of 1991, the Supreme Court changed its doctrine and allowed the sequence of events resulting in the calling of the Constituent Assembly on the grounds of original constituent power.

Imagine, however, a counterfactual scenario in which the Court had struck down the Assembly and the political elite had moved forward anyway, or in which an international body had believed the action to be "unconstitutional" despite the legitimation of the country's high court. A decision blocking the constitutional process may have prevented an exit from a deep political crisis, since the Congress and Supreme Court had stopped many previous efforts at constitutional change, leading critics to call Colombia in the 1980s a "blocked society" (Latorre Rueda 2011). And it would have stopped a process that, despite using extra-textual mechanisms, was highly consensual rather than unilateral: the resulting text was the result of broad agreement between various political movements, representing both the old party system and new insurgents. It also included input from a wide range of civil society groups (Segura & Bejarano 2004). Finally, the resulting constitution has been widely praised as strengthening rather than weakening Colombian democracy.

On the flip side, there are also cases where procedural rules have been followed but the process nonetheless raised significant risks of democratic erosion. The Hungarian case mentioned above is a good example – the Fidesz party arguably followed the relevant rules by gaining a two-thirds vote, but those rules allowed it to unilaterally dominate the process of constitutional replacement, resulting in a process that was neither deliberative nor inclusive, and which arguably worked a significant erosion of democracy in that country.

All of this may sound a bit too pessimistic: The fact that democracy clauses will sometimes be of little use in regulating constitution-making need not mean that this will always be the case. The point is simply that the attractiveness and feasibility of insisting on adherence to legality is very contextual. Imagine, for example, a case where the major political actors agree on a roadmap for a constitution-making process just before such a process is initiated. During the process, however, one of the actors (say a powerful president or party) reneges on the deal and changes the process in some substantial respect. In such a case, where domestic institutions are too weak to stop this action, it may make sense for international actors to insist that the existing legal roadmap be followed. Any legal claim to make a unilateral break with such a recently enacted procedural norm is probably weak, and the roadmap itself seems likely associated with positive normative values (democracy and social peace, for example) that could be imperiled by unilateral constitution-making. Even this use, however, would be a substantial expansion of the clauses beyond their current focus on military coups and similarly flagrantly illegal devices (Piccone 2005).

Procedural or Substantive International Norms

Some work has suggested that norms are emerging at the international level to govern either the process of constitution-making or the substance of constitutional texts. While it is possible that at some stage such norms would emerge, it is clear that we are far from such a situation. Moreover, it is unclear whether a transnational legal order of this type would be ineffective or even counterproductive.

The most commonly cited norm said to be emerging to govern the process of constitution-making, based both on treaties and custom, is one in favor of public participation (Franck & Thiruvengadam 2010; Hart 2010; Saati, Chapter ten this volume). It is not clear, though, how far such a norm would extend or what exactly it would encompass. Hart, for example, argues that the right could plausibly include three clusters of activities: electing representatives, voting in referenda, and offering input into the constitutional text. She notes that there is no clear guidance as to which mix of these forms of participation is appropriate in different circumstances. I will not, at any rate, analyze the question of whether such a norm exists or is emerging at the international level; I will instead simply point out that even if it were in the process of formation, it may not be an unalloyed good for domestic constitution-making.

Several commentators have noted the ambiguity in the concept of public participation in constitution-making. It encompasses a range of different activities, some more "active" and others more "passive" (Ginsburg, Elkins, & Blount 2009). Moreover, it appears to be easy to design popular participation mechanisms so that they appear to be robust, but actually play a function that is closer to window-dressing. Referenda or elections are of course very sensitive to the precise voting rules chosen, and can also be manipulated through outright fraud or subtler forms of influence. More active forms of participation, such as holding consultation sessions or encouraging popular input into the constitutional text, also vary widely. In some cases these may exercise significant influence on the final constitutional text. In others, however, their actual influence may be slight. In yet a third case, popularly-supported provisions, such as those governing constitutional rights, may actually be used as compensation for other provisions that support authoritarianism. Indeed, something like this may have happened in the 2008 constitution-making process in Ecuador, which both contained a large number of novel rights sought by civil society groups and instantiated a competitive authoritarian regime led by President Correa. So a mere requirement of participation, without much greater teeth, may do little to improve the outcomes of constitution-making.

In fairness, those supporting the emergence of such a requirement acknowledge its ambiguity – they argue that further practice will be needed to define its contours. But even a well-developed right to popular participation may involve trade-offs that have not fully been processed in existing work. The empirical literature gives little guidance as to which aspects of constitution-making actually result in more desirable outcomes. Some recent work suggests that public participation is correlated with those outcomes, while other work suggests more skepticism about their effect. At least in some cases, for example, inclusion of a full range of political elites – all or most major parties or movements – at the bargaining table may be more important than the level or type of popular participation in the constitution-making process. In those cases, an international mandate for popular participation may overshadow more important concerns.

More dramatically, pushing toward popular participation may actually make it less likely that designers of a process will achieve other goals. Some recent empirical work suggests that levels of popular participation are actually used to compensate for low levels of inclusion: when key sectors of political elite are excluded from a constitution-making process, constitutional designers compensate for this shortcoming by including passive forms of participation like referenda or more active forms like popular input into the text (Negretto forthcoming). Although participation and inclusion may act as substitutes for constitutional designers seeking legitimacy, they are not necessarily equivalent in terms of their effect on outcomes: leaving out a significant sector of the political elite may be especially destabilizing. Furthermore, as Elster points out, some forms of participation may also make it more difficult to reach elite consensus because different factions will be forced to play to their political bases rather than deliberating and compromising privately (Elster 1995: 388). Many of the Eastern European constitutions in the 1990s were written with relatively low levels of public participation but high levels of inclusion through round table talks and similar devices, in part because of this perceived need.

None of this is meant to argue that popular participation in constitution-making is a bad thing. Some empirical work suggests that it does improve outcomes, although this work is insufficient to make any definitive claims (Eisenstadt, LeVan, & Maboudi 2015). It may also be possible to design participation so that trade-offs do not materialize or are less sharp. Some analysts have suggested, for example, for an hour-glass shaped form of participation in which levels are high at the beginning of the process (to activate it and determine its basic procedural and substantive shape) and the end (to legitimate it), but lower in the middle to allow elite bargaining (Elster 1995). In particular contexts, this proposal or another one may make sense. But the imposition of a robust and more specific "participation" norm at the international level is at best premature and at worst may impose too much uniformity on design choices that should properly be dependent on context. We have not yet developed a plausible list of best practices in constitution-making, if such a list is even feasible.

Perhaps even more difficult would be the emergence of substantive norms or practices governing the content of constitutional texts. Given that democratic governance itself is not an international right, the possibility of international norms governing particular aspects of constitutional texts may seem very unlikely at least at the international rather than the regional level. But even were the emergence of such norms more imaginable, it is doubtful that they could be designed in an effective way.

The main reason lies in the dynamics of modern "hybrid" or "competitive authoritarian" regimes, which seem to rest on particular combinations of formal and informal norms. First, those regimes often seem to rely on particularly problematic combinations of formal norms, rather than any single provision operating independently. Scheppele has argued that the new Hungarian constitution created a "Frankenstate" composed of the aggregation of a large number of different elements that existed in other democratic states, although as problematic rather than salutary features (Scheppele 2013). The Hungarian constitution amalgamated all of these features – such as gerrymandering, restrictions on judicial jurisdiction, and less independent appointment procedures for courts and checking institutions – into a particularly virulent combination.

A related point is that the negative effects of new constitutions may rest heavily on contextual features, or on the interaction between formal and informal norms, rather than on isolated features of the text. In Venezuela, for example, President Chavez's constitution in 1999 did increase presidential power, but merely took a presidency that was perhaps the weakest in the region and made it one of the stronger ones, although still well within Latin American norms. The greatly increased effect of presidential power was caused by these formal changes coupled with other aspects of the constitution where the president warped or worked around formal norms; for example, by declining to effectively implement a civil society commission that was supposed to exercise a significant role over judicial appointments (Brewer-Carias 2010). By working around the commission, Chavez was able to control those appointments unilaterally.

In some cases, these problems may be overcome, although probably much more readily at the regional than the international level. It is imaginable, for example, that Latin America or Africa might eventually reach some consensus on the question of presidential term limits. Unlike many other parts of a constitutional text, the terms limits issue can arguably be analyzed in isolation, and at least within broad parameters in a universal way. Term limits at least in presidential regimes may exercise a clear influence on the political order irrespective of the content of the rest of the constitution. Although Latin America at least currently seems to be going the other way – more countries are currently removing term limits than adding them[6] – one could imagine the region eventually determining that at least some designs, like allowing presidents to serve for life with no break, were too dangerous or too associated with authoritarianism to be permissible. Even if some such norms eventually emerge, however, they are unlikely to play a major role in preventing democratic erosion.

6 Both Honduras and Ecuador, for example, removed term limits in 2015, in the Ecuadorian case through constitutional amendment and in the case of Honduras through a Supreme Court decision.

International Civil Society and Best Practices

This leaves a set of possibilities for transnational legal orderings that are more advisory, and perhaps less institutionalized, in scope. First, many commentators have noted the rise of involvement of international organizations and NGOs in constitution-making over the past several decades. In some circumstances, these groups can exercise a significant influence over the shape of constitutional process and the resulting constitutional text. For example, the international community has been heavily involved in constitution-making in some post-conflict situations. Across many other cases, international civil society groups have played a significant advisory role in the constitution-making process. An extreme example of this is the constitution of Bosnia and Herzegovina, where the constitution itself was drafted as part of an international peace agreement (O'Brien 2010).

The involvement of international organizations has plausibly improved constitution-making across a range of cases. That said, there are a few cautions before concluding that the involvement of these actors have effectively "internationalized" constitution-making and ameliorated the problems noted in Part I. The first is simply a point about selection. International involvement is not evenly distributed or a part of every constitution-making process: these entities are heavily involved in some processes but much less involved in others. The involvement of international actors may to some degree be endogenous to other characteristics of the domestic and international political landscape.

In part, levels of international involvement seem to depend on the interests of international actors and the perceived importance of the country in question. At the domestic level, involvement of international actors will often depend on the goals of dominant political actors. In the ongoing process in Chile, for example, the government has invited in a broad range of international actors, perhaps as a way to increase domestic legitimacy and support despite right-wing opposition. The Chilean government has been attentive, because of the domestic political context, to being seen as following international best practices. But in both Hungary (2011) and Venezuela (1999), international actors played much less role in discussions around constitutional process and text. In both cases, political leaders who had engineered a rapid and exclusionary process plausibly viewed international involvement as an obstacle to their aims. Those cases where democratic erosion is most possible may also be cases where international involvement tends to be slight.

The other major caution is about the state of the field, or the existing and perhaps inevitable gaps in our levels of knowledge. International involvement can without question be helpful in showing domestic designers the full range of comparative experience and in demonstrating the pitfalls and promise of approaches tried elsewhere. Still, best practices are sometimes formulated without a sufficient empirical base, or on a small number of case studies. The popular participation norm, for example, is one often pushed by international actors, sometimes based on the paradigmatic case of South Africa. But as noted in the prior section, the empirical evidence for the impact of participation is mixed, and we still do not fully understand its trade-offs with other aspects of the constitutional process. There are limits to the advice that can plausibly be given by international organizations and NGOs, and it is even possible that the involvement of these actors might worsen rather than improve some processes.

Advisory Bodies

Finally, in some cases advisory organizations at the international level have played a role in monitoring constitutional change and constitution-making, and this role could perhaps be expanded to additional regions and processes. A good example is the Venice Commission of the Council of Europe, which has become a relevant actor in some of the recent threats to democracy in Eastern Europe (Craig, Chapter six this volume). The Commission's mandate is advisory: it has the ability to review legal measures and other instruments and to make recommendations in order to move toward "the dissemination and consolidation of a common constitutional heritage" in Europe.

Since 2010, for example, the Commission has offered several opinions reviewing the new Hungarian constitution as well as laws intended to implement it. In Opinion 621 of 2011, for example, the Commission critiqued the exclusionary, non-participatory, and rapid and non-transparent nature of the constitution-making process. It also expressed concerns over some of the substantive provisions of the new constitution, such as the limitations on the jurisdiction of the Constitutional Court. The Commission also issued several opinions reviewing several of the "cardinal laws" intended to implement key parts of the constitution: It critiqued several aspects of the laws regulating the judiciary (663/2012), the Constitutional Court (683/2012), and the prosecution service (666/2012).

The Venice Commission's work in the Hungarian case, as well as other recent Eastern European episodes, has been subject to criticism as well as praise. Critics have argued, for example, that the Commission's analyses have tended to take pieces of legislation in isolation, rather than holistically – a variant of the "Frankenstate" problem noted above. They have also argued that the Commission has demonstrated insufficient knowledge of the facts on the ground. But at least potentially, an advisory commission approach offers advantages over other models on both scores. A body like the Venice Commission is not restricted to determining whether domestic actors have followed their own rules, or analyzing aspects of procedure or substance in isolation. It can instead potentially make a relatively holistic review of the effect of procedure or substantive provisions, and one based on the impact actions and provisions in practice, rather than simply on paper. Moreover, the Venice Commission is not restricted to identifying violations of domestic and international law, but can instead push states toward best procedural and substantive practices, in light of "common European heritage."

Of course, the advisory nature of the Commission's review may limit its effectiveness, which is another common critique (Nergelius 2015). The Hungarian government made some legal changes in response to the Commission's recommendations, but it did not change its approach; the changes were generally cosmetic. The review of an advisory body like the Commission could gain more teeth if it was utilized by other international actors with binding authority to sanction a noncompliant state. In Europe, this is at least a theoretical possibility because of the existence of actors like the European Commission. The European Commission in 2014 adopted a multi-step procedure for responding to threats to the rule of law, but it is too soon to know whether it will take effective action in response to significant problems noted by the Venice Commission, such as the recent erosion of democracy in Poland (Koncewicz 2016). Advisory bodies may also influence constitution-making through other routes: they might for example embolden domestic institutions like courts to take tougher stances against abusive constitution-making practices.

One could imagine seeking to generalize advisory bodies like the Venice Commission outside of the European context. President Marzouki's International Constitutional Court proposal envisioned an advisory role for the Court in developing best practices and analyzing national legal changes, in addition to an adjudicative role. But it would be very difficult to develop international best practices, at least in terms of constitution-making, for the reasons noted above. Perhaps more feasible would be the expansion of advisory bodies at the regional level, where problems of reaching substantive and procedural consensus might be less dire, if still complex.

Take Latin America as a potential case study. Although significant human rights and other regional institutions do exist in the region, the overall network of international institutions is much less dense than what is found in Europe, and those that do exist are less effective. It may not be easy for regional states to agree even on an advisory commission to govern domestic constitutional and legal design. Moreover, even if states did agree on such a body, it is unclear whether what a "Latin American heritage" in constitutional and legal design would look like.

The recent constitution-making experiences in the Andes, for example, offer both a procedural and substantive challenge to prevailing liberal models. From a procedural perspective, they permit exclusion of prevailing political elite in return for participatory processes that offer input to historically marginalized groups. From a substantive perspective, they perhaps weaken horizontal institutions of accountability in return for strengthening direct popular control over the governing class via devices like recalls and referenda and the inclusion of new forms of rights (McCoy 2010). In both cases, the basic idea is that liberal democratic models can stand as obstacles to the achievement of social transformation and the inclusion of marginalized groups.

In a sense, as noted above, the recent Andean constitution-making experiences are not just attempts to leverage gaps in the existing liberal-democratic constitutional TLO, but at least incipient challenges to that TLO. The existence of this level of contestation within Latin America shows that even within a region where there is broad agreement on basic norms of democracy, broad divergence in both the process and substance of constitution-making can persist. This disagreement does not make the establishment of advisory bodies impossible, but it does significantly complicate the task.

CONCLUSION

This chapter has had two major goals. The first is to argue that the particular institutional and legal circumstances of constitution-making mean that domestic restraint is often problematic, and this absence of restraint is associated with significant common problems: the erosion of democracy and increase in political tension. In other words, the dominant liberal-democratic constitutional TLO has gaps that are particularly salient during the constitution-making process. This is partly a product of the political context within which constitution-making is normally undertaken, and partly a product of the way the TLO itself has treated the process of constitution-making.

The second goal of this chapter is to undertake a critical review of potential ways in which the constitutional TLO could potentially be strengthened to focus more on constitution-making moments. The review concludes that this is a very difficult issue to tackle at the international level, perhaps suggesting the limits of a TLO framework to deal with certain types of problems. First, constitution-making is often carried out during periods of domestic institutional crisis, which may limit the ability of transnational norms to penetrate and constrain within domestic legal orders. Second, it is possible that the concerns involved in constitution-making are too localized, and its issues too politically charged and too close to the core of national sovereignty, for at least a strong transnational order to emerge in this area. More broadly, this study of the weaknesses of the constitution-making TLO may suggest that it is failing in part because of insufficient attentiveness to political context and considerations. The actors constructing the emerging TLO governing constitution-making have focused in large part on legal questions, such as the theoretical question of constituent power and the issue of whether actors have followed existing constitutional rules, rather than the issues of political context that animate how these tools are used. A successful legal TLO in this politically sensitive area would need to achieve greater integration between legal analysis and political context.

All of the plausible solutions surveyed in this chapter – democracy clauses, international norms, best practices, and advisory bodies – have substantial drawbacks. Some are very difficult to deepen; others might threaten to do more harm to domestic constitution-making than good, either by privileging the wrong goals or by imposing uniform models on what is a very contextual process. Still, some useful recommendations are suggested from existing models. For example, experience suggests that improved approaches are likely to emerge from a combination of approaches. For example, an advisory model like the Venice Commission shows perhaps the most promise in identifying problematic constitution-making processes; such an approach could be paired with other institutions that give a greater promise of effective enforcement. Given the importance of the threat posed by some acts of constitution-making, the most sensible solution is to seek realistic, incremental progress across a range of the models reviewed here aimed to strengthen a liberal-democratic constitutional TLO.

REFERENCES

Arato, Andrew. 2000. *Civil Society, Constitution, and Legitimacy*. Plymouth: Rowman and Littlefield.

Arato, Andrew. 2010. "Post-Sovereign Constitution-Making in Hungary: After Success, Partial Failure, and Now What?" *South African Journal of Human Rights* 26: 19–44.

Bánkuti, Miklós, Gábor Halmai, and Kim Lane Scheppele. 2012. "Hungary's Illiberal Turn: Disabling the Constitution." *Journal of Democracy* 23: 138–46.

Braver, Joshua. 2016. "Hannah Arendt in Venezuela: The Supreme Court Battles Hugo Chávez Over the Creation of the 1999 Constitution." *International Journal of Constitutional Law* 14: 555–83.

Brewer-Carias, Allan. 2010. *The Dismantling of Democracy in Venezuela*. Cambridge: Cambridge University Press.

Brown, Nathan. 2013. "Tracking the Arab Spring: Egypt's Failed Transition." *Journal of Democracy* 24: 45–58.

Cajas, Mario. 2008. *El control judicial a la reforma constitucional, 1910–2007*. Santiago de Cali, Colombia: ICESI University Press.

Cameron, Maxwell A. and Kenneth E. Sharpe. 2010. "Andean Left Turns: Constituent Power an Constitution-Making." Pp. 61–80 in *Latin America's Left Turns: Politics, Policies, and Trajectories of Change*, edited by Maxwell A. Cameron and Eric Hershberg. Boulder: Lynne Rienner.

Cepeda-Espinosa, Manuel Jose. 2004. "Judicial Activism in a Violent Context: The Origin, Role and Impact of the Colombian Constitutional Court." *Washington University Global Studies Law Review* 3: 529–700.

Colon-Rios, Joel. 2012. *Weak Constitutionalism: Democratic Legitimacy and the Question of Constituent Power*. Abingdon: Routledge.

Conaghan, Catherine M. 2008. "Ecuador: Correa's Plebiscitary Presidency." *Journal of Democracy* 19: 46–60.

Dixon, Rosalind and Vicki C. Jackson. 2013. "Constitutions Inside Out: Outsider Interventions I Domestic Constitutional Contests." *Wake Forest Law Review* 48: 149–210.

Dixon, Rosalind and David Landau. 2015. "Transnational Constitutionalism and a Limited Doctrine of Unconstitutional Constitutional Amendment." *International Journal of Constitutional Law* 13: 606–38.

Dixon, Rosalind and David Landau. 2016. "Competitive Democracy and the Constitutional Minimum Core." Pp. 268–92 in *Assessing Constitutional Performance*, edited by Tom Ginsburg and Aziz Huq. Cambridge: Cambridge University Press.

Eisenstadt, Todd A., Carl LeVan, and Tofigh Maboudi. 2015. "When Talk Trumps Text: The Democratizing Effects of Deliberation during Constitution-Making, 1974–2011." *American Political Science Review* 109: 592–612.

Elster, Jon. 1995. "Forces and Mechanisms in the Constitution-Making Process." *Duke Law Journal* 45: 364–96.

Feldman, Noah, David Landau, Brian Sheppard, and Leonidas Rosa-Suazo. 2011. Report to the Commission on Truth and Reconciliation of Honduras: Constitutional Issues, at http://papers.ssrn.com/sol3/papers.cfm?abstract_id=1915214.

Franck, Thomas M. and Arun K. Thiruvengadam. 2010. "Norms of International Law Relating to the Constitution-Making Process." Pp 3–19 in *Framing the State in Times of Transition: Case Studies in Constitution Making*, edited by Laurel E. Miller. Washington, DC: United States Institute of Peace.

Gamarra, Eduardo A. 2008. "Bolivia: Evo Morales and Democracy." Pp. 124–48 in *Constructing Democratic Governance in Latin America*, 3rd edition, edited by Jorge I. Dominguez and Michael Shifter. Baltimore: Johns Hopkins University Press.

Ginsburg, Tom, Zachary Elkins, and Justin Blount. 2009. "Does the Process of Constitution-Making Matter?" *Annual Review of Law and Social Science* 5: 201–23.

Halliday, Terence C. and Gregory Shaffer. 2015a. "Transnational Legal Orders." Pp. 3–72 in *Transnational Legal Orders*, edited by Terence C. Halliday and Gregory Shaffer. Cambridge: Cambridge University Press.

Halliday, Terence C. and Gregory Shaffer. 2015b. "Researching Transnational Legal Orders." Pp. 475–528 in *Transnational Legal Orders*, edited by Terence C. Halliday and Gregory Shaffer. Cambridge: Cambridge University Press.

Hart, Vivien. 2010. "Constitution Making and the Right to Take Part in a Public Affair." Pp. 20–54 in *Framing the State in Times of Transition: Case Studies in Constitution Making*, edited by Laurel E. Miller. Washington, DC: United States Institute of Peace.

Human Rights Foundation. 2010. "The Facts and the Law Behind the Democratic Crisis of Honduras, 2009." Available at http://humanrightsfoundation.org/uploads/The_Facts_And_The_Law_Honduras_2009.pdf.

Koncewicz, Tomasz Tadeusz. 2016. "Of Constitutional Defiance, Migration and Borrowing of Unconstitutional Tactics and European Resistance." *International Journal of Constitutional Law Blog*. August 17, 2016. Available at www.iconnectblog.com/2016/08/of-constitutional-defiance-migration-and-borrowing-of-unconstitutional-tactics-and-european-resistance.

McCoy, Jennifer. 2010. "Venezuela under Chavez: Beyond Liberalism." Pp. 81–100 in *Latin America's Left Turns: Politics, Policies, and Trajectories of Change*, edited by Maxwell A. Cameron and Eric Hershberg. Boulder: Lynne Rienner.

Landau, David. 2013a. "Constitution-Making Gone Wrong." *Alabama Law Review* 64: 923–80.

Landau, David. 2013b. "Abusive Constitutionalism." *University of California Davis Law Review* 47: 189–260.

Landau, David. 2015. "Honduras: Term Limits Drama 2.0 – How the Supreme Court Declared the Constitution Unconstitutional." *ConstitutionNet*.

May 27, 2015. Available at www.constitutionnet.org/news/honduras-term-limits-drama-20-how-supreme-court-declared-constitution-unconstitutional.

Landau, David and Rosalind Dixon. 2015. "Constraining Constitutional Change." *Wake Forest Law Review* 50: 85990.

Landemore, Hélène. 2015. "Inclusive Constitution-Making: The Icelandic Experiment." *Journal of Political Philosophy* 23: 166–91.

Lehoucq, Fabrice. 2008. "Bolivia's Constitutional Breakdown." *Journal of Democracy* 19: 110–24.

Latorre Rueda, Mario. 2011. "Colombia: una sociedad bloqueada? Articulo 120: espiritu nacional y partipacion adecuada y equitativa." Pp. 173–84 in *Partidos y elecciones en Colombia*, edited by Felipe Botero. Bogota, Colombia: Universidad de Los Andes University Press.

Levitsky, Steven and Lucan R. Way. 2010. *Competitive Authoritarianism: Hybrid Regimes after the Cold War*. Cambridge: Cambridge University Press.

Negretto, Gabriel. 2012. "Replacing and Amending Constitutions: The Logic of Constitutional Change in Latin America." *Law and Society Review* 46: 749–79.

Negretto, Gabriel. Forthcoming. "Constitution-Making in Democratic Orders." In *Constitution-Making in Democratic Orders*, edited by Gabriel Negretto. New York: Cambridge University Press.

Nergelius, Joakim. 2015. "The Role of the Venice Commission in Maintaining the Rule of Law in Hungary and Romania." Pp. 291–308 in *Constitutional Crisis in the European Constitutional Area: Theory, Law, and Politics in Hungary and Romania*, edited by Armin von Bogdandy and Paul Sonnevand. Oxford: Hart Publishing.

O'Brien, James C. 2010. "The Dayton Constitution of Bosnia and Herzegovina." Pp. 332–49 in *Framing the State in Times of Transition: Case Studies in Constitution Making*, edited by Laurel E. Miller. Washington, DC: United States Institute of Peace.

Partlett, William. 2014. *The American Tradition of Constituent Power*. Unpublished manuscript. Available at https://papers.ssrn.com/sol3/papers.cfm?abstract_id=2538970.

Partlett, William. 2012. "The Dangers of Popular Constitution-Making." *Brooklyn Journal of International Law* 38: 193–238.

Piccone, Theodore J. 2005. "International Mechanisms for Protecting Democracy." Pp. 101–26 in *Protecting Democracy: International Responses*, edited by Morton H. Halperin and Mirna Galic. Lanham: Lexington Books.

Scheppele, Kim Lane. 2013. "The Rule of Law and the Frankenstate: Why Governance Checklists Do Not Work." *Governance: An International Journal of Policy, Administration, and Institutions* 26: 559–62.

Segura, Renata and Ana Maria Bejarano. 2004. "Ni una asamblea mas sin nosotros! Exclusion, Inclusion, and the Politics of Constitution-Making in the Andes." *Constellations* 11: 217–36.
Stilt, Kristen R. 2012. "The End of 'One Hand': The Egyptian Constitutional Declaration and the Rift between the 'People' and the Supreme Council of the Armed Forces." *Yearbook of Islamic and Middle Eastern Law* 16: 43–52.
Tushnet, Mark. 2015. "Peasants with Pitchforks, and Toilers with Twitter: Constitutional Revolutions and the Constituent Power." *International Journal of Constitutional Law* 13: 639–54.

9

The Possibilities and Limits of a Constitution-Making Transnational Legal Order: The Case of Chile

Javier Couso*

INTRODUCTION: THE ROLE OF A CONSTITUTION-MAKING TRANSNATIONAL LEGAL ORDER IN THE DYNAMICS OF ENACTING NEW CONSTITUTIONS

Until the mid-twentieth century, constitution-making was generally considered to be a fundamentally national enterprise. Indeed, given that the constitution was not just the apex of the legal system but, more importantly, the foundational (or re-foundational) document of the nation and, therefore, a crucial element in the formation of its identity, emphasis on the national character of it was critical.

The intimate link between constitutions and national identity was a social construction largely disconnected from historical fact, since the borrowing of foreign ideas in constitution-making processes is as old as the emergence of modern constitutionalism. But it was a social construction that played an important legitimating role, in the context of the creation of new nation-states. Indeed, due to nineteenth-century legal ideologies linking the juridical system and, especially, constitutional law, to the nation-building process, constitutions were thought to embody the identity of a nation, something that made foreign influences in this domain unacceptable.

The national character then ascribed to constitutional law was, in turn, reflective of the influential work of Montesquieu, who, in the previous century, had defended the need of public law to be suited to the character of the people it was supposed to govern. In his own words:

* I am thankful to Fondap Project N° 15130009, which finances the Centre for Social Conflict and Cohesion Studies (COES), of which I am an Associate Researcher. This piece includes some ideas developed in an unpublished document written by the author. See Javier Couso, "Reflections on Latin American experiences in constitution-building from a Chilean perspective," in *Constitution-Building Processes in Latin America* (IDEA International, Conference Report, October 21–22, 2015). On file with the author.

> Besides the law of nations relating to all societies, *there is a polity, or civil constitution, for each, particularly considered* … Better is it to say, that the government most conformable to nature is that which *best agrees with the humour and disposition of the people in whose favour it is established* … the political and civil laws of each nation … *should be adapted in such a manner to the people for whom they are framed, that it is a great chance if those of one nation suit another.* They should be relative to the nature and principle of each government; whether they form it, as may be said of political laws; or whether they support it, as in the case of civil institutions. They should be relative to the climate of each country, to the quality of its soil, to its situation and extent, to the principal occupation of the natives, whether husbandmen, huntsmen, or shepherds: *they should have a relation to the degree of liberty which the constitution will bear, to the religion of the inhabitants, to their inclinations, riches, numbers, commerce, manners, and customs.*[1]

Montesquieu's defense of a heavily localized public law ought not to be taken lightly. In an era when natural law (the "law of reason") was still considered to be binding on every civilized nation, to argue that laws – and constitutional law in particular – ought to be suited to the "humour and disposition" (what we would now call "culture") of the people it was aimed to rule, was nothing short of revolutionary.

The fact that Montesquieu would have such an important influence on the United States' Constitution of 1787, as well as the compatibility of his constitutional thinking with other nationalistic forces in display at the time, contributed to the notion that the ancient practice of legal borrowing and transplants (Watson 1974) could not easily apply to the drafting of "political codes." In spite of this, the actual history of constitution-making and implementation departed significantly from this ideology. In fact, there was much exporting and importing of constitutional ideas and institutions from both the center to the periphery (if that category can be used to describe what happened two centuries ago), and within the periphery. An example of export is the active role played by Jeremy Bentham in influencing the process of constitution-building in other nations.[2] An example of import can be found in the way the Argentinean framers of the 1853 Constitution discussed the virtues and flaws of the constitutions of a number of countries, when faced with the task of elaborating a new one for their own nation. This can be appreciated in the seminal work of Juan Bautista Alberdi, who, from his exile in Chile, studied with care the constitutions of the United States; Germany;

[1] See Montesquieu (1757), I, 3. Emphases added.

[2] See M. D. A. Freeman (1998), p. 139.

Switzerland; Chile; Peru; Colombia; Mexico; Uruguay; Paraguay; and California. From this *tour de force*, Alberdi elaborated a draft that adapted foreign constitutional ideas to the perceived needs of his native country.[3]

The account of the relationship between constitution-making, transnational legal borrowing, and national identity just given is particularly well suited to the Latin American region at the time of its independence from Spanish imperial rule, in the early nineteenth century. Indeed, given that the wars of independence (1809–33) were waged against a monarchical regime, it was only natural that, once the new leaders consolidated their power and were confronted with the need to politically organize new independent states, they looked at the only country with a republican system at the time, the United States of America. The imperative to create a political regime as distant as possible from monarchical rule was so strong that the United States Constitution of 1787 served as the basic model for the bulk of the newly independent states of Spanish America, in spite of the fact that the US legal system was fully immersed in the so-called "Common Law tradition," resting on a completely different basis from the "Civil Law tradition" characterizing Latin America.

The dynamics of early constitution-making in Latin America continue to the present, involving a combination of transnational borrowing and domestic choice of constitutional design shaped by national power conditions. One of the crucial changes with regard to the former, however, is the transformation of what used to be merely a transnational borrowing into a fully formed transnational legal order (TLO), due to the sense that there are aspects of constitution-building that are not optional, but normatively compelled. This shift from optional borrowing to being obliged, practically speaking, to adopt some elements of liberal constitutionalism, has been happening in most of Latin America with regard to the bill of rights and, to a certain extent, with the very processes of constitution-making.

Having said this, I shall argue that, in spite of its success in the areas of rights and procedures, the dominant (liberal) TLO regulating constitution-making processes has not been as successful with regard to the sections of the constitution that organize political power. Indeed, as we shall see in some detail in the analysis of the case of Chile, it is extremely challenging for the constitution-making TLO to influence the distribution of powers section of constitutions, a domain where domestic power struggles define what gets done.

Thus, through the study of Chile, this chapter aims to contribute to the theorization of the constitution-making TLO, by noting that there are

[3] See Alberdi (2017, 1852).

historical and power politics contingencies that may either render this TLO incomplete or unable to display the influence it has shown in other areas. In the Chilean case, then, the liberal constitution-making TLO appears only partially institutionalized.

ACKNOWLEDGING TRANSNATIONAL INFLUENCES AND THE RISE OF A LIBERAL CONSTITUTION-MAKING TLO IN LATIN AMERICA

Notwithstanding the transnational features that processes of constitution-making have had since the dawn of modern constitutionalism in Latin America, the need to affirm national identity led to the evisceration of evidence of foreign influence in the constitutions of the newly emancipated countries of the region. Thus, whereas Andrés Bello (the region's great codifier of private law) had no problem in openly recognizing in the preamble to Chile's Civil Code of 1857 the foreign sources that he used to elaborate that celebrated code, the framers of the Latin American charters enacted immediately following independence from Spain were careful to omit any reference to the transnational sources used in their constitution-making efforts. This would change only gradually, as exemplified by the recognition by Juan Bautista Alberdi of the foreign constitutional sources that inspired his work.

The acknowledgment of the role played by transnational elements in constitution-making in Latin America increased in the early twentieth century, when many Latin American jurists and politicians openly recognized at constitutional conventions and assemblies the borrowing they engaged in, for example, concerning the adoption of the so-called "*social constitutionalism.*" This was the case of the most important actor behind the elaboration of Chile's Constitution of 1925, Arturo Alessandri, who openly invoked the work of the French scholar Leon Duguit in the constitutional convention that led to the introduction of the above-mentioned charter.[4] At any rate, the trend toward explicit constitutional borrowing would eventually be fully legitimized with the introduction of the Universal Declaration of Human Rights of 1948, which – due to its enormous prestige – became a standard transnational source for drafting bills of rights around the world.

The shift toward the embrace of the legitimacy of constitutional borrowing eventually led to the emergence of what Ginsburg, Halliday and Shaffer call a "Constitution Making Transnational Legal Order." According to these authors:

[4] See Dorner (1971), p. 85.

> The TLO framework brings together three concepts: (i) it focuses on the issue of order, a central concept in the sociology of law regarding the creation and settling of generalized normative behavioral expectations; (ii) it studies the role of law in such ordering processes, involving the use of legal form and legal institutions; and (iii) it examines the transnational nature of the normative ordering. Bringing these three concepts together, it defines a transnational legal order as "a collection of formalized legal norms and associated organizations and actors that authoritatively order the understanding and practice of law across national jurisdictions."[5]

The notion of a constitution-making TLO is helpful to identify a critical juncture experienced by processes of constitution-building and implementation in recent decades. Indeed, as we have seen, while there has always been exportation and importation of constitutional ideas and practices (notwithstanding the nationalistic rhetoric that opposed such practice in the past), *until recently this occurred without the normative spirit brought by the emergence of a "constitution-making TLO,"* which provides a sense of obligation to what was previously seen as merely an option. Indeed, as other chapters in this volume describe well, the emergence of a liberal democratic constitution-making TLO, which includes a set of human rights declarations, treaties, and other international human rights instruments, has helped to cement a sort of "global bill of rights" regarded as mandatory.

Thus, it can be asserted that, while the exportation and importation of constitutional law ideas and practices has been going on for centuries, the appearance of a transnational legal order regulating the elaboration and implementation of new constitutions signals a qualitative change in the meaning of practices that look otherwise similar. The key factor shaping the meaning of the practice of constitutional borrowing is the normative bent that characterizes a constitution-making TLO. To put it bluntly, it is one thing to engage in the cherry-picking of constitutional ideas and institutions when designing a new constitution, and quite another to feel forced to include what has become the canon of civilization in terms of constitutional law.

The influence of a liberal-democratic constitution-making TLO in the domain of fundamental rights in Latin America is apparent in the convergence that can be seen in the bill of rights of the constitutional charters enacted in the last three decades or so, such as the ones of Brazil (1988); Colombia (1991); Venezuela (1999); Ecuador (2008); and Bolivia (2009). Indeed, the analysis of these charters reveal that the fundamental rights they recognized are largely the same as those proclaimed by the Universal

5 See the Introductory Chapter of this volume.

Declaration of Human Rights (1948) and the American Convention of Human Rights (1969), both integral elements of the liberal constitution-making TLO. Furthermore, the impact of the latter is in fact so strong that even the constitution imposed in 1980 by General Pinochet in Chile, included a bill of rights largely aligned with the liberal TLO (although the charter included a transitory clause which made the entire rights section of the constitution inoperative until democracy returned in 1990).

As we have seen in this section, the explicit acknowledgment of constitutional borrowing that had taken place since the late nineteenth century in Latin America eventually led to the emergence of a true constitution-making TLO. This, however, has been so far only influential in the domain of rights, and – as we shall see below in this chapter – increasingly in the constitution-making process itself, but not in the way the distribution of political power is structured. In the following section, we shall analyze this dynamic.

LIMITS TO RESTRUCTURING POWER WITHIN THE STATE

We have seen that, with the appearance of a liberal democratic constitution-making TLO, the old practice of constitutional importation and exportation has acquired a new meaning, one that promises to enhance even more global convergence in the domain of fundamental rights (a trend that started at least from the time of adoption by the French of the Declaration of the Rights of Man). Furthermore, as other contributors to this volume show, the dominant constitution-making TLO includes "best practices" of how to go about debating and adopting a new constitution, using procedures that have been elaborated and promoted by international organizations such as International IDEA. These process norms are perhaps a distinctive feature of this particular TLO, relative to others out there.

Yet, contrary to what is the case with fundamental rights, or even with the norm of participatory and deliberative processes for constitution-making, promoted by the liberal-democratic TLO, the organization of state power remains staunchly national in character, resisting the global convergence forces at play in the domain of rights, or the norms regulating the process of constitution-making. One plausible explanation for the difference is that – even in this era of legal convergence – there is a sense that, while human rights are "universal" in nature, the decision on the specific arrangements of state institutions (such as the decision to adopt a federal or a unitary form of state, or a parliamentary or presidential regime) ought to be left to the sovereign states.

In other words, *while fundamental rights travel well across continents and legal cultures, the distribution of state power remains a highly localized affair.* In other words, actors involved in processes of constitution-making are more open to the importation of human rights than to the transplant of foreign institutions to the "engine room" (Gargarella, 2013) of their own constitution. One plausible reason for the different treatment of constitutional borrowing of human rights as opposed to techniques of organizing state power is that while the latter is typically done through the enactment of clear constitutional rules (thus making the political power distribution evident to all at once), the importation of universal rights would typically involve the introduction of open-ended clauses, which will necessarily require the interpretation of abstract principles and values done by the very institutions that the "engine room" of the constitution will set up. In light of this, it is only natural that the constitution-makers of a given country will be less open to let foreign ideas define the distribution of state powers than to adopt abstractly worded individual rights.

The Latin American constitutional landscape represents a good example of this. Even though there are a few commonalities in the way the organization of state power is set up – in particular, the central place that the executive branch plays in the structure of government – there are also strong divergences in terms of the organization of state power, including the spatial division of authority (with some countries having a federal system, while others a unitary one); the organization of the judicial branch (in terms of having a separate constitutional court or, instead, giving the supreme court constitutional adjudication powers); the electoral system; the existence of one or two legislative chambers; the way the legislative process is organized, and so on.

As relevant as the differences just noted is the almost complete lack of global normative prescriptions coming from the liberal TLO with regard to the organization of state power, in contrast with what happens in the domain of rights. In fact, there is little guidance provided by global norms within the dominant liberal constitution-making TLO in terms of how to structure state power.

Finally, even if there were a set of clear prescriptions coming from the liberal TLO in terms of how to structure a constitutional democracy (apart from the centuries-old notion of the need to have a separation of powers), the national power dynamics would be crucial in terms of which recommended structural reforms are accepted and which are not.

To sum up this section, considering that law – and in particular constitutional law – can fundamentally alter the political, economic, and social power relations of a given nation, one should expect that, even if a constitution-making TLO is in full display, the degree to which it will exert its force on a particular state will depend on the crude political and socio-economic correlations of power existing in a specific country.

THE EMERGENCE OF TRANSNATIONAL ACTORS IN CONSTITUTION-MAKING PROCESSES

In the previous sections, I have referred to just one of the transnational elements often present in constitution-making processes – norm-borrowing by national framers of constitutions – suggesting that, while it was already present in Latin America at the dawn of modern constitutionalism, its political legitimacy developed only gradually. Contrasting with norm-borrowing, transnational legal actors did not appear in the scene of Latin America's constitution-making processes until recently. Indeed, although by the 1920s and 1930s an active norm-entrepreneurship began to be deployed by US economists in the realm of fiscal and economic regulation (with several economic "missions" going to the region to advise governments to set up central banks, securities and exchange commissions, and other regulatory bodies), nothing like that was accepted in the domain of constitution-making or constitutional reform. In other words, Latin American states were traditionally happy to accept legal foreign assistance in the drafting of codes and economic regulations, but they were not ready to do so in the sphere of constitution-making. This disparity suggests that while legal assistance by foreigners was regarded as acceptable in the more "technical" domains of the law, it was not considered appropriate in the more "political" realm of constitutional law. However, over the last couple of decades, this second aspect of transnational constitution-making started to develop, particularly in countries of the so-called "Global South," that have accepted – or actively look for – the assistance of constitutional scholars from the "Global North" when confronting constitution-making processes.

The emergence of a set of transnational legal actors involved in the actual drafting of constitutions (or in the advice of domestic constitution-makers) started soon after the end of the Cold War, which coincided with state-building processes and transitions to democracy in many former communist regimes, including due to the emergence of new states following the dissolution of the former USSR and former Yugoslavia. This trend toward engaging transnational legal actors has been reinforced by the work of international organizations, such as International IDEA, which has played a crucial role in helping countries involved in constitution-making processes.

After the notion that expert knowledge in the domain of comparative constitutional law could contribute to national processes of constitution-making became legitimized in countries of the Global South, a variety of transnational actors began to deploy their "expert" knowledge in such processes, often with the help of Global North non-governmental organizations, as well as organizations linked to the United Nations system. Given the relatively recent emergence of these transnational networks of experts, we lack a reliable evaluation of their actual contribution. What we know, though, is that they have been playing a significant role in processes of constitution-making, typically by conveying the accumulated experience of constitutional bodies and structures of their own countries to the local politicians and scholars involved in the drafting of new constitutions. The very presence of such experts is not ideologically neutral, a fact that has led to a "competition" for influence between different sets of transnational experts for influencing particular countries engaged in these types of processes.

Thus, while in the early years of the so-called "*third wave of democratization*" (circa 1990) the upper hand belonged to constitutional experts linked to international financial organizations such as the World Bank and the IMF (who then promoted various forms of "neoliberal" constitutionalism), in recent years they have been challenged by another set of transnational actors espousing either "social-democratic" forms of constitutionalism or different types of "radical" constitutionalism.

Given this context, while in the countries where neoliberal constitutional experts prevailed the new constitutions introduced autonomous central banks and the strengthening of private property rights (among others economic clauses), in those where social-democratic experts managed to become hegemonic, a number of justiciable socio-economic rights were included in the new charters. Finally, in the case of the so-called "radical" democracies of Venezuela, Ecuador, and Bolivia, an entire different set of "experts" were called to help in the drafting of constitutions who aligned with the revolutionary character of those regimes (Couso 2014).

THE LIMITS TO THE CONSTITUTION-MAKING TLO: THE CASE OF CHILE

In the previous sections, we have outlined the emergence of a transnational legal order which regulates the many constitution-making processes taking place around the world. In spite of its success, however, there are important limits to the reach of this particular TLO. These limits result from the high stakes that any constitution-making process necessarily involves. Indeed, given the deeply political nature of discussing and adopting a new constitution, the specific configuration of power within a particular nation can fundamentally alter the impact of the transnational norms and orientations prescribed for national constitution-making processes. In this section, I shall illustrate this point through the analysis of the constituent process that took place in Chile between 2011–17. The case of Chile is of interest since, in spite of the fact that this country had everything going to conform to the liberal-democratic TLO for constitution-making processes, it ultimately failed to deliver a new constitution. This case suggests that, as opposed to less ideologically-charged domains, the creation and implications of a transnational legal order for constitution-making processes face political obstacles that can be impossible to overcome. In other words, Chile's recent history demonstrates that domestic politics sometimes inhibit full normative concordance between global and national constitutional norms, thus placing Chile partially outside the characteristic settlement of norms in TLOs elsewhere.

Chile is a mid-sized democratic state, with a prosperous economy and well-established rule of law. The country represents a rather successful story, in a region where there are only a handful of countries enjoying a similar experience. Chile has achieved its current situation in spite of having inherited a highly controversial constitution imposed upon it by the country's most violent dictatorship in its history, that led by the notorious General Augusto Pinochet.

Given its origin, Chile's Constitution of 1980 is regarded as illegitimate by a large percentage of its population. Aside from its violent imposition by a regime that inaugurated its rule by bombing the Presidential Palace ("La Moneda") and then went on to "disappear" and torture thousands of people and send into exile half a million citizens (around 5 percent of the population at the time), critics of the 1980 charter argue that it has a neoliberal economic bias and that it was designed to prevent the dismantling of the socio-economic model introduced by the military regime. Furthermore, according to a recent study (Luna and Vergara 2015), the political system structured by the 1980 Constitution of Chile has had the effect of weakening what O'Donnell once called "vertical accountability" – that is, the responsiveness of the political system to the people – since the elections, although clean and transparent, are rarely decisive. In consequence, even if a party or coalition obtains a strong majority of the votes, this result does not necessarily translate into policy changes demanded by the majority. This is due to requirement of legislative super-majorities to change important pieces of legislation and, more fundamentally, due to the existence of a highly conservative Constitutional Court that serves as a non-elected third chamber. The Court in recent years has been willing to actively strike down democratically-enacted legislation that departs from the model imposed by the dictatorship.

An important factor behind Chile's constitutional plight was the nature of its transition to democracy. This process took place under the constitutional terms set up by the military regime (Huneeus 2006; Karl 1990). In other words, the "price" of ending authoritarian rule was acceptance by the democratic opposition of the charter imposed by the dictatorship. The negotiated character of the transition to democracy may explain the fact that, although the constitution of 1980 had a clearly illegitimate origin (Fuentes 2013a), it took the Chilean population over two decades to start demanding a new one (Atria et al. 2013).

Both before and after the return to democracy, Chile's constitution experienced important amendments, but these did not by any means eliminate the constitution's "authoritarian enclaves" (Couso & Coddou 2010; Garretón 2003). The reason was that the nature of the 1980 document made it impossible for the center-left coalition that ruled Chile for two decades after the military regime to change the text without the consent of the right-wing parties that had supported the dictatorship. Due to this crucial constraint, during the first fifteen years of Chile's transition to democracy (1990–2005) the country had to endure the presence of a sizable group of non-elected senators (*senadores designados*), which gave the right-wing opposition parties control of the upper chamber of Congress, even though they were consistently defeated in the electoral process by the center-left coalition.

The anti-democratic institution of the "designated senators" was eliminated in 2005, when President Ricardo Lagos was able to persuade the right-wing opposition to end this anomaly, something it acquiesced to because – at that point in history – the institution was becoming more problematic for them than useful. Because the governing coalition had been able to appoint some of the designated senators, the non-elected senators' previous role in ensuring a right-wing veto point had eroded, at the same time that the political cost of appearing to benefit from an authoritarian enclave had increased (Fuentes, 2013b). This amendment, which was passed along with transition to civilian control of the armed forces, and the elimination of Pinochet's signature from the official text of the constitution, led some scholars to argue that the amended charter should be renamed the "Constitution of 2005," but that idea never took off.

The crucial factor explaining why the 2005 amendments were not considered to amount to the passing of a "new constitution" was the persistence of a number of clauses that had been designed by Pinochet's advisers to protect the main tenets of the conservative revolution introduced by the military regime. Chilean conservative parties used the counter-majoritarian features of the Constitution of 1980, including the super-majority (four-sevenths of the actual members of both chambers of Congress) required to amend or abrogate legislation of an "organic-constitutional" nature (e.g. the regulation of education, or the armed forces), and the "preventive" control of the constitutionality of laws by the Constitutional Court. Indeed, as discussed elsewhere (Couso & Toha 2009), important authoritarian enclaves were retained even after the major amendments introduced in 2005.

Already prior to 2008 a group of scholars had started to question the acceptability of Chile still being governed under a constitution imposed by a dictatorial regime, and a document with important democratic shortcomings at that. This objection to the country's fundamental law gained ground in 2009, when former President (and then candidate) Eduardo Frei Ruiz-Tagle included the introduction of a new constitution in his electoral platform. Then, in 2011, a final and more decisive turn against Pinochet's constitutional charter took place, when hundreds of thousands of students demonstrated for months in the streets of Santiago (and other principal cities of Chile) demanding a new constitution.

What is interesting about the students' call for a new charter is that it resulted from a realization that Chile's constitutional order posed significant obstacles to the introduction of public policies altering the socio-economic model left in place by the dictatorship. In their view, not only did the constitution exhibit a fatal legitimacy problem (having been imposed by a criminal regime), but also, just as importantly, it had an anti-democratic and neoliberal bias. These last points were crucial to popularize the demand for a new charter, because it helped to transform the – rather abstract – legitimacy objections into more concrete and forward-looking criticisms about barriers to progressive policies in important domains such as education.

Three aspects of the 1980 Constitution were identified as preventing the adoption of badly needed social change: the legislative super-majority needed to amend the so-called "organic laws"; the binomial electoral system, which made it extremely hard to translate even huge electoral victories into decisive majorities in Congress; and the "preventive" control of the constitutionality of legislation exercised by the Constitutional Court. This last aspect has been systematically used by the right wing to "abort" progressive bills before they are promulgated, transforming that body into a sort of "non-elected third chamber" (as identified by Alec Stone Sweet in his 1992 study of France's Constitutional Council). The binomial electoral system, eliminated from the permanent text in the 2005 amendment, nevertheless remained in place as a matter of electoral law, as did the exact same quorum for amendments.

Congress eventually replaced this system with a proportional one in 2015, voting in favor of a proposal by the government of President Bachelet.

Challenging those who advocated reform, the groups supporting the constitutional status quo argued that Chile had made an exemplary transition to democracy under the 1980 charter, adding that it was frivolous to create the institutional uncertainty associated with a complete constitutional change for the merely symbolic fact that the existing one was associated with Pinochet's regime. This body of opinion also downplayed the anti-democratic features of the Constitution of 1980. Progressives sought to rebut these objections by providing concrete examples of how conservative groups have used the 1980 charter to block social change. They pointed out that instead of uniting the Chilean people, the existing constitution is a source of deep divisions among them. Furthermore, they claimed that the transition to democracy was possible in spite of the fact that it occurred under an authoritarian constitution, not because of it, arguing that Chile's long republican tradition was the crucial factor explaining the country's successful return to democracy.

By 2013, calls for a new constitution had gone beyond intellectual and political circles, reaching important social movements and the general population. Given this context, it was not a surprise that in the 2013 presidential election all the candidates – with the exception of the right-wing candidate, Evelyn Matthei – included the introduction of a new constitution in their electoral platforms. More significantly, Michelle Bachelet made it one of her three programmatic priorities, and went on to win the election in a landslide. This appeared to give credibility to the goal of having a constitution discussed under democratic conditions.

Once President Bachelet was inaugurated, the question arose as to how exactly the government would proceed to elaborate a new constitution. In her program, Bachelet had anticipated that the procedure would be "democratic, participatory and institutional," but during the first eighteen months of her administration, little more was added to that statement of principle. While her administration was busy dealing with the implementation of other important structural reforms (such as an unprecedented tax reform and a radical modification of the education system), the constitution-building process remained a work-in-progress. In the meantime, the right-wing opposition continued to adamantly oppose the very notion of changing the constitution, hoping that Bachelet as President would abandon her campaign promise. Meanwhile, scholars and politicians who supported a new constitution debated endlessly over the most appropriate "mechanism" for achieving such goal (see Fuentes and Joignant 2015). While some ruled out a constituent assembly, others argued that this was the only way to get a legitimate constitution. What both groups had in common, however, was that they regarded the issue as fundamentally about finding the best "formula" from a legal–normative point of view, without giving much consideration to the institutional and political constraints that the Chilean context posed. The debate (framed in terms of being pro- or against a constituent assembly) drew heavily from the state-of-the-art of contemporary constitutional theory and comparative constitutional law, assuming that the resultant constitution-building formulae could be easily implemented in Chile. In this sense, it bore resemblance to how democratization experts bet on the virtues of "institutional engineering" in the 1990s, largely disregarding the role of historical, social, and cultural characteristics of different countries in transition.

The grip that this normative-driven search had on those involved in Chile's constitutional debate explains why even the social scientists involved in it did not pay attention to what Thornhill (2011) calls "constitutional sociology." One explanation for this is the idealized image still prevalent within Chile's progressive circles regarding constitution-building processes. Indeed, with a few exceptions, when Chileans get into a "constitution-making mode," they tend to imagine those processes as completely free from the miseries of everyday politics (with its harshness, abuse of positions of power, and influence peddling). It is as if those advocating a new constitution think that, by the mere inauguration of the constituent process, the hard realities of "normal politics" would be miraculously suspended, while an enlightened deliberation takes place: as if, as Habermas (1981) would have it, the subject matter can itself substitute "communicative rationality" for "strategic rationality."

Another idealized image underlying the excessively normative character of the Chilean debate concerns the most celebrated constitutions of the world (such as those of the United States or South Africa), and the constitution-making processes that led to them. The logic seemed to be that if something went well, the process must necessarily have been virtuous. A more historically-informed perspective reveals that the process of constitution-building in even the countries with the most attractive constitutions has rarely been commendable. Even a cursory review of the literature on the process that led to the US Constitution reveals that it was a messy affair, filled with the vices characteristic of "normal politics," such as the harsh display of power politics, manipulation, and a final text which was the subject of bitter criticism by the group defeated in the process, the Anti-Federalists (see Wood 1969).

The need to incorporate historical and sociological considerations when confronted with a constitution-building process rests on the premise that precisely because what is at stake at a "constitutional moment" is much more important than what is at stake in "normal politics," one should expect more, not less, conflict and tension in the course of the discussion. Indeed, because the drafting of a new charter opens the possibility of a fundamental adjustment of the basic rules of everyday politics, the constitutional debate can be very rough. The polarization generated in Chile due to the structural reforms initiated by President Bachelet in the first two years of her second administration (from March 2014 to March 2016) is illustrative, since it anticipated the polarization that later characterized the debate over the constituent process. Those who had more to lose (the Chilean right wing) spared no resources in trying to abort or attenuate the process.

In contrast with most progressive scholars and social and political leaders, President Bachelet gave consideration to the balance of political forces. Therefore, she resisted calls to enact a new constitution through a method which disregarded the rules regulating constitutional change contemplated in the Constitution of 1980. Bachelet's rationale seems to have been that, given that within her own coalition there were sectors who strongly objected to any mechanism that violated the Constitution of 1980 (in particular, the more conservative branch of the Christian Democratic Party), complemented by the fact of a conservative bias in the most influential media, even the slightest attempt to sidestep the Constitution of 1980 could lead to a major political crisis. Furthermore, all progressive heads of state in Chile remember very well the fact that the excuse for the military coup that overthrew President Salvador Allende was precisely that he had violated the Constitution of 1925 (Arriagada 1974). Finally, the fact that Latin American constitution-making experiences immediately preceding Chile's included violations of the previous constitutional regimes, and then led to radical governments (as was the case in Bolivia, Ecuador, and Venezuela) made the use of any similar mechanism a rather explosive proposition in Chile.

Given this historical and political context, President Bachelet had little option but to propose a mechanism of constitutional change that meticulously followed the rules set up by the Constitution of 1980. This path, although it could not be attacked by right-wing-controlled media made, however, the introduction of a new constitution impossible without the collaboration of the right-wing opposition.

The procedure and the itinerary for the elaboration of a new constitution were finally announced by President Bachelet in October 2015. The plan contemplated three different stages to be implemented during her administration, followed by three more to be executed during the next government. In terms of the liberal-democratic constitution-making TLO, the procedure announced by Bachelet was flawless.

The first, the "civic and constitutional information" stage, consisted of a media campaign aimed at informing the citizens about the entire constituent process (it was completed in March 2016). In order to avoid accusations of government manipulation, Bachelet ordered the creation of a Citizen's Council of Observers, made up of constitutional scholars (both supporters and critics of the government) and other academics, the media, figures from the entertainment industry, and even a sports celebrity. This council was given the task of making sure that the first stages of the constituent process were implemented with transparency and fairness. The second stage ("constitutional dialogues") consisted of a series of participatory channels including individual participation through the internet, local town halls, and finally, several regional and one national meeting, at which the citizens expressed their opinions regarding the content of the new constitution. The result of these constitutional dialogues was the so-called Citizen Bases for the New Constitution, which was ready by the end of 2017. The third – and most crucial phase – contemplated that the President send to Congress a bill reforming the Constitution of 1980, in order to enable the following legislature to discuss a new constitution. At the time of this writing, this critical vote had yet to happen, and the prospects are poor since the right wing, which returned to power in 2018, had already announced that a new constitution was not its priority. The end of Chile's constituent process was a foregone conclusion, in that Bachelet's popularity had taken a tumble because of a corruption scandal, and the right had no incentive to give her a significant political victory.

The Chilean case represents something of a paradox, because after having one of the best processes of constitution-building ever implemented in Latin America (in terms of public information and citizen participation, transparency, and procedural fairness), it ultimately failed to deliver a new constitution. This can be attributed to the persistence of normal politics during the whole affair.

CONCLUSION

After analyzing the transformation of what used to be disguised practices of constitutional export and import into a veritable transnational legal order regulating constitution-making processes, this chapter addressed both the possibilities and limits of the formation and institutionalization of such a TLO. Due to the high political stakes involved in creating a new constitution, the institutionalization or reach of a constitutional TLO can be severely limited because of national power relations. The chapter illustrates this point through its analysis of the process of constitution-making in Chile, a country which, in spite of having all the conditions for successfully implementing the orientations of what could be considered a hegemonic liberal democratic constitution-making TLO, failed to deliver a new constitution, due to the domestic political configuration. The Chilean case suggests that, for all its benefits in terms of regulating an important domain, the constitution-making TLO must acknowledge its limits, which seem greater than the ones facing other transnational legal orders.

Indeed, although it is clear that a liberal-democratic TLO can be identified as having a relevant role in processes of constitution-making in Latin America, its influence seems to be limited to the domain of rights and, to some extent, to that of the process of making a new constitution, without reaching the realm of the organization and distribution of state power. The reason for this discrepancy, I submit, is that national political actors are reluctant to let transnational regimes influence the organization of the very structures that define their political power. The lack of influence of the constitution making TLO in this sphere is relevant since – as has been highlighted elsewhere – the implementation of fundamental rights crucially depends on the existence of a state structure that is reasonably open and transparent.

Given the importance of state structure, it will be important for the consolidation and progressive influence of a liberal TLO that it incorporates norms regarding some elements of state structure, such as structures favoring judicial independence and forms supporting state transparency and accountability.

REFERENCES

Alberdi, Juan Bautista. (1852) 2017. *Bases y Puntos de Partida para la Organización Política de la República Argentina*. Red Ediciones, S.L.

Arriagada Herrera, Genaro. 1974. *De la "Vía Chilena" a la "Vía Insurreccional."* Santiago de Chile: Editorial del Pacífico.

Atria, Fernando, Guillermo Larraín, José Miguel Benavente, Javier Couso, and Alfredo Joignant. 2013. *El Otro Modelo: Del Orden Neoliberal al Régimen de lo Público*. Santiago: Random House Mondadori.

Couso, Javier. 2014. "Radical Democracy and the 'New Latin American Constitutionalism.'" In *Seminario de Teoría Política y Constitucional en Latinoamérica*. SELA. Retrieved from www.law.yale.edu/system/files/documents/pdf/sela/SELA13_Couso_CV_Eng_20130516.pdf. 4.

Couso, Javier. 2015. "La 'Solución Constitucional': Una Aproximación Desde la Sociología Constitucional." In *La Solución Constitucional*, edited by Claudio Fuentes and Alfredo Joignant. Santiago: Catalonia.

Couso, Javier and Alberto Coddou. 2010. "Las Asignaturas Pendientes de la Reforma Constitucional Chilena." In *En Nombre del Pueblo. Debate Sobre el Cambio Constitucional en Chile*, edited by Claudio Fuentes. Santiago: ICSO.

Couso, Javier and Carolina Tohá. 2009. "El Sistema Político y Sus Desafíos: Un Nuevo Arreglo Constitucional Para el Bicentenario." Pp. 167–88 in *El Chile que Viene: De Dónde Venimos, Dónde Estamos y A Dónde Vamos*. Santiago: Instituto de Políticas Públicas Expansiva-UDP and Centro de Estudios Públicos.

Dorner, Peter, ed. 1971. *Land Reform in Latin America: Issues and Cases*. Madison: Land Tenure Center at the University of Wisconsin-Madison.

Freeman, Michael, ed. 1998. *Current Legal Problems 1998: Legal Theory at the End of the Millennium* Vol. 51. Oxford: Oxford University Press.

Fuentes, Claudio. 2013a. *El Fraude. Crónica Sobre el Plebiscito de la Constitución de 1980*. Santiago de Chile: Editorial Hueders.

Fuentes, Claudio. 2013b. *El Pacto. Poder, Constitución y Prácticas Políticas en Chile: 1990–2010*. Santiago: Ediciones Universidad Diego Portales.

Fuentes, Claudio and Alfredo Joignant, eds. 2015. *La Solución Constitucional*. Santiago: Catalonia.

Gargarella, Roberto. 2013. *Latin American Constitutionalism, 1810–2010: The Engine Room of the Constitution*. Oxford: Oxford University Press.

Garretón, M. A. 2003. *Incomplete Democracy: Political Democratization in Chile and Latin America*. Chapel Hill: University of North Carolina Press.

Habermas, Jürgen. 1981. *Theory of Communicative Action, Volume One: Reason and the Rationalization of Society*. Boston: Beacon Press.

Huneeus, Carlos. 2006. *The Pinochet Regime*. Boulder and London: Lynne Rienner.

Huneeus, Carlos. 2014. *La Democracia Semisoberana. Chile Después de Pinochet*. Santiago: Taurus.

Karl, Terry. 1990. "Dilemmas of Democratization in Latin America." *Comparative Politics* 23(1): 1–21.

Montesquieu, Charles de Secondat, Baron de. 1989. *The Spirit of the Laws*, translated by Anne M. Cohler, Basia Miller, and Harold Stone. Cambridge: Cambridge University Press.

Stone, Alec. 1992. *The Birth of Judicial Politics in France: The Constitutional Council in Comparative Perspective*. Oxford: Oxford University Press.

Thornhill, Chris. 2011. *A Sociology of Constitutions: Constitutions and State Legitimacy in Historical-Sociological Perspective*. Cambridge: Cambridge University Press.

Watson, Alan. 1974. *Legal Transplants: An Approach to Comparative Law*. Charlottesville: University Press of Virginia.

Wood, Gordon. 1969. *The Creation of the American Republic, 1776–1787*. Chapel Hill: University of North Carolina Press.

10

Participatory Constitution-Making as a Transnational Legal Norm: Why Does It "Stick" in Some Contexts and Not in Others?

Abrak Saati

INTRODUCTION

Much has happened since James Tully stated that constitution-making is the single activity in "modern politics that has not been democratized" over the last three centuries (Tully 1995: 28). To be sure, over the past twenty-five years, the common perception of constitution-making as something reserved for political elites and lawyers to deliberate behind closed doors; as an exclusive domain for the chosen few, has been challenged (Ghai & Galli 2006: 5). In the wake of former UN Secretary General Boutros-Ghali's two influential reports *An Agenda for Peace* (1992) and *An Agenda for Democratization* (1996), constitution-making with the assistance of ordinary women and men has become part of a broader peace-building agenda that is envisioned to establish, promote, and strengthen democratic institutions and, in consequence, bring lasting peace and stability to post-conflict states and states in transition from authoritarian rule. Because of this, there has been an upsurge of what is now commonly referred to as participatory constitution-making (see e.g. Eisenstadt, LeVan, & Maboudi 2015; Brandt et al. 2011). Across the globe, in post-conflict states and in states in transition from authoritarianism in Africa, in Europe, in Latin America, in the MENA region, and in Southeast Asia, ordinary people have been invited to voice their opinions and convey their aspirations as to what they believe to be important to include in their country's founding laws as they move away from violent conflict and/or authoritarianism.

My argument here is that participatory constitution-making in post-conflict states and in states in transition from authoritarian rule has by now become something more than just a trend. I argue that it is, or at least that it is starting to, develop into a transnational legal norm and that the international community has been, and continues to be, important for the promotion of this particular norm. I have elsewhere (Saati 2015: 86–108) theorized participation in constitution-making, and suggested that we must approach this notion in a more analytically sharp and distinct way so as to be able to differentiate between different types of participation in terms of how much influence the public have been allowed to exert on the constitution through their, so-called, participation. Indeed, if we were to imagine a scale of participation in constitution-making processes, we would at the bottom of the scale find cases that have involved minimal public input, cases in which "participation" has been a mere act of window-dressing – i.e. cases where the general public have not been allowed to influence the content of the constitution even in the least.[1] Higher up on the scale we would find cases in which participation in the constitution-making process has been extensive in the sense that the public have been provided opportunities to actually influence the content of the constitution.[2] Between these two opposites on the scale, we would find a number of in-between cases in which participation has varied as to the extent of influence participants have been allowed to exert on the content of the constitutional draft.[3]

These differences of participation in practice suggest that the norm of participatory constitution-making for some reason, or reasons, "sticks" better in some contexts than in others. In some contexts, the norm is rejected altogether – national governments do not seem interested at all to adopt the norm and to include their population in the making of the constitution, not even in a cosmetic sense. In other contexts, the norm is at least institutionalized, meaning that the norm is incorporated into law. In these instances we find domestic legislation that stipulates that the public are to be consulted in the making of the constitution. The extent to which these words transcend the paper on which they are written and are effectively implemented is however a different matter. Finally there are contexts in which the norm is both institutionalized and internalized. This means that national governments live up to their rhetorical claims of wanting to include the citizenry, fully institutionalize the norm, and comply with it – leading to the general public being able to effectively participate, by exerting influence on the constitution.

1 Such was the case in the Iraqi constitution-making process that resulted in the 2005 constitution as well as the Nigerian constitution-making process that resulted in the 1999 constitution (see e.g. Saati 2015).

2 Such was the case in the Kenyan constitution-making process of 2009–10 (see e.g. Saati 2015).

3 Please be referred to Saati 2015 (86–108) for an exhaustive account of different types of participation in constitution-making processes and a categorization of twenty empirical cases illustrating how participation and the extent of influence granted to participants greatly differs between cases.

These differences of norm diffusion are intriguing and they beg the question: Why? Why do some countries reject this norm whereas it is institutionalized without any actual effect in others, and both institutionalized and internalized in yet others? Why and how do transnational legal norms, such as participatory constitution-making, travel? These questions constitute the focal point of attention in this chapter.

Although this is primarily a conceptual chapter that sets out to understand this particular transnational legal norm – participatory constitution-making – and how it can be diffused into domestic contexts, it also draws on empirical examples for purposes of illustrating differences as far as successful/unsuccessful norm diffusion is concerned. The empirical examples are also useful for being able to draw tentative conclusions as to *why* this norm appears to "stick" better in some contexts than in others. Related to the question of why this norm is more or less successfully diffused into domestic contexts, is another issue that this chapter also aims to discuss; namely if participatory constitution-making is entirely without risks or if it harbors potential dark sides as well.

The chapter is organized as follows: I proceed with a discussion of whether or not a case can even be made for participatory constitution-making evolving into a transnational legal norm after which I trace this development. This is followed by a section that, in brief, discusses potential risks of participatory constitution-making. A theoretical discussion concerning how norms diffuse follows, and in this context, I also discuss what is needed for a norm to transcend mere institutionalization to also become internalized. In the final section, conclusions are discussed.

PARTICIPATORY CONSTITUTION-MAKING – IS IT AN EVOLVING TRANSNATIONAL LEGAL NORM?

In order to understand if participatory constitution-making is a transnational legal norm, or if there are indications of it developing into a transnational legal norm, what is meant by the concept must first be established. In sorting this out, the theory of *transnational legal orders* can be useful. Now, what does transnational legal order (TLO) imply? In their edited volume, Halliday and Shaffer (2015) provide the following definition of a TLO. They state that a TLO is: "a collection of formalized legal norms and associated organizations and actors that authoritatively order the understanding and practice of law across national jurisdictions." It is relevant to understand that the object of "ordering" in TLO theory is normative understanding of appropriate behavior. The theoretical point of departure is that, at one point or the other, some actors come to understand that certain occurrences/behaviors are problematic at which point they will attempt to change these occurrences/behaviors by remaking the social order, in turn giving rise to new orders. Though this might sound like a fairly straightforward exercise, this is not so, because whether or not a specific behavior is construed as a problem is an area of debate and struggle between different actors (Halliday & Shaffer 2015: 7). In relation to constitution-making, a significant issue to address at this juncture is whether constitution-making is *one* coherent transnational legal order, or if it is an arena for a number of different, and perhaps even contending, transnational legal orders. As the chapters in this volume illustrate, different transnational orders appear to be in competition with each other as regards the content of constitutional texts (Ginsburg, Chapter two this volume), likewise different colonial heritages also appear to give rise to different systems of government that stand in contrast to each other (Law, Chapter five this volume). Adding to this, which ties into the focus of this chapter, constitution-making can also be viewed as a *process* during which it is possible to advance different norms, such as public participation, i.e. in the practice of *making* the constitution. Hence, it is perhaps more accurate to refer to a number of different transnational legal orders within the broader framework of constitution-making. This also leads us to another pertinent concept for the purposes of this specific chapter; transnational legal *norms*. According to Shaffer (2012: 15), transnational legal norms "embody prescriptions for the regulation of activities in particular functional domains," and they provide actors with tools and models so that they are able to redesign institutional arrangements to address specific situations.

The source, or sources, behind transnational legal norms can be different, ranging from international treaties to foreign legal models that are endorsed by transnational actors (Shaffer 2012: 9). In addition to providing definitional clarity to the concept of a transnational legal norm, Shaffer (2012: 8) makes a useful analytical distinction between the concepts of transnational law, legal norms, legal processes, and legal orders, and argues that "transnational law consists of legal norms that are exported and imported across borders, and which involve transnational networks and international and regional institutions that help to construct and convey the legal norm within a field of law."

When it comes to participatory constitution-making, there are signs suggesting that it has developed into a transnational legal norm since the notion as such, as well as its practice is, in fact, being exported and imported across national borders. However, it is not entirely accurate that the norm is firmly established as a transnational legal norm in the sense that it embodies clear prescriptions as to *how* the general public is to be involved in the making of their constitution. This can possibly be explained by the issue addressed above concerning the development of transnational legal orders as a struggle between different actors when it comes to the specific understandings and behaviors that are to be reconstructed. Though engaging the public in the making of their founding laws appears to be a trend that is here to stay, there are no exact rules, guidelines, or clearly formulated prescriptions regarding what stage of the process, and to what extent and with what amount of influence on the final draft the general public is to be involved – probably because the issue is still a contested one. Also, the spread of this norm, though transnational in some sense of the word, is still not universal[4] as it is primarily directed toward post-conflict states and states in transition from authoritarian rule, not toward stable democracies. This is indeed an important note to make; public participation is developing into a core norm for constitution-making not universally *but* specifically for countries that find themselves in a post-conflict state or in a transition from authoritarianism (see for example Miller 2010). By consequence, this implies that this is a norm that is most commonly expressed by different types of international organizations toward post-conflict states or states in transition from authoritarian rule; i.e. this is a norm that is being "downloaded" from international to domestic law.[5] The fact that the norm of directly engaging the public in the making of their constitution is, in some contexts, enforced from a higher standing authority (either an international treaty or an agent such as, for example, the United Nations) rather than from actors/organizations or institutions from the domestic environment, can perhaps serve to partly explain why it is not always successfully internalized in the recipient context, i.e. that there is a mismatch between the norm of participatory constitution-making endorsed from an outside force that does not fully resonate with existing domestic norms (see e.g. Shaffer 2012). I will return to and discuss this particular issue further below. For now, we shall direct our attention to analyzing the sources behind the development of participatory constitution-making processes into a transnational legal norm. As noted by Alldén (2009) and echoed by Halliday and Shaffer (2015), transnational legal norms do not travel by themselves, rather they originate from somewhere after which they are conveyed by different actors, such as

4 Therefore I do not agree with Franck and Thiruvengadam's (2010) view that participatory constitution-making is a worldwide trend. In regards to this, Halliday and Shaffer (2015) also make a useful point of separating "global" (law) from "transnational" (law). "Global" law suggests exactly that; that the law, or the legal norm, in question has global reach, while transnational law (or the legal norm in question) captures the phenomenon of legal ordering that goes beyond the nation-state but that does not necessary diffuse to all parts of the globe.

5 For a useful operationalization of transnational law, see Koh 2006.

international actors, domestic political elites, and/or agents within civil society organizations.

Normative Understandings of the Benefits of Direct Citizen Engagement in Political Decision-Making

If we were to trace the ideas of direct citizen involvement not only in constitution-making but in political decision-making in general, we would inevitably come across the writings of classical liberal theorists such as Mill (1862) and Rousseau (1762; 1971). To reiterate and analyze the complete set of arguments that these authors have emphasized in support of citizen involvement in matters of public relevance would require a full length book solely devoted to this matter, and this is not the place to provide such an analysis. Suffice it to say that much of their work, as well as the writings of contemporary participation theorists such as Pateman (1970), Arnstein (1969), Radcliff and Wingenbach (2000), and Finkel (2003) to name a few, spring from a highly normative understanding of public participation as something that *ought* to be pursued due to a number of perceived beneficial effects primarily for the individual who is engaging in the act of participation,[6] but also because of perceived positive outcomes at the macro level of analysis.[7] Over the course of years, and particularly from the beginning of the 1990s and the ushering in of the peace-building era, this normative understanding has also made its way into official policy documents of international organizations in which it is often stressed that public participation is more than the involvement of recipients of aid in the implementation of projects. Rather, public participation should be understood as a development strategy in its own right that serves to strengthen local ownership.[8] This development has in turn been a response

6 At the individual level of analysis, the educational merits of direct citizen participation in political decision-making are frequently brought to attention (see e.g. Pateman 1970, Arnstein 1969).

7 As people become more knowledgeable about the political system when they directly engage in political decision-making, social capital is also envisioned to be built. This will in turn lead to more support for government institutions, which will make people feel a stronger bond to democratic principles (Moehler 2008).

8 The 1993 Human Development Report, for example, states that: "Participation, from the human development perspective, is both a means and an end. Human development stresses the need to invest in human capabilities and then ensure that those capabilities are used for the benefit of all. Greater participation has an important part to play here: it helps maximize the use of human capabilities and is thus a *means* of increasing levels of social and economic development. But human development is also concerned with personal fulfilment. So, active participation, which allows people to realize their full potential and make their best contribution to society, is also an *end* in itself." Similar passages can be found in the 2002 Human Development Report.

to failed, or at least broadly perceived as such, top-down approaches to development and peacebuilding (Khwaya 2004) as well as in response to the abuse of sovereign power by governments during the recent past (Ghai & Galli 2006: 13). Hence, what we see here is a shift in ideas and conceptualizations as to how peace-building ought to be practiced, which has contributed to altering our understanding of how post-conflict constitutions are to be produced as well. This relates back to the earlier theoretical discussion about normative understandings as the focal point of TLO theory and also illustrates the theory's applicability in this context; i.e. previous social behavior in this specific context has heavily leaned toward top-down approaches to peace-building, and indeed also to constitution-making, which has long been the exclusive arena of political elites and lawyers (see e.g. Ghai & Galli 2006); in light of this having been construed as problematic, actors within the peace-building community are now attempting to reconstruct this behavior to instead engage local, bottom-up, initiatives to various peace-building activities including constitution-making.

Since the early 1990s, public participation, not only in the arena of constitution-making but in general, has become part of a broader development and peace-building agenda that emphasizes "the local" (Mac Ginty & Richmond 2013), "peacebuilding from below" (Ramsbotham, Woodhouse, & Miall 2016), and "grassroots peacebuilding" (Heathershaw 2008). Even though there are a few empirical examples of transitioning and/or post-conflict states that involved their respective populations in the making of the constitution prior to the 1990s,[9] the trend of participatory constitution-making has increased substantially from the 1990s and onwards. In the words of Samuels (2009: 5), constitutional theory, and I would argue constitutional practice as well, has first of all traditionally focused on constitutions in stable political contexts and not on the importance of constitutions in times of transition. Second, among constitutional scholars, focus has likewise, traditionally, been on the content of the constitution rather than on the *process* through which the constitution comes into being (Samuels 2009). From the onset of the peace-building era, however, both of these aspects have changed: (i) the constitution has become a prioritized area of concern in post-conflict states and in states in transition from authoritarian rule, and (ii) the process of constitution-making has gained increased attention. It is in

9 Uganda, for example, underwent a lengthy constitutional reform process (1988–95) in which the general public were invited to participate. In Brazil as well, constitutional reform with broad based citizen engagement took place 1987–88. In Nicaragua, the public were invited to participate in the making of the constitution during the constitutional reform process that lasted 1985–87.

relation to the latter aspect that the importance of including ordinary citizens has been emphasized by scholars and practitioners alike (Samuels 2009; Ghai & Galli 2006; Banks 2007; Brahimi 2011).

To summarize; within the political science, as well as the peace-building community, there is a long tradition and a strong bias, in favor of direct citizen involvement in political decision-making. This has influenced our thinking about constitution-making processes to the extent that participatory constitution-making is by now – and particularly since the onset of the peace-building era – a recognized concept, as well as an established practice. As a result, the once deeply-rooted idea that constitution-making should be limited to the smoke-filled chambers of political elites and lawyers, is no longer the dominant understanding, no matter how technically sound the constitutional content of such an elite-driven process may be.

With all this being said, it can still be discussed if it is accurate to refer to participatory constitution-making processes as a transnational *legal* norm, or if it is rather, and only, a transnational *political* norm. Against the latter, there can be no serious objections. Public participation in politics is generally viewed as the defining element of democratic citizenship (Dahl 1998; Verba, Schlozman, & Brady 1995), and although "participation" is most often construed as participation in free and fair elections, the range of issues that the public can influence through their participation, of course, exceeds merely electing government officials every four or five years. Among the range of issues, constitution-making can be included, which – in light of the upsurge of empirical cases of participatory constitution-making processes in various geographical locations around the globe – appears to be the case. Moreover, seeing how involving the public in the making of the constitution seems to have an appeal that is not limited to one specific geographic area in the world, it would likely not be too farfetched to refer to participatory constitution-making as a *transnational* political norm. However, it is still worthwhile discussing if it can also be considered as transnational legal norm. I turn to this issue below.

Legal Justifications in Support of Participatory Constitution-Making

In addition to normative reasons as to why ordinary people ought to be included in the making of their founding laws, there is a continuing debate concerning whether or not legal justifications can also be put forth in support of participatory constitution-making (see e.g. Hart 2010). Advocates of including the general public in the making of the constitution often refer to the International Covenant on Civil and Political Rights (ICCPR), and more specifically to article 25 of the treaty.[10] The article states that: "Every citizen shall have the right and the opportunity to take part in the conduct of public affairs, directly or through freely chosen representatives" (ICCPR, 1966, Article 25). Aside from article 25 of the ICCPR, article 21 of the UN Declaration of Human Rights (1948) has also been referred to, which states that "Everyone has the right to take part in the government of his country, directly or through freely chosen representatives." In a similar manner, article 5c of the International Convention on the Elimination of All Forms of Racial Discrimination has been referred to, in which the right to take part in public affairs is established. The European Framework Convention for the Protection of National Minorities has also been invoked, in which article 15 settles that persons who belong to national minorities must be allowed to effectively participate in cultural, social, and economic life as well as in public affairs. Adding to these international treaties, a number of regional charters also underscore the right to participate in public affairs. Examples include: The African Charter on Human and People's Rights of 1981, The Harare Commonwealth Declaration of 1991 and the Asian Charter of Rights of 1998.

Despite these legal instruments, two separate but related questions are relevant to consider. To begin with, one might ponder if constitution-making is in fact a *prior* condition for citizens to participate in the governance of their country (either directly or through freely chosen representatives), or not. If one would argue that such is the case, then public participation in the making of the constitution as such would likely have to be precluded from the right to participate in governance (Hart 2010: 21). On the other hand, it could also be argued that since it is the constitution that establishes the rules of the political game and in which it is decided how and through which institutional forms that the general public is going to be able to engage in the political process of their country, it is *when* the constitution is being produced that the public ought to have the possibility to voice their opinions. It could, indeed, be argued that this goes to the very heart of participating in governance.

The other issue that deserves consideration is what to "take part" actually means in the context of constitution-making. Even if article 25 of the ICCPR, article 21 of the UN Declaration of Human Rights, and article 5c of the Convention on the Elimination of All Forms of Racial Discrimination were unambiguous in supporting participation in constitution-making, "take part" is a vague formulation that provides little guidance as to how it is or should be practiced. In order to "take part," does it suffice to vote for members of

10 For a more thorough discussion and analysis of the ICCPR and how the treaty provides legal justification for public participation in constitution-making, see Hart 2010.

a constitutional assembly whose members then have the responsibility of formulating the constitution? Or does "take part" include having the possibility to vote on a draft constitution? Or is "take part" to receive constitutional education in order to then be able to actively participate in the making of the constitution in an informed manner? Undeniably, the concept can be interpreted in different ways. As noted by Hart (2010: 23), the regional charters, international treaties, conventions and declarations, when taken together, influence and frame our view on meaningful participation in political affairs even though they are not specific as to what "take part" means and even though they do not specially mention public participation in constitution-making. Of course, the fact that participation in constitution-making is not mentioned explicitly also ties into the question of whether or not it is accurate to refer to participatory constitution-making as a transnational legal norm. If one agrees with Shaffer's (2012: 32) understanding that transnational legal norms can encompass both soft as well as hard law, then participatory constitution-making could be referred to as a transnational legal norm to the extent one is at least willing to accept it as soft law. Yet, the legal aspects of the norm remain so unclear that they fail to embody prescriptions for the regulation of how exactly participation in this particular domain is to take form, leading to vast differences at the domestic level when the norm is adopted (see e.g. Saati 2015: 307–18).

Since clarifications in international law that directly mention public participation in constitution-making might be a lengthy process, Hart (2010: 31) suggests that it is now primarily a matter of seizing the momentum of including ordinary people in political decision-making in general to apply the norm to the arena of constitution-making; in this way, the norm can be diffused through international organizations and networks, giving rise to actual practice and new understandings ensuing from it. This leads us to a discussion of how norm diffusion is brought about and how a specific transnational legal norm is successfully adopted in some contexts and less successfully adopted in others. But before discussing this issue, we address whether direct public participation in constitution-making is entirely problem free or if it can contain potential risks as well.

PUBLIC PARTICIPATION – WITHOUT RISKS?

The norm of direct citizen engagement in issues of public relevance in general, including in constitution-making processes, is by now rooted to the extent that dark sides, or at least potential difficulties, are not frequently discussed or given much attention. Though actively engaging in deciding issues that affect one's life has many potential positive effects, as previously discussed, potential drawbacks must also be acknowledged. To begin with, though we are currently placing high expectations on participatory constitution-making in terms of various outcomes[11] (see for example Hart 2003; Samuels 2009; Widner 2005; Ghai & Galli 2006; Banks 2008; Eisenstadt, LeVan, & Maboudi 2015), participation is not a guarantee of any specific result. In an ideal scenario, by opening up the process for people to participate, the citizenry becomes better informed about their constitutional rights and are hence more disposed to defend those rights (Ghai & Galli 2006: 14). It is however not at all certain that a participatory constitution-making process leads to a more democratic constitution, even though this is an expected outcome (Interpeace/IDEA/USIP 2009). Such correlations have yet to be empirically substantiated and experts within the field have even warned against rash as well as spurious correlations (Interpeace/IDEA/USIP 2009: 44). Actually, there are a number of proposed outcomes of participatory constitution-making processes that still remain understudied. Ginsburg, Elkins, and Blount (2009: 219) capture this challenge by stating that: "On the theoretical side, we find a broad consensus in the literature about the importance of public involvement as well as an apparent trend in practice. Yet many of the assumptions of proponents of participation remain untested, and the precise relationships between participation and desirable outcomes remain underspecified."

Recent studies (see Eisenstadt, LeVan, & Maboudi 2015; Saati 2015) have endeavored systematic analysis of public participation in constitution-making and whether or not it has an effect on democratic outcomes at a macro level of analysis, as well as whether or not active participation effects the individual's sense of viewing the constitution as a legitimate one (Moehler 2008), but a lot of systematic empirical work remains before we can determine that public participation does lead to all of the positive outcomes scholars and practitioners have proposed, and perhaps also, intuitively, expect.

In addition to empirical gaps about the proposed benefits of public participation in constitution-making that still need to be addressed, potential drawbacks of participation must also be brought to light. To begin with; as amply put by Ghai and Galli (2006: 15), who "the people" are that are envisioned to participate is not as clear as one might believe. There is

11 Proposed benefits of public participation in constitution-making range from increased legitimacy for the document, to reconciliation between former adversaries of violent conflict, to it being a needed exercise in democratic practices that can lead to increased levels of democracy at a macro level of analysis.

no homogenous entity that encapsulates the notion of "the people." Rather "the people" consist of numerous different groups ranging from religious groups, the disabled, youth, women, indigenous people, even warlords, and so on. Some of these groups might be better organized, better equipped, and hence better positioned to participate whereas others might not be organized and therefore unable to participate in any effective manner. Because such discrepancies affect the equal ability to participate, this poses challenges for processes in practice. Some of these groups, for example former combatants, guerrilla groups and war lords, might manipulate the process in order to secure constitutional guarantees that are particularly lenient toward them, such as provisions granting amnesties for example (Brandt et al. 2011: 87–8).

Furthermore, does a participatory process imply that every single individual within, for example, all religious groups, all women's organizations, and so forth, is to actively participate, or does it mean that representatives should be chosen that speak on their behalf? If the latter, does this not go against the idea of public participation in the process – i.e. that people are to engage directly for purposes of legitimacy, learning democratic practices, encountering opponents face to face in order to identify common ground? On the other hand, is a completely inclusive process in a war-torn country, logistically, possible? Related to this issue, the management of people's expectations is relevant to consider. Though Ghai and Galli (2006: 14) contend that participation, even if only ceremonial, will lead to a higher commitment to the constitution among the populace, this is a question that should be problematized. Perhaps if people are properly informed at the very outset of the process that their participation is merely ceremonial and that they hence should not expect to be able to influence the content of the constitution, then it is possible that people are content with this ceremonial type of participation. If, on the other hand, people are expecting to participate with at least some extent of influence, and then denied this influence, potential problems might arise causing frustration and even violence. At the same time, if the outspoken agenda and ambition from the outset of the process is that the population shall participate with actual influence, proper mechanisms must be installed so that this is indeed made possible, mechanisms that can systematically gather, analyze, and categorize submissions to balance them vis-à-vis each other for subsequent inclusion in the constitution – something that can prove to be cumbersome due to many, and often times conflicting, interests and opinions (Brandt et al. 2011: 89).

Though the above account is not exhaustive in discussing all potential risks of participatory constitution-making, it is still important to bring attention to some aspects of its practice that might be problematic. This is particularly important in light of the increasing strength of this norm transnationally. In the next section, we attend the question of how norm diffusion occurs and why it is more or less effective in different contexts.

HOW CAN NORMS BE DIFFUSED?

Though it is today generally accepted that norms matter, the issue is how norms diffuse and how they work their effects in the domestic arena. My argument is that the international community – as part of a broader peace-building agenda – brings the norm of direct citizen participation in political decision-making in general, and in constitution-making in particular, into post-conflict states and states in transition from authoritarian rule. The UN, particularly through its Department of Political Affairs (UNDPA), the United States Institute of Peace (USIP) and the International Institute for Democracy and Electoral Assistance (IDEA) are important actors for the promotion of participatory constitution-making in these types of contexts, and they encourage this practice via interactions with actors at the domestic level who are then expected to understand, incorporate, and conform to this norm. Hence, what we are currently observing is something that can be referred to as *norm enforcement from above*, alternatively *vertical norm diffusion* (Alldén 2009: 19; Koh 2006: 745–6). At the same time, these actors, as just stated, interact with domestic actors; meaning that they do not bring this norm into an empty void. Whether or not norm diffusion is successful depends on actors that operate on both of these levels. To be sure, international as well as domestic actors can be norm entrepreneurs. When it comes to actors within the domestic arena, a further distinction must be made between national elites at the formal state level and the people at large – i.e. civil society (Flockhart 2005). This distinction is needed because it is not unlikely that while a specific transnational legal norm is embraced by the people and by the civil society of a given state, it is not accepted by national elites (Flockhart 2005).

When it comes to participatory constitution-making specifically, there are some empirical cases that demonstrate this division between elites and the people at large. The struggle for constitutional reform with broad-based citizen engagement in Kenya, for example, was initially driven by elites within Kenya's civil society (Bannon 2007). Their claims were, however, not met with sympathy from the ruling elite who had no interest in initiating a constitutional reform process that would most likely endanger their positions of power (Bannon 2007). The consistent efforts of Kenyan civil society actors did, nevertheless, lead up to the 2001–05 constitutional reform process which was a highly participatory endeavor (see e.g. Bannon 2007; Saati 2015). The same holds true for the Zimbabwean constitutional reform process of 1999–2000. Just as in Kenya, it was civil society organizations, and primarily the National Constitutional Assembly (NCA), that insisted on a people-driven constitutional reform process even though the Mugabe regime was very much against it (Ndulo 2010; Dorman 2003). In Colombia as well, it was primarily youth and student organizations that put constitutional reform with broad-based public participation on the political agenda in response to wide spread corruption and violence in the country during the 1980s. By mobilizing their efforts, these groups were successful in persuading both the sitting president (Virgilio Barco Vargas) and the Supreme Court of Justice to allow the Colombian citizenry to vote on the matter of establishing a constitutional assembly for subsequent constitutional reform (Fox, Gallón-Giralodo, & Stetson 2010). Indeed, the election for the Constitutional Assembly in December of 1990 was unique in the sense that it was the first time that members to a constitutional body were not only representatives of established political parties but also representatives of a number of citizens' constituencies and, perhaps more importantly, they were elected by universal suffrage (Marulanda 2004). Though the subsequent steps of the Colombian constitution-making process were less successful in terms of ensuring the full participation of the general public, the efforts of the youth and student organizations must be acknowledged since, without their struggle, constitutional reform in the beginning of the 1990s might not have occurred.

Though these empirical examples capture instances of a particular norm being embraced by segments from the civil society sector of a given country, on a theoretical level, the opposite might of course also occur; that national elites embrace a specific norm while it is simultaneously rejected by the general public and/or domestic civil society organizations.

In order to make us better understand the ways through which transnational legal norms can be diffused, and how it is, in fact, an interplay between the international and the domestic level, Harold Koh (2006: 745–6) provides a useful analogy with the internet. He says that the best operational definition of transnational law is:

> (1) law that is "downloaded" from international to domestic law: for example, an international law concept that is domesticated or internalized into municipal law, such as the international human rights norm against disappearance, now recognized as domestic law in most municipal systems; (2) law that is "uploaded, then downloaded": for example, a rule that originates in a domestic legal system, such as the guarantee of a free trial under the

concept of due process of law in Western legal systems, which then becomes part of international law, as in the Universal Declaration of Human Rights and the International Covenant on Civil and Political Rights, and from there becomes internalized into nearly every legal system in the world, and (3) law that is borrowed or "horizontally transplanted" from one national system to another: for example, the "unclean hands" doctrine, which migrated from the British law of equity to many other legal systems.

In keeping with Koh's definition, when it comes to participatory constitution-making processes in post-conflict states and in states in transition from authoritarian rule, it is primarily a matter of the norm being "downloaded" from a higher standing authority (which signifies a vertical form of norm diffusion – i.e. norm diffusion from above), or that is being "horizontally transplanted" from one national system to the other. As regards the first one of these modes, it is, as previously mentioned, mainly international organizations and institutions that encourage, and sometimes enforce, this norm upon post-conflict states and states in transition from authoritarian rule. For example, following its declaration of independence from Serbia in 2008, the leadership of Kosovo had no choice but to invite the population of the province in the making of the new constitution. Kosovo had committed itself to the prescriptions in the Ahtisaari plan, which stipulated that a participatory constitution-making process was to be carried out (Comprehensive Proposal for the Kosovo Status Settlement 2007). The Ahtisaari plan, though facing challenges of being approved in the UN Security Council due to Russia threatening to use its veto, was endorsed by an "international steering group" consisting of several countries, including the USA and the UK.[12] The mandate of the steering group, in turn, was to support the full implementation of the Ahtisaari plan. Hence, in this specific case, the norm of participatory constitution-making was, in a sense, downloaded from a higher standing authority, or perhaps more accurately, enforced from above.[13]

As regards norms that are horizontally transplanted, the norm of participatory constitution-making has indeed also traveled between different post-conflict states and between different states in transition from authoritarian rule. The South African constitution-making process of 1994–96, frequently

[12] The members of the International steering group were the UK, France, Germany, Italy, the US, Austria, the Czech Republic, Finland, Sweden, Turkey, Belgium, Denmark, Hungary, Slovenia, and Switzerland.

[13] It is however difficult to imagine that the extent of public input to the process can have been anything but limited since the time period between the declaration of independence (February 17, 2008) and the finalization of the public participation phase of the process was a mere fortnight (March 2, 2008) (Saati 2015: 100–3).

brought to attention for its highly participatory features, has, for example, become a reference point for many other countries that have set out to include their respective populations in the making of their constitution (see e.g. Ebrahim & Miller 2010).

Regardless of a particular norm being downloaded or horizontally transplanted, it is a matter of rooting the norm in the recipient country, which commonly implies that domestic actors reconstruct the norm so that it fits with existing norms and norm hierarchies – something that Acharya (2004: 241) describes as a process of "localization." Hence, norm diffusion is seldom a matter of downright rejecting a norm or wholeheartedly accepting a norm. A more nuanced understanding of how norms diffuse can be reached by acknowledging that domestic actors build congruence between transnational legal norms and local beliefs and practices (Acharya 2004). In consequence, in contexts where a specific norm does not successfully diffuse, the case might be that domestic actors have not been able (or allowed) to find a way to harmonize the norm with local norms and practices, leading merely to a symbolic acceptance of the norm, or to the norm being formally institutionalized but not internalized.

Different Steps of "Norm Localization"

Acharya (2004: 251) envisions norm localization as something that occurs in several steps. The first step is that of *prelocalization* during which local actors might resist the new external norm out of concern that it will undermine local practices. The norm might however be localized if some domestic actors start to consider the external norm as something that could potentially strengthen already existing institutions. This line of reasoning finds resonance in Shaffer's (2012: 37) discussion about how transnational legal norms invariably depend on local supporters and perhaps primarily the support of domestic political elites.

Acharya refers to the second step as *local initiative*. This stage of the localization process implies that local actors frame the external norm such that the value of it becomes clear to the local population. In order for the general population to accept the norm, it is also imperative that they do not view the domestic norm entrepreneurs who support the external norm as puppets of outside forces.

The third stage that Acharya envisions in the localization process is that of *adaptation*. This implies that the external norm is reconstructed so that it concords with local norms and practices at the same time as local norms are adjusted in order to find similarities with the external norm. This entails that the external norm is redefined and local actors manage to relate it to existing norms in the domestic environment, or that some parts of the external norm are accepted whereas other parts of it are rejected.

The fourth, and final, stage is *amplification and "universalization"* which means that new instruments and practices are developed that reflect local influences. This aspect of the localization process finds echo in Risse and Sikkink's (1999: 11) discussion about moral consciousness-raising which implies that domestic actors, elites, members from the civil society sector or domestic NGOs try to convey the universality of the norm and, by so doing, try to evade arguments against the norm on the basis of it being alien to the culture and way of life in the norm-recipient country. This form of consciousness-raising can be done through a variety of techniques ranging from persuasion, to actors invoking emotional appeals, to actors presenting logically sound arguments. According to Risse and Sikkink (1999: 15) moral consciousness-raising often also involves a process of "shaming." This holds particular relevance when a norm-violating state does not adhere to human rights norms. States that do not comply with the norm are exiled from the group of "civilized states" which is, in turn, expected to work as an incentive for norm-violators to change their behavior and be persuaded to conform to the human rights norm. Once the ruling elite in the norm-violating country starts referring to the norm – in this case, to participatory constitution-making – and makes tactical concessions and references to it in political rhetoric, it will sooner or later have to start to make behavioral changes as well. In a sense, they will become entangled in their own rhetoric, making it difficult not to follow up "talk" with rule-consistent behavior (Risse & Sikkink 1999: 20). Taken together, from the stage of local initiative, to adaptation, and lastly to amplification and universality, the norm is incrementally acknowledged and adopted in the norm-recipient country which in turn facilitates its institutionalization (Risse & Sikkink 1999: 17).

These separate stages of the localization process set aside, the fact remains that in some contexts external norms are simply more difficult to diffuse than in other contexts; sometimes the process of norm diffusion is more challenging and sometimes the incremental process as displayed above does not occur. Why is this so? According to Checkel (1997), Cortell and Davis (2000), as well as Shaffer (2012), it is, in a sense, a matter of cultural match. In order for external norms, or transnational legal norms in keeping with Shaffer's terminology, to have an impact, they must resonate with domestic norms and domestic understandings. In contexts where the transnational legal norm is in agreement with prevailing cultural and institutional norms, it is more likely to diffuse than in contexts in which this agreement is absent. Also, and perhaps equally important, the question of whether or not norm diffusion is successful depends on local power hierarchies and how incumbent persons in government positions as well as members of the political opposition believe that the norm in question will help them advance their own agendas and objectives. If current power-holders suspect that by opening up the process for public input, a new institutional order that undermines their positions will see the dawn of day, they may be quite reluctant to give the general public this opportunity. Institutionalizing and internalizing a norm can also be challenging if citizens in a given country are not adequately informed about the benefits of the reform in question. Hence, even though they might benefit by it, they might still resist it due to poor information (Collier 2007). Hence, the obstacles of norm institutionalization and even more so, norm internalization, can be substantial. At this point it becomes relevant to make an analytical distinction between the two, because while institutionalization is a necessary condition for successful norm diffusion, it is not a sufficient condition (Alldén 2009). For norm diffusion to be successful, institutionalization must be followed by internalization which, again, puts the issue of agency at the front and center of attention (Alldén 2009). It is in this context that the notion of *capabilities* becomes central, and more specifically, an individual's "capability to function" as referred to by Alldén (2009: 30–1).

Capabilities

The *capabilities approach* is perhaps most commonly associated with Amartya Sen (1999) and focuses on the quality of life that individuals are able to achieve. One could say that the approach centers not only on an individual's understanding of how satisfied she/he is with what she/he *does*, but also on what the person in question is in a position *to do*. It is the latter aspect of the approach that is of relevance when we try to understand how a transnational norm can become internalized. To place this idea in the context of constitution-making would imply that an individual, to be able to effectively participate in the making of his/her country's constitution, must be equipped with the relevant skills in order to be able to do so; i.e. the person must be *capable of functioning* in this specific context. As expressed by Robeyns (2008: 84), "capabilities are real opportunities to functionings ... such as being literate, being well fed, being healthy, being educated, being part of a social network, having a decent job and so forth." Hence, these aspects are not, primarily, important in themselves but more than anything else, important because they enable people to be capable to function. Many times, however, a variety of obstructions impede an individual's capability to function, ranging from the social institutions of a given country (e.g. the political system, the educational system), to the social norms that exist in a particular country (e.g. religious norms, moral norms, cultural norms) to environmental conditions in a given country or region within a country (e.g. lack of physical infrastructure, high levels of violence) (Robeyns 2008: 84–5). Such impediments are quite prevalent, particularly, in many post-conflict states which, in turn, poses certain challenges for the norm of participatory constitution-making to transcend institutionalization to also become internalized. Let me illustrate this with some empirical examples, starting with the case of Afghanistan.

When one studies the mandate and the work plan of the Constitutional Commission in Afghanistan, one cannot deny the commission's high ambitions to include the Afghan people in the making of the draft which resulted in the 2004 constitution. The Constitutional Commission was, among other things, to make information about the constitution-making process available to the public for the duration of its work; carry out consultations with ordinary Afghan citizens in each province of the country as well as with Afghan refugees in Pakistan and Iran as regards what they believed to be important to include in the new constitution; receive written constitutional submissions from ordinary Afghans from inside as well as outside of the country; analyze the input given through written constitutional submissions as well as oral statements; produce a draft, and disseminate and educate people on the draft constitution (The Secretariat for the Constitutional Commission in Afghanistan 2003; Brandt 2005). Though the aspirations of the Constitutional Commission were noble, to properly engage the Afghan citizens proved to be challenging due to a number of reasons. For one, it turned out to be difficult to include people, engage people, and gather ideas from people when they had not received constitutional education prior to the commission setting out to solicit their views (Brandt 2005). Indeed, for people to be able to genuinely participate, they must first of all have a good understanding about the issue(s) about which they are to voice their opinion. In Afghanistan, the illiteracy rate was a huge obstacle to genuine participation, as was poor infrastructure, as were prevailing social norms that made it difficult to engage women in particular (Brandt 2005). Hence, a number of circumstances made it difficult for people to acquire the needed capabilities necessary for the norm to transcend institutionalization to also become internalized.

The same type of circumstances prevailed in East Timor when this country embarked on what was supposed to be a participatory constitution-making process following the vote for independence in 1999 (Brandt 2005). Here as well, the East Timorese were not extended the opportunity to acquire the necessary skills in order to be able to genuinely participate (Saati 2015: 309). The United Nations Transitional Administration in East Timor (UNTAET) carried out a civic education campaign but it did not include education on constitutional issues. Hence, when the Constitutional Commission conducted hearings throughout the country in order to gather suggestions from the population, it was difficult for the general public to provide informed input. Adding to these unfavorable circumstances, the opportunity for the public to comment on the proposed draft constitution was also severely circumscribed, as it was published in Portuguese, which not everyone in the population reads and speaks. In some sense, the opportunity for norm internalization was lost in East Timor when the Security Council on repeated occasions chose to disregard the East Timorese civil society organization's plea for sufficient time and resources in order to be able to first inform and educate the citizenry in order to include them in a genuinely participatory constitution-making process (Brandt 2005). The two empirical examples of East Timor and Afghanistan can be contrasted with the Eritrean and South African experiences of public participation in constitution-making.

Eritrea, to begin with, faced numerous challenges to ensure genuine participation in its 1994–97 constitution-making process – much like the challenges faced in Afghanistan and in East Timor. Through a range of different measures, however, the Constitutional Commission in Eritrea managed to overcome many of these obstacles and by so doing, it was successful in equipping parts of the Eritrean citizenry with the necessary capabilities to be able to effectively participate in the making of their country's constitution (Selassie 2010). The mandate of the Constitutional Commission in Eritrea was, just as the mandate of the constitutional commission in Afghanistan, quite ambitious. Its members were to: (i) organize and manage a wide-ranging and all-embracing national debate and an education campaign with public seminars and a lecture series on constitutional principles and practice, and (ii) organize and conduct – or cause to be organized and conducted by the appropriate bodies – seminars, symposia, educational lectures, and discussions on constitutional principles and practices (Proclamation 55/1994). These efforts were to be done through the mass media and were to be aimed at educational and civic establishments as well as other appropriate institutions.

The difference between the Eritrean case and the cases of Afghanistan and East Timor is that these promises made their way into actual practices. Over a period of three years, Eritreans within the borders of the country as well as the diaspora community were involved in the constitution-making process (Selassie 2010). Constitutional education programs were held in all languages spoken in the country. Measures for reaching the illiterate were also taken, as were non-traditional forms of outreach, among other things conveying the principles of constitutionalism through puppet shows and poetry sessions. Contests and debates on the radio and television were also part of the civic education programs (Selassie 2010). Hence, the Eritrean population was much better equipped with the necessary skills to be able to participate in their country's constitution-making process compared to the general public in East Timor and in Afghanistan. In Eritrea, they were, in other words, more capable of functioning in the specific context of constitution-making. The fact that the constitution that emanated from this highly participatory process was never enacted and to this day remains on the shelf, is a separate matter. As far as ensuring that ordinary Eritreans were able to participate in the making of the constitution in an informed manner, the process was undeniably a fairly successful endeavor.[14]

South Africa is another empirical example of public participation in practice where the population have been extended the necessary capabilities to effectively engage in the making of the constitution (Ebrahim & Miller 2010; Haysom 2001). What is important to note, however, is that the South African constitution-making process was a two-step endeavor in which the first phase of the process was completely elite-driven without public participation (Mbete-Kgositsile 2001; Haysom 2001). Let me linger a bit at this particular constitution-making process since it has, and continues to, receive a lot of attention from the scholarly community as well as by practitioners in the field.

The South African process was divided into two separate steps. During the first stage of the process, negotiations between all major political parties produced an interim constitution with guidelines for the transitional period from the apartheid system to a democratic order (Haysom 2001). In the second stage, a popularly elected Constitutional Assembly was established to create and adopt a final constitution (Ebrahim & Miller 2010). Although the mandate of the assembly granted it sole responsibility to formulate the constitution on its own, its members felt that public involvement in the process was necessary to assure the legitimacy of the final product (Mbete-Kgositsile 2001; Ebrahim & Miller 2010).

A Constitutional Committee, drawn from the members of the Constitutional Assembly, was established after elections in April 1994 (Ebrahim & Miller 2010). The Commission envisioned three phases for the process. The first step would involve the participation of the public and the

[14] For a comparison of this case with nineteen other cases of participatory constitution-making, see Saati 2015.

writing of a draft text; the second stage would include circulation of the draft for further input from the people; the final stage would include negotiations and, finally, adoption of the document by the Constitutional Assembly (Mbete-Kgositsile 2001; Ebrahim & Miller 2010; Haysom 2001).

As the members of the Constitutional Assembly knew that a large portion of the South African public was composed of illiterate rural residents with no access to electronic media, they understood the importance of education programs to raise consciousness about the issues (Ebrahim & Miller 2010). The Commission agreed that the best approach would be to carry out constitutional education before soliciting public input, and to continue with education programs during the second stage of the process as well. During the first phase of the public participation program, a media campaign was launched which was complemented with advertisements on television, radio and in local newspapers (Ebrahim 2001; Ebrahim & Miller 2010). The set-up of the television programs was designed so that members of civil society could question assembly members from different political parties about their views on human rights, separation of powers, and other issues in question. Moreover, the communication process was structured to enable feedback. All submissions were recorded or written down and then translated for the members of the assembly to take into consideration (Ebrahim 2001). By the end, two million submissions had been written by the South African public and sent to the Assembly (Ebrahim & Miller 2010).

To be sure, the South African experience of participatory constitution-making stands in stark contrast to the experiences of Afghanistan and East Timor. In South Africa, substantial efforts were made by the Constitutional Assembly and the Constitutional Commission to properly prepare the South African population so that they could genuinely participate in the making of their founding laws. I have argued elsewhere, that it appears that the increasing power and strength of the "participation-norm" in constitution-making processes is being nourished by the South African case (Saati 2015: 273–4). Indeed, this case was impressive in terms of the many avenues through which people were able to get involved in the process; there is no denying this fact. Nonetheless, in the somewhat idealized story that has developed around the South African process, it is often "forgotten," or at least not mentioned, that the participatory elements of the process were preceded by elite negotiations on the highest political level. The South African political elites had, in fact, reached consensus on a number of contentious constitutional issues *before* the South African population at large were invited to participate, and even when the people had done so, final authority over the content of the constitution was still not directly vested in their hands (Haysom 2001; Ebrahim & Miller 2010).

The purpose of directing attention to the four empirical examples of Afghanistan, East Timor, Eritrea, and South Africa is to show that participation in practice differs immensely from one context to the other and that we may start to understand the reason behind these differences by making an analytical distinction between norm institutionalization and norm internalization. Indeed, as these empirical examples illustrate, it is one thing to provide a right (to participate in the making of one's constitution), and another for individuals to be able to actually access that right (to have the capability to really participate). Moving from norm institutionalization to norm internalization, in the context of participatory constitution-making, can be eased by a number of different measures, including awareness-raising of particularly marginalized groups who have traditionally been excluded from the political arena. Judging by the empirical examples above, however, the carrying out of various types of constitutional education programs before, during and perhaps even after the constitution-making process, stands out as a particularly effective measure for this specific norm to move beyond institutionalization to become internalized.[15]

CONCLUSIONS

Whether or not transnational norms, be they legal, political, or social, diffuse into a specific domestic arena can certainly depend on a variety of different reasons, and the answer to why successful norm diffusion has occurred in one context and not the other will invariably differ. In cases of norm diffusion from above, the issue of cultural mismatch should not be downplayed, especially if it is a case of norm *enforcement* which would make it difficult, if not entirely impossible, for domestic actors to try to reconstruct the norm so that it can become harmonized with already existing local norms, institutions, and beliefs. At the same time, the issue of cultural match should not be overemphasized as the most important factor for why transnational norms diffuse successfully or not.

It is easy, and perhaps also convenient, to become entangled in a postcolonial line of reasoning that reduces international organizations as

[15] The importance of constitutional education programs and their sequencing is further discussed in Saati 2015 where the comparison of twenty cases of participatory constitution-making processes illustrates the relevance of these types of programs, particularly in the early phases of the process before setting out to solicit input from the general public.

culturally ignorant enforcers of western norms. This is a one-dimensional analysis that does not fully resonate with reality – but then again, it depends on the norm in question. If one finds that enjoying political rights is a natural component of an individual's life, then the norm of participatory constitution-making should not be regarded as an alien concept to nations outside of the West. This is not to say that people must necessarily exercise this right – but that they ought to be equipped with the proper capabilities in order to do so if they are to engage in participatory constitution-making. Here, again, the matter of capabilities becomes central.

Though seldom discussed in the literature on participation in political decision-making in general and in constitution-making in particular, participation may not always be problem-free. Public participation in the making of the constitution, which is among other things envisioned to reconcile former adversaries of violent conflict, might also bring about the precise opposite – increased polarization between different groups in society. This risk is more imminent if some individuals and segments of the population are better positioned to participate in terms of being more educated, more familiar with the workings of the political system, and more used to participating in various deliberative forums; i.e., simply more capable of functioning in the context of constitution-making. Hence, in order to decrease the possibility of increased polarization between various groups in society, it is worth carefully considering how constitutional education programs can be designed to suit different segments of the population based on their previous level of knowledge, so that the possibilities of participating on an equal basis increases.

Another potential risk with public participation in the making of the constitution is that it increases people's expectations of having their input reflected in the final draft. When these expectations are not met, frustration might follow which can potentially lead to violence. With this potential risk in mind, it might be a sound idea to investigate if public participation in the making of the constitution can be sequenced to junctures that are more suitable for involvement. Though this is an issue that deserves further systematic empirical research before any general suggestions can be made, the South African experience is valuable in terms of starting a discussion on how these processes can be sequenced, and if it is a sound idea to allow the first stage of the process to be limited to negotiations between political elites and the following stages to be open to public input. Again, however, this is a field of research that must be probed further – and perhaps this is where our attention needs to focus so that potential perils are avoided, while institutionalization and internalization are facilitated.

REFERENCES

Acharya, Amitav. 2004. "How Ideas Spread: Whose Norms Matter? Norm Localization and Institutional Change in Asian Regionalism." *International Organization* 58: 239–75.

African Charter on Human and People's Rights. 1981.

Alldén. Susanne. 2009. *How do International Norms Travel? Women's Political Rights in Cambodia and Timor Leste*. (Dissertation) Umeå. Print & Media.

Arnstein, Sherry R. 1969. "A Ladder of Citizen Participation." *Journal of the American Institute of Planners* 35 (4): 216–224.

Asian Charter of Rights. 1998.

Banks, Angela M. 2007. "Challenging Political Boundaries in Post-Conflict States." Faculty Publication, Paper 5. William and Mary Law School.

Banks, Angela M. 2008. "Expanding Participation in Constitution Making: Challenges and Opportunities." *William and Mary Law Review* 49 (4): 1043–69.

Bannon, Alicia L. 2007. "Designing a Constitution-Drafting Process: Lessons from Kenya." *The Yale Law Journal* 116 (8): 1824–72.

Brahimi, Lakhdar. 2011. "Foreword" in Michele Brandt, Jill Cottrell, Yash Ghai, & Anthony Regan. *Constitution Making and Reform: Options for the Process*. Switzerland: Interpeace.

Brandt, Michele, Jill Cottrell, Yash Ghai, & Anthony Regan. 2011. *Constitution Making and Reform: Options for the Process*. Switzerland: Interpeace.

Brandt, Michele. 2005. "Constitutional Assistance in Post-Conflict Countries: The UN Experience: Cambodia, East Timor & Afghanistan." United Nations Development Programme.

Checkel, Jeffrey T. 1997. "International Norms and Domestic Politics: Bridging the Rationalist-Constructivist Divide." *European Journal of International Relations* 3 (4): 473–95.

Collier, Paul. 2007. *Post-Conflict Recovery: How Should Policies Be Distinctive*. Oxford: Centre for the Study of African Economies, Department of Economics, Oxford University.

Cortell, Andrew P. and James W. J. Davis. 2000. "Understanding the Domestic Impact of International Norms: A Research Agenda." *International Studies Review* 2 (1): 65–87.

Dahl, Robert. 1998. *On Democracy*. New Haven: Yale University Press.

Dorman, Sara R. 2003. "NGO's and the Constitutional Debate in Zimbabwe: From Inclusion to Exclusion." *Journal of Southern African Studies* 29 (4): 845–63.

Ebrahim, Hassen 2001. "The Public Participation Process in South Africa." Pp. 153–61 in *Constitution-Making and Democratisation in Africa*, edited by G. Hyden oran and Denis Venter. Pretoria: Africa Institute of South Africa.

Ebrahim, Hassen and Miller, Laurel E. 2010. "Creating the Birth Certificate of a New South Africa: Constitution Making after Apartheid." Pp. 111–57 in *Framing the State in Times of Transition: Case Studies in Constitution Making*, edited by Laurel E. Miller and Louis Aucoin. Washington, DC: United States Institute of Peace.

Eisenstadt, Todd A., A. Carl LeVan, and Tofigh Maboudi. 2015. "When Talk Trumps Text: The Democratizing Effects of Deliberation during Constitution-Making 1974-2011." *American Political Science Review* 100 (3): 592–612.

European Framework Convention for the Protection of National Minorities. 1995.

Finkel, Steven E. 2003. "Can Democracy Be Taught?" *Journal of Democracy* 14 (4): 137–51.

Flockhart, Trine. 2005. "Complex Socialization and the Transfer of Democratic Norms." Pp. 43–62 in *Socializing Democratic Norms: The Role of International Organizations for the Construction of Europe.*, edited by Trine Flockhart. Basingstoke: Palgrave Macmillan.

Fox, Donald T., Gustavo Gallón-Giralodo, and Anne Stetson. 2010. "Lessons of the Colombian Constitutional Reform of 1991: Toward the Securing of Peace and Reconciliation?" Pp. 467–82 in *Framing the State in Times of Transition: Case Studies in Constitution Making*, edited by Laurel E. Miller and Louis Aucoin. Washington, DC: United States Institute of Peace.

Franck, Thomas M. and Thiruvengadam, Arun K. 2010. "Norms of International Law Relating to the Constitution-Making Process." Pp. 3–19 in *Framing the State in Times of Transition: Case Studies in Constitution Making*, edited by Laurel E. Miller and Louis Aucoin. Washington, DC: United States Institute of Peace.

Ghai, Yash and Guido Galli. 2006. *Constitution Building Processes and Democratization*. Stockholm: International Institute for Democracy and Electoral Assistance.

Ghali, Boutros B. 1992. *An Agenda for Peace: Preventive Diplomacy, Peacemaking and Peace-keeping*. United Nations (A/47/277 – S/24111).

Ghali, Boutros B. 1996. *An Agenda for Democratization*. New York: United Nations.

Ginsburg, Tom, Zachary Elkins, and Justin Blount. 2009. "Does the Process of Constitution-Making Matter?" *Annual Review of Law and Social Science* 5: 201–33.

Halliday, Terence C. and Gregory Shaffer, eds. 2015. *Transnational Legal Orders*. Cambridge: Cambridge University Press.

Harare Commonwealth Declaration. 1991.

Hart, Vivien. 2003. "Democratic Constitution Making." United States Institute of Peace [online]. Available at www.usip.org/files/resources/sr107.pdf [accessed December 26, 2016].

Hart, Vivien. 2010. "Constitution Making and the Right to Take Part in a Public Affair." Pp. 20–56 in *Framing the State in Times of Transition: Case Studies in Constitution Making*, edited by Laurel E. Miller and Louis Aucoin. Washington, DC: United States Institute of Peace.

Haysom, Fink 2001. "Special Features and Mechanisms in Negotiating the South African Constitution." Pp. 93–113 in *Constitution-Making and Democratisation in Africa*, edited by Goran Hyden and Denis Venter. Pretoria: Africa Institute of South Africa.

Heathershaw, John. 2008. "Unpacking the Liberal Peace: The Dividing and Merging of Peacebuilding Discourses." *Journal of International Studies* 36 (3): 597–621.

International Convention on the Elimination of All Forms of Racial Discrimination. 1965.

International Covenant on Civil and Political Rights. 1966.

Interpeace/IDEA/USIP. 2009. Workshop Report: Dilemmas and Opportunities of Public Participation in Constitution Building (April 2–5, 2009).

Khwaja, Asim I. 2004. "Is Increasing Community Participation Always a Good Thing?" *Journal of the European Economic Association* 2 (2–3): 427–36.

Koh, Harold H. 2006. "Why Transnational Law Matters." *Penn State International Law Review* 24 (4): 745–53.

Mac Ginty, Roger and Oliver P. Richmond 2013. "The Local Turn in Peace Building: A Critical Agenda for Peace." *Third World Quarterly* 34 (5): 763–83.

Marulanda, Iván. 2004. "The Role of Constitution Building Processes in Democratization: Case Study Colombia." Stockholm: International Institute for Democracy and Electoral Assistance.

Mbete-Kgositsile, Baleka. 2001. "The Principal Actors in the South-African Constitution-Making Process." Pp. 25–42 in *Constitution-Making and Democratisation in Africa*, edited by Goran Hyden and Denis Venter. Pretoria: Africa Institute of South Africa.

Mill, John S. 1862. *Considerations on Representative Government*. Norrköping: Föreningens boktryckeri.

Miller, Laurel E. and Louis Aucoin. eds. 2010. *Framing the State in Times of Transition: Case Studies in Constitution Making*. Washington, DC: United States Institute of Peace.

Moehler, Devra. 2008. *Distrusting Democrats: Outcomes of Participatory Constitution Making*. Ann Arbor: The University of Michigan Press.

Ndulo, Muna. 2010. "Zimbabwe's Unfulfilled Struggle for a Legitimate Constitutional Order." Pp. 176–206 in *Framing the State in Times of Transition: Case Studies in Constitution Making*, edited by Laurel E. Miller and Louis Aucoin. Washington, DC: United States Institute of Peace.

Pateman, Carole. 1970. *Participation and Democratic Theory*. Cambridge: Cambridge University Press.

Radcliff, Benjamin and Wingenbach, ed. 2000. "Preference Aggregation, Functional Pathologies, and Democracy: A Social Choice Defense of Participatory Democracy." *The Journal of Politics* 62 (4): 977–98.

Ramsbotham, Oliver, Tom Woodhouse, and Hugh Miall. 2016. *Contemporary Conflict Resolution*, 4th edition. Cambridge: Polity Press.

Risse, Thomas and Kathryn Sikkink. 1999. "The Socialization of International Human Rights Norms into Domestic Practices: Introduction." Pp. 1–38 in *The Power of Human Rights: International Norms and Domestic Change*, edited by Thomas Risse, Stephen Ropp, and Kathryn Sikkink. Cambridge: Cambridge University Press.

Robeyns, Ingrid 2008. "Sen's Capability Approach and Feminist Concerns." Pp. 82–104 in *The Capability Approach: Concepts, Measures and Applications*, edited by Flavio Comin, Mozaffar Qizilbash, and Sabina Alkire. Cambridge: Cambridge University Press.

Rousseau, Jean-Jacques. 1971. *The Social Contract and Discourse on the Origin and Foundation of Inequality among Mankind*. New York: Washington Square Press.

Saati, Abrak. 2015. *The Participation Myth: Outcomes of Participatory Constitution Building Processes on Democracy*. (Dissertation) Umeå. Print & Media.

Samuels, Kirsti. 2009. "Postwar Constitution Building: Opportunities and Challenges." Pp. 173–95 in *The Dilemmas of Statebuilding: Confronting the Contradictions of Postwar Peace Operations*, edited by Roland Paris and Timothy Sisk. New York: Routledge.

Selassie, Bereket H. 2010. "Constitution Making in Eritrea: A Process-Driven Approach." Pp. 57–80 in *Framing the State in Times of Transition: Case Studies in Constitution Making*, edited by Laurel E. Miller and Louis Aucoin. Washington, DC: United States Institute of Peace.

Sen, Amartya. 1999. *Commodities and Capabilities*. New Delhi: Oxford University Press.

Shaffer, Gregory. 2012. "Transnational Legal Processes and State Change: Opportunities and Constraints." University of Minnesota Law School. Legal Studies Research Paper Series. Research Paper No. 10–28.

The Secretariat of the Constitutional Commission of Afghanistan. 2003. *The Constitution Making Process in Afghanistan*. March 10, 2003.

Tully, James. 1995. *Strange Multiplicity: Constitutionalism in an Age of Diversity*. Cambridge: Cambridge University Press.

UNDP. 1993. *United Nations Human Development Report 1993*. New York, Oxford: Oxford University Press.

UNDP. 2002. *United Nations Human Development Report 2002*. New York, Oxford: Oxford University Press.

United Nations Declaration of Human Rights. 1948.

Verba, Sidney, Kay Lehman Schlozman, and Henry Brady. 1995. *Voice and Equality: Civic Voluntarism in American Politics*. Cambridge: Harvard University Press.

Widner, Jennifer. 2005. "Constitution Writing and Conflict Resolution." *The Round Table* 94 (381): 503–18.

Index

CPSIA information can be obtained
at www.ICGtesting.com
Printed in the USA
LVHW040138290920
667310LV00012B/96

9 781108 460989